"At a time when an accurate and positive und [the Roman Catholic Church is most importa [volume makes a unique contribution. The greater portion of the book is a detailed, balanced and readable account of the two-thousand-year history of ministry in the Church. His knowledge of the subject is thoroughly up to date; he draws from and then synthesizes the best of current Catholic scholarly research.

"Two elements in the book deserve special recommendation: Bernier ends his historical sketch with a careful analysis of Vatican II's teaching on the matter of ministry. Though acknowledging the historical turnabout represented by Vatican II's recognition of the active discipleship of all the laity, the author pays special attention to the council's view of the presbyterate. He then goes on in the volume's final chapters to suggest the future development of ministry and to formulate a theology of ministry that could guide that development. His outlook is carefully forward-looking, open to the newest movements of the Spirit in the Christian community."

Bernard Cooke
Author of *Sacraments & Sacramentality*
and *Ministry to Word and Sacraments*

"Father Bernier's *Ministry in the Church* should be required reading for all seminarians and pastoral ministry students. He provides a clear, concise history of ministry in the church from its New Testament beginnings to the present day. Sensitivity to the historical context of ministry shows the reader that changes in external forms and their theological legitimation were dictated by needs within the community.

"This book is not merely a survey of the past. Fr. Bernier sees the need for new forms of ministry today. The shared ministry of all the baptized requires both ordained leadership and the active participation of lay persons. He reminds us that all ministry grows out of basic Christian spirituality: faith in the Lord and love for the Church."

Pheme Perkins
Professor of New Testament, Boston College

"Paul Bernier's book has gathered the best of current scholarship into a comprehensive overview of the varied developments of ministry in the Church. In these days when the gifts of all the baptized and the charisms of leadership are in constant dialogue this book should help that conversation mightily. For the sophisticated reader *Ministry in the Church* is a tour de force through the centuries giving us firm grounding in our present efforts to be an effective collaborative Church."

William J. Bausch, Pastor
Author of *Ministry: Traditions, Tensions, Transitions*

"The author's vision for a new era in the church focuses on the need to revitalize ministry. Since a knowledge of history is essential to understanding ministry today he details those historical developments that affected ministry. Tradition has always been a strong argument for Catholics, even though we have often been unhistorical. However, the author meticulously examines history and tradition, sifting through the data, raising questions that others have passed over. He focuses on the past to bring light on the present. He reappraises old structures of ministry, suggests new ones based on the collective insights of those he calls 'architects of the future.' ...This book is a superb foundation for all who work in ministry. It is a great gift and answers a real need....Intended for Catholics it can't be ignored by any Christian tradition; focused on ministry it also serves as a fine history of the Church, of the papacy, and of lay life."

Leonard Doohan
Gonzaga University

"Paul Bernier's *Ministry in the Church* is a compact yet comprehensive survey of the historical development of ordained ministry. Well grounded in both historical sources and contemporary scholarship, *Ministry in the Church* offers the reader a clear picture of how the early believers viewed church and ministry. The author then documents the changes in perspective that led to the clericalization of ministry and the reduction of the laity to the status of non-clerics who passively received the sacraments. In the final portion Bernier deals with the changes in perspective brought about during the Second Vatican Council. These observations also offer the reader some important insights into what the fully developed RCIA process can help achieve in renewing the contemporary Church.

"Another basic perspective in Bernier's book is that of the believing community's on-going confidence in the Holy Spirit's presiding over the development of Church structures and practices. Adaptation of ministry to the needs of the People of God is not viewed as a threat to order in the Church, but as a hallmark of the Spirit's guidance.

"*Ministry in the Church* is a timely book, surveying the post-Vatican II perspectives on such key issues as the active role of the laity, mandatory priestly celibacy, and the ordination of women. Ecumenical in tone, Bernier's work also explores the implications of the ministerial service rendered by leaders of those Christian churches and communities not in communion with the Bishop of Rome."

Robert Obach, Ph.D.
Adjunct Professor at Wright State University,
Antioch University, Mount Saint Joseph College,
and RCIA Coordinator, St. Mary's Parish in Dayton

MINISTRY IN THE CHURCH

A Historical and Pastoral Approach

PAUL BERNIER

TWENTY-THIRD PUBLICATIONS

Mystic, Connecticut 06355

Third printing 2000

Twenty-Third Publications/Bayard
185 Willow Street
P.O. Box 180
Mystic, CT 06355
(860) 536-2611
(800) 321-0411

© Copyright 1992 Paul Bernier. All rights reserved. No part of this publication may be reproduced in any manner without prior written permission of the publisher. Write to the Permissions Editor.

ISBN:0-89622-536-4
Library of Congress Catalog Card Number: 92-64051
Printed in the U.S.A.

Preface

Mention the word "ministry" in any church group, and most people will automatically think of the ordained ministry. Perhaps they might include religious nuns and brothers among those who have a ministerial role in the church, but most others are de facto excluded. Ministry, in other words, is generally seen as a function of only a small minority of people. The laity are somehow excluded from any active role in the life of the church. Authentic ministry, however, is not the private preserve of the vowed and ordained. It is the service that God requires of all the baptized.

The title of this book is meant to indicate that it aims at treating ministry in a much broader context—as something flowing from the nature of the church itself. This is exemplified, generally, by using a historical approach. Especially because there have been many changes in the practice of ministry through the ages, it seemed helpful to situate this development in its general historical context. Nothing happens in a vacuum. Being able to correlate developments in the life of the church with similar currents in society at large should yield a better understanding of the whys and wherefores that underlie change.

Much of what has happened to church ministry was not reasoned out clearly ahead of time, but was a practical response to needs. When we have a clearer idea of how church ministry has developed through the ages, we can become more aware of the various influences that have affected our present practice.

When the Roman Empire collapsed, the bishops found themselves in the position of trying to maintain not only the church but the social order as well—a far different task than that envisaged for the bishop by Ignatius of Antioch! When feudalism took over as the dominant social system, the church was directed in the same manner as the secular state. With monasticism the ideal of all fervent Christians, its way of life also became the pattern expected of all clerics.

At the time of the Reformation, when many were challenging the accepted order, the church tended to stress mainly what was being denied by its opponents, and to downplay whatever aspects of the church its opponents insisted on. None of these were examples of reasoned or planned change. It was more a question of reacting to the pressures of the times as best as one could. These changes took place in view of a more effective ministry. As Pope John XXIII would put it, they flowed from pastoral concerns rather than abstract biblical or dogmatic principles. Taking account of the signs of the times was then, as it should be now, a valid hermeneutical principle.

We do not have to fault people for choices that were made in the past. At times they were the only choices possible. But we need not necessarily feel bound by patterns that have evolved over the years if they no longer correspond to present-day needs. The purpose of ministry always was to facilitate the growth of the Christian community. That is one of the few constants we should keep in mind.

To a large extent, the major influence in this book is the work of Edward Schillebeeckx, *The Church with a Human Face: A New and Expanded Theology of Ministry.* That is, I accept the fact that there has been a development in the practice and theology of ministry in the church, and the normative value of earlier church practice in solving the problems of ministry in the church today. This is rooted in the conviction that ordination is radically grounded in the vocation to mission common to all baptized Christians. There is an interplay between ordained and non-ordained ministries in the church. Every believer has some charism (ministry) to offer others, but not all possess the unique gift of leadership that guides and sustains the community. Those who do may be ordained to serve the church.

Another thread that runs through the book is what Schillebeeckx calls the right of the church to Eucharist or, more fundamentally, the apostolic right of Christians to ministry. The first five centuries never had the problem that now besets the church: vast numbers of people who are priestless and, consequently, who have to live for months and months without Eucharist. We risk protestantizing the church by forcing people to live only by the word of God. And the growing practice of having laity preside over a pseudo-Eucharist (or dry mass) with hosts imported from elsewhere trivializes the Eucharist itself and treats the consecrated hosts in a quasi-magical way.

It is a sad fact that the 1990 Synod on the *Formation of Priests in the*

Present Day brought no new insights or approaches to these problems. Church leaders could do little better than to give the same answers we have been using for the last 400 years. Seminary formation was visualized more after the pattern of the Tridentine seminary than from the perspective of the needs of the People of God today. We were told that what was needed was that we do better what we were already doing. We might call this a functional approach to ministry. The reasoning goes somewhat like this: If young Catholic men were more generous, we would have no shortage of vocations. If priests prayed more and led deeper spiritual lives, we would have a more effective presbyterate, and fewer would leave. More, more, more.

There are major problems with this approach. It ignores the fact that priests today are perhaps more fervent and dedicated (to say nothing of more overworked!) than they have been at any time in our history. How much "more" can we expect them to do?

All such solutions remain on the functional level. It is assumed that everything will be well if we could somehow only get people to improve whatever it is they are already doing. No thought is given to the possibility of structural changes that might better correspond to the needs of the church today. Hence the unwillingness to even consider questions like mandatory celibacy, the ordination of the heads of the basic ecclesial communities in the Third World, the ordination of women, or the effectiveness of the seminary structure as we have known it since Trent.

Perhaps we need new answers to meet new pastoral needs. This is another reason for the historical approach. If it is true that there have been numerous changes in the practice of church ministry through the centuries, we might ask why the process of trial and error in pastoral exploration should suddenly come to an end in our time. Much more is possible in the community of Christ than we might imagine. Or, to put it another way, much less is absolute than most people think. As Schillebeeckx notes, it can be liberating to discover from historical material that in other times the accents did not lie where they do now.

In outlining the historical development of ministry, few books are more helpful than Bernard Cooke's *Ministry to Word and Sacrament*. I have used this massive work throughout, not always properly footnoted, I fear. The structure of this book also makes it difficult to refer to properly in the suggested readings at the end of each chapter. It is divided into five general parts: 1) Ministry as the Formation of Community; 2) Ministry to God's Word; 3) Service to the People of God; 4) Ministering to God's Judgment; 5) Ministry to the Church's Sacramentality.

Each of these is treated chronologically. Since I have organized this book differently, there would be five sections to refer to for each of my historical periods, a space-consuming and unwieldy proposition.

We have inherited a view of ministry and the priesthood that is the end result of a long process of development. To a large extent our present understanding was fixed in its present form by the spirituality of the French School in the seventeenth century. At the heart of this view lies the conviction that Jesus was a priest on the basis of his divine nature, rather than his humanity. The French school had an enormous influence in upgrading the quality of priests and in deepening priestly spirituality. But one obvious result of its theological bases was the sacralization of the very idea of priesthood, and a reinforcement of the secondary status of the laity.

In the course of 2000 years, there have been quite fundamental shifts in theory and practice. No radical breaks can be noted, however. There are real threads of continuity. This book attempts to schematize these in the various historical periods studied. We have, then, the following broad development:

1. The generalized reality of ministry in the foundational period and the second generation, as witnessed in the New Testament period, when ministry tended to be characterized by charismatic signs, and where there was greater diversity and common involvement.

2. The conceptions of ministry in the second and third centuries, as our present patterns begin to emerge, and ministry becomes more structured and centered around the bishop.

3. The fundamental shift in the fourth century that led to the mystique of the consecrating priest and the sacerdotalization of ordained ministry itself.

4. The feudal period, with the monastization of ministry and the relegation of laity to second-class citizenship in the church.

5. The Scholastic period, with the identification of ministry with the hierarchy. The great theologians of the age, who have given us a (false) "timeless" understanding of the ministry of their own period, with the definitive linking of priest and Eucharist.

6. The changes wrought by the Reformation (O'Meara calls it the *pastoralization* of ministry) and the resultant efforts at church reform that came with the Council of Trent.

7. The fortress-like understanding of church that resulted from the Counter-Reformation along with the strongly sacral image of the priest that was given us by the French School, and the emergence of the pope as the source of all ministry.

8. The rejection of the scholastic and/or Tridentine model of ministry by the Second Vatican Council, and the more holistic view of ministry that resulted from that council.

9. The unanswered questions as to what directions we will take in the future.

The church of the future lies in the hands of present believers. The book tries to suggest only what the future *may* bring, based on the lessons of the past. The theological vision and fidelity to Christ of present believers will determine how the church responds to the needs of the age. If we are truly able to read the "signs of the times" we can draw on the experience of the past to draw from our storehouse things both old and new.

* * * * *

This book is the end result of several years of teaching the course on Ministry at Maryhill School of Theology, in Quezon City, Philippines. I felt that few current books on the subject were comprehensive enough to serve as a basic text. (Kenan Osborne's excellent study, *Priesthood: A Study of the Ordained Ministry in the Roman Catholic Church*, had not yet appeared.) Other works and articles that have somehow influenced this book are listed in the suggested readings at the end of each chapter.

I am indebted to Dr. Leonard Doohan for the extensive quotes from his book, *The Lay-Centered Church: Theology and Spirituality* (Minneapolis: Winston Press, 1984) that appear on pages 264-68 in this volume.

Contents

Introduction

In his book on ministry, Thomas O'Meara makes the pertinent point that thinking about ministry is thinking about what it means to be church.[1] Questions of ministry are essentially ecclesiological questions. Any discussion of ministry should begin with our understanding of the church itself.

What is this reality we call the church? A building for worship? A salvation club? Or a community of people?

What does it mean to be a Christian? To receive grace and salvation? To be able to receive the sacraments, especially the Eucharist? Or to make salvation a reality for the world?

What did Jesus expect of his followers? Avoiding sin? Liturgical participation? To form warm intimate communities? Or to transform the world?

What if the plan of God was that *everyone* should serve Christ and the world? What if action on behalf of the community and the world were an ordinary part of being Christian, if ministry were the glory and responsibility of all the baptized? What if Christ intended the church to be essentially and unavoidably ministerial?

While this book focuses more on the role of the special or ordained ministry within the church, it also stresses that ministry is a facet of baptized life, not the vocation of the few. In the New Testament, Jesus does not invite his followers to a decent but passive secular life, but to a life of faith in service to the Kingdom of God. The church and the world are the foci around which the streams of creation, sin, and grace swirl.

The attention given to ministry is not simply the latest program to improve the parish or to make up for the shortage of priests. It is a way of confronting the reality that has absorbed most of our attention in the last 400 years: What is the church itself? And how can it be faithful to its mission?

There has been much study on the history and theology of ministry in the church following the Second Vatican Council. Most of this has been enriched by the deeper ecclesiological awareness that has resulted from that council. It has also profited from the better historical and scriptural studies that are ours today. Further, the efforts that have been made in ecumenical relationships, especially the bilateral discussions of the last twenty years, have been very fruitful. All these have helped us develop a more open and less defensive theology.

It is also true, however, that much of this scholarship is undigested by the church at large. Older categories of thought have often remained unchanged. This is true for several reasons.

1. The spirituality and practice of the past 400 years are deeply entrenched, not only in books and schools of spirituality, but in the minds and hearts of many of the faithful. Thus, the reverence accorded priests, the fact that they are thought of as being "apart" from the laity—indeed, everything that comes from regarding priests as *sacred*—is a case in point. All of this helps to reinforce the differences between priest and laity, to the neglect of what we all hold in common as members of the People of God.

2. The prevailing Roman theology and canon law still treat priesthood as a theology of power, sometimes quite apart from good Christology and ecclesiology. Our theology of the ordained ministry is often about who has the power to do what to whom, or who has jurisdiction and authority over others. In the first millennium we were content to see those ordained as exercising a pastoral office by their public and official witness to the faith of the church. Scholastic theology, however, began to see the ordained as having special ontological powers inherent in their persons enabling them to act as public persons. Thus, the power to consecrate the eucharistic bread and wine or to ordain others to the church's ministry can be completely divorced from their proper ecclesial context and still be considered valid.

3. There are very simplistic ways in which we have understood the history of the church. Perhaps it would be better to say that the understanding of church is largely *unhistorical*.[2] Thus, many exhortations of popes and bishops speak as if Jesus conducted the first ordinations in the church at the last supper, and as if priestly ministry depended simply on an unbroken transmission of power from the apostles to bishop and bishop through the ages.

We have been so conditioned to thinking unhistorically that it is difficult to reflect in any other way. Furthermore, new ways of thinking are sometimes feared as if they challenged the foundation of everything that gives meaning to Christian life. We should, perhaps, try to see our tradition in such a way that it becomes an ever more creative power in any given situation.

With a less polemical and more nuanced view of our past, we need no longer simply assume that:

•Jesus clearly and deliberately founded the church as we know it today, and willed it to be just as it is;

•from the beginning the church was divided into hierarchy and laity, an arrangement whereby the only active members of the church are the ordained;

•Jesus explicitly instituted the seven sacraments and gave us directions as to how they were to be celebrated, and by whom;

•the threefold ministry of bishop, priest, and deacon comes from Jesus and was the pattern throughout the church from the very beginning;

•the first ordination took place at the last supper, and Jesus gave priests the exclusive power to change bread and wine into his body and blood;

•after ordaining his apostles priests, Jesus ordained them bishops and instructed them to ordain successors—and to exclude women from ordination;

•Peter was the founder and first bishop of Rome, and was recognized from the outset as the church's first pope.

While there might be significant symbolic meaning to all of the above, none of them correspond to actual historical events. Does this mean that there are no evangelical norms to guide our understanding of church ministry? Not at all!

A theology of ministry is thinking about how the church should live today. There is a dialectic at work here. On the one hand, we will have an interest in the forms and models through which the church has developed its ministry and styles of ministry. We are looking for the form clusters that tell us something about the life of the church and how it thought of itself in various periods. We want to know *why* the church in this or that era interpreted itself so—how, for example, it went from being the new Israel to the new Rome. Then we are in a better position to see the limitations history has imposed on us, along with the essence of Christian ministry.

Edward Schillebeeckx has noted that fidelity to the living tradition of the church is not to be found in simply doing today what has always been done in the past. Rather, fidelity lies in responding in new and creative ways to the most basic mandates of the gospel. It means trying to be in our time what Jesus was to people in his time so that we can translate the gospel imperatives in our own historical moment in accord with the new cultural situations in which we find ourselves.

Gregory Baum likewise points out that the church's ministry will be truly apostolic not because of its material fidelity to some ecclesiastical structure of the past (whether of the apostolic age, or of the post-apostolic period in which the monarchical episcopate developed), but because of formal fidelity to the divinely given norms revealed by Christ and the apostolic witness.[3]

Baum reminds us that Christ's revelation is not extrinsic to world history. Rather, it clarifies God's redemptive presence in our lives.[4] Jesus' own ministry and that of the early church reveals what leadership in the church should be like; this becomes normative for all times. This goes beyond organizational patterns to give us the principles by which any ministerial pattern must be tested.

The church exists in history. A theology of ministry is first and foremost a study of history: Forms of ministry come from different periods of history. Being grounded in history gives us hope of remaining in touch with reality. When we think and act as if present forms are timeless and eternal, we risk being left behind by change—and we turn the church into a museum. To identify the church with any particular age or form is to lose sight both of the universality of the church as well as the needs of the world we are called to serve. It is only by knowing our history well that we can discover what is normative in our past.

There are varying ways of being church. Seventeenth-century Spanish Catholicism—which still provides a heavy overlay in the Philippines or Latin America—is very different from Swiss Calvinism. Society in the Middle Ages has little in common with American pluralism. No church today is structured as were any of the churches in the first century. We must learn to discern the principles that underlay the various changes that have occurred.

The church has expressed itself differently in different periods and places. The more we enter into the history of the church, however, the less we need fear history. Social forms, liturgical signs, styles of praying, charisms, and ways of ministering are the flesh and blood of the church's life, for through them grace acts on us—or fails to act. Knowing our past helps us determine our future more effectively.

Thus, living fidelity to our tradition implies a *critical remembering* of our past, along with an openness to what God's Spirit is telling us in our present moment. Looking for forgotten insights of the past, we should be aware of any distortions that history might have introduced into our practice. An example here might be that the apparent acceptance of slavery by the early church does not mean we must practice it today. We can admit that this was because of an uncritical acceptance of societal norms and assumptions that we now know to be evil.

One important consideration that we should be aware of is that we are on the threshold of at last becoming a world church. By the year 2000, more than 70 percent of the world's Catholics will be in third world countries.[5] Most of these will come from Latin America, Africa, or from the Philippines in Asia. The center of gravity has shifted from the first world to the third. The 500th anniversary of Columbus's discovery of the new world served to remind us that these peoples received a Hispanic Christianity and that they still suffer from lack of any real inculturation. Perhaps this is one reason they still lack ordained ministers.

We could make a similar assertion about the United States or any country that received its Christianity from abroad. In considering our forms of ministry the time has come to realize that Europe (which bequeathed us the Christianity we know and which continues to control our thinking with largely European forms) is passing away. What forms of ministry based on our own experience and needs can we share with the universal church? We need only think of the basic ecclesial communities, with their origin in Latin America, to see one gift of the Third World to the entire church. What is our gift?

Something that all countries experiencing a priest shortage need to ask is how we ever got to the point where we had to worry about being able to do the work that needs to be done as a church. This never seemed to be a problem in the early church, when ministries spontaneously arose to meet needs. This forces us to ask if there are other ways in which people might be cared for, or whether their fate rises and falls with the priesthood as we know it today.

Regarding ministry itself, it is easier to speak about it than it is to define it. Schillebeeckx speaks of ministry as "the specific crystallization of a universal charisma of the Spirit," and also "a gift of the Spirit reserved for certain Christians with a function in the church."[6]

Although this is not the clearest definition, he has made three important points: 1) Ministry is rooted in the gifts of the Holy Spirit; 2) ministry is both universal and particular; 3) ministry is a function more than a state. That is, one doesn't become a priest to become a priest, or to enter the priestly state. One is ordained to *do* ministry, to fulfill certain specific, permanent functions within the church.

Yves Congar, one of this century's greatest ecclesiologists, used to speak of various *levels* of ministry. He suggests that there are three. The first is general ministry, expressed in occasional, passing service to others (e.g., parents catechizing their children, helping others who might be in need, leading Bible study groups, etc.). The second is publicly recognized ministries more directly related to the habitual activities of the church (e.g., permanent catechists, lectors, eucharistic ministers, etc.). The third level would be the ordained ministries, which are public offices with a sacramental base.

The Lima Statement on Ministry makes a similar distinction between general ministry, which is rooted in the gifts of the Holy Spirit and bestowed on every member of the church, and ordained ministry. *Baptism, Eucharist and Ministry* predictably has difficulty with defining the necessity or importance of the ordained ministry in the church. But it makes the point that if everything is ministry, then nothing is ministry.

McBrien summarizes the views of Congar, Schillebeeckx, O'Meara, and Lima by noting the four following constants[7]: 1) ministry is rooted in the Holy Spirit; 2) there is a distinction between general and particular ministry; 3) all ministry is functional, that is for the benefit of others, not primarily the minister; 4) ultimately, all ministry is for the sake of the kingdom of God, which is the object of the church's ministry.

This notion of ministry being for the sake of the kingdom of God is very important. In other words, the church is a community with a mission. The church is first called and then it is sent. Like Christ, the church "receives the mission to proclaim and establish among all peoples the kingdom of Christ and of God."[8] According to Vatican II, the church has a single purpose: that God's kingdom may come and that the salvation of the whole human race might come to pass.[9] Since this same kingdom was at the heart of Jesus' ministry, what he lived and died for, this should not be surprising. What the Second Vatican Council taught us to avoid is the ever-present temptation to identify the church with the kingdom.

Vatican II also clarified the relationship between our efforts to build the kingdom and the workings of God's grace and Spirit: "Earthly progress must be carefully distinguished from the growth of Christ's kingdom. Nevertheless, to the extent that the former can contribute to the better ordering of human society, it is of vital concern to the kingdom of God."[10] Our human efforts do not create the kingdom, but they do have a significant connection with it.

Notice that nothing has been said so far about the celebration of the Eucharist, something that has been intimately associated with ordained ministry in the church. There are several reasons for this. The first is that priestly ministry goes far beyond liturgical or cultic functions. The second is that in the early centuries, at least, the connection between presiding over the Eucharist and ordination were not clear. This is a question that will be taken up especially in its historical development.

Problem Areas

Many people today speak of a "crisis" in ministry. They point especially to what Ivan Illich has called "the vanishing clergyman." Over 50,000 priests have left the ministry since the Vatican Council, and the number entering the seminaries has gone down. Illich himself is a former priest. The U.S. bishops recently issued a report detailing identity crisis, burnout, and other problems affecting priests in the United States. Given the current lack of vocations to the priesthood, many already ordained have trouble defining their role in relation to the future.

We can focus on issues such as these and think, for example, that we need better work conditions, or that we had better improve our recruiting techniques or diocesan personnel policies. We might be deluding ourselves, however, by concentrating only on symptoms rather than on the main problem. There is too little space to treat most of these issues. Important as they are, however, they are hardly the main problem; they are more indicative of something that besets the entire ecclesial body. Our socio-cultural milieu is very different from that of Europe after the Council of Trent, yet our ecclesiology and practice are still governed by that model of church. Why cannot our structures be adapted to achieve a better discharge of ministry?

One obvious symptom that has been with us for almost 1500 years is the dichotomy between clergy and laity. We have succeeded in making the laity as passive as sheep in an age when many of our people are well educated and have enormous social responsibilities. Though the Vatican council has told us that baptism gives us radical equality and constitutes us all as members of the People of God, this insight has not yet begun to affect church structures to any large extent. Very little has changed.

Most of these problems seem to reduce themselves to a proper ecclesiology, rather than to the personal identity problems of priests or laity, or to doctrinal justification for present church practice. The focus of this book will be to stress what has been and should be the *object* of the church's ministry in the world in the various periods of its history. This will help us devise workable structures. For the question of ministry (or ministries) is not mainly a question of persons, nor is it a problem raised by one category of Christians. The basic question is how the church itself could (or *should*) discharge the ministry needed to be faithful in the service of the Good News given it by Jesus.

The Basic Tasks of Ministry

What does it mean, then, to minister as Jesus did? What aspects of the church's task must be kept in mind if it is to be whole? Ministry has basically the five following tasks:

1. *Building community.* The task of the church is to reverse Babel, to break down whatever it is that alienates people one from another, to bring the world back to the harmony that characterized Eden. Hence the necessity of being able to understand and speak the language of the various cultures we are trying to serve, lest we confuse bringing the message of Jesus with forms of religious or cultural imperialism based on previous expressions of the tradition.

2. *Storytelling.* The good news must be proclaimed to the ends of the earth. The story of salvation must be seen for what it really is: the manifestation of God's loving kindness toward all peoples and God's desire to save. The Bible is the manifestation of this loving kindness in history. Ministry has to root Christians in, and offer to all peoples and cultures the reality of, God's revelation as shown in salvation history.

3. *Prophesying.* The word of God is not simply a consolation for the sorrowing. The challenge of the gospel stems from the image of Christ condemned by the powers of the world of his day because his message challenged the smug assumptions of his age. The gospel sides with freedom against the forces of oppression. Hence the new consciousness we have today about the necessary link between social justice and the proclamation of the gospel. It is in this sense that Christians should always be in the world but not of it.

4. *Nurturing.* The transcendent mission of the church is not only to witness to the truth and justice of the gospel, but to bring people into a new relationship with God—and with each other. Hence the need for the humble service that has been the glory of the church through the ages: care for the poor and needy, education, and works of charity. Ulti-

mately, the communion symbolized by the Eucharist must lead to a nurturing community, one aware and open to the needs of the world around it.

5. *Missioning*. Finally, the task of the church is to empower others to be what they are by reason of baptism. That is, it must inspire its members to carry on the work of Christ. All are called to be active in the church and to build the Kingdom for which Jesus lived and died.

Indeed, one of the principles running through this book is that the ministry of the church is the common responsibility of all Christians, although in diverse ways. As will be obvious from the ecclesiology of the New Testament, there is no foundation there for the priest/lay distinction most people take for granted today. If the church is identified with the clergy and the laity with the world, both sides lose, and the church itself is impoverished.

It would be ideal if we were able to eliminate the priest/lay dichotomy (for which there is no foundation in the New Testament) as a concept governing our thought, and replace it with the general concept of ministry. This would make it possible to consider the specific character of the ordained ministry and the new relation that exists between the object of ministry and the person of the minister (what might be properly called priestly spirituality) within its proper context. It would also help to make us aware of the organic link that exists between ministry and the local church.

Summary

1. One cannot understand ministry without first understanding the church. Likewise, we can see how the church understands itself at different periods of its history by examining its patterns of ministry. Many changes in ministerial practice were responses to social developments in the world.

2. Knowledge of history is essential to understanding ministry today, for it helps us to appreciate where we have come from and to extract from our tradition those primal insights that are normative for the present and future. This is a *formal* fidelity rather than a *material* fidelity to ancient structures.

3. Although there are different approaches to ministry in recent theological writings, certain important points have been agreed on: a) ministry is rooted in the Holy Spirit; b) there is a distinction between general and particular ministry; c) all ministry is functional, i.e., for the benefit of others, not primarily the minister; d) ultimately, all ministry is for the sake of the kingdom of God, the object of the church itself.

4. The mission of the church is the establishment of the kingdom. Ultimately, all ministry is for the sake of the Kingdom of God and not an end in itself. This teleology is also a principle that helps us determine choices and options for our present forms of ministry.

5. Ministry (in its various forms) is not a vocation of the few, but a facet of Christian life incumbent upon all the baptized. Ordained ministry is a further precision of this baptismal commitment for those with the charism to lead the community.

Discussion Questions

1. Try to come up with a workable definition of ministry, one that is linked with the nature and mission of the church. Note how different definitions tend to reflect fundamental differences in how we understand the nature of the church itself.

2. What ministries could the church easily do without because they have outlived their usefulness or purpose? What types of ministries will the church have to develop if it is to be viable in the next century?

3. If you were bishop of a diocese, what would you like to do most about the ministries of the diocese? If you were parish priest, what would you do about parish ministries?

4. What are some principles of church ministry that we can note from our general understanding of the gospel and the vision and ideals of Jesus?

5. What are the main problems with ministry today? What might be possible solutions? Why?

Suggested Readings

Bühlmann, W., "From Western Church to World Church," *The Church of the Future: A Model for the Year 2001*, Maryknoll, N.Y.: Orbis Books, 1986. Chap. 1, pp. 3-11.

McBrien, R., *Ministry: A Theological, Pastoral Handbook*, San Francisco: Harper & Row, 1987.

O'Meara, T., "Ministry: Between Culture and Charism," *Theology of Ministry*, Mahwah, N.J.: Paulist Press, 1983. Chap. 1, pp. 3-25.

Schillebeeckx, E., *The Church with a Human Face: A New and Expanded Theology of Ministry*, London: SCM Press, 1985, pp. 1-10, 115-123.

1

The Foundations of Ministry

This period takes in only the first generation of what is now known as Christianity. It runs from the ministry of Jesus around the year 27 through the destruction of the Temple in the year 70. During this time the foundations of the church were laid.

The year 70 is not an arbitrary demarcation point. By that time the great apostles Paul and Peter had been killed. With the razing of the Temple there came a definitive break with the Jewish religion that had served as the womb from which Christianity was born. Before this point Jewish Christians still regarded themselves as Jews. The destruction of the symbol of Jewish life occasioned an identity crisis. This, and the opposition of the Pharisees who led Judaism after the Roman victory, necessitated what was, for many, a painful choice. In the aftermath of this difficult struggle, Christian self-consciousness came of age. That will be the matter of the next chapter.

Before the destruction of the Temple, however, Jerusalem remained the spiritual home of the new Christian movement. Here Christianity developed mainly as a sect within Judaism, that is, Jews who believed that Jesus was the messiah (cf. Acts 24:14). We should be careful not to imagine that the day after the resurrection the early Christians thought of themselves as a new religion, with the necessity of establishing all the structures implied thereby.

Nevertheless, during this period, especially because of the writings of Paul, we have foundational documents that eventually guided the growth of what we now so easily call the church. Note that most of the other New Testament writings will be considered in Chapter 2, since they belong more properly to the next generation of Christian Scriptures.

Christ's Ministry

Though they may neglect it in the course of their practical activity, Christian churches in all periods of history admit in some form the principle that Christ alone is the ultimate possessor of priesthood, ministry, and authority in the church. Thus, knowledge of his ministry is determinative for any true understanding of Christian ministry, whether it be the ministry of the community as a whole or any individual within it. Knowing what Christ did and what he is still doing lies at the heart of what church is all about. Hence the importance of a solid Christology to ground our ecclesiology.

Catholics tend to see Christ's death and the last supper he had with his disciples as the key events defining his priesthood. But if Christ's death is the culminating moment, his public ministry must be seen as a preparation for that action. Jesus' preaching and ministry of compassion were all geared to making God's kingdom present in some fashion here below. Everything in his ministry was meant to form the community of faith that eventually emerged. His death is but the final moment in a whole lifetime of service. Furthermore, there is no doubt that the early Christians saw themselves as entrusted with the God-given role of continuing Christ's public ministry, not just his last supper.

A category that helps illumine this is the presentation of Jesus' ministry in terms of *service*. Jesus was *the* Servant, a characterization that seems rooted in his own self-identification. This indicated a specific service, however, one seen as fulfilling the expectations expressed in the Old Testament ideal of the Suffering Servant.

Mark's gospel and numerous other New Testament texts seem to indicate that this explanation of the servant ideal was part of the primitive baptismal catechesis. A Christian was called to serve even as Christ had served us. The notion of service is very close to the term *diakonia*, often used for the ministries of the early church. The diakonia of Jesus, as well as that of the disciples, is thought of in terms of Isaiah's fourth servant hymn (cf. Matthew 20:26–28). A minister (*diakonos*) of Christ is useful to him in fulfilling his purpose in the world. So closely do Christian workers see themselves as belonging to Christ that they are proud to call themselves slaves (*doulos*) of Christ (cf. Romans 1:1).

Challenging our tendency to associate Christ's ministry with only "the sacrifice of the cross," and to see it mainly in cultic terms, is the fact that one of the most striking features of the early Christian decades is their strongly a-cultic character. We begin to see an active and reflexive cult only in the middle of the second century; the earliest decades of the church are not characterized by an institutionalized ritual of worship. This has unavoidable implications for our study of ministry in these decades. It makes it difficult to maintain that cultic functions were central to Christian ministry in the primitive church. Cult was subordinated to service.

Also, with only one exception, no New Testament book refers to Jesus himself as a priest. He was not one of the priestly class, and never performed cultic actions in the temple in his own lifetime. The Letter to the Hebrews is the one exception in calling Jesus a priest; but it does so only to point out that his "priesthood" is so unique as to force a redefinition of the concept itself. His death itself was a public execution, a most unholy event. By it, Jesus broke the barrier separating the sacred from the profane.

The Letter to the Hebrews is so strong about Jesus' priesthood being in a class all by itself and so all-sufficient in its saving power, that the Letter says nothing about cultic priestly activity on the part of Christians. No individual Christian is called a priest anywhere in the New Testament. But, because our lives are somehow caught up with Christ's, perhaps the various places in the New Testament where aspects of Christian life are spoken of as "worship" should be taken strictly—although it will require adjusting our ideas of worship!

At the risk of gross oversimplification, let us make the following summary statements about the way the early church saw both the basic ministry of Christ, and their own link with him:

1. The New Testament writings show that the early church saw a continuity between the historical Jesus and the risen Lord, who continued to have an influence in their lives and destinies. The meaning of his life, death, and subsequent glorification transformed the meaning and purpose of their own existences. Furthermore, his Spirit moved in their midst to animate and direct their communal and individual lives, transforming them into children of God.

2. The Pauline perspective (which is not singular in the New Testament) saw Jesus as a contemporary reality with whom we are still in contact. Paul saw his own role as co-worker with and ambassador for Christ (1 Corinthians 4:1, 2 Corinthians 5:20); he speaks of himself as introducing others into the life of Christ (1 Corinthians 4:16); and as exercising the authority of Christ himself (1 Thessalonians 4:2).

This, incidentally, is also the viewpoint of the later New Testament period. The tenth chapter of Matthew (and the missionary discourses in the other synoptics) reflect the manner in which Christian evangelization was looked upon as being provided by Christ himself. The Lukan viewpoint is dominated by the risen Lord whose presence to the community is a replacement of the *kabod* (glory) attached to the Temple. The Johannine literature is unintelligible apart from the living Lord who imparts eternal life to those who accept him in faith (John 6), and who invites his disciples to abide in him as he abides in them (John 15).

3. The ministry of the community is one of witnessing (Revelation 1:5), of reconciliation (Colossians 1:22), of granting the spirit of adoption and giving life (Galatians 4:4; John 6), of redemption from wickedness (Galatians 1:4). Basic to these is the formation of community. The risen Christ has unified humankind in himself and reunited it to God (2 Corinthians 5:19, Galatians 4:4), reconciling those who had alienated themselves from the divine (Colossians 1:22). This reconciliation also has a horizontal dimension, breaking down the walls of division that separate people from one another (Galatians 3:26–29; Ephesians 2:11–16).

4. Probably in no place does the community-forming function of the risen Christ find such profound expression as the Pauline usage of the *body of Christ*, and the Johannine usage of the *vine*. Paul's usage of the phrase *en Christo* also stresses the corporal reality of our union with Jesus. The risen Christ acts as a source of life and unity. What binds the community together is a common bond with the person of the risen Lord who abides with them and gives them his very Spirit, all in order to bring believers into deep communion with the heavenly Father.

5. Aware of the unique character of a community that was able to form a social unity because of the risen Christ, we note the key biblical category of *covenant* that underlies it. It is hard to find a more pervasive manner of thinking in both Old and New Testaments. Jesus' death and resurrection is seen and presented in the New Testament as the establishment of the new covenant foretold by Jeremiah 31:31–34. It embraces the entire relationship of humankind with God.

6. Jesus' public ministry is to be seen as both announcing and inaugurating the new covenant community that took shape after his resurrection. It was governed by that goal. The last supper is only the culmination of an entire lifetime of commitment. The whole of Jesus' work, then, was normative for the early Christians in their own lives and action. The "work" of Christ is somehow to be carried on in the church through the power of his Spirit.

7. At first sight, it seems that the ministry of the early community is *ad intra*, in building up the church itself. Even in the early days, there was some movement *ad extra*, though there was not a refined understanding of the church's role in relation to the world. The priestly overtones of all such ministry, though, are quite interesting. The phrase in 2 Corinthians 9:12, referring to the collection that Paul was taking up for the poor in Jerusalem, uses liturgical terms: *tes leitourgias tautes* (the administration of this public service).

8. The *whole* church shares in the ministry of preaching the good news and of witnessing to the death/resurrection of Christ. This seems to be accomplished in large part by the very intrinsic growth in the loving community of the people themselves. Their daily life is their sacrifice (Romans 12:1). They have their diverse functions for the sake of the whole body (Colossians 3:16). Living out its faith in daily life is the sacrifice of the community (Philippians 2:17). This is linked to Jesus' own servant ministry, extolled in chapter 2 of the same letter. Paul seems to place stress on the sufferings of the early Christians as some sort of prophetic witness (e.g. Philippians 1:27–30).

9. Though the nurture of community among themselves is basic to the common ministry of all Christians (it is also a fundamental objective of the charismata given individuals), one cannot conclude from the New Testament evidence that this ministry was seen as extending outward toward forming community among all humankind. We can draw these conclusions theologically from the principles contained in New Testament literature, but the evidence is scarce that the early church saw itself in this way, despite Paul's vision of God having reconciled the world to himself in Christ, where the church's role is one of working to make this a reality (Ephesians 1:4–14, Colossians 1:9–23).

10. A category that runs through all these others is that of *service*. Jesus is presented as the Suffering Servant, one who came not to be served but to serve others. His disciples are called upon to continue that service to each other and, eventually, to the world.

The Starting Point

There are many possible starting points for a study of ministry in the church today. Even examining the New Testament foundations for present church practice leaves us with many possible avenues of approach. Bernard Cooke makes it clear that the *community* dimension of Christianity deserves initial emphasis.[1] When one turns to the biblical evidence, the emphasis on community is quite evident. God's gratuitous revealing action began with the formation of a special people,

Israel. The historical evolution of that people under divine influence constitutes what we now call Old Testament revelation. Christianity itself starts as a community of believers united in their consciousness of being a renewed Israel in the risen Christ whom they saw as messiah and redeemer—as the apex of God's revelation to humankind.

If it seems relatively obvious that the formation of human community through shared community with Christ is a key aspect of Christianity's early existence and activity, many question how central it is. Does it lie at the very heart of "salvation," of "worship," of "giving glory to God," of "forgiveness of sins," or is it a somewhat peripheral result of the cumulative salvation of individual humans? Catholicism has always tended to see community as the central means whereby God's grace and life is mediated. Non-Catholic churches, on the other hand, tend to have a more individualistic ethic.

Unless we know what kind of church we are talking about, however, it will be impossible to discover the essential elements of Christian ministry and priesthood. For if ministry has any purpose at all, it is directed to nurturing the life and activity of the community—the church—as a whole.

Specialized Ministries Within the Community

We should begin by stressing how difficult it is to present a clear account of ministry in the early church. We have to deal with very meager sources. None of the New Testament books is concerned about setting forth in any full or systematic way how the church was structured, or how its ministry was carried out. Any reconstruction of the church's ministry must depend on the implications of a few scattered passages. We must also resist the temptation to think that what we find in one place was likewise the practice of the entire church.

Only three New Testament writings give lists of ministries: Romans 12:4–8; 1 Corinthians 12:4–12; and Ephesians 4:11–14 (which would be second generation). The lists seem illustrative rather than exhaustive. They tell us more about the theology than the structure of ministry. That is, it is easier to conclude that ministry was active, diverse, and flexible than it is to derive job descriptions of the various ministries listed.

None of the lists includes *episkopos*, from which our term "bishop" derives. There is no mention of *priest*, of course, but neither is there of *presbyter*, although Luke indicates that they were present in the Jerusalem community. The various leadership ministries are given different names, seeming to reflect a flexible terminology and practice. We have not reached the point where these are titles of all-powerful leaders.

Paul's enumeration of ministries is not intended to present an ecclesiology. His flexible use of terminology indicates to us that ministry then was diverse, that it flowed from the life of the community, and was significant because of its importance for the continued strength of the community. *Apostles, prophets,* and *teachers* seem to have been the most prominent ministries in the Pauline lists. This prominence survived even into the second century. The *Didache* will state that their importance led to apostles and prophets being the ones who preside over the Eucharist. Bishops would come only later.

These three activities—external evangelization, inspired preaching, and teaching—formed the core of the cluster around which the other ministries seem to revolve. The other special charisms and functions were meant to increase the vitality of the community itself. They are various forms of *diakonia*, and *diakonia* implies the building up of the community. Paul's writings are explicit in this matter. There is a constant stress of sharing, unity, and concern for one another.

The communities served by these ministries were not basically a matter of social arrangement in the minds of the New Testament writers. Rather, we have the deeper reality of people sharing a common insight into the meaning of life. Based on Christ, it impels them to work toward a more mature and concerned love of people for one another, no matter what their backgrounds or specific historical situation.

In facing questions about the nature of ministry today, it is important to keep in mind that this more profound level of Christian community must be seen as one of the governing objectives of ministry. In other words, rather than trying to resurrect ancient forms or canonize older structures, we should recognize that all external forms brought into being or sustained by the church are for the sake of this basic communion in love and worship. The ideal will be incarnated differently in different times and places. All questions about reshaping, retention, or evolution should be answered in the light of this finality.

All Christian churches agree with this, at least theoretically. Controversy comes when one begins to ask whether some particular structures (e.g., episcopacy, diaconate) were not willed by Christ to be indispensable for the well-being of the church. In other words, what is part of our unchangeable Tradition? It is highly doubtful whether this can be settled on the basis of New Testament evidence; too much variety is found there. Here, history can come in to show how certain forms and patterns became normative.

We should not assume that the ministries that were exercised in the early church were neatly defined in a hierarchical structure such as we have today. In the first generation, there were very few well-defined roles, and much more room for the charismatic exercise of one's gifts and talents. Furthermore, there were different patterns in different churches. Raymond Brown's book, *The Churches the Apostles Left Behind*, clearly shows how the second generation came up with different ways to survive after the death of the foundational apostles.

Before we take a closer look at New Testament developments, let us pause briefly to see to what extent Christianity was influenced by the Jewish religion from which it sprang.

Relation to Jewish Ministry

The religion of Israel was surely the most important of the many influences that impinged on the early church. Not only was Jesus Jewish, but so were the earliest converts to the new Way. The idea that there was a radical distinction vis-à-vis Judaism took time to develop. Two areas need to be studied carefully: the manner in which the early church's view of itself as a priestly community corresponded with that of Israel, and the respective views of the two communities regarding the role of ministerial groups in fostering the community's life.

New Testament evidence points to a tension in early Christianity's relation with Judaism. After decades of conflict, there was an eventual separation, which served to emphasize the differences separating them. Nevertheless, some ideas and themes were retained: The church was the renewed Israel; its community existence was grounded in the new covenant effected in the blood of Christ; this covenant is the fulfillment of the Sinai covenant (Jeremiah 31:31); all of Christ's life was "that the Scriptures might be fulfilled." Yet, while a deep current of continuity existed, it tended to flow at the level of the God of history rather than at the surface level of religious institutions.

In contrast to Old Testament Israel, where religious life not only depended on external structures of social and political life but was practically indistinguishable from them, the early Christian communities were based almost exclusively on faith in Jesus as messiah. Common culture, common social customs, and common national or political affiliation were not the basis of unity in the early decades. After a period of hesitation, Christianity broke with Jewish religious cult, law, and the authoritative guidance of the priesthood.

Even more important, there seemed to be no inclination to substitute for these forms. There was an early enough insight into the universality of the gospel, which militated against limiting it by particular laws and customs. Surprisingly, perhaps, there was little felt need to provide for the church any of the priestly mediation so important in Judaism. This is even more striking because, as Acts tells us, a fair number of early converts were priests (6:7). This stands in distinction to the stand taken at Qumran; there the Jewish priesthood was replaced by one of their own. Of the three key "offices" of mediation in the Old Testament—king, priest, and prophet—only the *prophet*, in its charismatic and non-institutionalized form, seemed to exist in the church (note the Pauline lists). There were also two other groups:

1. *Elders.* These had recognized roles in Judaism at the time of Jesus. Their role increased in importance after the exile, especially in those communities not in close contact with Jerusalem. Even in Jerusalem, the Sanhedrin, which functioned as a supreme tribunal, was composed of key elders. Their influence extended even to Jews of the diaspora. Though they may not have recognized the authority of the priesthood, dissidents like those at Qumran retained the pattern of a ruling group of elders for their own communities. All indications seem to be that many of the early Christian communities also gave a body of elders (*prebyteroi*) some power of guidance over local communities, a pattern that would remain until the fourth century.

Interestingly, neither in the Old nor the New Testaments are claims made that this is of divine institution (as opposed to claims made for the priests, prophets, and kings). Rather, their role seems to arise simply from the needs of the group, as a sort of outgrowth of clan and family structures, and seems to have been judicial in nature. In the early Christian churches, neither the origin nor the function of the elders is clear, but the existence of a group of guiding *prebyteroi* became a common, if not universal, pattern. The presbyterate does not seem to have come from the special corporate role of the Twelve, that is, as "successors of the apostles" (though it seems to have emerged in Jerusalem only after the Twelve had gone). Nor did it derive from the special charism given prophets or apostles.

Rather, quick emergence of elders seems to have come from natural leadership, along with some special designation by the community.[2] For example, Paul, as founding father, would at times leave elders in charge after he left (though he does not use the word elder). It seems that the concrete needs of the early communities dictated their existence and precise functions. There is evidence that it would be wrong to see their role as an *office*, or as a precise function over against prophets or teachers. From the New Testament and other writings, their roles seems to overlap (or not overlap) with *disdascalos*, or *prophetes*, or *episk-*

pos, not in formal description of function, but in the applicability of two or more of these terms to the same individual.

2. *Teachers*.[3] Just as the role of elders seems to have arisen from the needs of the community, as in Judaism, so also did teachers. In both groups, their activity was directed in unifying the people in faith. The understanding they possessed was not for their own sake, but a heritage to be passed on for the sake of the people. All gifts were to be shared.

3. *Prophets*.[4] We have already mentioned that prophets were among the leaders of the community in the Pauline lists. This charismatic role seemed quite common in the early church. In 1 Corinthians, the whole community seems to take turns at prophesying. We learn from Acts 2:17 that the ecstatic utterances of the apostles at Pentecost were seen as a fulfillment of the prophesying promised by Joel for the final times. In the early church, prophets helped the community discern what God's will was in contemporary events. Because of their wisdom, they became the gifted leaders of many of the early congregations. We might note references to this in places like Romans 12:6; 1 Corinthians 12:10; 28ff; Ephesians 2:20; 3:5; 4:11. Significantly, the prophets included both men and women.

Thus the strongest continuity or influence we can see between Israel and Christianity lies in the "non-office" roles of elder, teacher, and prophet far more than with the classic priest and king roles. This extension of the role of the prophets, rabbis, and the elders seemed to provide adequate leadership in the beginning, and may help explain why there seemed no felt need to set up a formally institutionalized priesthood at first.

In comparing the notion of ministry in early Christianity with that found in Judaism, however, there seems to be a basic difference in how the ministry of the community as a whole was seen. Israel had a sort of narrow self-focus; if salvation was open for others, they had to come to Israel. Christianity, on the other hand, was marked almost immediately by an outward thrust in both evangelization and service. The mission was good news to the ends of the earth.

In such a context, the role of ministers takes on a different orientation. While they function as guides and stimulants for the well-being of the community itself, they also direct it outward in witness and service. Paul often urged his converts to be as he was (1 Corinthians 11:1). This approach affected their attitude to leadership. Pentecost was a democratizing experience, and the gifts of the Spirit were to be used by all for the good of all.

At the same time, the New Testament testifies that the key ministerial roles of Israel found an idealized fulfillment in the new Israel. Basic to this view is the way Jesus is seen to recapture these roles in his own ministry of service. Though he occupied no political office, nor did he seek to, he is shown as the messiah who realizes the ideal unattained by the historical kingship of Israel. Definitely not a priest, his death replaces the sacrificial ritual of Old Testament law. Without formal rabbinic training, he is the supreme teacher who reveals God to us. He is also the great prophet who fulfills all that the Old Testament prophets were all about.

Called to a discipleship that is not one of *succeeding* Christ in his historical role, but rather where the Lord remains present to them and works through them, the Christian communities saw themselves as sharing in this fuller ministry. Like *the* Servant whose death brought life to all, so their service was to build the kingdom of saints. Their mediation is not as much through office, as through their lives.

The Earliest Church Communities

The experience of God's concern for humanity, embodied in the message and life of Jesus, gave rise to the church. At first this group was overwhelmingly Jewish, and continued to think of itself as such. They held, however, to the common conviction that Jesus was the promised messiah. For most of these "Christians," the experience of the historical Jesus was not the direct foundation of their faith; they had never met him. Baptized in his name, however, they were filled with his Spirit and convinced that Jesus had been raised from the dead by the power of God to become life-giving Spirit (1 Corinthians 15:45).

Initially, the community centered around Jerusalem. The first twelve chapters of Acts show the Twelve assuming the leadership of this group, with Peter as head. Problems with the Hellenistic Christians were solved (temporarily) by allowing them to appoint their own leaders (6:1–6). The Twelve receive and distribute the goods given for the poor (2:32ff; 4:42ff), judge the erring (5:1–11), send Peter and John to Samaria (8:14) and Barnabas to Antioch (11:22). After this, the Twelve seem to disappear, and the leadership of the Jerusalem church fell to James.

James had respect because he was a relative of Jesus. As leader of the Jerusalem community, he preached, taught, judged, interpreted the law, and presided. He never became a missionary, but remained in Jerusalem, a sort of prototype of the monarchical bishop and guardian of the tradition. We are told by Eusebius that he was succeeded by

Symeon bar Clopas, an uncle of Jesus. Jesus' family maintained control in Jerusalem, in fact, until the destruction of the Temple.

The Jerusalem church under James was indeed the mother church of primitive Christianity, judging disputes and guarding tradition. This church continued to have a say in the affairs of the other churches up to the destruction of the Temple. As the center of what today might be called the conservative wing of the church, we can note their role in the enormous struggle over the reception of the Gentiles into the church (which takes up several chapters of Acts). Upholding the more progressive wing would have been Paul. Peter spent much time trying to hold these two together.

With James, according to Acts, we find the first evidence of a group of elders, patterned on the Sanhedrin, guiding the early community. These presbyters had real authority and could make decisions affecting the community. In the so-called Council of Jerusalem (chapter 15), they are active in formulating the final decision. Thus they seem in many ways to be like wise counselors.

The Twelve

The role of the Jerusalem church is related to another sticky question: the role and significance of the "Twelve." Among Catholics, the Lukan version has served as the basis for understanding both apostolic ministry and episcopal office. The scenario goes something like this: Jesus called the Twelve, commissioned them his apostles, and ordained them at the last supper. This divinely-appointed college likewise ordained successors, who are the college of bishops in the church. This is the view taken by Vatican II (*Lumen Gentium*, 22) and by many others.

The assumption is often made that the "Twelve" and the "college of apostles" are one and the same. New Testament exegesis, however, shows that the earliest traditions about the Twelve make no such assumptions. The concept of apostleship goes far beyond the Twelve, to include Barnabas, Paul, Apollos, and others. We have apostles mentioned well into the second century. Even Luke, who is the main one to give the Twelve the name apostles, is not entirely consistent in this matter, conceding the title also to Paul and others. (Note that John never uses the term apostle for the Twelve; Mark and Matthew do so only once.)

Aside from this, we have the curious fact that by the time most of the New Testament was written, the Twelve seem to be only a hallowed memory. They belong more to the past, and are contemporaneous only with Jesus' own ministry and the earliest days of the church. Their function is generally symbolic and eschatological. They point to the Kingdom in which Jesus' disciples will rule the twelve tribes of the renewed Israel. Nowhere are they understood as having any successors as a "college."

The Lukan view equally does not portray them as early bishops (i.e., heads of local churches), nor as sacramental practitioners. Raymond Brown suggests that they emerged as a sort of "Council" in matters that affected the church as a whole.[5] Their stature—both as historical figures and as immortalized heroes—derives from their being the closest followers of Jesus, rather than his deputies or vicars. In that sense, they were irreplaceable.

The Pauline Churches

In Jerusalem, however, there were also Hellenistic Jews who became members of the community. Driven out of Jerusalem at an early stage, they were responsible for founding the first mission communities. Of these, the greatest was Antioch, and it was to this community that Paul became attached and from which he began his own ministry. Since Paul's letters are the earliest writings we have that witness to early church organization and practice, we will touch on how he saw some of the characteristics of the churches of the Gentile mission.

Paul's preferred metaphor for the church was the "Body of Christ" (cf. Romans 12 and 1 Corinthians 12). Keeping in mind the smaller house churches of Paul's time, we can well understand his fervent appeals for unity and solidarity. However, Paul's expression is more than a convenient metaphor. He is thinking in more cosmic terms as well, and his metaphor is meant to express the reality of Christ's presence in the world.

Concerned with how Jesus made it possible for us to escape the trap of inauthenticity in which sinful humanity was mired, Paul insisted that it was only by living "in Christ."[6] This is something that he understood very concretely, and it underlies his concept of the Body of Christ.

Since we live in the real world, all of us are surrounded by people and a climate that is either healthy (virtuous) or unhealthy (sinful). The problem lies in the fact that before we can live virtuously, we must somehow be delivered from the power of relatives and friends—any atmosphere that breathes of sin. Somehow, we have to be taken out of that unhealthy environment that prevents us from living authentically.

The solution is to live "in Christ"—to enter a new environment, one provided by the Christian community, which is Christ's Body here on earth. There we can find new role models, encouragement, people to inspire us and to pray with us; in short, we can become part of a dynamic community that is truly alive with the very life of God. Without this immersion in a truly Christian community, authentic behavior is impossible. Because of the power of the Holy Spirit, the resurrected Christ continues to live in his church for our salvation.

Paul often returns to this analogy of the Christian community being the Body of Christ. Some of the more important references here would be Romans 12:4-8; 1 Corinthians 10:16; 11:29; 12:12-27. The same theme is also developed in Ephesians 1:22-23; 3:6; 4:3-6; 4:11-16; Colossians 1:18; 3:15. There are several things to note:

1. Paul is thinking in terms of organic unity; he is not merely using a descriptive analogy. In other words, the analogy of the body was chosen because Paul felt that we were as connected and necessary to one another as members of a human body are interrelated. If one is sick, all suffer; when all are well, the entire organism functions smoothly. There is need for diversity, just as there is need for a healthy relationship between the parts.

2. Each of the parts is necessary. Paul never stresses in his letters that some ministries are "higher" or better than others. He is also careful to note that one should not feel that those who seem to play more important roles in the body are better as a result. All the members are needed for the body to function smoothly. There will obviously be diversity, just as there is in a human body, but this is the nature of all organisms. Each person should perform his or her own function as well as possible or the community will suffer.

3. The different gifts that each possesses are not for one's own use, but for the good of the whole. Paul regards the gifts and abilities that we each have as being given for the sake of others—just as Christ lived not for himself, but for others. The quote from Romans 12 explicitly states this.

4. Human beings are never defined autonomously. Paul would not have agreed with the Aristotelian definition of a person as a rational animal, nor with the Cartesian *cogito, ergo sum*. He would have thought it impossible to define a person independently of other persons. To be human is to be a relational being, and hence to be defined relationally. Biological existence is not the most important aspect of humanity. To be fully human (as Christ was) is to be actively concerned about one's brothers and sisters.

5. The eucharistic applications that Paul makes give a sense of personal, intimate relationship to the analogy. Ultimately, what enables

the body to function is love and concern for one another. Thus, there is a warmth that enlivens and makes the mutual responsibilities flow from an inner sense of obligation, not the external constraint of law.

This having been said, we cannot deny that within the community, with its multiplicity of gifts, there are some categories of people that seem to be essential to building it up. Paul himself, for example, is an apostle, and quick to vindicate that position (cf. Galatians; 2 Corinthians). Further, Paul's apostolic ministry is supported by a large number of associates: workers, co-workers, prophets, teachers, brothers. These terms are not used loosely, but seem to be somewhat technical for him.

Worker (*ergates*, *kopiontes*) indicates one who has a special responsibility for the Christian mission. Workers are helped by:

Deacons (*diakonoi*), a special class whose members include *teachers* and *preachers*, and who are entitled to pay and support from the community. Among the diakonoi are also:

Apostles who carry out a commission from the risen Lord in relative independence and develop their own groups of co-workers. Finally, there are the

Brothers (*adelphoi*), a term sometimes used for Christians in general, but having a more restricted meaning in Paul. When he uses the term with the definite article he is referring to a limited group that has the Christian mission as their primary occupation. Like the deacons, they could teach or preach, or simply act as messengers for Paul or another apostle.

Co-workers (*synergoi* [cf. Romans 16:3, 9, 21]), seem to be local converts who participate in the Christian mission and continue it after the apostle passes on.

Prophets, who tend to rank higher in the lists of gifts than "administrators."

Paul explicitly includes women among the leaders of local churches. Phoebe is a deacon (Romans 16:1), while Prisca and her husband Aquila are co-workers (16:3), as Paul and Apollos are in 1 Corinthians 3:9. Maria (Romans 16:6) has worked hard for the church, and Junias (16:7) is called outstanding among the apostles. They were not automatically excluded from key church roles because of gender.

Close to 150 of these co-workers of Paul are named. Despite that, they cannot be fitted into one neat pattern of church office. Besides their large number, they cut across the traditional religious lines of Jew and Gentile, slave and free, male and female; and they have no official titles. The harmony in church life and belief that characterized them are summed up in the ultimate title of brother or sister—in Paul's mind, perhaps the most important title they could hold.

Paul never uses the term "elder," and "bishop" (*episkopos*) occurs only once, and this itself is a disputed reading (Philippians 1:1). The above does not prove too much. It bears witness, perhaps, that titles and jobs were still rather fluid at this stage, and that there was no exclusive ministerial pattern throughout the church at this time.

If there is a cluster of insights we can gain from this foundational period, they might be:[7]

1. *Christian ministry is not sacral office.* While cultic priesthood is as old as the human race, the earliest Christian ministers were neither liturgists nor mediators for humanity. They ministered to the lives of the people and revealed moments of God's presence among them, especially as seen in Jesus and his example of justice, love, and compassion. The basic goal was community service, which explains why sacral terms are not used to describe any of them.

2. *Christian ministry is action.* The early church described its ministry as actions, not as honorific offices. There was no gulf between title and work, because the name of the ministry is both the title of the minister and the service performed.

3. *Ministry is service to the kingdom of God.* Paul has a variety of terms: gospel, life, grace—but he is referring to the loving kindness of God that has been manifested in Christ. Ministry, like the church, serves something outside of itself. The dynamic of the church is pointing to and realizing that which it serves. Secular jobs are not ministries unless they further the gospel, or (as Paul would say it) build up the body of Christ. Ministry is a visible expression of the existence, goals, and values of the Kingdom of Christ preserved by the church.

4. *Christian ministry is universal and diverse.* Ministry is for each baptized person; it is charismatically given in a universality and particularity that should not disturb the harmony of the community. This is the gift of the Spirit, who always works for the good of the whole. Paul's letters were addressed to communities and not individuals, because individual ministry is always within the context of the entire church. Whatever law and constitution there is in the church today, it must aim at holding together a voluntary association of men and women who are both community and service.

Summary

Let us isolate some developments that seem to have characterized this first generation in the early church:

1. Central to understanding ministry is the distinctive position of

Christianity's founder to his community. As head of the body, Christ abides with it and acts through it for the redemption of humankind. This alters the outlook on authoritative office within the Christian community, for it is Christ alone who holds authority in his own name. While there is some "delegation" of that authority, it is not in the sense that others exercise authority in Christ's stead. Rather, they minister to his continuing function of preeminent charismatic leadership. They bear witness to his presence, and allow his Spirit to work through them for the direction and nurture of the community.

2. To an extent that is hard to parallel in other religious communities, Christianity exists apart from civic involvements. The kingdom it works to establish is "not of this world." With a naïve simplicity that history and its own missionary thrust would soon alter, the early church saw itself as an "otherworldly" movement, "in the world, but not of it." Unavoidably, this conditioned the manner of discovering or devising ministry. It excludes the political model as an apt parallel. "The lords of the Gentiles dominate their subjects; it is not to be that way with you...."

3. As they saw it, the early communities not only owed their origin to the event of Christ's death and resurrection, but they continued to live that event. As they gathered in Eucharist, they were constantly formed by their meals with the risen Christ as the central element of their experience. Their worship, then, took on a distinctive character: It was a "memorial" in a new sense, and was tied to the communal life of the people rather than to designated shrines or to detailed ritual. In such a context there was little need for a priestly group. Such a group would probably have been seen by most as in competition with the Temple priesthood.

The early church used what we would today call liturgical language to denote the concern we owe one another. Caring for the people was an expression of their proper worship. In some ways we are back to the primitive sociological family or clan structure of life and social order, where cult can be assured without need of special ministers.

4. Of the three prominent mediatorial functions the early Christians would have known from their Old Testament heritage, that of the prophet gained ascendancy. Significantly, this was the least structured and institutionalized of the three. Even here, the model was not the organized prophetic groups but with the charismatic prophets whose vocation was independent of official recognition, deriving directly from divine choice. Moreover, the office of prophet absorbed into itself the idealized functions of both priest and king. This was true of Jesus and

also of the disciples. Even worship was subsumed under this prophetic function, as there are clear indications that Eucharist was seen as proclamation of the Word, and until the end of the century the prophets would be the main presiders at Eucharist (cf. John 6).

5. Prophetic ministry would seem to be the essential pattern of pastoral service within the infant church. Those who with special designation provided for the faith and unity of the churches did so basically through the witness of their words and lives. To some extent, this was not restricted to a special group; all who belonged to the community had a prophetic task. This seems to be the message of Acts 2, where the explanation of Pentecost given by Peter is that the gift of the prophetic Spirit is communicated to the entire assembly. Perhaps our understanding of distinctive functions within early Christianity must distinguish different aspects of prophecy, rather than trying to distinguish prophecy from other roles.

6. Attention should be drawn to an element connected with Christian prophecy—the notion of discipleship. This is more than the founder's immediate followers having a special role to play. Here the followers not only spread the teaching of the master, they are the very embodiment of his continuous teaching and witness. They are themselves the living instance of the mystery they proclaim. In personifying the message, they become signs, sacraments, of Christ's redeeming activity.

7. In both Palestinian and Gentile communities, prophecy seems to have been a prized manifestation of the Spirit. Some of these inspired teachers may have been responsible for the formation of a Christian literature (e.g., a passage like 1 Corinthians 2:6–16, or the "Q" source of Luke). They may also have played a prominent role in the liturgical assemblies. These included both men and women. Paul ranks them high after apostles.

8. During the first generation, no single pattern of leadership emerged as one "willed by Jesus," or which was normative for all the churches; rather, ministry and leadership were extremely diversified.

9. Whether Hellenized or Hebrew, the first Christians were essentially a sectarian movement within Judaism. Missionary communities, however, were not simply transplants of the Jerusalem church. They developed their own style and a special ministry to the Gentiles. Despite Paul's tendency to downplay its influence, however, there was a special status accorded Jerusalem in the early days.

10. Missionary apostles like Paul were active within twenty years of Jesus' death. These included both men and women, and each apostle

appears to have freely developed his or her own group of associates in the missionary ministry. If Paul's case is typical, the apostle was surely the supreme authority in matters of doctrine and discipline for his communities. There is evidence that Paul put leaders (elders? overseers?) in charge to continue pastoral supervision after he had gone.

11. Ministry seems to have been regarded as a function common to many, rather than a hierarchical possession restricted to a few. There is no evidence that these earliest Christians attempted to establish a priesthood parallel to the Temple, as did the community at Qumran.

12. From the classic passages concerning gifts, charisms, and ministries of various kinds (1 Corinthians 12:4-11; Romans 12:6-8; Ephesians 4:11-16 [though this is later than Paul]), we find ministries of preaching, instruction, healing, miracle-working, prophecy, discernment, interpretation of tongues, teaching, exhortation, almsgiving, presiding, mercy, administration, as well as the ministry of apostles, evangelists, and pastors. Thus, there was a variety, and probably a variety of combinations as well. All served to build the community; the gathering rhythm was basic, at first.

Discussion Questions

1. What distinction between the various ministries do we find in the first generation? How were the five basic tasks of church realized in this first generation?

2. What are some of the conclusions (if any) that can be drawn from knowing that there was no class of people called priests in early Christianity?

3. Can we argue to the classic understanding of bishop from the practice of Peter and the Twelve? from James? from Paul? Why or why not?

4. What understandings of church ministry can we learn from the first century that are still valid for us in the church today? Which do you consider most important and why?

5. Are there any similarities between the church in our country today and the church in the time of Peter and Paul? How so? Are there any lessons we can learn from the past for our practice today?

Suggested Readings

Brown, R., *Priest and Bishop*, Mahwah, N.J.: Paulist Press, 1980.

Lemaire, A., "From Service to Ministries: *Diakonoi* in the First Two Centuries," *Concilium*, 10, 8 (December 1972), 35-49.

Mitchell, N., "The Earliest Patterns of Christian Ministry," *Mission and Ministry: History and Theology in the Sacrament of Order*, Wilmington, Del.: Michael Glazier, 1982, Chap. 2, pp. 72-136.

Mohler, J., "Christian Presbyters of the New Testament," *The Origin and Evolution of the Priesthood*, New York: Alba House, 1970, Chap. 2, pp. 11-32.

O'Meara, T., "Primal Ministry," *Theology of Ministry*, New York: Paulist, 1983, Chap 4, pp. 76-94.

_____."Ministries in the New Testament," *Biblical Theology Bulletin*, 3 (June 1973), 133-166. This provides an excellent summary of literature on the subject up to 1973.

O'Toole, R. J., "New Testament Reflections on Ministry," *Biblical Theology Bulletin*, 10 (October 1980), 140-148.

Schillebeeckx, E., "The Changing Meaning of Ministry," *Cross Currents*, (Winter 1983), 432-45, (Spring 1984), 65-82.

_____. "Jesus Christ and His Messianic Communities," *The Church with a Human Face: A New and Expanded Theology of Ministry*, London: SCM Press, 1985, Chap. 1, pp. 13-39.

_____. "The Practice and Theology of Ministry in the Early Communities of Christian Believers," *ibid.*, Chap. 2, pp. 40-124.

2

Ministry as Charism

Though comprising only some forty years, this is a varied period and perhaps even more important than the foundational period of the first generation. In a way it was a time of re-foundation. The razing of the Temple in the year 70 was more than the ruin of a building, it was the final destruction of a way of life, a way of thinking for both Jews and Christians. A rethinking of enormous proportions was necessary. This is reflected in the remaining books of the New Testament, all of which were written at this time.

In this one generation the church spread into many different lands as well as in cities and villages; this brought about a pluralism of practice that we are only beginning to appreciate. Finally, as Christians began to realize that the *parousia* was a long time in coming, greater concern began to be shown for developing permanent structures to provide for the long haul.

The first generation had been largely Jewish, or people who accepted the legitimacy of the Jewish religion and its Law. Without a Temple, there was no longer a priesthood. And the consolidation of the remains of Jewry was brought about by the Pharisees, no friends of those sectarians who believed that Jesus was messiah. Shortly after the destruction of the Temple, Christians were excommunicated from the synagogues: "Let the Nazarenes...be destroyed in a moment... Let their names be expurgated from the Book of Life and not be entered with those of the just."[1]

Compounding the problem, the great apostles were no longer around to provide guidance. This had to come from within. The Letter to the Hebrews, that daring fresh look at the meaning of Jesus' life, was written during this period. It was also the time of the *Didache*, and the letters of Ignatius and Clement, writings that some churches considered part of the New Testament canon. As the new faith spread to all corners of the Roman world, some stabilization and a greater uniformity of practice did set in, though there was still great variety.

After the disappearance of the first generation, the problems of ministry began to be more urgent. People did not occupy themselves so much with structures, but with a sort of theological reflection on needs and on practice. The need to provide leadership for a new generation is seen in the pastoral epistles, for example, whose very pseudonymity shows the desire to provide links with the founding generation. They show the importance of an organic link to justify the practices of a later age. Ministry is seen as insuring the fidelity of the community to its apostolic origins and orientation. Proclamation, leadership, and building the community in accordance with its apostolic foundations is also the purpose of Ephesians, as we will see.

Ministerial Structures in the Post-Apostolic Age

One interesting thought for those who think of Jesus as having provided the blueprint for his new community is that the one structure that is attributed to him—the college of the Twelve—did not last. After Judas's betrayal, the Eleven thought it important to replace him in order to keep the number at twelve. But nothing more is heard of the Twelve after a few more years. They were only a hallowed memory at the end of the foundational period. In Jerusalem, leadership of the church was taken over by James, a non-apostle. Never again do we hear of the necessity of perpetuating an apostolic college.

We can perhaps make too much of the eschatology that characterized the church in its first decades of existence. Without having to view these people as unrealistic visionaries who sat around waiting for the final coming of Christ, and the next generation as slightly disillusioned realists who decided to make the best of a bad situation, we can see that there was surely need for some adjustment as it became more obvious that the parousia was not around the corner. The church began to make realistic provisions for its own continued existence. The emphasis on the Kingdom of God began to shift somewhat to the church itself, and those who guided the church were regarded in a new light. Attention was drawn to what was necessary to make an earthly "kingdom" run effectively. The question also rose as to what role Christianity would play in its continuing historical existence.

The question facing the church at this point was (theologically), who had the right and responsibility of teaching authoritatively in the name of Jesus? How could one be sure that teaching was authentic? Matthew's warnings against false prophets (7:15–23; 24:11, 24) seem to indicate that the second generation was beginning to challenge the authority of the prophets in this regard. Ephesians, another second generation document, also seems to indicate that prophets, like apostles, were part of the church's *past*. It speaks (2:19–20) of the church founded [only] on "apostles and prophets" with Jesus Christ as capstone. In 4:11–12 it adds "evangelists and pastors" to the Pauline list of church ministries. These terms appear in documents only after 70 C.E. Eusebius also associates them only with the post-apostolic generation. Though prophets continued to play an important role well into the second century (and even into the third), they began to be viewed with increasing suspicion.

By the end of the first century, church order was insured in many places by a group of "presbyters." These presbyters were also sometimes called *episkopoi*, for some of them had the function of overseeing. There are many shifts in the meaning of the term "presbyter" at this time, as well as in the functions of the prophets. (It would seem that presbyters and prophets were two of the more important groups in this period.) New terminology and specific functions began to be defined, though it is not always clear what the ancient understanding may have been. We should be careful not to simply transpose our modern understanding of terms on ancient times.

It is important to keep in mind is that no single solution emerged to the crisis in leadership for these later Christian generations. Different communities responded in different ways, and it was well into the second century before there began to be more standardized ways for providing continuing leadership. Raymond Brown gives a number of examples of how the various churches reacted in different ways to the challenge of survival. Brown lists seven distinct communities:[2]

1. Antioch, where Matthew was written
2. The community of Ephesians and Colossians
3. The community where Luke/Acts was written
4. The community where John was written
5. The community in which 1 and 2 John were written
6. The community where 1 Peter was written
7. The community of the pastoral epistles.

One preliminary conclusion we can draw from all this is that there was still no set pattern to either the names or functions of Christian ministers at the close of the New Testament period. There was a continuous development according to the needs of the various communities.

Brown should be read for a far more complete explanation. Here we will content ourselves with noting only a few of these areas of development.

The Teacher/Scribe in Matthew

Matthew has well been called the gospel of church order. In no other gospel is such attention given the role of the apostles, or to the leadership role of Peter. He softens the stark harshness of Mark's presentation. As regards his treatment of prophecy, Matthew seems custodial and conservative. He struggles to insure that Jesus' words are not distorted by prophetic interpretation, thus seeming to oppose prophetic innovation. He appeals to the Jewish tradition of the teacher/scribe, whose primary job is to hand on what has been received rather than to create new traditions. We are dealing with the needs of an established community.

Matthew 7:22–23 hints at the gospel writer's attitude. Persons condemned here are precisely those who have prophesied in Jesus' name. In contrast, Matthew 8:19 speaks of a scribe who is eager to become Jesus' disciple with its hardship and homelessness. Then Matthew will amend Marcan passages like "prophets and apostles" to read "prophets and wise men and scribes" (23:34), implying that wise men are now the guarantors of the Jesus tradition formerly taught by the apostles. Finally, at the end of the gospel, Matthew omits any references to charismatic signs and wonders accompanying the preaching of the gospel (28:18–20).

"Every scribe who is learned in the reign of God," says Matthew, "is like the head of a household who can bring out from his storeroom both the new and the old" (13:52). For Matthew, the *past*, the gospel's carefully controlled portrait of Jesus, has become normative for the church's present and future. He looks to teacher/scribes who will sustain the "little ones" in a life of fidelity.

Who were these teacher/scribes? There obviously seems to be some parallel between the Jewish scribes and the Christian teachers. Scribe may simply be a way of indicating *true* prophets/teachers, as opposed to those who are false. We do not have enough evidence to say it represents a new ministry emerging in this period, but it may represent a different emphasis given an older ministry. If so, then where the first generation scribe was a charismatic innovator, Matthew sees second generation scribes as the custodians of established tradition, well authenticated by the community.

The Johannine Alternative[3]

If Matthew was convinced of the need for authoritative teaching, he rejected the method of worldly rulers, who lord it over others (20:25–30). This was in keeping with the basic equality of all Christians. More radical still was the approach taken by the Johannine communities, which seem to have resisted investing any human minister with final authority in teaching or discipline. Rather, the Spirit was to be the guarantor of truth and fidelity.

Commentaries on John's gospel show the tension between the Johannine and the apostolic community. He is strangely silent about any authority given the Twelve or to Peter. In fact, we have the figure of the mysterious disciple whom Jesus loved (not to be confused with St. John) who is the central witness of his gospel, and who "believes" even while Peter is still confused about the meaning of the empty tomb (20:3–9). In the gospel, the beloved disciple's witness and the presence of the Spirit seem sufficient to ground the community's faith (19:35; 21:24).

Raymond Brown has shown convincingly in his *Anchor Bible* commentaries on the Johannine Epistles and in an accompanying book (*The Community of the Beloved Disciple*) some of the problems that arose from this approach. The leader of this community was unable to resolve conflicts in any way except by appealing to the Spirit; but his opponents could (and did) make the same appeal. There was no external authority to make decisions stick. Ultimately many of the dissidents slid off into Gnosticism, while those who remained faithful adopted some Matthaen authoritarian structures. Note that in the appendix to John's gospel (chapter 21), there is reluctant admission that Peter's authority is real, being rooted in his love for Jesus.

The World of the Pastorals[4]

Johannine communities knew of the practice of others. The author identifies himself as an "elder" (*presbyteros*), even if he doesn't attach much authoritative significance to the term. Most scholars seem to agree that this term and concept was taken over from Judaism. As derived from synagogue practice, it referred to a group of people respected for their age and wisdom, a sort of proven virtue. They formed a consultative or advisory group that helped guide the community. This pattern would surely have begun in Jerusalem and eventually spread into other areas. Acts, for example, presumes there are presbyters at Ephesus (20:17), as well as in cities evangelized by Barnabas and Paul on the first missionary journey (14:23), a fact not attested in the epistles.

Later literature, from around the year 100 on, has rather frequent references to this group of individuals (cf. 1 Timothy 5:1,17,19; Titus 1:5; 1 Peter 5:1; James 5:14 [?]). Sometimes we are given their qualifications: "irreproachable, married only once, the father of children who are believers and known not to be wild and insubordinate" (Titus 1:6). Similarly, 1 Timothy 5:17 insists that "presbyters deserve to be paid double, especially those whose work is preaching and teaching." Surely by this time, most Christians were familiar with the presbyteral pattern of local leadership.

According to Ernst Kasemann, the churches addressed in the pastoral epistles were originally part of the Pauline mission field and were trying to rally around the traditions of Paul's gospel. Faced with various types of outside opposition, the communities looked to recognized office-holders to guarantee the "deposit of faith" (1 Timothy 6:20).

In both their ecclesiological assumptions and their views of church order, however, the pastorals depart from what we find in Paul's genuine letters. Paul saw the church as the body of Christ in which all the members were endowed with gifts of mutual service; the pastorals see it as the household of God exposed to external dangers and needing protection. Such guidance is supplied by leaders whose qualifications are like those of the head of a family, as one can see from their lists of required qualities. (cf. 1 Timothy 3:2–7 [episkopos]; Titus 1:6 [presbyteros]; 1 Timothy 3:8–13 [diakonos]).

Brown agrees with this, and shows how the setting of the letters imagines Paul as he approaches death and his thoughts turn to the Christians he is leaving behind. The letters are thus more pastoral than missionary. The danger now seems to be false teachers (Titus 1:10; 1 Timothy 4:1–2; 2 Timothy 3:6, 4:3). The solution is clearly an answer in terms of church structure. Presbyter/bishops are to be named in every town (Titus 1:5,7); their authoritative guidance will preserve the churches from disintegration. Guidance, not sacramental ministry, was thus the main role of the presbyter/bishops in the pastorals. (Note that there is evidence in the Essenian communities of having both presbyers and certain "overseers," also described as shepherds, besides presbyters.)

First and foremost, the presbyter/bishops were the official teachers of the community. Second, because the church is the household of God, they were to administer it well. The standards set are rather pedestrian, but they are standards nonetheless. As the church became more organized, it began to determine which men would guide it best, and was willing to sacrifice charismatic qualities for standards that, in the long run, would provide for harmony and growth. Thus, the right of the church to set requirements seems to have been established even in the New Testament period. This is the famous "institutionalization," which is a bad word in some circles.

There are strengths and weaknesses in this approach.

1. Impressive stability and solid continuity are marks of an institutional structure. If the bishop must "hold fast to the firm word as it was taught" (Titus 1:9) it is because other teachers are introducing new ideas (Gnosticism). Stringent control of teaching is an essential weapon in times of doctrinal crisis, and prevents the church from being destroyed from within.

The great danger of too exclusive a stress on officially controlled teaching, however, is that it can become cant. It can easily lead to the image of a safe-deposit box sterilely protecting what was put into it in the first century. Constructive insights to augment and nuance doctrine become suspect. This attitude is the ancestor of the theology of a deposit of doctrine, ecclesiastical approval of professors, imprimaturs, and an index of forbidden books.

2. The total orientation is toward pastoral qualities in the officials: safe, institutional virtues. Paul himself would have hardly fit this pattern. If the entire thrust is toward highly prudential leaders holding on to the past, this creates an orientation that is not going to favor the innovations necessary for a dynamic mission. This can lead to the "Caiaphas principle," where individuals can be sacrificed for the "good" of the community.

3. Timothy 3:1–9 is hardly kind toward false teachers. Is differing from standard teaching, however, always a mark of false teachers, or can it be a mark of constructive teachers whose ideas may lead the church to perceive more clearly what has been entrusted by the Holy Spirit? Remember Galileo.

4. Another weakness is the attitude taken toward those who are taught; "weak women," is used as an example of those who are ignorant, impulsive, and easily misled. We so easily refer to "the simple faithful," that we can get a picture of church as made up of presbyters and a fixed class of those taught who, if not instructed by the official church, will all be deceived by false teachers. It was O.K. to "remind the people to be submissive to rulers and authority "(Titus 3:1); but the fact that "remind them to contribute to the church by being construc-

tive" did not make it into the same letter makes the first statement rather determinative of our approach.

The World of Colossians and Ephesians

By way of contrast, we have another Pauline strain: the churches represented by Colossians and Ephesians. These seem more directly connected to Paul than the church of the pastorals. Colossians may have been written only a decade after Paul's death. These letters also give authoritative guidance to the church, seen as "the household of God," but also "built upon the foundations of the apostles and prophets, with Christ Jesus himself as the cornerstone" (Ephesians 2:19–20).

Instructions for the ethical behavior of members of the household are supplied in somewhat similar manner to what we have in the pastorals, but an awareness of a charismatic church structure is shown in Ephesians 4:11, which lists apostles, prophets, evangelists, pastors, and teachers. There is no stress on apostolic succession or the institutional aspects of the church. We see nothing significant about the functioning of the pastors and teachers—despite the onslaught of false teaching (Colossians 2:8–23; Ephesians 4:14). Rather than responding to error by emphasizing official teachers they offer instead an expanded, idealistic view of "the church."

They adopt Paul's image of the Body of Christ and develop it in a new way to fit a massive emphasis on the church. Despite the corporate understanding, the church never becomes a corporation (unlike the pastorals). The theme of love between Christ and the church is very strong, and holiness is an important characteristic. Matthew's explanation of the parable of the weeds planted and allowed to grow would illustrate this attitude. The church itself, however, is glorified and almost identified with the Kingdom.[5]

There are strengths and weaknesses in this approach also.

1. The Body of Christ approach personalizes the church and encourages our love for it. It's much easier to love "mother" church than the "institutional" church. Christ gave himself up for her (Ephesians 5:25), and Paul completed in his flesh what was lacking to the sufferings of Christ for the sake of the church (Colossians 1:24). This personalization and love is a logical derivative of the ecclesiology of Colossians/ Ephesians.

2. The holiness of the church that is part of the picture is also an element that allows the church to survive. The author of Ephesians knew well of the many sinful situations Paul described, yet he could still refer to the church as a spotless bride, holy and without blemish. This is no

starry-eyed romanticism, but mystical vision. Those who follow his example will be able to acknowledge sin and still put this into perspective through love for the church.

It is difficult, however, to think of reforming a spotless bride. If the members are knit together in a growth that comes from God, and are being built up in love, is there any place for defects, or for corrective operations? This is more the high Catholicism of the Eastern churches. There may be a stimulus to triumphalism here.

The emphasis on holiness can also be a defect if it begins to mask existing faults. It can lead to hiding the sins and stupidities of church figures. On the other hand, it is said, if all the dirty laundry is put out to public view, many may find it difficult to cope with this or feel dedication to such a flawed organization. These are the inherent tensions.

The emphasis on "the" church in these letters can weaken the role of the local churches in ecclesiology. This has been very obvious in the Catholic church. The theology of the local churches almost has to be rediscovered in our age. Finally, if there is too strong a concentration on the church as the ultimate goal of God's plan, a large part of the world seems to be left out.

Another Look at Presbyters, Deacons, and Bishops

From the different approaches of the above-mentioned communities, we can see that the very "facts" had different meanings for people living at roughly the same time. The use of the two terms presbyter and bishop, for example, did not necessarily indicate separate or distinct offices or categories of leadership at this time. (Later they surely do.) A common opinion is that "presbyter" and "bishop" are virtually interchangeable. Some refer to them as presbyter-bishops. While not seen as successors to the Twelve, they might be seen as successors to the Pauline missionary apostles, inasmuch as they exercised care in the communities that the apostles had founded. This is Brown's opinion, though he cautions against taking it as a universal rule or practice.[6]

Can we draw any conclusions from the New Testament evidence about the roles of presbyters and deacons, or even bishops? Let us begin with the latter term first, because it is the easiest to deal with.

"Bishops" in the New Testament World

The term "bishop" is found only in Acts and 1 Peter. We have mentioned that the most esteemed ministerial roles for Paul were those of apostle, prophet, and teacher. This is equally true for Acts, which though it mentions "bishop," does so only once. What can be said of

the title is that it is taken from secular usage, and has no religious con-
notations. A bishop would have some authority, but his main role was
of service in building up the community and holding it together. This
would seem to be the way it was used in Acts [20:17–20], where we are
told that Paul tells the elders at Miletus to be responsible overseers of
the people of God. Here, however, it is difficult to distinguish whether
there is any distinction between elders/presbyters and bishops/
overseers.

Note that nowhere in the New Testament does it say that the apostles, or the Twelve, were bishops. This equation was made by Cyprian
at a much later date. There is no evidence for linking the "college of
apostles" and the "college of bishops." To say that the apostles were
the first bishops goes beyond New Testament evidence. The apostles
were surely the first chief leaders of the Christian assembly, but they
neither had the title bishop, nor did they function the way bishops
would function later in the church.

Presbyters as Role Models

Presbyter is a much better attested title in the New Testament. It is
found in Acts, in the pastorals, and in the Johannine material. As has
been mentioned before, however, there is considerable disagreement
about what these presbyters did, or even if they did anything. We have
seen that to a large extent their existence is based on a previous Jewish
model. This being so, one thing we can affirm about them with certainty is that liturgical functions were not part of their role. Much of the ink
that has been spilled over exactly what their functions were, and how
they differed from bishops, may come, in part, from thinking of them
as modern "priests," which they certainly were not.

The solution may be quite simple. Many think that the evidence
shows that "presbyter" is only a status title.[7] The terms "bishop" and
"deacon" would be titles related to ministries. In other words, "presbyter" in itself did not apply to a specific ministry within the community, but to the status accorded those who were senior in authority. This
status, with its prestige and respect, belonged to those whose conversion and rebirth through faith had been longstanding and fruitful. The
presbyterate, thus, was not a category of office, or a college of ministers, but a designation for those whose lives demonstrated a fruitful
Christian maturity. Age was not necessarily a factor; it depended more
on having given oneself fully to Christ. This conception accords well
with the role of elders at Qumran.

Powell argues further[8] that the controlling image that stands behind the notion of presbyterate is not the "head/body/members" metaphor of 1 Corinthians 12, but the "first fruits/final harvest" image of 1 Corinthians 15:22–24. All Christians are part of this; presbyters can only claim special recognition because of the quality of their conversion; as Christ is the firstfruits of those that sleep, so the presbyters are the firstfruits harvested in the apostolic mission.

This would help explain the apparently overlapping terms used in the pastorals. The "presbyters" of 1 Timothy 5:17,19 and Titus 1:5, for example, are not an additional category of ministers (like bishops or deacons) or a governing council (college), or an alternative designation for bishop. *Some* of the presbyters undoubtedly do perform the ministries of bishop and deacon, but they will acquire specific functions only as we approach the *Apostolic Tradition* of Hippolytus.

If this analysis is correct (and it would seem the most logical), we can conclude that the pastorals deal with, at most, two ministries: bishop and deacon. Unfortunately, no detailed job description is given for either. The *bishop's* responsibility seems to have included three major areas: 1) overseeing and regulating the community's life (which might result in correcting abuses, or censuring offenders—Titus 1:9–11); 2) administering its fiscal resources (thus the emphasis on good household management—1 Timothy 3:3–4); 3) teaching sound doctrine (Acts 20:28–29). These requirements clearly point to a local leader whose acquaintance with the local community is longstanding. And, if he were taken from among the presbyters, it is understandable why one recently baptized would be considered an inappropriate candidate. By their very nature, presbyters could not be recent converts.

The Role of Deacons

What do deacons do? It is common teaching today that the office of deacon goes back to our origins. This, however, is a term used only by Paul and in the pastorals. It does not appear in Acts. Calling the Seven Hellenists who were set aside to minister to the Greek-speaking "deacons" goes beyond New Testament evidence. They function more as leaders and apostles. Though the Pauline writings mention deacons, the nature of their ministry is not specified.

We have to allow that "deacon" at this time may be simply a further specification of the bishop's ministry. In Philippians 1:1, for example, there is no overwhelming indication that bishops and deacons are two distinct offices; the phrase may simply refer to all who exercise leadership in the church. Some would translate this "...to all the holy ones in Christ Jesus who are at Philippi, especially those who teach and preach." (Note that many consider *episkopos* here as a later textual addition.)

Paul described his own ministry as missionary/apostle with the word *diakonia* (2 Corinthians 3:6; 4:1); and the household of Stephanas, the "first converts in Achaia," is to be obeyed and recognized because of their *diakonia* (1 Corinthians 16:15–16). In other words, Stephanas and his co-workers seem to "bishop" precisely because they "deacon." It may well be that the ministerial function of episcopacy (literally, "overseeing") is expressed through the function of deaconing (literally, serving others).

Some hold that *diakonos* has a slightly more technical meaning in both Paul's letters and the pastorals. Deacons may have formed a special class of teacher/preacher who assisted the Pauline workers, and were thus entitled to support from the local congregations. Paul even described himself and Apollos as *diakonoi* (1 Corinthians 3:5). It might shed light on Timothy being called a *diakonos* (1 Timothy 4:6); as Paul's co-worker and companion, though Timothy acts more like a missionary.

What it comes down to is that here also the evidence is not conclusive. Presbyter/deacons may have been church leaders recognizably different from presbyter/bishops, but it is impossible to identify the exact difference. Both are expected to be good heads of households; this would seem to imply types of ministry that are local and residential in nature. André Lemaire argues that deacons had missionary responsibilities, noting that in 1 Timothy 3:8–13, "hospitality" is omitted in the qualities of deacons.[9] While this may have been accidental, it could make sense if the deacons had itinerant ministry. All this remains conjectural. The one thing we can say with certainty is that the pastorals do not attempt to arrange "presbyter, bishop, deacon" into a hierarchical pattern of superior and inferior leaders.

We might summarize the existing evidence as follows: The ministry of deacons, as some form of subsidiary ministry, goes back to the time of the apostles, but no precise descriptions are given of their roles. At times there seems to be an overlap with the presbyters or with the bishops. The ministry of deacons, however, is one in which women are specifically mentioned by Paul.

Ordination in the New Testament

Many people feel that, if sacraments came from Christ, some form of ordination must have taken place during his lifetime, or at least within the New Testament era. This may well be, but we have no historical proof of it. To begin with, first-century Jews were not familiar with an ordination for priests (priesthood was a matter of genealogy, not vocation). Some ceremonies seem to have existed after the Exile, but these did not "make" a person a priest, they simply marked the solemn beginning of ministry. Thus, even those most attached to their Jewish background (James and the Jerusalem church) had neither an ordination ceremony to inspire them or ever thought of themselves as priests to begin with. Nor were there any rabbinic antecedents at this time.

This still leaves us with the question as to whether or not there was some form of ritual appointment to authoritative offices or roles in the church. The crux of the problem, however, goes much deeper than this. The theological question is what is a priest, and who deserves this title in the church of Christ? Let us mention three indisputable facts of the New Testament.

1. No Christian is ever called priest in the New Testament. This was a cultic word, and was reserved to the Jewish or pagan priests. It was consciously avoided by the New Testament writers when it came to any ministries in the community of Jesus.

2. There are several passages in the New Testament where the entire community is called priestly. This is the origin of the teaching on the common priesthood of all believers. Basically what is at stake here is the radical equality that baptism brings to all in the church. Ministries are a form of service within the community in order to make it what Jesus intended. No ministry is one of status only. And there seems to be no distinction between sacred and profane ministries.

3. Jesus himself is a layman, as far as the New Testament is concerned. There is only one writing in the New Testament that ever calls Jesus a priest: the Letter to the Hebrews. It does so, however, only by redefining what priesthood itself is. It goes out of its way to point out that if Jesus were still alive he would not be considered a priest, since Jewish priests were such by genealogy, not special vocation. Thus, no one would have thought of calling him a priest until after long meditation on the meaning of his life and death.

If we accept that Jesus is a priest, however, we have the further statement of Hebrews that he is the *only* priest. He exhausts the category completely. Thus, calling the present ministers of the church *priests* is legitimate only if we are aware that this is an analogical use of the term, one that finds no warrant in the New Testament, and would have been understood quite differently then. It began only in the third century, mainly because of the renewed influence of the Old Testament in the preaching and teaching of the Fathers.

Thus, we can assert that Christian priesthood cannot be understood unless we understand the priesthood of Jesus; and then it can be understood only as an analogical concept. This will be an underlying theme throughout this book. That having been said, reflecting on the "lay" reality of Jesus' life and death should serve as an inspiration for *all* in the church. The greatest imitation of Christ does not depend on ordination. It requires only that one try to be to people in our time what Christ was to people in his. This can and must be achieved by everyone who has been baptized.

With these cautions, let us return to the question of whether or not we have any examples of "ordination" ceremonies in the New Testament.[10] We do have several instances of the laying on of hands (it is mentioned nine times in the New Testament). What this might mean, however, is debatable. In many cases it designates a way of sending people on a particular task (as in sending Barnabas and Paul on the first missionary journey [Acts 13:2–3]). Whether any of these refer to ordination is questionable.

The clearest hint of such a practice comes from 1 Timothy 4:14, where we read: "Do not neglect the gift you have, which was given you by prophetic utterance when the council of elders laid their hands on you." The passage occurs as part of an exhortation to fulfill what we might call today a ministry of the Word. It all sounds like an official ordination.

Edward Kilmartin, using this and other texts, argues that we can discern the outlines of an ordination rite in the New Testament.[11] As he sees it, this would have resembled the following:

1. The candidate is "elected" through an inspired utterance from the community's prophets (cf. 1 Timothy 1:18; 4:14).

2. A recitation of basic elements contained in the gospel entrusted then follows (a kind of *traditio symboli*, or profession of faith [cf. 2 Timothy 2:2]).

3. The candidate promises to guard the teaching faithfully (cf. 1 Timothy 6:12).

4. Thereupon, hands are imposed by the elders of the community. Prayer would probably have accompanied this action.

Kilmartin notes that the imposition of hands is intimately linked to a charism that supports the candidate in the ministry of the Word (cf. 1 Timothy 4:11–13; 2 Timothy 1:6). The rite does not bestow personal authority on the candidate, but acts to mediate a charism that comes from God. The charism is one *for* office, not one *of* office. Any authority the person might possess stems from faithful fulfillment of the service.

This is admittedly an attractive reconstruction, and would show a New Testament basis for what surely became common by the third century. But Kilmartin admits that his ordination liturgy is very unclear. As a ritual gesture, the laying on of hands means many things in Scripture. Furthermore, in 1 Timothy 4:14, those laying on hands are the elders, not bishops.

In passages that deal with this, for example, Acts 12:1–3 or 1 Timothy 4:14, the gesture of laying on of hands is directed toward people who are missionaries. The same might be said for Acts 6:6, which deals with the Hellenists, Stephen, et al. By contrast, residential leaders (bishops) are never described as having hands laid on them. It is probable that the laying on of hands is a type of commissioning gesture for people designated for missionary work. If we keep in mind the crisis in leadership that the church experienced at this time, and the suspicion of wandering prophets, it would have made sense to know that people had been officially commissioned by specific communities.

1 Timothy 5:22 is adduced at times to show that Timothy was a bishop who ordained presbyters. He is warned not to be hasty in the laying on of hands. The larger context, however, suggests that the warning is given precisely because Timothy belongs to that select group of presbyters; because presbyters are linked with the laying on of hands for those in functional ministries, Timothy is advised to be cautious.

In summary, the question of whether there were or were not ordinations in the New Testament is the wrong question. We should really ask how Christian communities in the first three generations recognized leaders, and how these leaders gained authoritative status. It is clear that recognized leadership did exist. We cannot say that anyone could exercise any role in the church. Paul certainly thought of himself as an authority to be reckoned with. By the second or third generation, however, it is more difficult to discern who might legitimately have a "mandate" for ministry. In local churches, resident leaders could probably be chosen through election, because their quality of life and teaching were well known and long observed.

Increasingly, "missionaries" presented a problem. How reliable were they? Ritually designating them was one way to help prevent self-appointed prophets from wandering about disturbing the faithful. It helped fix and conserve in approved channels the heritage left by Christ.

Ministry and the Celebration of Eucharist

Many people raise the question about who presided over the celebration of the Eucharist in the early church. Though today we tend to associate ordination with "the power to celebrate the Eucharist," this was beside the point in the early church. Life then did not organize itself around the liturgy, but around building up the community's life.[12] Eucharist was but one aspect of that larger reality. Preaching, admonition, and works of charity are far more central than questions about "who presides" at baptism or Eucharist. The fundamental purpose of New Testament ministry is to preserve the community's self-identity as the community of Christ, and to help it discover the gospel in the changing circumstances of life.

For this reason, New Testament literature shows almost no interest in questions of "presidency" at Eucharist.[13] Paul seems to be cast in this role in Acts 20:11, but he never mentions presiding at Eucharist; and he seldom baptized. The pastorals say a good deal about bishops and deacons, but they never list "leading the church at Eucharist" among any of their tasks. Furthermore, there is absolutely nothing in the New Testament about a chain of sacramental power passed from Jesus to the Twelve, to the missionary apostles, to the bishops, etc. The most we can say (with Brown) is that *someone* must have led the church at Eucharist. For we know that weekly celebration became the norm soon after the resurrection as an expression of the life of the community.

Not only did someone lead the church at Eucharist, but leadership to do so must somehow have been recognized by the community. We are never told, however, how anyone got that position, nor whether it was permanent or ad hoc. Nor are we told that it was an exclusively male prerogative. It seems most likely that in the house churches that were common, the host—or hostess—presided. Note that the New Testament refers explicitly to women whose houses were used for Eucharists (cf. Colossians 4:15). It is likely that it was those already considered competent to lead the church in matters of public responsibility who were ipso facto considered competent to preside at Eucharist as well, without need for any special authorization to do so. Surely there was no problem about *having* Eucharist. This was the nature of the church.

What all of this indicates is this: Any arguing about New Testament ministry that begins with Eucharist and proceeds to ministry is not evident in any New Testament writing. Rather, the argument must proceed in the opposite direction: from the ministry of leadership over the community to a consequent liturgical or sacramental leadership. In other words, it is not because New Testament ministers have the power to consecrate the Eucharist that they are ministers of the Christian community; it is because they are leaders that they preside over the community's public prayer. It is ministerial leadership that is emphasized in Acts and the epistles; almost nothing is said of sacramental, much less eucharistic, leadership.

This should not be taken to mean that eucharistic presidency was a free-for-all, or that anyone could preside whenever he or she felt like it. There is a temptation to understand the New Testament teaching about the common priesthood of all believers to mean that everyone is a priest, or to interpret the injunction given at the Last Supper, "Do this in memory of me," to mean that any baptized person could preside. This is equally without scriptural foundation. Nowhere does the early Christian community seem to be an amorphous, leaderless mass. Ministerial leadership is evident in the earliest New Testament writings, a leadership that formed the general basis for eucharistic leadership.

We will see in the next chapter that presidency over the Eucharist was not confined to bishops, and that presbyters were never said to have presided. Early church ministry is far more focused on the presidency over the community. Eventually this provides the basis for an exclusive presidency over the Eucharist. As we will see in the course of this study, a theology that bases priestly ministry almost exclusively on celebration of Eucharist gave rise to many distortions that Vatican II tried to correct.

Summary

1. The early church seems to have been characterized by having a number of local leaders (teachers, prophets, evangelists, etc.) along with a leadership that surpassed that of the local level. Paul would have represented this latter type. Although the term apostle was not a title to any formal office, the apostles were part of the origins of the local churches. They also had authority in the particular churches that they had founded, though this was more of a moral nature by reason of their relationship with the communities they had founded.

2. Alongside the apostles, Paul's fellow workers also seemed to have some sort of authority over the local leaders. From the beginning, for example, Paul's missionary journeys were a collective effort by the church at Antioch; he formed part of a sort of mission team that functioned collegially. But it also seemed to have some sort of supervisory role over the local communities they had established, and Paul lists over 100 people who helped him in his apostolate.

3. Common to the different social roles in the communities is that they all began as manifestations of the charisms of the Holy Spirit. Formalization only begins to set in toward the end of this present period.

There was also a tendency toward a more uniform institutionalization as we enter the second century. It is not so much that what was formerly charismatic was now becoming institutional. Rather, local leadership was appropriating the authority of the former prophets and teachers. This tendency was especially obvious in the case of those called bishops.

4. In this period, we hear nothing of the Twelve, nor of anyone replacing them as a group or as individuals. They made no efforts to replace themselves either. Therefore, the second generation, faced with the problem of survival, had to determine who could function authoritatively in the community and how to remain faithful to the faith they had received. Different churches answered this in different ways.

5. Matthew's solution to survival lay in preserving the tradition. He tends to downplay the role of prophetic elements in favor of recognized leaders. Peter, among the Twelve, comes in for special treatment, and is given a leadership role. His communities are characterized not so much by charismatic signs and wonders, but by solid teaching by people who have been deputed for this task within the community.

6. The Johannine communities were more egalitarian. The role of the Twelve is not emphasized; indeed they are never called "apostles." Closeness to Jesus is based especially on love, and in this the "beloved disciple" excelled, even though he was not one of the Twelve. Based on this love of Christ and guided by the Holy Spirit, his community was to be held together and remain faithful to its ideals. John also has the highest Christology in the entire New Testament. Some who tried to go even higher soon found themselves sliding into Gnosticism.

7. The Pastorals faced the problem of survival by stressing the role of the recognized leaders and some form of apostolic succession. They required the same qualities for their leaders that made one a good manager of a household. The chief emphasis here was stability, not charismatic leadership (or the very qualities of one like Paul, who had founded them). There was a difference between a missionary situation and the ability to withstand persecution and survival. Their solution was to look to church leadership (the presbyter/bishops, in their case) for authoritative direction. Brown sketches the strengths and weaknesses of this position well.

8. The church of Colossians/Ephesians relied on a vision of the church as Body of Christ. There is little stress on apostolic succession or on the institutional aspects of the church. Rather, the church is seen as an organic unity based on mutual love. This is appealed to as a universal reality that transcends the strictly local levels, and makes for unity

in the entire church. The inner dynamic here is love, both for Christ and his earthly body, which is the church.

9. The presbyters, bishops, and deacons mentioned especially in the Pastorals are very difficult to define in terms of both title and function. There is no general agreement here. The most probable opinion is that, like the elders of the Jews and of the Essenes, presbyters were older men of proven virtue who were given status and perhaps even supervisory roles within the community. Some of these eventually became bishops or deacons, positions that had more definite responsibilities. Bishops, for example, were expected to manage finances, oversee the life of the community, and teach. The role of the deacons is unclear at this time, and may even be a sort of synonym for bishop.

10. There is no clear evidence of ordination rites at this time. Some have tried to interpret 1 Timothy 4:14 in this way because of the mention of the laying on of hands, now such an important part in the ritual of ordination. The real question is not whether they had specific rituals but, rather, how they recognized or commissioned leaders within the community. This they surely did.

11. It is embarrassing to try linking presiding over the Eucharist with any of these leadership positions or roles. The sources are silent about this. Even the bishops did not preside with any regularity until after the first century. The chief emphasis in church documents at this time is not on presiding over the liturgy or about passing on a chain of unbroken sacramental powers, but on building up the community.

12. The early church did not use the title "priest" for any of its ministers, even though it was readily available. They seemed to go out of their way to avoid it and adopted secular titles instead.

13. Christian ministers of all ranks are not self-appointed or simply community appointed. Rather, ministry is seen as a charism, a gift coming from the Lord through the Spirit. The community, however, is shown as having a role in the recognition and selection process, especially because ministry was seen as a collegial reality.

14. Though the New Testament names certain ministerial functions, it tells us far more about the spirit in which all ministry should be performed. It also enumerates the qualities of those who exercise the principal functions of leadership in the community.

Discussion Questions

1. What structures did the early church use to build itself as a commu-

2. To what extent were the people of God prevented from using their gifts and talents in the church's ministry at this time?

3. What seemed to be the most important ministries at the end of the first century? Why? Could there have been any other development? Give examples.

Suggested Readings

Brown, R., "Biblical Background of the Catholic Priesthood," *Priest and Bishop*, Mahwah, N.J.: Paulist Press, 1980, Chap. 1, pp. 5-45.

_____, *The Churches the Apostles Left Behind*, Mahwah, N.J.: Paulist Press, 1984.

_____, "Episcopos and Episcopoi," *Theological Studies*, 1, 2 (June 1980), 322-338.

_____, "Rethinking Priesthood Biblically for All," *Critical Meaning of the Bible*, Chap. 6.

Burke, M., "Reflections on Church Order in the New Testament," *Catholic Biblical Quarterly*, 30, 4 (October 1968), 493-511.

Elliott, J., "Ministry and Church Order in the New Testament," *Catholic Biblical Quarterly*, 32, 2 (July 1970), 367-391.

Legrand, H.-M., O.P. "The Presidency of the Eucharist According to Ancient Tradition," *Worship*, 52, 5 (September 1979), 413-438.

Lemaire, A., "From Service to Ministries: Diakonoi in the First Two Centuries," *Concilium*, 10, 8 (December 1972), 35-49.

_____, "Ministries in the New Testament," *Biblical Theology Bulletin*, 3 (June 1973), 133-166.

Meier, J.P., "Presbyteros in the Pastoral Epistles," *Catholic Biblical Quarterly*, 35, 3 (July 1973), 323-345.

Mitchell, N., "Ministry in the Later New Testament Period," *Mission and Ministry*, Chap. 3, pp. 137-200.

Mohler, J., "Christian Presbyters of the New Testament," *The Origin and Evolution of the Priesthood*, Chap. 2, pp. 11-31.

O'Meara, T., "Primal Ministry," *Theology of Ministry*, Chap 4, pp. 76-94.

Osborne, K., O.F.M, "Ministry, 27 to 110 AD," *Priesthood: A History of the Ordained Ministry in the Roman Catholic Church*, Mahwah, N.J.: Paulist Press, 1988, Chap. 3, pp. 40-85.

O'Toole, R.J., "New Testament Reflection on Ministry," *Biblical Theology Bulletin*, 10 (October 1980), 140-148.

Schelkle, K., "Ministry and Minister in the New Testament Church,"

Schelkle, K., "Ministry and Minister in the New Testament Church," *Concilium*, 43 (1969), 6-19.

Schillebeeckx, E., "The Practice and Theology of Ministry in the Early Communities of Christian Believers," *The Church with a Human Face*, Part 2, pp. 40-124.

Tillard, J.M.R., "Apostolic Foundation of Christian Ministry, *Worship*, 63, 4 (July 1989), 290-300.

3

From Ministry to Bishop

Historically, this period runs from the New Testament period to the beginnings of the Constantinian church, with a bit of overlapping to include witnesses that are contemporary with the later New Testament canon. During this time the Christian communities experienced an explosive spread throughout the Roman Empire, going from house churches to basilicas; from simple, community ministry to the emergence of monarchical bishops. With Constantine, the church was legitimized (eventually to become the religion of the empire).

We read in Acts that the church first spread because of persecution. This is probably a larger fact of church life in this period than we imagine. Sporadic persecutions, often very violent, erupted until they were brought to an end by the Edict of Milan in 313. In the second century, especially, someone would blame the decay of the empire on the displeasure of the gods, and the Christians would again be singled out for persecution.

Despite (or because of) this, it was a period of enormous growth. With the help of the Roman road system, the church began to spread. It is estimated that by the end of the first century there were already half a million Christians. There were two million by the end of the next century, and four to five million at the end of the third. By the time that Christianity became the religion of the empire, it numbered roughly 10,000,000 out of the 50,000,000 people in the Roman empire.

These were particularly critical years not only in physical growth, but in the development of Christian ministry both within the church and to the world. Within, diminution of fervor brought on by greater numbers was countered by the catechumenate, developed to safeguard and foster the ideals and spirit of the community. And the sacrament of reconciliation was brought into play to take care of those who slid from their first fervor.

During this time the church's structure became more uniform, and the New Testament canon was determined. The church also had to face a number of heresies that threatened the understanding of the faith. The doctrines and practices of the church were worked out against the strict monotheism of the Jews, and the Gnosticism and Montanism of the second century. By the time of the Council of Nicea (325), the first really general council, the church saw itself as a universal reality.

Mention should also be made of the subject of martyrdom. One reality that unified the church during this period was the very real possibility of (and desire for) *martyrdom*. From Stephen, Ignatius, and Polycarp, we have the unquestioned conviction that life could not end more happily than enduring suffering and even death "for the name of Christ." Its possibility was built into the catechesis of baptism; living and dying like Christ were but the natural outcome of baptismal initiation. By the time of Cyprian there was a thoroughly developed ideal of martyrdom, an explicit recognition that it constituted the highest ideal of Christian perfection. There were several consequences of this that affected church structure and ministry:

1. It made for a radical equality of all in early Christianity. One's status came more from being able to suffer for the sake of Christ than from any position within the church.

2. Confessors were considered as having been anointed by the Spirit and therefore no ordination was required for them to function as presbyters in the church.

3. The heroism displayed by many served as a stimulus to others in the community, as well as an example to those outside the faith, showing that Christians were "not of this world."

4. The sad experience of defection, especially in the Decian persecution (mid-third century) led to a painful reevaluation of Christian life and institutions. Out of this came penance practice, a modification of the catechumenate, and the evolution of office within the church. Judgment was passed on leaders who failed to measure up to expectations in time of trial.

Not all were called to martyrdom. Yet, all were called to bear witness to the gospel in their daily lives in some form. Thus, the ideal of heroic witness to the ideals of Christianity on a daily basis became a goal. Justin and others were able to appeal to the practice of lofty ethical principles. This ascetical ideal would eventually find its flowering in the rules of Basil and Augustine.

The Earliest Christian Writings

Valuable insight can be gained into the practice of ministry in the early church from writings that have come down to us from this period. Along with the Johannine material, and perhaps the pastorals and 2 Peter, all of which are now part of the New Testament canon, there are a number of other contemporary writings, especially the *Letter of Clement* around the year 95, the *Letters of Ignatius of Antioch* around 110, and the *Didache*, which give us a glimpse into church life and practice at the turn of the century.

Other writings of the second century that we will mention will be the letters of Polycarp, the *Shepherd of Hermas*, as well as the writings of Justin and Irenaeus. At the very end of the century we have Tertullian. And, at the beginning of the third century there is the *Apostolic Tradition* of Hippolytus, a landmark in terms of sacramental liturgies, and the *Didascalia Apostolorum*. We will be able to highlight only a few of these.

First Clement

The "First Letter of Clement," actually a letter from the church at Rome to the church at Corinth, was written around the turn of the century.[1] It is a topic of great interest among scholars, because of its early date and its information about church order, as well as the advisory role of the Roman church in matters concerning the internal affairs of other churches. The immediate occasion was a rebellion against the elders ("presbyters") at Corinth. Clement insists that the rebels (the "youngsters") must repent and submit to the presbyters, since these latter are part of the God-willed order that has been handed on by Christ through the apostles. The incident was one that divided the community and caused scandal to the pagans.

> It would not be a slight fault for us to expel from the office of bishop those who have presented the gifts [*prosenegkontas ta dora*] in a holy and blameless fashion.... Fortunate are the presbyters who have run their course and have completed a fruitful and perfect life.... We see some whom, in spite of their good conduct, you have discharged from their functions, which they exercised with honor and in blameless fashion (44, 4-6).

It is church order, which Clement calls divinely willed, that is the main focus of this letter. Clement holds up the picture of Jesus sending his apostles to preach the good news, and these apostles appointing others to act as leaders of future believers. Thus, he conjures up an ideal community based on God's cosmic order, soldiers under authority, the mutual subordination of members of one body, and (more biblically) the example provided by the levitical hierarchy.

Clement's idea seems to be that each person has a proper place in the church. He presupposes that, as in civil society, all have their own rank and complementary roles to play in the assembly. Everything must lead to the harmony of the community. If there is anything surprising in Clement's approach, it lies in his description of the composition of the church. The laity (the word *laikos* appears twice in the sentence referring to the levitical hierarchy) are here mentioned for the first time in Christian literature as opposed to those who lead the community. No one else will pick this up until another Clement (of Alexandria), 100 years later.

Throughout the rest of his letter Clement uses various terms to describe Christians: for example, "brethren," "the elect," "those called and made holy," "the holy portion," "sharers in the Father's election." The phrase that occurs most frequently is "Christ's flock." All have their own *leitourgia* to fulfill. "In the same way, may each of our brethren, each one keeping to his own rank, please God by acting with a right conscience, with dignity and without infringing the rules prescribed for his function."

This leaves us with the questions of who were the presbyters and bishops Clement refers to, and what was their role in the life of the church. At first glance their exact identity seems confusing, for we are told that "the apostles appointed their first converts, testing them by the Spirit, to be *bishops and deacons* of the future believers." Later, though, we read that the Corinthians have removed some of the *presbyters* in spite of their good service. Here we find the same kind of shifting reference to bishops, deacons, and presbyters that we saw in the pastorals.

Keeping in mind Powell's distinction between status and function, however, we might suggest that Clement's presbyters are those senior in status, worthy of respect and imitation by all. *Some* of these presbyters have specific ministries to fulfill: as deacons and bishops. The primary ministry is that of preaching the Good News, then offering gifts and sacrifices, almost surely a reference to presiding at Eucharist.

In this order of status (presbyterate) and ministries (diaconate and episcopacy), Clement sees a divinely willed "succession." The apostles received the gospel from Christ; they in turn transmitted it to their "first converts," the "bishops and deacons of the future believers." The reference to first converts fits in perfectly with the notion of presbyters as the firstfruits of the apostolic mission. This order of authority and ministry is similar, he argues, to the ordinances of Jewish life and worship.

In Clement, church order, status, and ministry are not merely practical conveniences, but divinely revealed realities that form part of the tradition coming from Christ. Hence, rebellion against the presbyters is tantamount to rebellion against Christ. An incipient theology of church order and ministry has begun to emerge here that Ignatius will carry further.

Ministry for Clement is radically Christocentric. It is the Lord who appoints church ministers. Any self-appointment is out of the question. Christian ministers are beginning to have liturgical functions, and a distinction is already being made between clergy and laity. There is still fluidity of terminology, however. "Bishops" is always used in the plural, so we are clearly removed from the mono-bishop of Ignatius.

The *Didache*
The first problem with the *Didache* is dating it. Expert estimates vary considerably. It seems probable, however, that it was written in two parts, one of which dates from the latter part of the first century, the other at the beginning of the second century, and comes from a Syrian/Palestinian milieu. Mention of ministry is not extensive here, but what is there is intriguing.

"Prophets" receive the greatest attention. They are called high priests and, along with the apostles, are the regular celebrants of the Eucharist. Later the same document speaks of choosing bishops (always used in the plural) and deacons to fulfill the ministry of the prophets and teachers. There is no mention of presbyters. Nothing is said of what the bishops and deacons do or how they are related to each other. But it is evident that the bishop is not yet the main minister.

Schillebeeckx suggests, as do others,[2] that the *Didache* represents a community whose patterns of ministry and worship are undergoing transition. Earlier sections of the *Didache* describe the breaking of the bread, and link "making Eucharist" with the prophets (9-10), while the section seemingly added later outlines Sunday worship and mentions bishops and deacons along with the prophets (14-15). This later section also reveals a liturgy that had become more elaborate, fixed on Sundays, and thus seems to reflect a later period of history. (Note that dating the _Didache_ to a large extent depends on what presuppositions one has about what liturgical forms were like in the early church.)

For the _Didache_, the successors of the apostles were the prophets. In these days the prophets (as well as the latter-day apostles) would have been wandering charismatics or missionaries. Surprisingly, bishops, who are mentioned only in passing, exhibit none of the strong characteristics of the Ignatian bishop. They seem to be just beginning to emerge as a recognizable and authoritative group in the church.

Ignatius of Antioch

By the time we reach Ignatius of Antioch, it is clear that, in his church, the bishops are presiding over the Eucharist. "Let that be considered a valid Eucharist which is celebrated by the bishop, or by one whom he appoints....is not lawful either to baptize or to hold an agape without the bishop" (Smyrnians 7:1–2). Note that Ignatius also thinks of one bishop for each church. We might contrast this with the _Didache_, also from Syria, which does not seem to reflect such a prominent role for the bishop.

Thus, although the New Testament does not link the ministry of leadership to eucharistic presidency, Ignatius, at the turn of the century, has begun making this connection. Though the eucharistic role of the bishop is highlighted, it is not clear whether this presumed that these presiders needed some ritual authorization in order to lead the community in the breaking of the bread.

In Ignatius, we see a pattern of local church leadership that is not otherwise mentioned until the middle of the second century: mono-episcopacy—the pattern of a single leader at the head of each church. Ignatius is the first witness of this.

The most striking feature of Ignatius is the role of the bishop. From Clement we get the impression that several bishops minister in Corinth; in Ignatius he is a single individual who can be addressed by name.[3] Only in the church at Rome does Ignatius not mention a bishop.

While not a monarch, the Ignatian bishop functions as the source of unity for the community. Likened to God the Father, he is also the visible representative of Jesus Christ, who is every church's "unseen bishop." Apart from the bishop, no legitimate Eucharist is possible, and he is the leader who gathers the assembly, writes to other churches, supervises marriages, and watches over widows. He is thus a principle of unity without which the people are only a disordered crowd.

Deacons, too, are important ministers for Ignatius. They are frequent emissaries from one church to another. He insists that deacons are "true servants" of the church, using here the term that Paul used (*hyperetes*) in relation to the missionary apostles. Deacons are expected to be subject to bishops and the presbytery. The Ignatian picture of bishops and deacons is reasonably clear. But once again we have to ask who the presbyters were in his churches. Consistently, they are compared to the "council of the apostles"; in fact, the apostles themselves are called "the presbyters [not the bishops] of the church."

Does this mean that the presbyters are a group of ministers, superior to deacons but inferior to bishops in power? Probably not. Like the presbyters of the pastorals and Clement, they seem to be distinguished by status, not specific function. The functional titles belong to the bishops and deacons. This helps explain the consistency of Ignatius's typology. Presbyters are always the type of the *apostles*, the first disciples of Jesus. One could say their status comes from being models of discipleship, types of those who first heard the gospel, believed it, and had grown faithful in conversion of life. The presbyters are revered because their lives reveal mature faith, not because they perform a ministry or have a specific job to do. They are *types* in the radical sense of the word (cf. 1 Peter 5:3; Romans 5:14): not examples *we* choose to follow, but examples authenticated by God, like the first apostles.

Ignatius and Clement seem to agree that "presbyters" refer to a status group, rather than to specific ministers. Those who carry out the ministry are "bishops and deacons." Ignatius, however, does indicate that the presbyters act as a consultative body for the bishop. The image of the bishop surrounded by his presbyters and assisted by deacons is a clear and powerful one, and will return as a characteristic of the church in the ordination ritual found in the *Apostolic Tradition*.

Church Structure: From Prophet to Bishop

As we move beyond the New Testament, we find aspects of church government becoming more and more sharply delineated. Descriptive names become specialized offices. Older offices are replaced by newer ones. We learned from the *Didache* and other sources, for example, that going into the second century, one of the most respected church roles was played by the prophets. These were soon replaced by the emerging bishops witnessed to by Ignatius.

Obviously, prophets did not utterly disappear in second-century Christianity. Nor did bishops appear out of nowhere. The *Shepherd of Hermas* (c. 140-150) is the work of a prophet from Rome. He gives valuable information about prophecy at mid-century, and outlines rules for recognizing true and false prophets. Aside from this, however, we also learn something surprising about church order at Rome at this time. Despite the list Irenaeus later gives, there seems to be no one bishop of the Ignatian type there. Note the following run-down:[4]

• 1 Clement (c. 95): no reference to a bishop at Rome. At Corinth, the _episkopoi_ are apparently a group.
• Ignatius (c. 110): no reference to a bishop in his letter to Rome (though one is mentioned for every other church he writes to, usually even by name).
• Justin (c. 150): from Rome he uses only the general word _praestos_ for the presider at Eucharist (1st Apology, 65-67).
• Hermas (c. 140-150): refers only to "bishops" of the Roman church, who "sheltered the destitute and widows" (Sim IX:27:2). Also: "apostles and bishops and teachers and deacons who have walked according to the holiness of God, and who have sincerely and reverently served the elect of God" (Vis III:5:1).

Hermas elsewhere speaks of "presbyters who direct the church" (Vis II:4:3). These seem to be the ultimate authorities; some of them are also bishops. The intriguing question here is when did the Roman church move to the Ignatian model of a single bishop? We know that this was the case by the time of Hippolytus. Hermas tells us that prophecy was still alive and well; it did not conflict, apparently, with either the "apostles, bishops, teachers, deacons" or the "presbyters who direct the church." The presence of other ministries has not eliminated the prophets' role, though at times there is some suspicion about them.

The institutional patterns that developed in the second century witness to a greater standardization than in the first century. The presbyterate became the most prominent agency for directing and nurturing the life of the community. This implied a sort of corporate leadership, although, as we see from Ignatius and others, it was, however, usually headed by a bishop, picked from their ranks. The main surprise is that despite Ignatius's witness to a strong bishop at the beginning of the second century, there did not seem to be a bishop in Rome at least until the middle of the second century. With the emergence of bishops, however, other roles of leadership begin to fade.

Already at the beginning of the second century, Ignatius had claimed prophetic gifts for the bishop in the performance of his role. Cyprian made the same claim in the middle of the third century. The _Didascalia_ indicates that at least in the third-century Syrian church, the episcopacy laid exclusive claim to authoritative teaching. By the time of Nicea, the episcopacy had clearly taken over full authority for the direction of church life. Though bishops may not have personally exercised all roles, the official authority of the church was vested in them, and theirs was special guidance to safeguard the faith. Fortunately, enough of them were great theologians.

The use of the term "bishop" can obscure for us the fact that in the earliest days this leader directed the activities of only one church (much like the pastor of a large parish today) with a clerical staff to help him. This head pastor was thus usually much closer to his people and, since he was chosen by them, less authoritarian than we might be tempted to think. However, the rise of strong church leaders led to a suspicion of competing voices from former key ministries like prophets and apostles. It was too difficult to control wandering charismatics.

As local churches became more stable, they increasingly depended on members from their own community to act as teachers and prophets. Itinerant ministry tended to vanish as its functions became absorbed by competent resident ministers. This did not happen overnight; both teachers and prophets are in evidence well beyond Nicea. However, the third century provides no example of prophets with the influence and autonomy of Hermas, nor teachers with the independent status of Clement of Alexandria and Origen.

The bishops clearly saw their role as preserving the unity of the body of Christ. Since the two great threats to this in an age of growth were false teaching and sin, it was inevitable that the episcopacy increasingly concern itself with maintaining unity of belief and purity of life; hence, the emphasis given the teaching role of the bishop and his role in the reconciliation of sinners. Furthermore, the threat of persecution and heresies helped the church to close ranks around their leaders. Community leadership became a full-time occupation.

Liturgically, we can say that in general, the textual evidence of the second and third centuries points to four situations where the role belonged to the bishop: baptism, Eucharist, ordination, penance. In the initiation ceremony there is a diversity of roles, with deacons and deaconesses performing the prebaptismal anointings, and the presbyters handling the baptizing, with the bishop presiding over the entire ceremony, doing the final anointing, and presiding over the Eucharist that followed. It was also the bishop's responsibility to see to the admission, training, and testing of the catechumens.

When we come to the penitential discipline of the period, clear evidence comes only in the third century, with only traces before this. Tertullian gives us the sharpest picture prior to Cyprian. His writings reflect a discipline of penance and reconciliation that is already well established. Tertullian argues against a laxist approach by some bishops; but it is taken for granted that the bishop plays the chief role, both for assigning the penance and reconciling the penitent to the church.

The very growth of the church also made for increased centralization of administration. In the middle of the third century, Cornelius, bishop of Rome, found himself with approximately 50,000 Christians out of a population of a million or so. He complained about the complexity of church life there, with its 46 presbyters, 7 deacons, 7 subdeacons, 42 acolytes, 52 exorcists, lectors and doorkeepers, hundreds of lesser ministers, and 1500 poor needing daily care.

Probably, in the context of administrative activity and supervisory responsibility, it was inevitable (especially with the reemergence of Old Testament notions and the Byzantine idea of *basileus*) that the ministry of bishops increasingly took on overtures of "ruling." The change from a mono-episcopate to a monarchical episcopate was an easy step to take in imperial Rome.

This is not to say that many bishops did not see themselves as servants and shepherds. Both the *Didascalia* and Cyprian bear witness to the use of that term. The *Apostolic Tradition,* in its ordination rite, prays that the bishop "feed his holy flock." In fact, the image of shepherd is rather constant right through the Middle Ages. In the actual exercise of ministry, however, bishops depended more on the model of government provided by those in secular positions around them. This too often led to an authoritarian style, and eventually to theoretical justification of an authoritarian and hierarchical structure for the church.

The *Didascalia Apostolorum* was written in Syria in the first half of the third century. Chapters 4-11 are devoted to the functions and qualities of the bishop. He is the center of the whole community, holding the place of God in governing God's people.

> He is your chief and leader and your almighty king. He rules in the place of the Almighty. Let him be honored by you as God, for the bishop sits for you in the place of God almighty (9).

Here is a regal, almost divine person, supreme judge of all with the God-given power of binding and loosing.[5] Fortunately, the author also adds that he is the guardian of the poor and those in need, protecting the widow and orphan, giving alms. Worthy of honor because, after God, he is both father and mother to the Christians, he is also to be revered and supported as a ruler and king. To be worthy of all this, his life should be irreproachable: married, over 50, etc.—the rather prosaic qualities noted in the pastoral letters.

Though we can see the beginnings of the process whereby the bishop and his presbyters and deacons were set apart from the masses, it is important to stress that the bishop at this time was still elected by the church at large, and regularly used to consult the community in matters of church or public life. Cyprian explicitly witnesses to the tradition noted by Hippolytus earlier in the century. As Cyprian wrote to his presbyters "I decided to do nothing of my own opinion privately without your advice and the consent of the people" (L. 4, 14).

This aspect of assent was a principle of pontifical and canonical tradition for centuries, at least in theory. The councils of Orleans (549) and Paris (557) even quoted Pope Celestine (d. 432), "that a bishop must not be imposed on a people against their will." Leo I (d. 461) said, "He who rules over all should be elected by all." The writings of Gregory the Great (d. 604) show that this is still common for Italy, Gaul, and some northern missions. The will of the community was central, and could veto an unpopular selection.

Although the term "laity" began to be used in the third century, there is some evidence that the distinction was not so much between laity and clergy, but between the dedicated or educated men of the community as opposed to the hoi polloi. These were examples for the rest of the flock, perhaps best described as the "one-woman man" of the pastorals, or the "true disciples" of Irenaeus. Note that this excluded women and perhaps the majority of the men.

It is difficult to generalize about this. The question has practical import, however, in regard to the church policy of consulting the laity in matters of church discipline and polity. Who was really included in this group? Everyone? Men only? *All* men, including catechumens, penitents, children? Though it is certain that there was far greater equality in the early days, and that the people were consulted in church matters, there were certainly variations in *how* this was done.

Paradoxically, it is the practical application of universalism in later centuries that eventually weakened the democratic principle. Church councils always seemed to have the presence of active laity (*periti*), which made the direct intervention of all the people impossible or unnecessary. What tended to happen was that the laity were informed of decisions after the event, and asked for their approbation only.

Soon enough, unfortunately, the term "laity" was seen as the opposite of clergy: All who were not priests and who belonged to the church were laypeople. Since they were not as perfect as might be hoped for, they must be cared for like children, that they might grow in the life of Christ (so the *Didascalia*). They had to be "ministered" to.

Origen, meanwhile, softened some of this by seeing the church as inspired by a dual movement. One came from the clergy, the other from the ascetics and theologians. He also spoke often of the priesthood of all believers, which the baptized enjoyed.

The Sacerdotalization of Ministry

Parallel to the episcopal centralization of the church with its reduction of ministerial diversity or charisms was the sacerdotalization of ministry. The bishop was not only regarded as the administrator of his church, he became the "high priest" of the community. This priesthood was linked especially to his role in the eucharistic celebration.

As noted previously, the New Testament was not concerned with specifying whose lot it was to preside at eucharistic assemblies. There are only allusions to the celebrations themselves. If Acts 13:1–2 describes a eucharistic celebration, it was prophets or teachers who presided. There is never any mention that a cultic, priestly qualification was required to preside at Eucharist.

If we may dip back to the *Didache*, we note that presiding over the Eucharist was primarily the prerogative of the apostles and prophets in the first century; in their absence, the *presbyteroi* or *episkopoi* chosen by the community could so function because they shared the direction of the community—not because they were seen as "successors to the apostles." Nothing is said about any sacerdotal denomination at this time.

In the letter of Clement, bishops/presbyters, established in succession to the apostles, preside over the church and the Eucharist. Here it would seem that the presiders at the Eucharist are the presidents of the local community. Its bishops and presbyters (the terminology is still fluid) were established by the apostles "or afterwards by other eminent men with the consent of the whole church" (44, 3). This indicates that it is not so much a question of linear succession from the apostles, but the assumption of office with the consent of the community.

Are these men "priestly" persons? Not yet. Clement uses comparisons which, by his deliberate choice of non-ritual terms, preclude assimilation of New Testament ministers to Old Testament priests. It is simply that those who preside over the church ought to preside over the Eucharist because "we ought to do in orderly fashion all those things the Master has ordered us to perform" (40, 1).

For Ignatius, as is well known, the bishop, as principle of unity in the church, is the one who firmly controls the rituals of baptism and Eucharist. Thus, in his letter to the Smyrnians:

> Apart from the bishop no one is to do anything pertaining to the church. Only that Eucharist is to be considered legitimate [bebaia] which is celebrated under the presidency of the bishop [he hypo episkopou ousa] or under that of the one he appoints [epitrepsi]. There where the bishop appears, let the community be, just as where Jesus Christ is, there is the whole church. It is not permissible, apart from the bishop, either to baptize or to hold an agape. But, whatever he approves is also pleasing to God—so that everything you do may be secure and legitimate. (8,1-2)

The key to his insistence on the role of the bishop is a mystique of unity of which the Eucharist is the sacrament. There is no mention in his letters that he feels only bishops have priestly qualifications (for he never applies this terminology to them). Nor does he trace them back to the apostles or employ the terminology of succession.

To summarize the thought of Ignatius: The bishop, guarantor of the unity of the church, presides over the sacrament of unity. Apart from him the Eucharist is illegitimate, not secure. Others, however, may act as celebrants by his authorization. Is the one so delegated a member of the presbytery? This is generally assumed, but we really do not know. It's astonishing that Ignatius does not mention the presbytery in this context when he is so pleased to speak about it elsewhere. Questions like these, however, obscure the basic perspective that the one who presided over the church presided over the sacrament of the unity of the church.

Saint Justin tells us: Those who preside over the church preside at its Eucharist. Writing around 150, he describes two Eucharists, one baptismal (1 Apol 65), the other a Sunday Eucharist (1 Apol 67). In both of these the role of the president is clearly distinguished from that of the assembly. Thus, we read in chapter 65: "Bread and a cup containing water and wine mixed with water are brought to him who presides over the brethren. He takes them and offers prayers, glorifying the Father of all things through the name of the Son and of the Holy Spirit; and he then utters a lengthy Eucharist....When he has finished, all the people present give their assent: Amen."

The same thing is true in chapter 67, 5. The presidency in both cases is the act of a single individual to whom a specific role is attributed, clearly distinguished from the role of the people.

Appeal to the testimony of Justin is clouded because some dispute the passages where he speaks of *ho proestos* (the president) of the eucharistic assembly. Many argue that this president is identified with the bishop, which would reinforce the role of the bishops envisaged by Ignatius. It is he who explains the meanings and implications of the day's readings and who prays the eucharistic prayer over the gifts, which are thereby transformed into the body of Christ.

It may well be that this presider was a bishop, but it cannot be proven from Justin. He makes no effort to make him a successor to the apostles, because he passes up the chance to do so when arguing against the cult of Mithra (chap 66, 3–4). Here he concludes the institution narrative with the remark: "He gave [the bread and the cup] to them [the Twelve] alone." His meaning here is that it was given only to the Christians, for he adds: "And the evil demons have imitated this and ordered it to be done also in the mysteries of Mithra."

Saints Irenaeus and Anicetus tell us: The bishops preside at the Eucharist. Toward 190, Irenaeus intervened in the controversy concerning the date of Easter, which had led to a conflict between the bishops of Asia Minor and the Roman See. Eusebius of Caesaria has recorded for us his letter of mediation in which he appeals to a precedent dating back to the year 154: "[Polycarp and Anicetus having been reconciled] entered into communion with each other, and Anicetus ceded the Eucharist to Polycarp, obviously out of deference, and they parted in peace" (Eccl Hist V, 24, 17).

In Hippolytus the picture is quite clear. It is the bishop who presides over the church and its Eucharist by virtue of an ordination conferring an apostolic charism. The descriptions of the rites of ordination of bishops, presbyters, and deacons give us invaluable insight into the understanding of these offices and, in the rite of initiation, of the bishop in action. Here we are given a picture where the regular celebrant is the bishop, accompanied by his presbyters and assisted by his deacons. Aside from where need required, and the presbyters presided at Eucharist, the normative liturgy had the bishop as its head.

There are interesting bits of information that can be gleaned from Hippolytus. We learn that the one to be ordained bishop "has been chosen by all the people" and that to ordain him other bishops "lay hands on him" while the presbytery is to "stand by and be still." According to the ordination prayer, the bishop is, to begin with, one who receives the apostolic charism, and it is his role to "feed the holy flock and to exercise the high priesthood...and to offer the gifts of the holy church." The eucharistic prayer of the Eucharist in which the ordination is situated is recited alone by the new bishop, surely, because in those days it was still improvised.

Hippolytus witnesses to the continuity we have been seeing: The one who presides over the church presides over the Eucharist. However, he is more explicit than those who preceded him with regard to titles of this president: elected by all, ordained, having the apostolic charism, a pastor, high priest. This latter attribute will appear more and more frequently in subsequent documents.[6]

Thus, if it became axiomatic in the second century that whoever presided over the Christian community presided over its liturgy, what was added in the third century was the perception of the one who presided over the Eucharist as a priestly figure. Hippolytus, Tertullian, the *Didascalia*, and Cyprian are the first to speak in this way.

Tertullian tells us, "We receive the Eucharist from no other than our presidents" (de corona 3, 5). Only proven elders [presbyters] receive this office of presidency (Apol 39, 5; Pud 14, 16). Presidents exercise "priestly charges" (de Praesc 41, 8; de Exhort Cast 11, 1–2). They are high priests (de Bapt 17, 1; Pud 21, 17). His evidence is confusing, however, because Tertullian also says that in case of necessity a layman can celebrate with the title of his [common?] priesthood.

M. Bevenot, a specialist in this period, feels that "One cannot be certain that the *sacerdos* is so named because he celebrated the Eucharist, nor that, granted that he did, that was the primary reason for so naming him....Tertullian never says that it is because of this function that a bishop is named *sacerdos*."[7]

In other words, Tertullian does not base the presidency of the Eucharist on a specifically priestly qualification. To "preside" in his vocabulary means to be at the head of the community, to have care of its life as a whole. Thus, it would seem that presidency of the Eucharist is based essentially on the presidency of the Christian community rather than on a priesthood that pertained exclusively to ordained ministers.

This seems all the more probable when we consider the text: "Where there is no body of ordained ministers in residence, you laymen celebrate the Eucharist, you baptize and you are yourself your own priest, for where two or three are gathered, there is the church, even if these three are laymen" (de Exhort Cast 7, 3). He asserts here that when ordained are lacking, laity can exercise their cultic functions. Note that he reproaches the Montanists at this time for confiding sacerdotal functions to laymen (de Praesc 41, 5–8) because they did so without necessity.

(Tertullian is the main witness of this practice. Augustine would later oppose the practice, proof that it was still going on. It is also historically attested that, at the beginning of the fourth century, the first lay evangelizers of Ethiopia celebrated Eucharist.)

If there is some confusion as to how Tertullian and Hippolytus understood the priestly qualities they attributed to the bishop, marked progression in the use of priestly terminology comes especially with the *Didascalia* and with Cyprian. The *Didascalia* is explicit: Not only are bishops kings (as we have already seen), they are also the high priests of the new Israel. Here we have a clear reappropriation of Old Testament categories for New Testament ministries.

> Then were the first fruits and tithes and part offerings and gifts. But today the oblations are offered by the bishops to the Lord God, for they are your high priests. The priests and Levites now are the presbyters and deacons and the orphans and widows. But the Levite and high priest is the bishop. He is the minister of the word and mediator; but to you a teacher and your father after God who begot you through the water (9).

Cyprian (c. 250) tells us: The bishop, the bond of unity, presides at the Eucharist. In so doing he is *sacerdos* and symbolizes Christ. Cyprian is the first to note that the bishop presides at Eucharist *vice Christi* (in the place of Christ), a theme that would have an interesting medieval destiny and a modern reincarnation in the spirituality that saw the priest as "another Christ." This was so disputable that Vatican II chose to ignore it entirely.

Cyprian also tells us that, exceptionally, presbyters delegated by the bishop may preside at the Eucharist. This is the first written testimony of a celebration of Eucharist by presbyters, although Cyprian reserves the title "priest" exclusively for the bishop.[8]

Applying priestly terms to the ordained ministry comes from Cyprian's predilection for Old Testament vocabulary. He speaks of the emptiness of the Old Testament rites and their replacement by the sacrifice of Christ.[9] In this regard, Augustine would not follow his fellow Carthagenian; he always remained quite reserved about priestly descriptions of episcopal and presbyteral ministry.

Without doubt, however, Cyprian's principal emphasis is that there can be no Eucharist *against* the bishop. He is obsessed with this question, whereas he does not pose Tertullian's question of Eucharist *without* a bishop. In his eyes the union of bishop, church, and Eucharist is so close that to separate oneself from the bishop, to oppose him, is to become an enemy of the altar, a rebel in relation to the sacrifice of Christ.

To attempt a Eucharist in rivalry with the bishop is a profanation of the divine victim, a sacrilege. We find this position held throughout the first millennium, up to Peter Lombard.

Why does the presidency of the Eucharist pertain to the bishop? First of all because it is the sacrament of unity (Ep 45) and because the bishop is the guarantor of unity in the church. "You should know that the bishop is in the church and the church is in the bishop, and that if someone is not with the bishop, he is not in the church" (Ep 66,8).

Even aside from Cyprian, three influences can be seen at work in appropriating priestly terminology to the role of the bishop:

1. The first was the natural desire (and expectation on the part of the church) to have priests like every other religion. Separated from the synagogue, Christians could not be considered as a legitimate religion without some priestly structure.

2. Perhaps more important was the a-historical rereading of the Old Testament. Whereas the early church had seen Old Testament priesthood as being fulfilled in Christ, the later church saw the Old Testament as a prescription for church organization. Thus levitical sacerdotalism and the image of the priesthood of Melchisedech filtered into church mentality.

3. This was helped along considerably as theology began more and more to see the Last Supper as a sacrifice, which gave it a cultic rather than profane aura.

The emergence of a largely eucharistic church had enormous influence on ministry. The Roman gift for distinction and order resulted in both lessening the diversity of ministries within the community and also the separation of the church community into two classes: clerical and lay. The move from houses to church buildings, especially after the year 300, would greatly facilitate this shift.

The Question of Ordination

The first real evidence we have for any ordination comes from the *Apostolic Tradition*. Here we have detailed ceremonies for the ordination to the ministries of bishop, presbyter, and deacon. Though it dates to the beginning of the third century, it probably witnesses to earlier practice and understanding.

By the beginning of the third century, then, three distinct offices had emerged in the church: bishop, presbyter, and deacon. The *Apostolic Tradition* makes it clear that they ordinarily attained their position through some form of election, together with a ritual of ordination that included prayer and the laying on of hands. This document reflects the practice at Rome:

> Let him be ordained bishop who has been chosen by all the people; and when he has been named and accepted by all, let the people assemble, together with the presbyters and those bishops who are present, on the Lord's day.
>
> And when a presbyter is ordained, the bishop shall lay his hand on his head, the presbyters also touching him.
>
> When a deacon is ordained, let him be chosen according to what was said above, the bishop alone laying on hands.

At this point it is clear that the "laying on of hands" is a part of the ordination rite. How did this become the norm? Despite Kilmartin's tempting theory that this goes back to New Testament practice, there is no sure way of demonstrating this hypothesis. Laying on of hands was surely used as a general rite of commissioning, and is hence not necessarily an indication of ordination. Sources like the *Didache*, *First Clement*, and the letters of Ignatius never mention the imposition of hands, even though they refer explicitly to the election or appointment of bishops and deacons.

Earlier Christian literature is silent about any ritual of ordination for local church leaders. In his description of church worship, Justin Martyr outlines the eucharistic celebration and speaks of the "one who presides" at it, but says nothing about his position, nor about an ordination that would have qualified him for it. In *Adversus Haereses* Irenaeus provides us with a list of "bishops" of the Roman church, but never alludes to an imposition of hands or any way by which the office was transmitted from one to the other.

Some scholars have seen a reference to the laying on of hands for ordination in the *Acts of Peter*, probably written in Asia Minor toward the end of the second century. In the section of this document that describes the call of the apostles, we are told that Christ "chose and laid hands on them." Since Jesus is not represented in Scripture as having used this gesture in calling the apostles, some have argued that it shows the common custom at the end of the second century. As Kilmartin himself notes, however, the larger context does not really support this interpretation. More probably the laying on of hands here signifies Jesus' forgiving of the disciples who had doubted him.

We could use the argument of silence, but there is evidence that some churches developed customs for designating leaders that did not include a laying on of hands. In Letter 146 of St. Jerome (written to the presbyter Evangelus during the episcopate of Damasus [366-384]), there is a description of an earlier custom used at Alexandria for the selection of bishop:

> At Alexandria, from the time of Mark the evangelist until the time of Bishops Heraclus (232-247) and Denis (247-264), the presbyters always installed one elected from among themselves as bishop, whom they then enthroned—much like soldiers designate their "emperor" or deacons elect as archdeacon one of their own number well known for his industriousness.

Here it would seem that the very act of seating the bishop-elect was considered sufficient. The Alexandrian custom would thus have resembled the form of installation used for public officials. Taking his chair was a person's first public act, effectively fixing him in his new position. Jerome would have us believe that this was the custom since apostolic times. It is difficult to confirm the accuracy of his report, as it is mentioned by no one else; and it certainly differs from Hippolytus, where we see a clear distinction between the bishop's *election* "by all the people" and his *ordination* "by all the bishops." Besides, Jerome's vigorously anti-episcopal feeling and his contempt for ordination customs are well known. There is a growing consensus among scholars, however, that he was not fabricating in this case.[10] There is even reason to believe that a similar custom may have obtained at churches like Antioch, Lyons, and Rome.

Thus, though there may have been different ways of setting people apart for certain ministries, at least some of the early churches did so by imposing hands on them. Some feel that designating *episkopoi* and *presbyteroi* in this way is at least as old as the pastoral epistles. Only in the *Apostolic Tradition*, however, do we have some explanation of the rites and prayers. We can offer the following summary:

1. The imposition of hands for episcopacy was strictly by one or more other bishops (at least three).

2. In presbyteral ordinations, it involved the whole presbyterate, though the bishop's imposition had special significance.

3. In both instances, there is evidence of being accepted into some collegial reality.

4. In both, the imposition is associated with the giving of the Spirit.

5. In both, the action is finalized with the collegial celebration of Eucharist, which accents its cultic orientation and the relationship or func-

tion that results from the ordination.

Lest this minimalist discussion seem shocking to those who regard laying on of hands as a constant going back to our origins, one should remember that ritual validation is only *one* means used by churches to designate ministers. Cyril Vogel[11] has noted that ultimately the essential item is *the mandate of the church*. Liturgically, this mandate may have ordinarily been expressed by the laying on of hands. But there seems to be no particular reason why churches would need this particular gesture to "ordain" anyone.

Similarly, in Cyprian's defense of the election of Cornelius as bishop of Rome (c. 250), nothing is said about the laying on of hands. Because Cyprian held that this constituted valid episcopal consecration, it seems strange that he did not allege it in Cornelius's case, as it would have bolstered his argument. Perhaps Rome did not yet use laying on of hands. It should be remembered that Hippolytus was leader of a dissident group within the Roman church, and his views were not necessarily those of the party in power. In the earliest Roman ordination ritual written in Latin (manuscript c. 725), absolutely nothing is said about the imposition of hands for a bishop. Vogel has commented that:

> In spite of the booklet's rusticity of language and its evident brevity, one finds gathered there a number of details relating to gestures, vestments, prostrations, and chants. Under these conditions it is difficult to believe that if, during the period when the redactor of Ordo 34 compiled his directory in a decadent Rome, the rite of imposing hands had the least prominence, it would not have been mentioned.[12]

Thus, evidence for the imposition of hands as a prominent element in the ordination rites of the Roman church is scanty, at best, during the first several centuries of the Christian era. We are forced to conclude that this was not a prominent feature of "ordaining" church leaders in the second century and even later. It is only in the third century that we encounter Hippolytus's insistence on this rite as part of ordination. Even here it is impossible to conclude that *all* churches would have regardedthis rite as essential in all circumstances.

In this period it is Cyprian who gave the greatest development to the process of ordination. Several distinct elements comprised the activity of ordaining.[13]

1. *Election:* In the case of a bishop, election to the office must include the people, the local clergy, and the neighboring bishops.

2. *Divine Investiture*: The church saw an intimate link between the people's call and God's choice of a minister.

3. *Ecclesial Investiture*: The church is the concrete historical agent that calls a person to ministry. But actual installation requires action by the bishops, who alone have the right to "ordain" them.

4. *Imposition of Hands*: Cyprian upholds the laying on of hands mentioned in the *Apostolic Tradition* as the recognized rite for ordination.

5. *Conditions*: The validity and legitimacy of an ordination require the fulfillment of two conditions: It must be in accord with "apostolic tradition," that is, the church and the candidate must live and believe according to the tradition of the "first witnesses of Christ's mission." Second, the ordination must occur in a community that lives in communion with the whole church. Apart from these two conditions, apostolicity and catholicity, no valid ordination can occur. For Cyprian, a schismatic community would not have valid ordinations.[14]

6. *Effects*: Ordained persons form the *clerus*, and have an authoritative role in directing the community's life. Their powers are spiritual, rather than socio-political. All powers are radically rooted in the church itself of which they are, after all, *ministers*.

7. *Loss of Ecclesial Mandate*: Cyprian vigorously believed that the people not only had a right to choose worthy bishops, but to reject unworthy ones. The mandate could be lost through the minister's unworthiness.

8. *Approval by Others*: The unity of the churches in love was safeguarded by requiring the approval of the neighboring bishops. This also showed the collegial responsibility shared by the ordained.

All of these make up "ordination." The ritual act is but one element of a much larger process, and is indeed subordinate to election, worthiness, and the conditions of apostolicity and catholicity. There is nothing here of the ritual bringing about an ontological change or indelible character, though obviously it had public effects and consequences.

One of the most strongly held assumptions of early Christianity was a quasi-unanimous understanding of ordination as requiring attachment to a particular community. Persons were chosen by and ordained for a particular community. No one could be ordained "in general," or "absolutely." (This church rootedness was later referred to as the "title" to ordination.) So strong was this conviction that two centuries later the Council of Chalcedon prohibited absolute ordinations, declaring that these were not only "null and void," but utterly "non-existent."

Further Reflections on Ordination

It is one thing to speak of ordination in the third century, however, and quite another to translate its meaning into our modern categories. The danger is to think that the ancients understood ordination the way we do today, or to imagine that they saw it as being of equal importance with baptism and Eucharist, for example. Thinking of "Holy Orders" as a sacrament grew very slowly. In the earliest texts, the significance of ordaining someone to the clerical ministry was not generally described in sacramental terms. What, then, did it mean?

Tertullian, for example, uses "ordain/ordination," not in a distinctly theological sense, but more in the ordinary, non-technical sense of the word. According to a recent study by Pierre van Beneden[15] there are at least three different senses:

1. in the general sense of directing a person in a new direction. Thus we say that "he is ordering his life to new goals," etc.

2. in the sense of installing a person in a position, rank, or role. This implies an action having public consequences. Though there is definite authority involved here, there is no implication of a permanent or unalterable "state of being."

3. in the sense of ratifying an event or a person's role. We use this language with treaties, for example, and there are definite implications for relations between peoples, etc.

As Tertullian used them, the terms clearly had consequences for the church's life, unity, and integrity. But they did not refer primarily to the liturgical or "sacramental" acts of designating clergy; still less did they imply some indelible, sacerdotal character possessed by the persons ordained. The main emphasis was on giving and receiving a mandate to serve the church. This thought was that of Cyprian also, who reminded us that ultimately it is God who ordains, but this ordination is mediated through the church's action. This implies several distinct elements.

1. Ministry is entrusted only to those who have been chosen by the local church, which is the concrete historical agent calling a person to ministry. This approval also extended to bishops in other regions (to safeguard the unity of the church).

2. The actual installation comes through the bishop (and presbyters), who have the right to ordain them.

3. Hands are often laid on the persons as one of the primary rites (at least in the West).

4. The validity and legitimacy of an ordination requires two things:

that it be in accord with "apostolic tradition" (i.e., the church and candidate must live according to the tradition handed on from the "first witnesses to Christ's mission"); then, it must occur in a community that lives in communion with the whole church (i.e., "apostolicity" and "catholicity").

5. Ordained persons have an authoritative role in directing the life of the community; they also possess honor and dignity. Their powers are spiritual in nature, and not socio-political. Bishops, in particular, possess power related also to liturgical functions, for example, baptism, reconciliation of penitents, ordaining others, presiding at Eucharist. These powers are radically rooted in the church itself, of which the bishops are ministers.

6. Cyprian vigorously believed that the people not only had the right to choose worthy leaders, but also to reject unworthy ones. He knew of no permanent indelible mark caused by ordination. In fact, the ecclesial mandate could be lost through unworthiness. Since the mandate was mediated through the church, it could be revoked by the church. (There was absolutely no distinction at this time between a "power of orders" [irrevocable or indelible] and the "power of jurisdiction" [revocable]. Ministry was totally rooted in church service, not personal power.)

This should make it clear that the act of commissioning ministers is but one element of a much larger process involving several closely related elements. The mandate of the church was perhaps the most important element here. The liturgical ritual was only one component; it was neither the only nor the most important one. Note especially that the mandate to serve the church could be (and at times was) revoked by the same church who had mediated it in the first place. In those days the minister simply returned to the ranks of the laity.[16]

A canonical tradition deriving from the time of Hippolytus tells us that a confessor can take his rank without ordination among the presbyters, and preside at Eucharist by virtue of this fact. We read in the *Apostolic Tradition* (9), "A confessor, if he was in chains for the name of the Lord, shall not have hands laid on him for the diaconate or priesthood, for he has the honor of the priesthood by his confession. But if he is appointed bishop, hands shall be laid upon him."

Among other legislation derived from this are the Canons of Hippolytus and the *Testamentum Domini*. These provide that even slaves could become priests by having confessed the faith (slaves were never ordained in antiquity). Here, presbyteral ministry is accepted as such without the necessity of ordination.

This willingness to accord official ministerial status without any ritual intervention gives us an important clue for our understanding. Ordination was seen as recognition of the action of the Holy Spirit already present in the person (i.e., the status of proven virtue expected of elders); it was not so much a human choice that the Spirit was expected to ratify. Ordination would not, then, be expected to infuse qualities that were not already present in those being ordained. Persecution made for radical equality, and also allowed the cream to rise to the top.

To summarize the testimonies of the pre-Nicean church, a general perspective emerges. The bond between the apostles and the presidents of the Eucharist is found (perhaps) only in Clement and (to some degree) Hippolytus. The perception of the president of the Eucharist as an explicitly priestly figure is not attested before the beginning of the third century (Hippolytus, Tertullian, Cyprian). On the other hand, it is axiomatic with all the other witnesses that those who preside over the life of the church preside over the Eucharist.[17]

The Role of the Presbyters

The only second-century source to speak of presbyters' roles is Polycarp's letter to the Philippians. It outlines their duties: to bring back the straying, visit the sick, care for widows, orphans, and the poor, serve as "judges," and avoid avarice. These sound so like the duties of Ignatian bishops that some have suggested that Polycarp's presbyters are really bishops (or that Smyrna knew only collegial ministry of presbyter bishops and had not adopted yet Ignatius's model of mono-episcopacy).

However, there is no special difficulty in the duties outlined. There is no mention of the "sacramental" functions that Clement and Ignatius reserve to bishops. More probably, Polycarp was bishop chosen from among the presbyters, surrounded by a "college of apostles"—presbyters who are types of those first disciples who believed and converted.

Otherwise, there is little in second-century sources to indicate any specialized ministerial functions attached to presbyters as such. They are neither emissaries from one church to another nor presiders at Eucharist. Even at the end of the century Irenaeus (c. 180) speaks of them as "disciples of the apostles" (Adv Haereses, II:33:3). For Irenaeus, the importance of presbyters lay in their role as teaching authorities responsible for authentic teaching of Scripture and doctrine.

In this, Irenaeus may be following Papias, who was supposedly bishop of Hierapolis in Asia Minor (and whose five books entitled *Exegesis of the Lord's Gospel*, though lost, are quoted by Eusebius). Though the exact meaning of presbyter in Papias has been disputed, it appears to signify an old and revered person who is cited with respect, whether he is an ecclesiastical writer, or the source of an oral tradition, or one who hands on an earlier tradition.

In using the term "presbyter," Irenaeus may have narrowed its meaning, making him a vital link in the chain of doctrine that constitutes "apostolic succession." One can understand that, in combatting heresies, he would have been anxious to establish unbroken authoritative teaching; hence the idea of Christ, apostles, presbyters (apostles' pupils), as well as bishops drawn from the presbyterate.

Today people tend to assume that presbyter equals priest. At this time, however, there was still a great reluctance to use priestly terminology for those who led or guided the churches. If it was used, it was applied to bishops, though even this began only in the third century. Ignatius, despite his exaltation of the bishop, never calls bishops priests (or their ministry priestly), though he does refer to the Jewish priests, as does Clement. The term "High Priest" is used by him, at times, but only to refer either to Christ or to the Jewish priesthood. The only unambiguous reference to Christian ministers as priestly is found in the *Didache*.

In the *Didascalia* presbyters are hardly mentioned, compared to the bishops and deacons. Interestingly enough, in contrast to the *Apostolic Tradition*, they are chosen by the bishop himself. Hosea 1:10 is used as justification, the king taking from the people the administrators needed for the multitude: "So now does the bishop also take for himself from the people those whom he accounts and knows to be worthy of him and his office, and appoints them presbyters as counselors and assessors" (9). In Syria at this time, however, the bishop was chosen by the laity.

The *Didascalia* does give presbyters a special place in the liturgical assembly, at the east end where the bishop also has his throne. They still seem definitely outclassed by the deacons, who are the official representatives of the bishop to the people as his "hearing, his voice, heart and soul." The deacon is said to hold the place of Christ (the bishop holds the place of God); hence the people should go through them to approach the bishop. The presbyters, be it noted, are compared only to the college of apostles.

By the third century, the bishop was the recognized chief celebrant of the liturgy. Liturgical activity by the presbyters was seemingly very limited. This may not be the case, however. Though presbyters were overshadowed by the bishop in the situation described in the *Didascal-*

ia, the remainder of the third century seems to point to situations where Eucharists were presbyteral celebrations under the presidency of the bishop. We would thus have a form of concelebration. Concelebration here was more than a formality or added solemnity. It manifested the nature of the church and the roles of each within the community.

Furthermore, according to Cyprian, presbyters were beginning to be allowed to preside over the Eucharist alone in the absence of the bishop (Cyprian L 12,1; 16, 4). Both presbyters and deacons could also hear the confession of one about to die if there were no bishop to do so (18, 1). Tertullian seems to give them a role in the discipline of penance a half century earlier. The few texts we have seem to assume that the presbyters are the proper agents to be selected by the bishop if the latter is unable to carry out the function himself. The one area where the presbyters functioned by right, however, was in the anointing of the sick. What is occurring in this period, then, is a process of clericalization.

By the beginning of the fourth century, both East and West were beginning to possess a developed notion of cultic priesthood, shared in differing levels of dignity by bishops and presbyters. The actual understanding of Eucharist that emerges from this period is inseparably linked with the evolution of thought about the nature of the eucharistic action. As the Eucharist becomes more and more cultic, the function of the liturgical leadership is also increasingly seen as cultic. This development becomes even more accentuated in the post-Constantinian period.

Summary

1. The trend manifested in the pastoral epistles toward authoritative residential leaders of the presbyter/bishop variety received further development in this period, with the bishop emerging as the primary leader of the local church. He replaced the apostles and prophets in power and influence, combined many of the tasks done by others into one role, and became the full-time leader of the community. At the same time he became the principal one to preside over the emerging cult.

2. The New Testament offers no unambiguous evidence for *ordination*, though the gesture of laying on of hands does suggest at least commissioning for missionary tasks. Similarly, there seems to be no linking of ministry with sacramental leadership. This fell into place during this period, with ordinations for bishops, presbyters, and deacons. While the bishop is the undisputed leader of cult at the end of this period, the presbyters are at times allowed to function in this capacity with his approval.

3. By the early second century a rather clearly defined "hierarchy" of local leaders (i.e., bishops, presbyters, and deacons), evident in the letters of Ignatius of Antioch, begins to emerge. This model gained greater popularity, so that by the end of the century it was the ordinary pattern. Rome seems to have acquired a bishop by the last half of the second century.

4. The direct application of priestly or cultic vocabulary to Christian ministers begins only in the third century. We do see the beginning of parallels between Old Testament priests in the later second century, though these same sources say nothing about liturgies of "ordination." Laying on of hands does not seem to be essential to commissioning church leaders.

5. There is a beginning of efforts to link Christian ministry with an order "willed by God." First Clement connects church order with Christ and the apostles and the cosmic order of creation itself. Irenaeus connects episcopal ministry with a succession of authoritative teaching traced back to the "apostles." In the *Didascalia* the bishop holds the place of God.

6. Clement's letter to the church at Corinth reveals a rebellion against the presbyters for apparently no good reason. The letter suggests that the presbyters somehow derived their leadership from the apostles, and ultimately from Christ. Hence, to obey them is obedience to the Lord himself. Here we see theological justification being given to the presbyteral structure that was in place at the end of the century at Corinth. And we know that they had some sort of liturgical role as well.

7. Theological justification of the role of the bishop is even stronger in Ignatius of Antioch, where the bishop is clearly distinguished from presbyters and deacons. Serving as the bond of unity of the church, he is president of the presbyteral college. The presbyterial college is an earthly type or model of the heavenly Jerusalem. The bishop represents God, the presbyters, the apostles, and the deacons, Christ himself. Earlier prophets' and teachers' roles are swallowed up in that of the bishop. Remember that this was a time of persecution.

8. At this time we witness the emergence of bishops and deacons as functional ministers in virtually all the churches. "Presbyter," on the other hand, is primarily a status title. Presbyters do not form a hierarchy of prestige only, however; they form the bishop's council and have a role in judicial matters affecting the church. The bishops are usually elected from their ranks.

9. Some distinction between clergy and laity is in evidence rather

early. Clement had a brief reference to it, saying that each should work in his proper order in the church. However, until the *Didascalia*, all still seem to function within the basic unity of the local church. In the *Didascalia* the bishop possesses a kind of regal/priestly eminence that lifts him (and by association those close to him) to a distinct level above his people. They are more his charges and subjects than they are fellow Christians.

10. One of the great equalizers in these first centuries was the fairly frequent occurrence of martyrdom. Though a large proportion of those singled out for persecution by the civil powers were the leaders of the church, many of the faithful courageously faced torture and death. Martyrdom was one of the highest ideals, and it formed its own hierarchy of potent witness to the power of the gospel at the very heart of the apostolic ministry itself. Thus, with many "confessors of the faith" commanding their own respect, it was hard to view the clergy as "better" Christians. Confessors did not even need presbyteral ordination.

11. One indication of the importance given the laity at this time was their right to elect or at least assent to their leaders, and to be consulted in matters of church policy. Ordination was not understood theologically at this time as creating any metaphysical difference between the ordained and the rest of the community. It was a question of a different relationship to the community.

12. Bishops saw their role as preserving the unity of the Body of Christ. This ability to gather and protect the flock led them to arrogate to themselves the teaching and prophetic roles formerly exercised by others. At the same time, as the church grew in size, their work became more administrative.

13. The usual link of the bishops with the people was through the deacons, who handled day-to-day activities, the dole to the poor, and were considered the bishop's right-hand men. The fact that there were seven deacons in Rome (but 46 presbyters) is because each was in charge of one of the seven districts of the city.

14. This period also made an explicit link between presiding over the Eucharist and priesthood. The bishops not only presided, they were the high priests of the new Israel. By the end of this period, the Latin term *sacerdos* [= priest] was the normal way of thinking of the bishop.

15. The laying on of hands, which eventually became the standard gesture of ordination in the Latin church, surely began to emerge at least in the third century. The *Apostolic Tradition* is proof of this. We should learn to distinguish, however, the mandate of the church from the way in which the church indicates its mandate.

16. Though the ordained played an authoritative role within the community, they could be rejected by the community if they proved unworthy for some reason.

17. That ordinations were always incorporated into the eucharistic liturgy is of great importance in helping us to understand how they did not see the creation of orders or classes as being divisive. First of all, there could be no ministry *outside* the community, or parallel to it; all ministry was identical with the church body. As the Body of Christ, the church existed as a manifestation of Jesus' own ministry in the world.

18. Saying that no ministry could be understood outside the community was understood strictly. It was the community that prayed or that exercised charity. Bishops were not delegated authority by the community, nor did they represent it. These terms are juridical, and led eventually to a separation of the ordained person from the community: to act *on behalf of* the community implies standing *outside* the community because it means to act in its place. Understanding ministry communally is to affirm that ministry cannot stand outside or above the community.

19. To say that the ministry belongs to the community places the entire matter of ordination outside the dilemma of choosing between an ontological or a functional understanding. That is, does ordination bestow something indelible on the one ordained, or merely empower him to function for a certain purpose? If we understand ordination existentially, this distinction is misleading and inappropriate, since there is no charism that can be possessed simply as individuals.

20. Ordination to the ministry in eucharistic communion implies that the seal of the Holy Spirit cannot exist outside the receiver's essential relationship with the community. Its indelible character can best be compared to that which is possessed or given by love. Outside this existential bond with the community it is bound to die, just as the Spirit who gives this charism constantly sustains it for the good of the community.

Discussion Questions

1. What changes would take place in the present structures of church ministry were we to return to a third-century understanding of church hierarchy?

2. How might church ministries have developed if the church had taken root in the twentieth century? Would this be an improvement over what we now have? How?

3. Does it surprise you that the only "priests" in the early church were the bishops? And that this understanding came only in the third century? What could happen to the Eucharist if we did not see it in cultic terms?

4. Do you think it was necessary that the bishop take over the functions of other ministers in the church? Was it good?

Suggested Readings

Brown, R., "Are the Bishops Successors of the Apostles?" *Priest and Bishop*, Chap. 2, pp. 47-86.

Bevenot, M., "'Sacerdos' as Understood by Cyprian," *Journal of Theological Studies*, 30 (October 1979), 423-429.

Echlin, E., "The Deacon's Golden Age," *Worship*, 45 (1978), 37-40.

Faivre, A., "The Laity in the First Centuries: Issues Revealed in Historical Research," *Lumière et Vie*, 42 (1984), 5-25.

Legrand, H.-M., "Theology and the Election of Bishops in the Early Church," *Concilium*, 7, 8 (September 1972), 31-42.

Mitchell, N., "A Christian Priesthood," *Mission and Ministry*, Chap. 4, pp. 201-259.

Mohler, J., "Presbyters Become Priests: Third Century Church Order," *The Origin and Evolution of the Priesthood*, Chap. 4, pp. 51-70.

_____., "Prophets and Presbyters of the Second Century," *The Origin and Evolution of the Priesthood*, Chap. 3, pp. 33-50.

O'Meara, T., "Primal Ministry," *Theology of Ministry*, Chap. 4, pp. 76-94.

Schillebeeckx, E., "Organization and Spirituality of Ministry in the Course of Church History," *The Church with a Human Face*, Part 3, pp. 125-139.

Stockmeier, P., "The Election of Bishops by Clergy and People in the Early Church," *Concilium*, 137 (1980), 3-9.

4

Priesthood as Ministry

Before this period, the Christian religion had been officially pro-scribed. Believed to be enemies of the state, Christians had been severe-ly persecuted. This was the glorious age of martyrs. It ended once and for all when an edict of toleration was issued in 311 by the Emperor Ga-lerius. Constantine ratified this in 313 with the Edict of Milan.

A far more significant event occurred two generations later (381) when Theodotius declared Christianity to be the religion of all the people in the Roman empire. Christianity thereby took on the task of safeguarding the empire, a task that had formerly been exercised by the pagan religion. Christianity was now the state religion. Empire and church entered into a partnership, a coalition based on mutual interests that was to have incalculable consequences for Christianity to this day.

Church and state were united. The emperor thought of himself as protector of the church; it was his concern to foster its growth and ward off whatever would harm it. Though this seemed to promise short-term benefits, it was to lead to bitter conflicts over the years as each side fought the other for freedom, autonomy, or supremacy. Often the only thing holding the alliance together was the threat of outside enemies. It is important to note that despite the many changes that have occurred over the centuries, Constantinian Christianity has survived to this day, at least as an ideal, to govern the relationships of church and state.

As persecution ceased and government patronage increased, fourth-century Christianity grew rapidly. Those flocking to the church did not always do so from the purest of motives. The vast increase in numbers and new official religious duties had to be accommodated, forcing a re-structuring of the ministry. Synods and councils from Arles (314) to Chalcedon (451) set down canons that were to regulate ministry for the next millennium.

In some ways the fourth to the sixth centuries are different from the years that follow, because East and West were still closely united. The development of the episcopacy was one feature of these centuries. Some of greatest Fathers of the church lived during this period. The Edict of Milan allowed bishops to emerge from the era of persecution as the unquestioned leaders of the community. Many of them dominat-ed the life of the church.

Another consequence of acceptance was large-scale conversion (the church practically doubled in size—from five to ten million by the time Theodotius made it the religion of the state). This tended to introduce greater complexity and institutionalization into church organization. Furthermore, as the church went from persecution to official accep-tance, bishops found themselves almost immediately in the position of functionaries in the civil sphere. Assignments were given them by the emperor; episcopal courts were given civic recognition; bishops were often called upon to insure domestic tranquility.

Perhaps one of the more important changes was the subtle shift in the imagery applied to the church and, derivatively, to the episcopacy. As an officially identifiable and accepted social entity, the political model of society was applied (unconsciously at first, perhaps) to the church and its leaders. So also was imagery regarding Israel and the high priest borrowed from the Old Testament.

Thus, one of the striking features of the fourth and fifth centuries is the extent to which the episcopacy developed after Nicea. Bishops con-tinued to solidify the position that they had gained in previous years. The same is not true of the presbyterate, which began to lose its relative independence and initiative. Its role as chief council for the church and the bishop, as well as its corporate identity and functions, disappeared as presbyters began to be used more as helpers of the bishop and to be given individual assignments as "little bishops" in branch communi-ties. They became part of the bishop's work force, rather than fellow members who chose him to head their college.

Freedom from persecution did not automatically result in peaceful growth and development. It is almost as if added leisure freed the church to speculate on the mysteries of the faith—often resulting in het-erodox opinions and heresy. Four general councils were called (often by the emperor) to try to restore unity within the church itself. Though known mainly for their dogmatic importance, all issued disciplinary canons that were to regulate ministry for the next millennium.

1. Nicea(325) dealt with the divinity of Christ as opposed to the teaching of Arius.

2. Constantinople (381) dealt with the divinity of the Holy Spirit, as opposed to the teaching of Macedonius.

3. Ephesus (431) dealt with the divine motherhood of Mary, as opposed to the teaching of Nestorius.

4. Chalcedon (451) dealt with the two natures of Christ, declaring him to be both true God and true man.

This was the golden age of the Fathers. In many ways an impressive synthesis of faith was built up. However, the church was delivered a rude shock (in the West, at least) with the barbarian invasions and the collapse of Rome. Suddenly, the bulk of the people were illiterate warriors, and the faith once again had to be rebuilt—a process that took centuries.

Though the Fathers of the church dominate the era, it is impossible to give their teaching any decent treatment here. A few will be called upon to illustrate the major trends that developed during this period, some of which might be described as the primacy of bishops, an increase in the number of ministries and the rise of a powerful diaconate, the conversion of presbyters into priests with the consequent beginnings of celibacy, an increased clericalization of the church, and a separation of the clergy from the laity.

The Primary Role of Bishops

Christians of the fourth century saw a marked difference between early church forms and what had begun to emerge by the time of Nicea. Ambrosiaster, for example, said that in the early church anyone could teach and baptize; he justified the newer structures by saying that "when we do everything, this is irrational, vulgar, and abhorrent." We could also cite the increasing absorption of cultural traditions, or the rapid social evolution of the church after the Edict of Milan. But nowhere are changes more evident than in the position of the bishops and the subsequent evolution of presbyters into priests.

The bishops of this age clearly dominate the life of the church. Some of them were tremendously gifted men. Many were also powerful in both church and state. Ambrose of Milan, for example, is a classic instance of a bishop wielding power and influence far beyond what flowed intrinsically from his episcopal authority. Men like him were given special assignments by the emperor by reason of their acknowledged ability and influence. This is the period when the metropolitan sees acquired considerable prominence, and the patriarchates emerged (Alexandria, Rome, Antioch, and Carthage were joined by Milan, Caesarea, and Constantinople). The church was now a culturally identifiable and accepted social entity.

A new "ecclesiastical cosmology" arose, perhaps seen best in Augustine's *City of God*, where a highly developed explanation of the functioning of the world clearly has the church at the center. This had enormous impact on later ecclesiology. In this view, perfection consists in occupying one's place with fidelity and humility; the notion of the church as hierarchical was cast, however, in the image and likeness of Roman society.

At the time of Nicea, the episcopate began to move aggressively to exploit the potential that Milan had opened up. The role of the laity in the church is reflected in Canon 18 of Ancyra (319), which said that if a bishop were not acceptable to the people of his diocese, he must return to the rank of presbyter. Moreover, if he were dissatisfied with this and caused dissension, he was to lose the dignity of the presbyterate. Now, as bishops consolidated their position, canons of councils from Nicea to Chalcedon began to determine that they would be chosen by their fellow bishops with only "some" consultation of the people.

As the fourth century progressed, greater emphasis was placed on the episcopal choice of bishops and less on the participation of the people. In some places the participation of the people survived only as a type of assent. The ordaining bishop would ask if the candidate was worthy, and the congregation would answer "axios!" (he is worthy).

As regards universality, however, there was always a recognition that church leadership involved more than the local church. The Synod of Arles (314) canonized what was begun in the *Apostolic Tradition*, insisting that bishops be ordained by more than one bishop—a rule still in effect in the church:

> Concerning those who claim for themselves alone to have the right of ordaining bishops, we decree that no one take this upon himself unless he be accompanied by seven other bishops. If seven is impossible, they should not dare ordain without three others (Canon 20).

Nicea reiterated this, even going so far as to say that bishops should be consecrated by all the bishops of the province, if possible. At least three were required; those absent should give their consent in writing, confirmed by the metropolitan. This shows the importance given to communion with the larger church.

There was one (and only one) bishop for each local area. Under Augustine, for example, a meeting was held in Carthage in 411 attended by 268 Catholic and 279 Donatist bishops—more bishops than in the entire United States today! When Gregory the Wonderworker was named bishop, there were only 17 Catholics in his "diocese." What this comes down to is that today where we would have a priest-pastor, in those days they had a bishop-pastor.

Bishops of lesser towns would have had a metropolitan head, and they soon began to meet in regional synods. This collegial cooperation assured each area of apostolic succession—not only of bishops in communion with each other, but joined in orthodox teaching from the apostles as well. There was intense conciliar activity during this period. More than 75 councils met in the fourth century. Cyprian's idea that the bishops were apostolic because they succeeded the apostles in an identity of function and power is a type of theology that grew enormously and was never questioned during this period.

Episcopal collegiality was perhaps at its strongest during this time. The various forms this took (letters, synods, councils, etc.) gave this collegiality a spiritual and ecclesial depth that helped shape understanding of what a bishop should be. The college of bishops was not simply the sum of individual bishops. And it is fundamentally the college of bishops that is the successor of the "college of apostles." Individual bishops do not succeed individual apostles.

At the same time, we note the beginning of a new dynamic: the role of the bishop of Rome. In this model, each individual bishop is bonded more and more to the pope so that the monarchical aspect of papal power is highlighted. Only in relationship to the head was a bishop theologically understandable, either as an individual or as part of the college of bishops. This was given quasi-canonical status with the election of Gregory the Great (d. 604), whom we will consider in the next chapter. He has rightly been called, "the last of the Fathers and the first of the popes."

As the church became more structured, the wandering apostles and prophets were put out of circulation. In many cases, they were simply made to settle down as ruling bishops. To stem the number of wanderers, however, and to stop jurisdictional problems, there were a number of disciplinary decrees. For example, bishops and other clerics were not allowed to change dioceses (Arles 2, 21; Nicea 15; Antioch 21; Rome [402] 16), nor to interfere or assume episcopal functions in another diocese (Arles 17, 26; Sardia 11; Rome 15). Bishops were not to receive a person excommunicated by another bishop (Elvira 53; Arles 16; Nicea 5; Rome 16). Neither should they persuade people from another diocese to come to them so they might ordain them (Nicea 16).

Fourth-century legislation pointed up jurisdictional disputes between bishops, as well as a legal system ranging from local courts to the provincial sanhedrin of bishops, from which appeal could be made to Rome if the decision was not unanimous. The bishop was supreme in his diocese, although in cases of need he could delegate his priestly powers (except that of ordination) to presbyters.

All was not politics and administration, however. To a surprising degree the bishops of this period retained the primacy of preaching in their ministry. They saw this as their prerogative. If presbyters preached, it was by the bishop's delegation (and often with his training). They saw this responsibility as coming from their position as successors to the apostles and the tradition that came from them, and also in their role as shepherds.

In the doctrinal ferment that raged in these two centuries, practically all the great theologians were bishops. Prosper of Aquitaine, a layman, stands out as an exception. His presence, and the fact that he was often consulted by bishops, shows that theology, theoretically, was open to all. But even if some scattered laypersons could avail themselves of it, access to culture and education was not widespread in these years after the fall of Rome. Thus, we see the beginnings of regarding bishops as the official teachers of the church, a claim that generally went unchallenged.

Impudent Deacons

In many ways, deacons were the important men in the third and fourth centuries, far more than the presbyters.[1] They were in the front lines in the daily running of the church. They were the bishops' link with the people, in charge of church temporalities, and receiving strangers. The leader of the deacons in Rome, the archdeacon, often became pope (until at least the ninth century). In light of this, it was a normal reaction for them to think themselves superior to the presbyters. This led to some abuses that synods of the next two centuries tried to correct. By the end of this period, the diaconate was relegated to the final step of the ladder leading to the presbyterate.

Some of this seems petty to us today. It simply reflected a growing sense of independence, and a desire to stretch the limits of their responsibilities. Nicea, for example, reacted strongly to the presumptions of deacons who put themselves ahead of presbyters and even the bishop:

> It has come to the knowledge of this holy synod that in certain places and cities the deacons give the Eucharist to the presbyters, whereas neither canon nor custom allows that they who have no authority to offer should give the body of Christ to those who do offer. It has also been made known that now some of the deacons receive the Eucharist even before the bishops. Let all such practices be done away with and let the deacons keep within their proper bounds, knowing that they are the ministers of the bishop and inferior to the presbyters....[2]

Ambrosiaster, who lived under powerful Roman deacons and saw two of them (Ursinus and Damasus) struggling for the bishop's chair, wrote against their presumption. So did Jerome, who could bring a savage pen to the fight. To counter them, he strongly asserted the dignity of the presbyters, saying that there was nothing the bishop did that presbyters could not do, except ordain.[3] Jerome compared the bishop, presbyters, and deacons with Aaron, his sons, and the Levites. Deacons should recognize this, and be content with their levitical ministrations, said he. The power of the deacons began to be eroded by the increased pastoral ministrations of the presbyters, especially as they began taking on sacramental ministry. By the high Middle Ages, the diaconate became only a step toward a sacralized priesthood.

Already at the beginning of the third century, women had been recognized as deaconesses in the church. Origen explained the text in Romans concerning Phoebe by saying, "This text teaches with the authority of the apostles that even women are instituted deacons in the church." The *Didascalia* a few years later proposed a novel typology in their regard. For them, the bishop was the image of God the Father, the deacons of Christ, and the presbyters of the college of apostles. Deaconesses were said to be the image of the Holy Spirit, perhaps because in Hebrew and Syriac, Spirit is feminine. This is found nowhere else, however.

Unlike male deacons, who were the right arm of the bishop and had extensive duties, the responsibilities of deaconesses, it would seem, were mainly with the women in the church. In this period, they had taken over many of the functions of the earlier order of widows, especially visiting the sick and helping at baptisms. It would seem indisputable that they were thought part of the clergy. They participated with them and with them alone in the Eulogies (i.e., the distribution of the surplus of unconsecrated bread offered by the faithful for Eucharist). Hands were imposed on them as for other clerics, as the bishop prayed:

> O Eternal God, Father of our Lord Jesus Christ, Creator of man and of woman, who replenished Miriam with the Spirit, and Deborah, Anna and Huldah; who did not disdain that thy only-begotten Son should be born of a woman; who also in the tabernacle of the testimony and in the Temple did ordain women to be keepers of thy holy gates, do Thou now look down upon this thy servant who is to be ordained to the office of a deaconess, and grant her thy Holy Spirit, that she may worthily discharge the work that is committed to her to thy glory and the praise of thy Christ... [4]

From the sources that we have, it would seem that though deaconesses flourished from the fourth to the sixth centuries, they did so in the East more than in the West. Ambrosiaster categorically rejected them. In Latin canonical sources after the fourth century there are many references to deaconesses, but this seems to have been an honorary title for the professed widows.

They reappear in the fifth century, as is evidenced in the following curious text: "Deaconesses are absolutely not to be ordained; and if there are still any of them, let them bow their heads under the benediction that is given to the congregation" (First Council of Orange, canon 25). A still more curious passage comes from a letter of Pope Gelasius to the bishops of Italy, wherein he protests the fact that "Women discharged altar service," and "performed all other things which had been assigned to the ministry of men only." He emphasized the enormity of this situation and blamed those bishops who permitted these things as well as the silent complicity of those other bishops who did nothing about it. [5] This is an area where we would wish for more texts and clarifications about the actual situation.

The fact remains that in many ways and in most places women were still regarded as inferior to men, and even those ordained deaconesses did not have the same importance or exercise the same functions as their male counterparts. Eventually deaconesses passed from the scene, victims of the idea of the natural superiority or primacy of man over woman.

Priestly Presbyters

Narsai, the bishop of Nisibe, summed up what the priest is and what he does in this fifth-century sermon:

> The priest has received the power of the Spirit by the laying on of hands. Through him all the mysteries of the church are performed. The priest consecrates the font with the water for baptism, and the Spirit gives the baptized person adoptive childhood. Without a priest, no woman would be given to be married to a man; without a priest their marriage obligations are not completed. Without a priest the water would not be blessed and the house would remain impure. Those who do not possess the *ordines* cannot celebrate the Eucharist, however pious they may be. For through their purity the righteous cannot bring down the Spirit, but a sinful priest cannot prevent the descent of the Spirit through his sinfulness....
>
> As priests they perform on earth the mystery of the inauguration of the Kingdom of Heaven....To this end the high priest [bishop] gave the priesthood to new priests, so that people could be made priests and forgive sins on earth.[6]

This alone is enough to tell us that we have come a long way from the understanding of presbyters that obtained in the first two or three centuries. The presbyters have vanished. They have become priests, and a very cultic kind of priest.

Actually, by the time of Nicea the old presbyterates were beginning to disappear. The main pressure was the expansion of the city churches into what we would today call dioceses. Here the bishop presided in the titular church and sent his presbyters into the neighboring towns and country districts. The presbyters traded their disciplinary and judicial roles to the bishop for a share in his cultic role. Now both bishops and presbyters belonged to the priesthood of the altar.

Of course, the situation in which Christianity found itself under Constantine and Theodotius meant that the pagan conception of religion at that time was transferred to some extent to Christianity. Clerics were equated with the pagan priests and exempted from all duties. This forced the ordinary believer more into the background under the leadership of the clerics—at least in the eyes of the pagans. Some of this was bound to rub off.

With Christianity the official state religion, things like Trinitarian belief were also mandated by the state; hence the gospel was opened for all sorts of misunderstanding. But with the emphasis on *religio*, theology (especially with the help of the Old Testament) began to move the priesthood into the realm of the holy and the sacred. John Chrysostom could write that priestly life is a "terrifying existence, full of fear and trembling." However, the Theodosian sacerdotalizing of ministry had a long prehistory.

Perhaps one of the most potent forces in the cultifying of Christianity at this time was the influence of the Old Testament. We know that by the year 70 there had been a definite break with Judaism, as the radical transformation of the Old Testament wrought by the New became evident. Nevertheless, soon enough Old Testament categories and attitudes began to creep back in and they allowed for a much different interpretation of the gospel than had been the case in the first two generations. The mentality behind it was a typology grounded in the historical evolution of the process of salvation, which was seen as organic development, despite the quantum leap represented by Christ. Even today, we still find it hard to keep a clear vision of the uniqueness of Christianity as well as its bond to Israel. At any rate, in the third century, Christians began to drift back to the Old Testament way of viewing even the redemptive work of Christ. Perhaps with distance, the polemic that accompanied the separation of church and synagogue tended to lessen. And the theological awareness of the first two centuries changed.

This was also true in the East; the *Didascalia* also shows the influence of Jewish thinking. The impact of Old Testament patterns of thought and practice on episcopal and presbyteral ministry becomes increasingly noticeable over the succeeding centuries. It would affect the notion of sacrifice, the hierocratic theories of papal and episcopal authority, the understanding of the efficacy of priestly action in the sacraments, and would become one of the major factors in the overconcentration on the cultic that tended to obliterate somewhat other aspects of Christian ministry. As this affected the Eucharist, for example, the presbyter went from being one who unified the community in faith and charity to a dispenser of graces. The Eucharist was now seen mainly as a source of saving grace.

Along with this came vestments. Many presbyters also began to wear special clothing even outside the liturgy, thus separating themselves symbolically from the laity. After the year 400 we find the tonsure being prescribed in some areas. This was part of Egyptian and monastic spirituality. And, of course, we see the beginnings of celibacy. This will be treated below.

To sum up, by the end of the fourth century, sacerdotalism had become the ordinary way of thinking and speaking of the clergy. They were the priests of the New Israel, replacing their Jewish predecessors of old. Commonly accepted by the Fathers, sacerdotalism is clearly reflected in Chrysostom's treatise on the priesthood.

One consequence of this was a widening gap between the clergy and the laity. Also, as the presbyter/priests became identified with their sacramental roles, it could be argued that they were essentially the same as bishops, except for the right to ordain. From the bishop's side, this led to the perspective of the late Middle Ages, seeing the episcopate only as the "fullness of the presbyterate." They were defined as being priests—only more so.

It might be good to recall that the understanding of ordination in the church entering the fourth century owed much to Cyprian. Before Nicea, it was accepted that the mere liturgical ritual did not guarantee the existence or validity of an ordination; other ecclesial and juridical conditions had to be met. One of these conditions was rootedness in a particular community to which one was called to minister. There could be no such thing as a priest without a community.

It was this principle that the Council of Chalcedon wanted to preserve when it ruled in canon six that ordinations that were not rooted in a community were invalid. The community provided a person his title or right to ordination. This is still the law in the East. In the West, it lasted for more than a millennium. There was a double focus here. In the first place, priests were supposed to have a particular church function. This was the essence of church ministry, and the very reason for ordination.

Linked with this, unless priests had a particular ministry, they had no right to an imperial salary. This economic interpretation was taken a step further at the Third Lateran Council (1179). Pope Alexander III there interpreted the "title" of ordination to mean that the cleric should have enough to live on. This became the exclusive focus in 1198, when Innocent III argued that even a priest ordained absolutely still possessed and retained his "presbyteral" quality. In other words, the ordination ritual alone made a person a priest—forever.

Augustine can be blamed for this, in part, because of his fight against the Donatists.[7] They insisted that personal holiness was essential for membership in the true church; an unworthy Christian or minister would need rebaptism or reordination, etc. as the case may be. Since *nemo dat quod non habet* (nobody gives what he doesn't have), they argued that only worthy ministers (those in the state of grace) celebrated valid sacraments.

The Donatists posed a serious threat. The challenge they posed for Augustine was a subtle one. Instinctively he had to admit that though they were heretical, they still celebrated valid sacraments. Otherwise, he would have implicitly admitted their principle of rebaptism.

Augustine put forth the principle that sacramental incorporation into the church by itself gave one a *character dominicus* (which would lead in later centuries to the notion of an "indelible quality"). Drawing a distinction between a valid and fruitful sacrament, he had argued that even a heterodox community's baptism gave the *character domini-cus*, that is, it permanently claimed and marked the individual as belonging to Christ, even if that claim remained unfruitful in the person's life. This distinction between a valid sacrament and a fruitful one enabled him to affirm three things:

1. He distinguished between a sacrament's validity and fruitfulness. It could be valid even if the minister were unworthy or heretical, since God does not penalize people because their leaders are corrupt, and God—not the minister—is the ultimate source of sacramental grace.

2. Because even heretical communities celebrate valid sacraments, one need not rebaptize or reordain if they return to communion with the church; the ordination of heretics simply remains unfruitful while they persist in heresy.

3. Even a heterodox community's sacraments create a *character do-minicus*, that is, they permanently claim the individual as one who belongs to Christ—even if that claim remains unfruitful throughout the person's life.[8]

These distinctions became more important in the late Middle Ages. In Augustine's day, however, they had but minor influence on the theology of ordination, or the transformation of presbyters into priests. For this latter step, the main influence was far more prosaic: physical growth. The bishops (read: parish priests) were no longer able to care for their growing flock. At the beginning of the fifth century, Innocent I wrote to Decentius, bishop of Gubbio, explaining how the whole community of Rome could not possibly be accommodated in a single church on Sundays. As a result, presbyters presided at other places, and a fragment of the consecrated bread was sent to each of them as a sign of communion of the entire church with each other and the bishop.

This marked a significant change in the understanding of presbyters that obtained in the first two centuries. From being the role models of the community they had evolved into sacramental practitioners. With a tradition that stretches back through Cyprian to the *Didascalia* we note an increasing emphasis on cult. As this happens, both the presbyters and the *episkopoi* become cult personnel not only in their activity, but in popular understanding.

Whereas up till then the term *episkopos* described the basic function of pastoral supervision and care for the community, the new cultic emphasis soon resulted in preferring the term *hiereus [sacerdos]* for bishops (as well as priests). When Cyprian wrote to give reasons why bishops should remain with their congregations during times of persecution, the reasons given have almost exclusive reference to their being needed for liturgical activity. We have here an evolving recognition that certain worship officials are necessary for the church.

The Rise of Celibacy

The law of celibacy did not emerge in a vacuum. Its beginnings in this period were influenced by three trends that negatively influenced the theology and spirituality of all the baptized in the fourth century. These would be dualistic philosophies and heresies, the development of monasticism, and the increasing institutionalization of the church. A word about each.

The second-century church struggled against *encratism, Gnosticism,* and *montanism.* All three tended to look on matter as evil. Among other things, sexual activity was frowned on. With Plotinus (203-279) and the rise of neo-Platonism, even the Fathers of the church were affected with a dualism that viewed the material aspects of daily life in a negative way. This led to an exaggerated spiritualism, and helped fuel the second trend: flight from the world.

One of the equalizing factors in the first three centuries had been persecution. Those who suffered and died for the faith came from the entire spectrum of the church, clergy as well as lay. These heroic witnesses were looked up to by all. But with the legitimization of Christianity, martyrdom came to an end. Who were the new heroes of the faith? Those who embraced monasticism, a well-established phenomenon by the fifth century. By their giving up worldly values, monks were soon regarded as being in a "state of perfection"—an expression found in the Code of Canon Law until 1983. These became the spiritual elite. In the beginning, it should be noted that the line of division fell between the monks, on the one hand, and the clergy and laity, on the other. Clerics in these days were still married.

The third trend was the increasing institutionalization of the church that came with legitimacy and growth in size. Bishops became civil officials, with special privileges and tax exemptions. With the fall of the Roman empire to the barbarians, they emerged as the only ones who could maintain order and provide services. This made them seem a class apart, well above the layperson (a term that was coming to mean one without particular skills in a given field).

One finds traces of celibacy attached to priesthood even before Nicea. There are frequent discussions of remarriage on the part of bishops and presbyters. By the third century, 1 Timothy 3:2, advocating that the bishop be a man of one wife, was usually understood as a prohibition of remarriage for both a bishop or presbyter whose wife had died, or a prohibition of ordination for one who had married a second time. One also finds texts extolling celibacy, attributing to it a kind of angelic superiority, a purity from earthly contamination. This made it especially appropriate for those who ministered at the altar.

The exact roots of Christian thinking on celibacy are hard to determine. The exhortation of Paul and a few New Testament texts ("there are some who have made themselves eunuchs for the kingdom...") did influence people like Origen and Athenagoras. But there is no real New Testament tradition in this regard. Given the philosophical mood of the day, however, we now know that the preference for celibacy was strongly tinged with a depreciation of the bodily and material, which is more neo-Platonic than Christian.

Tertullian is an interesting case. From a beautiful eulogy of Christian marriage in *ad uxorem*, he speaks of remarriage as legalized debauchery in *de exhortatione castitatis*. He refers here to an undiscoverable text of Leviticus to justify the ban on remarriage for presbyters (an interesting conjunction: Christian presbyters = "priests," and so should be governed by the Old Testament law on priests). On the authority of Prisca, the montanist prophetess, he links celibacy with ministry on the basis that one must be pure to deal properly with holy things. Thus, the marital restrictions of Leviticus could be applied with a vengeance.

Also, in the developing theories of asceticism and contemplation that came from Origen and flowed into the emerging monastic movement, sexual abstinence was considered well-nigh essential to contemplation. Passion tended to be seen as destroying the impassibility and self-possession needed for contemplative insight. This idea may have originated more in stoicism than in the New Testament, but ideas like this held popular sway.

At the dawn of the fourth century, the first known law on the subject came from the Council of Elvira (305?) (always on the strict side of every church issue). This was a law of continence for all clergy; they were required henceforth to abstain from their wives when they were to minister at the altar. But they were not to separate from them! This was the first in a series of such laws, until the Lateran Councils I and II (1123 and 1139) took the final step of declaring the nullity of any marriage of a cleric in major orders. From an initial desire to live a "more perfect" form of life, the marriage of clerics was portrayed as an unmitigated evil to be extirpated at all costs.

Was it necessary? Audet chides us for looking at early ministry and focusing mainly on the evolution of hierarchy, the role played by the deacons, or some such issue.[9] All these clearly need studying, but he feels that we can become so concerned about the divisions of functions, powers, and authority that we do not look closely at the conditions that helped make up the effectiveness and continuity of pastoral service in the church of old.

How much real attention, for example, have we given to the domestic content of the original ekklesia? Almost certainly, all the New Testament writers and many writers of the early church were married men (or women). And the early churches were "house churches," providing the hospitality that was such an important element in the spread and solidification of the faith. It was the home context that made it possible at that time for the gospel and the ekklesia to be the leaven in the lump.

The pastoral metaphors of flock and shepherd were first developed in relation to the service of the assembly, rather than to that of the apostolic message. These images suggest above all closeness, watchfulness, day-to-day care. And such was indeed the character of service that the ekklesia could, and should, expect from those placed at their head to preside over the assembly.

In the early days, no one envisaged such an abstract alternative as "celibacy or marriage" to be evaluated in the light of some hierarchy of the relative perfection of different "states of life." What was actually considered was *style* of life—and that was something that could be determined from the facts, especially how one ran the household, which was the normal context for the assembly.

From the New Testament, the text that will be used over and over again is the injunction found in the pastorals that the bishop should be a man of one wife (*mias gunaikos andra*). Now, it has been thought (and is still quite generally thought) that this is a pronouncement against choosing bishops who had remarried (cf. Titus 1:6–9; 1 Timothy 3:2, 8,10, 12). But is this how the phrase is to be translated? Husband of a single wife is perhaps too simple.

There are three choices. It could forbid polygamy. But this was taken for granted in those days. Thus, some translated it to mean either conjugal fidelity or married only once. Audet argues that neither of these is sufficient. He suggests that the literary make-up of the phrase gives the clue to its meaning. We say a man of action, or a man of one idea, or a man of his word, and understand these figuratively. In the same way, a "man of one wife" would mean "undividedly attached to his wife." The qualification stipulated is a harmonious and stable marriage. Whether first or second does not matter.[10]

It may be argued that many of the Greek Fathers interpreted it to mean married only once. However, their interpretation may have been dictated by their own preferences or philosophical biases. Theodore of Mopsuestia's interpretation is substantially that given above (Commentary on Epistle of Paul: 1 Timothy 3:2). The pastorals also required a hospitality that was the basis of the church's pastoral service and that seem to flow from a well-ordered household.

A factor that is seldom considered in this respect is that it was only in the third century that the place of assembly was no longer the homes of the faithful. When the church went from house churches to fixed meeting places, a tremendous transformation took place in the physical setting of the community, one that would affect the style and quality of hospitality, to say nothing of the style of life of the bishop.

Another thing to consider is the genesis of the Pauline injunction to remain as he was (i.e., unmarried). There were two actual ministerial situations in the early church: one spread the word by apostleship, the other solidified what had been begun. It would seem that if anything, it would be the travelers who would find celibacy advantageous, while the residential leaders would be better served by the more usual domestic arrangement, with its wonderfully rich and strong customs of hospitality along with the marriage that constituted its essential and permanent reality.[11]

Two centuries later, however, the Council of Elvira proposed conjugal continence. A point of capital importance is that from now on it was not the service of the Word as apostle that formed the call to leave wife and family, but the pastoral service of the church itself. To be more precise, it was not so much the pastoral service of the church as it was the service of the sacraments, especially the Eucharist. This marked a shift from a focus on *styles* of life to *states* of life.

The influences here were asceticism and monasticism, to be sure, and also the very change in locale from homes to churches, which was bound to make Mass more impersonal and "organized." Perhaps more important than either of these was the perception of the impure and of the sacred. The desire to honor the Eucharist led to the conclusion that it was incompatible with the exercise of sexuality, since this was seen as somehow unclean. Remember, the other aspects of marriage were not touched at first.

This resulted from an enormous change in attitude. In the early church, none of the terms used to signify service of the gospel or of the church were taken from the sacral world of the Jews or of the pagans. They come directly from secular speech, and indicate that the group did not think of its ministers as forming a sacred caste like the members of the Levitical priesthood. The same attitude can be observed with regard to the places and furniture used for worship. We are dealing with homes, tables, cups, and plates, rather than "sacred vessels."

It is not till the beginning of the third century, when we begin to note the use of a more "priestly" vocabulary being applied to some of the services of the church, that we sense a change of attitude in regard to "holiness." Cyprian surely took a lead in this in the West. He defined pastoral care not in terms of people in need, but first and foremost in terms of "a service of the altar and sacrifices." Priestly service was seen as a sacred function, a *ministerium sacrum*. From that center— the altar of God—the sacred went out to communicate itself to the pastoral world as a whole. Beyond this, of course, lay the world of the impure, the profane, and the secular.

When the *Apostolic Tradition* used the word "ordination," it was a secular term. Following Cyprian the word "consecration" was introduced. Now bishops were not only ordained, they were consecrated to the service of the Lord. The ritual itself did not have any act of consecration. But the door was opened for the entry of various Levitical prescriptions and their application to the priesthood of the church. Eusebius of Caesaria (325?) was able to write:

> For those who have been consecrated, and have engaged themselves to serve God, it is fitting to abstain afterwards from relations with their wives.[12]

Here consecration is used as the reason for this fittingness. In this he was following the lead of Elvira. Nicea also considered an affirmation of the canon of Elvira, but was dissuaded by Paphnutius (though some hold this to be apocryphal). What is important here, however, is the reason being given. The argument depends on a particular perception of the sacred, yet uses the archaic distinction between pure and impure. Explicit support is sought by comparing the new priesthood with the old. It was in this form that Ambrose presented the argument at the end of the fourth century.

You who have received the grace of the sacred ministry with an untouched body, an untainted modesty, to whom also all conjugal relations are unknown, you know that you must be sure of an unhindered and spotless ministry, which must not be profaned by any conjugal relation. I have not wanted to pass over this matter in silence, for in many farther-off places clerics have had children during the exercise of the ministry, and even of the episcopate. Furthermore, they defend their behavior by citing ancient custom, when the sacrifice was only offered at intervals. In truth, even the people purified themselves for three or four days in order to become pure for the sacrifice, as we read in the Old Testament [Ex 19:10]. They also used to wash their clothes. But if their piety was so great in the time of prefiguring, what should not ours be in the time of the reality? Priest and Levite, learn what it means to wash your clothes, in order to present a pure body to the sacraments you must celebrate. If the people of Israel were forbidden to take part in their offering without having washed their clothes, would you dare to offer for others with a defiled mind as well as a defiled body? Would you dare to act as their minister?[13]

By the sixth century the terminology Ambrose uses here as well as the attitudes expressed had already become quite common. It is sacred terminology from beginning to end. The argument hinges on the ministry precisely insofar as it is seen as sacred and not profane. This requires a certain style of life in the one who exercises it. Above all, the ministry excludes the taint that any kind of sexual relations would bring. Using the Old Testament, Ambrose argues how much *more* holy we should be in the reality of the New Testament. The sacred character of the Eucharist spreads through the ministry right to the actual person of the one chosen to perform it.

Note that the growing custom of more frequent Eucharists in the church (more so in the West than the East) made it practically impossible for a minister to ever sleep with his wife. When children were born, priests could be accused of irreverence toward the altar or of sin. As Innocent I wrote to Victricius of Rouen (404), "Let deacons and priests have no sexual relations with their wives, for they are engaged in the needs of a daily ministry...."

Thus, there were many forces at work. There is the question of attributing priestly status to the ministers of the church. And there is the aversion toward sexual relations that was common at the time. Augustine was to hold that even between married couples, it was at least venially sinful. The amazing thing is that priests and deacons were allowed to be married at all. They were, however; they simply were not to use the sexual aspects of that relationship. It was only in the twelfth century that marriage itself was forbidden, and that we acquired the present legislation regarding a celibate priesthood in the Western church.

Several observations can be made about all this.

1. In the patristic age, especially, clerical continence became a critical symbol of the otherworldliness of the clergy, of their independence of the affairs of ordinary life.

2. It became the key issue in the whole matter of clerical morality and good example. This was tied in with a shift in thinking about morality in general. Charity had been the dominant theme in the first three centuries; sermons now emphasize chastity.

3. At every step of the way, for eight centuries, the extension of celibacy was a matter of legislation, enforced by means of threats and coercion. Few were convinced by appreciation of celibacy's intrinsic worth or inspired by others. It was ultimately made possible only because of powerful and absolutely monarchic popes.

Final Remarks

One byproduct of the developments of the fourth and fifth centuries is that the three divisions (clerics, monks, lay) that have come down to us today became firmly fixed. It was at this time that the term "lay" came to mean more or less what it does today: all Christians who are not clerics. Unlike in the second or third centuries, women were now surely included with the laity. Excluded from lay status, after the rise of monasticism, were the monks, as well as the emperor, who surely did not think of himself as "lay." Unfortunately, the term "laity" was not used to designate specific Christian responsibility in the church. It soon provided justification for lay non-involvement.

There are remnants of ancient lay involvement in some of the Eastern churches. The Syrians and (until 1920) the Melchites give an advisory voice to laymen in selecting bishops. Though Pius IX was concerned lest this should be seen as a constitutional right among the Armenians, Leo XIII confirmed their right.

Despite the significant change that took place in the sacerdotalization of the official ministry, there was actually little theological reflection on the nature of priesthood during this period. From the evidence we have, it seems that the principal effects of ordination were to situate a man in a given order or position in the church, that is, having the right and responsibility of performing certain functions for the sake of the community. As regards theologizing from the rite, the *Apostolic Tradition* is the only work we have to go on. It was still too early to speak of the *sacrament* of orders, or of a sacramental character. This came only with later reflection on Augustine's theology.

In the beginning, the church was far more concerned with *styles* of life than with *states* of life. Little thought was given to priesthood as a vocation. We actually have only three works from the patristic period that were devoted specifically to the priesthood. The first was the short work of Gregory Nazianzus, usually always referred to by its Latin title, *De fuga* (c. 362). Then there is the longer treatise of John Chrysostom, *On the Priesthood* (c. 385). (Though these spoke of priesthood, they were referring primarily to bishops.) Two centuries later, Gregory the Great would write his *Book of Pastoral Rule* (590). All of these are concerned with the dignity of the office and the consequent behavior or spirituality that should result. Chrysostom expresses it thus:

> The work of the priesthood is done on earth, but it is ranked among the heavenly ordinances. And this is only right, for no man, no archangel, no other created power, but the Paraclete himself ordained this succession and persuaded men, while still remaining in the flesh, to represent the ministry of angels. The priest, therefore, must be as pure as if he were standing in heaven itself, in the midst of those powers (III.4).

Summary

1. This was not only an age of great bishops, it was an age in which bishops themselves achieved undisputed headship as a ministerial group within the church. They were able to claim for themselves the teaching and prophetic roles in the church, and they became the chief liturgists as well. Baptism, confirmation, Eucharist, and reconciliation were all theirs by right. If the liturgy were presided over by a presbyter, it was only by the bishop's permission and authorization.

2. As the period began, the entire people of God had some say in the choice of bishops. As the period wore on, this choice was made more and more by the other presbyters or bishops of the region, and only submitted to the people for a general sort of approval.

3. By the fifth century, the church had adopted the structural organization of the Roman state. Dioceses were co-terminous with state boundaries, and many bishops exercised both ecclesiastical and civil roles. This strengthened the monarchical aspects of the hierarchy. Many of

the problems of bishops among themselves were jurisdictional problems, which could be appealed to Rome if they were not solved on the regional levels.

4. The sub-ministers who achieved the greatest "power" during this time were the deacons. Bishops and popes were often chosen from the deacons. They had far more effective leadership than the presbyters, who were (at least at the beginning of this period) seen as an advisory council to the bishop.

5. The major development in the presbyterate is that an almost complete change took place in the function of presbyters. They had begun as the wise men of the church, those who could be looked up to by others, and the advisory council of the bishop, who was often chosen from their ranks. This was gradually replaced by their being given a semi-autonomous sacramental and pastoral role by the bishops in areas where people could not get to the cathedral church for Sunday Eucharist. They became extensions of the bishops' work force outside the cities.

6. At the same time, both priests and bishops began to be identified more and more with their sacramental roles as "priestly" figures. Even the name "presbyter" was dropped, and the newer title "priest" began to be used instead. This was so much the case that men like Jerome could argue that there was very little difference between priests and bishops, since in the essentials of their ministry, they had equal powers.

7. With the change from presbyter to priest, a change also took place in how people viewed this priesthood. There began to be a subtle shift from a functional role with the church to a state of life within the church. The chief models for this were provided by the Old Testament rules and regulations governing priests. The main emphasis was on their cultic responsibilities.

8. The understanding of ordination at this time was still one that involved the whole process of election, worthiness, and attachment to a particular community. The ordination rite was part of all this. There was no thought of ordination being so permanent that a person could not be removed from his position if he were not fit for it.

9. There was still a strong sense that priests and bishops were ordained for the service of some local community. The Council of Chalcedon, in fact, decreed that an absolute ordination was an impossibility, and would be non-existent.

10. During this period, with greater emphasis being placed on the sacred nature of priestly ministry, we see major efforts to link priesthood with a type of cultic purity that would result in the law of celibacy in

the Western church. At first, the main effort was to prevent married priests or bishops from having sexual relations with their wives. Celibacy was eventually imposed as a means of achieving this.

11. The two major streams of influence here were the Old Testament regulations on priests ministering in the Temple, and the neo-Platonic philosophies that were common at the time. Sexual activity, if not seen as positively sinful, was at least looked down on as opposed to contemplation and definitely harmful to the life of the spirit. The "spiritual" man was supposed to be above all this. Celibacy became an independent value.

12. One area that still needs to be studied in this connection is the influence of the shift that resulted in going from house churches to basilicas, from pastoral qualities modeled on the hospitality of the household to the cultic functions of a priestly class.

13. From this time we see the priest being referred to as a person "consecrated" to the *sacred* ministry, not the profane. Thus, emphasis shifts from focusing on a *style* of life to making it a *state* of life. The argument is that if a certain holiness was required in the Old Testament, how much more should be required in the New, in which the priesthood was so much higher.

14. It should be remembered that at this time (and all along the line) the discipline of continence or celibacy was not voluntarily accepted by priests and bishops as it was by the monks. It is something that had to be imposed over and over again over a period of 800 years before it became a permanent feature of Western church law.

Discussion Questions

1. Was it necessary that the shift from presbyters to priests should have taken place? Should the advisory role of the presbyterate have been retained? How might this be done today?

2. Despite the political push that gave the bishops undisputed power in the church, is this a good feature of church life today? Could it be modified today without causing anarchy?

3. Despite the problematic way in which celibacy began in the church, in what sense is the lifestyle of the priest important to the effectiveness of his ministry?

4. What are some of the consequences of rootedness in a local community that could be effectively used in priesthood today?

5. From the limited role played by the laity at this period of church history, what aspects could be used by the church today to involve them more in the life of the church? How, in practice, might this be done?

Suggested Readings

Audet, J.P., *Structures of Church Ministry*, New York: Sheed and Ward, 1969.

Cowdrey, H., "Dissemination of St. Augustine's Doctrine of Holy Orders During the Later Patristic Age," *Journal of Theological Studies*, 20 (1969), 448-481.

Crehan, J.H., "Priesthood, Kingship, and Prophecy," *Theological Studies*, 42 (1981), 216-231.

Mitchell, N., "A Christian Priesthood," *Mission and Ministry*, Chap. 4, pp. 201-259.

Mohler, J., "The Sacred and the Secular: Fourth Century Sacerdotalism," *The Origin and Evolution of the Priesthood*, Chap. 5, pp. 71-108.

Schillebeeckx, E., "Organization and Spirituality of Ministry in the Course of Church History," *The Church with a Human Face*, Part 3, pp. 140-155.

Vogel, C., "Le passage à l'Eucharistie communautaire à la messe privée," *Revue des Sciences Religieuses*, 54 (1980), 231-250.

5

The Monastery as Minister

The Western Roman empire collapsed completely at the end of the fifth century. After 486, there was no longer any emperor in the West. In this vacuum and with the need for rebuilding society, the stage was set for a power struggle among three sovereigns: the pope, the patriarch of Constantinople, and the emperor of Byzantium. The pope won.

On Christmas Day in 496, Clovis, the King of the Franks, was baptized, thus inaugurating the conversion of the barbarians, a task that would occupy much church energy in this period. One hundred years later, Gregory of Tours, in his *History of the Franks*, called Clovis "a new Constantine"—a conscious effort to deny this legacy to the emperor in Constantinople. Thus, a fourth player entered into the contest of pope, patriarch, and emperor: the king of the Franks and his successors. The struggle was on between East and West.

Some 250 years after the baptism of Clovis, Pippin the Younger was honored by Pope Stephen II (754) with the title *Patricius Romanorum*: protector and defender of the Roman church and the Catholic faith. It matters little that the immediate cause was the Lombard threat. This sent a clear and irritating signal to the emperor in Constantinople (who held this title) that the link between the pope and the head of the Eastern Roman empire had been severed. On the political level, at least, a Rome/France axis was now a reality. Pope Leo III, no mean political player, cemented the papal position half a century later on Christmas Day, 800, by crowning Charlemagne (to his surprise) emperor in Rome.

Four years earlier, Charlemagne had written to the pope:

It is our task with God's help to defend the holy church of Christ everywhere with the force of arms against attacks from without by the heathens, and the ravages of infidels, and to strengthen the knowledge of the faith within the church. Your task, most holy Father, is to help our armies by lifting up your arms to God, as Moses did, so that through your intercession and God's command, the Christian people may always and everywhere win the victory over the enemies of his holy name, and the name of the Lord Jesus Christ be glorified throughout the world.

The split between East and West was abetted by the breakneck speed with which Islam expanded. Across Africa into Spain and even France, as well as up through Constantinople and toward Vienna, it caught the West in a pincer movement. This effectively cut off East-West communications. Missionary work and the outward thrust of the church was stifled. The Christian Middle Ages owes much, perhaps, to the fact that Islam acted as an incentive to turn inward.

As this period ends, the Photian Schism of the ninth century was glued into place with the excommunication of the Patriarch, Michael Cerularius in 1054. The split between East and West was irrevocably made and the Western church developed on its own, apart from some few uniate churches that maintained affiliation with Rome. Theology during this time tended to be more and more Augustinian, and to be little influenced by Eastern theology. Until the discovery of the new world, the vision of the Western church remained largely turned in on itself.

The Ministerial Expansion of the Monastery

In this unsettled age, in 529, Benedict founded a monastery at Monte Cassino. This was not the first monastic effort in the church, Basil and Augustine laying claim to this honor in the previous century. And the Celtic monks, already well established in Ireland and England, had already begun the chain of monasteries that would dot Europe. But the birth of new Visigoth and Frankish churches became the reality they did because of the efforts of Western monasticism. In a way the period can be divided between two Gregorys, both monk popes. Gregory I (the Great) was pope from 590 to 604, and Gregory VII (Hildebrand) reigned from 1073 to 1085. Both helped to stamp the church with the vision of the monastery.

Probably the most obvious case of monasticism "absorbing" Christianity occurred in Ireland. So strong were the monastic foundations there that they overshadowed the established hierarchy. In some instances bishops became chaplains for large monastic foundations, under the jurisdiction of the abbot or abbess. On the continent, however, the form that proved most durable was that started by Benedict.

During the great patristic period, regional synods and councils—exercising a practical collegiality—had become the prominent guiding principle of church life. The function of these synods declined to some extent during the Merovingian period, though they were energetically rejuvenated by Charlemagne, and played a decisive role in the church of the ninth century. They added much to the traditions of past councils that formed the foundation of canon law in the later Middle Ages. Even more pervasive, however, though not as easy to document, was the influence of the monastery.

To churches whose diocesan structure was weak, and whose local clergy but feebly prepared, the great monasteries and monastic families must have appeared as the true image of what the church should be. They set the ideal that all should strive for. The ministry of the local church was, of course, in the hands of the bishops and priests. The bishops were in one of two positions, however: Either they struggled against being controlled by the local princes, or they were themselves part of the feudal principate. Priests, often uneducated, had to find a place in a civil as well as ecclesiastical feudalism.

Many of the more notable bishops had been monks. Monastic renewal for the local church came from a sincere desire to renew the offices of bishop and priest. The monk became tutor to the priest. If fifth-century bishops like Martin of Tours, Paulinus of Nola, and Augustine had favored a monastic life for their priests, by 814 councils were urging the spirit and practices of the monks upon all diocesan clergy. This movement reached a further stage in the transformation of the clergy into canons regular. At the Roman Council of 1074, Gregory VII tried to enforce vows of poverty for the clergy, in imitation of the life of the Twelve, and a sort of monastic common life.

By the eighth century there were 17,000 abbeys and priories in Europe. On a practical level they spearheaded both economic and technological development. Over the years the monasteries produced 24 popes, over 200 cardinals, 1600 bishops, 43 emperors, 44 kings, 1560 saints, and 5000 blesseds. This gives some idea of the pervasive influence of monasticism on the church.

Local bishops could not compete with the resources of the monastery in these centuries of instability. In the East and in Ireland, monastic community was the normal setting for ministry. The great cathedral schools were monastic in both format and theology. Influenced by Origen and Pseudo-Dionysius,[1] many proposed an ecclesiology whereby monks were the first class in the church. By the year 1000, the monasteries set the tone for the church. Their remoteness made them secure islands for prayer, contemplation, and an austere spiritual life in an unsettled age.

Despite the vow of stability made by the monks, after Benedict's death Pope Gregory the Great tapped the monasteries as sources of missionaries among the Germanic peoples. This earned Benedict the title "Father of the West." The achievements of the monks can be summarized by the cross, the book, and the plow. Even anticlerical Gibbons stated, "A single Benedictine monastery may have done more for the cause of knowledge than Oxford and Cambridge combined." Naturally, the style of church they built tended to be monastic.

The monasteries did yeoman service in creating all four of the bases on which medieval civilization was to rest: 1) economic revival; 2) fusion of the Latin and Teutonic people; 3) the afterlife of Roman law in the monastic Rule, the canon law of the church, and the Holy Roman Empire; 4) the feudal system, which set up new hierarchies of power and enabled the monasteries to extend their influence and their benefits greatly.

In the monasteries, however, both a feudalization of the ministry and a sacerdotalization of monasticism itself occurred. In many ways ministry was reduced to jobs within the monasteries themselves and to liturgical priesthood. The great liturgies as well as the private Mass were both considered ministry par excellence. With the abbey church the geographic and spiritual center of monastic life, the liturgy and *opus Dei* (divine office) became the main ministries of grace. Some former ministries never survived monasticism, while others emerged: abbot, abbess, prior, hebdomadary, porter, for example.

With no competitors, monastic theology and spirituality influenced all areas in the church. Conversion, or perfection in the life of grace, usually meant entering a monastery. Flight from the world, not involvement in its struggles, was the accepted ideal. As this period ended, Bernard of Clairvaux was able to drag practically his entire family into the monastery. Entering a monastery had replaced martyrdom as the accepted means of expressing Christian idealism. Little wonder that those in full-time church ministry were colored with monastic ideals. Some results of this were:

1. The bishop came to resemble an abbot, rather than a coordinator of ministries. Ideally, he was to be a father of his people and the spiritual director of his priests. In the East, monastic leaders were chosen because their skill in the life of the Spirit was recognized. Even today, the bishops in the East are chosen from the monks. In the West, this ideal was often paid only lip service. The bishop became the centralizing figure in the church at this time, strengthening the process of hierarchization.

2. Perhaps more important, Christian life was seen not as a life of activity or mission in the public forum, but as an inner spiritual life where all were urged to practice monastic detachment and contemplation. The services of the local community apart from Mass and sacraments were the monastic offices. The divine office (breviary) was even imposed on the secular clergy under pain of mortal sin, and the clerics began to imitate monastic dress as well. (In the fifth century, Pope Celestine had written to clerics, telling them that they should be known by their behavior, not by their clothes!) Celibacy received the added push it needed, and was the final monasticization of the life of the diocesan priest.

The influence of the monastery lasts to this day in ways as diverse as the idea many have of what it means to be holy: much popular piety, the divine office, celibacy, clerical clothing, and liturgical forms. Many rubrics and institutions that seem to us eternally ecclesial and deeply Christian are monastic. In this period, the monastery was the source and standard of ministry. Drawing people into the inner life of the soul and to the eschatological liturgy, assuming or absorbing the diversity of ministry, it bequeathed its own unique spirit and style of life to the entire church. Begun as an isolated outpost in an expanding church, the monastery became the church itself.

Church and State

During this feudal period, church structure took on new forms in the West. This resulted largely from the Frankish structuring of the church and the development of what is called the proprietary church structure. One consequence of this was to make the priests almost independent of the bishop (they were more directly dependent on the proprietor or landlord). This separation of bishop and presbyter is the key to both the early medieval development and the later scholastic definition of priesthood.[2]

In 476, the last Roman emperor was sent packing off to Constantinople, capital of the Eastern empire. Europe was left without any central government. The bishops were alone to step into the breach. They were already administrators of land and wealth. Now they became a self-perpetuating government as lay election began to disappear. But they had no armies. So they had to come to terms with the invaders.

The Germanic tribes were converted with amazing rapidity, however. This may have had little to do with an individual choice for the faith. The barbarians were illiterate, and usually followed the religion of their rulers. The missionaries were smart enough to concentrate on the leaders of the clans and tribes. And as Christianity started to emerge once again, the bishops began to see themselves as rulers of a Christian Europe. Unfortunately, the lord of the region not only prescribed the religion of the people, he also had the exclusive right to build churches and monasteries on his land along with the right of patronage, the ability to name pastors and abbots—an eventual source of trouble for the independence of the church.

This led to an almost complete union of church and state. The church (and in these days "the church" meant the clergy, especially bishops) found itself involved in maintaining the basic needs of any society: order, unity, provision for the poor, law, and justice. They were aided and abetted in this by the rulers. A highly complicated ecclesiastical world came into existence. It worked. No matter what else can be said, church activity at this time did translate to a certain view of ministry and priesthood in which service to people was a dominant element.

Thanks to donations of land by Pippin and his son Charlemagne, the bishop of Rome was also king of central Italy. Bishops elsewhere had similar holdings. The feudal system was basically a pyramid, with peasants on the bottom being protected by and paying taxes to the local landlord, who in turn owed allegiance to their own lords, and so on up.

There were thus two lines of authority in medieval Europe: Political authority traced itself down from the sovereign through his vassal lords to the peasants; spiritual authority traced itself down from the bishops (later in the period with the pope above the bishops), through the clergy, to the same peasants. But these lines often intersected, since the bishops, as members of the upper class, were often related to the rulers; indeed, they were usually even named by them.

What was important (theoretically, at least) was that all cooperate so that society be regulated by the will of God. The Carolingian kings were more than willing to enforce this concept of the perfect society, thus often giving political muscle to ecclesial decisions. Liturgical reforms and Roman uniformity were hastened because of the efforts of the emperors. It was sometimes hard to see the distinction between the civil and the ecclesial realms.

In this somewhat ill-defined period, however, East and West were developing separately and under different pressures, before going their own ways. The church was perhaps a bastion of stability at this time. Though ministerial patterns were still quite fluid compared to today, sacramental roles were rather well established. There were also attempts to regulate dress, employment, recreation, celibacy, and other aspects of life.

Sociologically, there was a radical change in self-image in the West, inasmuch as it was becoming common to think in terms of Europe as a Christian society. During this time the church maintained a rather clear notion of itself as the Body of Christ, with Christ alone as its true king and head. At the same time there was an increasing emphasis on the pope and bishops as being mediators or vicars for Christ. Without any denial that Christ is the head of the church, popes began to claim that they were heads of the body, something we would never find in Leo I.

Though they were still ordained as priests, bishops were now primarily rulers. When they met, it was usually to discuss disciplinary matters, not doctrine. Nevertheless, this period still held to the more pastoral notion that three elements entered into the selection of a bishop: the voice of the members of the local church, ordination by the surrounding episcopacy, and approbation by the "higher" authorities. After all, St. Leo the Great had said: "He who must preside over all must be chosen by all." In this period, however, whatever claim the laity had in the selection process was claimed and exercised by the secular rulers.

The tradition going back to Cyprian stressed a fundamental collegiality and co-responsibility within the episcopacy. It left room, however, for a Roman primacy *within* the episcopacy. With Leo I (440-461) we have the beginning of a more vertical image of the source of authority, as given from Christ to Peter and through him to the other apostles. So does the pope receive supreme authority, which he then mediates to the episcopacy. This view was reinforced by Gelasius and Gregory I, and represents the oft-expressed policies of the ninth-century popes.

Developments like these, along with the rise of the monarchical episcopate, were bound to influence the manner in which people understood authority in the church. Far-reaching changes took place in terms of church ministries. One of the shifts in understanding was the rise of a theology of ordination that emphasized the personal powers and "unalterable character" that was attached to ordained ministers as individuals. Priesthood was losing its rootedness in the life of the community.

Bound up with this was the unfortunate development in the West of the idea of *jurisdiction*, whereby a split was made between the power of orders and the ability to use that power (jurisdiction).[3] This was somewhat dubiously grounded in earlier tradition, often deriving its justification from the "tradition" of forged decretals. This was a feature of Latin canon law; the East never developed the idea of jurisdiction.

The distinction between orders and jurisdiction reveals an understanding of church quite different from seeing the church as a "sacrament" of Christ; it requires an external authority besides that attached to its sacramental existence. Because ordination in itself no longer sufficed for one to exercise ministry, jurisdiction soon began to overshadow ministry or ordination. In itself, jurisdiction was seen as guaranteeing the validity of priestly actions. The emphasis shifted to the *ex opere operato* effects of sacraments given by duly designated ministers.

This shift also meant that the mere appointment to a position was presumed to give a person the qualities needed for the job. When a person was canonically installed in a church office, he was assumed to receive the accompanying charisms. Juridical appointment rendered discernment secondary, if not unnecessary. We have here the beginning of a great reversal: symbols and legal positions dispensing grace, rather than grace begetting life through visible charisms subsequently realized in office and service.

If seen essentially as jurisdictional realities, pastorates eventually become simply benefices yielding an income to those named to them. However, because of the size of dioceses or parishes, and the other responsibilities (or preferences) of the bishops and higher clergy, the one who was assigned to them often hired some vicar to do the actual work of the parish. The bishop's role in all this was mainly to exercise jurisdiction and supervise the activity of the lower clergy.

The priests were the ones in the most immediate contact with the people. Priests fell into two classes. Those in the cities tended to be better educated, and formed a distinct social group. Those in the country were quite like the peasants they served—except when celebrating the liturgy, when they would don vestments and use Latin that they had memorized. Their main duties were liturgical, not pastoral, and they did little preaching.

Church Hierarchy and Structures
We have mentioned the monasticization of the church at this time, but there were other more prosaic problems with which it had to deal: the interference of the rulers in the life of the church and the struggle for power or control. As mentioned in the previous section, the feudal or proprietary church structure tended to put the local church more under

the control of the local lord than of the bishop. This would culminate in the investiture struggle that came to a head at the end of this period and was faced squarely in the Gregorian reforms.

It has been mentioned that the bishop by this time had become a public dignitary, a member, in fact, of the medieval aristocracy. As dioceses grew, the bishops became distant administrators, no longer able to have personal contact with each of the faithful. This same growth made it difficult for believers to worship as one congregation. The link with his people was further weakened because the bishop was often named for political reasons. Indeed, some bishops never even set foot in their dioceses; they simply collected the revenues.

In actuality, there was considerable variety in church life and practice. On the one hand were the large dioceses. These were more characteristic of the urban centers. Here there was strong episcopal leadership, and the general pattern that had been set since the fourth century. On the other hand, there were the rural areas, which tended to come more under the influence of the local lord. These had their own juridical structures, their own form of appointment to presbyteral leadership. They enjoyed a sort of localized autonomy, with little or no tie to the episcopal, urban church.

This feudal practice eventually caused many monasteries to place themselves under the patronage of the local lord. (The phenomenon of religious orders having their links directly to the pope exemplifies the same principle, and a consequent weakening both of the authority of the bishop and the diocesan structure.)

Another wedge driven between the bishop and his people resulted from the growing custom of changing a bishop from diocese to diocese. Nicea had declared that for a deacon, priest, or bishop to pass from city to city was against received tradition and that such moves were invalid. This was reaffirmed by many other councils. A bishop was considered as married to his diocese, according to St. Athanasius, and he ought not to seek another "lest he prove an adulterer." Such moves were accepted only when approved by the synod. For this reason, it was the end of the ninth century before one already a bishop was named pope. Before this, some priest (or, as often as not, the archdeacon) would be chosen.

This was a time when the powers of the popes were considerably expanded. Even in the time of Gregory I they were engaged in doctrinal, liturgical, and disciplinary affairs far beyond the diocese of Rome. In their own words, they bore the *cura omnium ecclesiarum*. But prior to Nicea there was no evidence whatever that the bishops of Rome claimed to be the source of authority for their brother bishops—nor that bishops thought of their authority as coming from the pope.[4]

That was to change in the Middle Ages. Popes not only consolidated their preeminence over the political powers, they also strengthened their control over the church. At the end of the fifth century, Gelasius already claimed ultimate spiritual power. It was Gregory the Great (594-604), however, who gave a "theological" basis for the contours established by Leo I. He wrote:

> To all who know the Gospel, it is obvious that by the voice of the Lord the care of the entire church was committed to the holy apostle and prince of all the apostles, Peter.... Certainly, in honor of Peter, the prince of the apostles, the title "universal" was offered to the Roman pontiff by the venerable Council of Chalcedon (Ep 5, 37).

In the seventh and eighth centuries, the most influential theorizing on the episcopal role came from Gregory's *Cura pastoralis*. Here there was still a strong emphasis on preaching and teaching. At the same time the teaching role is combined with the image of the physician entrusted with the *cura animarum*. Those in power are to admonish the people, leading them to repentance and conversion, reminding them of the "four last things," and inspiring them with (largely legendary) stories of the saints. In contrast to the effort to create theological accuracy in the people's understanding (characteristic of the patristic age) one finds a fostering of credulity in order to obtain better moral behavior. Even Scripture was bent to this end, and tended to become a collection of moral aphorisms or examples of virtue.

Officially at this time, the bishop had control of the sacrament of penance, which was still public and limited to once in a lifetime. This began to break down at the beginning of this period (against the protests of several church councils) with the introduction of the Celtic practice of frequent confession. The point here is that the clergy alone were seen as having the power to open the gates of heaven for people.

Gregory had a lasting influence on the liturgy. The sacramentaries that were written under him eventually became the norm for all of Europe. Likewise, the seventh-century idea of priest had an enduring influence on Latin Christianity. This view is one where the priest is seen as a mediator between the people and God. In the liturgy he is the sole agent of the sacred action, which he performs on behalf of the assembled people. Note that he acts *on behalf of* the people, not as the liturgist of a sacrificing community. He was more the sacred actor performing the mystery rite than he was the prophetic herald of a Christian community. By the eighth century, as these ideas progressed, the Eucharistic Prayer was said silently, and the people were reduced to silence and to roles of passive witness.

Gregory was also the first pope to send Christians officially on missionary work. Before this, mission outside the empire had been regarded as a natural act that would be done by anyone: merchants, traders, prisoners, or monks and members of the clergy, for example. Evangelization was a responsibility of all Christians, to be carried out by all when the conditions were propitious. Now, the pope was officially directing and encouraging the missionary effort of the church.

Rome also came into the local dioceses by way of the pallium. This was offered to archbishops (the Western equivalent of metropolitans) by the pope. Originally a liturgical gesture, it soon acquired juridical overtones. Jungmann states that a new bishop "was neither to officiate at the consecration of suffragans nor to occupy the throne" until he had received the pallium. In this way archbishops were made more and more the agents of the pope.

The rise of the papal states also helped this process. In 774, with the backing of Charles the Great, the papal states were allowed to secede from the empire, and the pope became a sovereign ruler. No longer did the emperor's name appear on documents and coins; from now on it was the papal name and image. Popes became temporal rulers in their own right over the "patrimony of St. Peter." They were perhaps the most influential rulers in all of medieval Europe. Adding political clout to their spiritual power gave the popes influence and control in areas of the church never before enjoyed.

The strengthening of papal power by the end of this period led to bishops being more and more dependent on the pope. Previously, the emphasis had been on the collegiality of local bishops, as could be seen in the days of Cyril of Alexandria, Cyprian, Augustine, and Basil. This restructuring would lead in the scholastic period to the idea that the bishopric was only a position of jurisdiction and dignity.

Such papal claims were not universally welcomed. The Gallican bishops in the ninth century handled the affairs of the church quite by themselves. In 833, for example, when Pope Gregory IV appeared in Gaul just prior to the deposition of Louis the Pious, the bishops informed him that he had no right to interfere in their dioceses, and that "if he came to excommunicate, he should return excommunicated himself."

The fact remains, however, that the pope's power did increase during this period. In many cases, his intervention was requested, by both bishops and princes, against the pretensions of other rulers. Ultimately, at least theoretical supremacy of the spiritual over the political was established, and the church gained quasi-independence from the rulers. Episcopal collegiality was a casualty of the power politics of the age.

In the Middle Ages, the laity were further relegated to the background. In canon law they were lumped together with the unlettered, the *idiota*, the poor and fleshly man of the world. The powerful laity—princes and kings—that we hear about at this time were really not regarded as laity at all, especially in view of the consecration they received. Hincmar of Rheims even drew up a ritual of coronation in 877. The king was then anointed like a priest, and considered a *christus domini*, separated from the laity. Thus was theological support given to a situation that would eventually cripple the church.

Canon lawyers at this time divided the church community into two states (which had even ethical consequences): *duo ordines, clericorum et laicorum; duae vitae, spiritalis et carnalis*. The neo-Platonic spirit of the Pseudo-Dionysius is evident here, where the higher stage possesses to an eminent degree what the lower possesses only in a limited way. The competence of ministry—of all forms of service—is to be found in absolute fullness only at the top stage, the episcopate. Thus, all power was seen as coming "from above." This fueled the hierarchical development of the church, and identification of "church" with clergy. The people eventually became simply the object of pastoral concern, with no real role in the church.

Summarizing some of the developments that occurred during this period, we can note the following:

1. The tradition developed in both East and West at this time saw the church as definitely hierarchical, with bishop, priest, deacon, and various minor orders, and so on down. Since the heritage of the great Fathers was considered to be of apostolic origin, hierarchical orders were also considered "apostolic." The kind of ministry that had taken root was thought to have existed from the beginning.

2. The ministry of the hierarchy was beginning to be seen as largely sacramental, and was greatly influenced by the works of Gregory Nazianzen, John Chrysostom, and Dionysius the Areopagite.

3. As the pope gained more and more importance and power, the role of the bishops was equally diminished, and episcopal collegiality declined in the West. It continued to be the model in the East.

The Eucharist in the Late Middle Ages

In the sixth and seventh centuries the narrowing down of ministry to the celebration of the Eucharist was aided by a theological interpretation that was to have far-reaching consequences. The clearest indication of this is a famous text from the *Leonianum*, a collection of liturgical prayers that goes back to the time of Leo the Great, if not to Leo himself. The text runs: "As often as the remembrance of the sacrifice which is well pleasing to you is celebrated, the work of our redemption is made present (*exeritur*)." The word *exeritur*, which is rare, was not understood by later copyists. In the *Vetus Gelasianum* (c. 750) the word was changed to *exercitum* and still later to *exercetur*, which means "the work of our redemption is carried on (or *completed*)."[5]

What in the original text was a happy statement about the relationship between the Eucharist and the cross (i.e., the Eucharist makes the sacrifice of the cross present) began to be regarded in the Middle Ages instead as the Mass being a *renewal* of the sacrifice of the cross, which is certainly a substantial distortion of Leo's quote. This would ultimately lead to the conviction that the Eucharist was a bloodless repetition of the sacrifice of the cross—leading to one of the great protests of the Reformation.[6]

In the early centuries, the Eucharist was generally celebrated weekly, with the exception of certain feasts, when it was also celebrated. Two changes occurred in the medieval period. One was the rise of daily celebrations and, especially from the eighth century on, the rise of the private Mass. What brought this about, and what were the consequences for the theology and practice of the church?

As might be expected, several factors were at work in both cases. As regards the frequency of eucharistic celebrations, we might note the influence of the veneration of relics. In some cathedrals of the late fourth century (for example, Milan, or North Africa—in the West rather than the East), we already have some evidence of daily celebrations.[7] In later centuries we often see fourteen side altars (two rows of seven). These were so that Masses could be said over the relics of the saints; church rules from the fourth and fifth centuries on forbidding Masses "in private oratories" should be interpreted to mean in a place with no reliquaries. This antedates the custom of Masses for the dead, or votive masses.

Though the Eastern church never fully accepted daily Masses as did the Western church, frequency in both areas was bound up with the growth of the liturgical cycle. Besides the regular Sunday celebrations, feasts and liturgical seasons dictated the frequency, not simply someone's "devotion."

A second major factor favoring a multiplicity of celebrations was a desire to offer Masses for the dead, something that fit in with the medieval system of penitential tariffs. This led to many monks being ordained simply so that they could celebrate the Mass.[8] The custom of offering stipends for this purpose would lead to the abuse of priests celebrating a dozen or more times daily, often with no congregation at all present.

As a result, spirituality became markedly individualistic. Private Masses and votive Masses "for particular intentions" became established by the ninth century. And the increasing ordination of monks—whose only pastoral responsibility was "saying Mass"—further eroded the concept that ordination was for the sake of a particular community. The Eucharist was again taken away from the laity and made the responsibility of the priests.

As a result, by the tenth century, the conception of the priestly role became increasingly ritualistic. In other words, the liturgy was seen more and more as the work of privileged specialists. It also led to priests celebrating alone, and hence to the notion that only he was essential to the celebration. This de facto situation—the rise of the private Mass—would be given theological justification in the scholastic period.[9]

The gap between priest and people became almost deliberately emphasized at this time, for the priest began to turn his back to the people, and they were to receive communion on their tongues rather than in their hands. By the ninth century, too, the host had replaced ordinary bread, thus removing the eucharistic bread from the realm of the profane. Shortly after this the cup was no longer given the laity. Mass, as the synopsis of salvation, became the exclusive preserve of the clergy. To compound the insult, in many churches a *schola cantorum* of specialists took over the singing as well.

This, incidentally, had an effect not only on the relationship of priest and people, but on that of priest and bishop. If the priest was ordained to celebrate the Mass (and as this began to be seen as the whole purpose of his existence), then the sacramental functions became the primary definition of priesthood. The sacrament of orders was defined by priesthood, since this is where one received the power to consecrate the Eucharist. Being a bishop was seen as more of a jurisdictional reality. Thus, if one were named bishop in this period he first had to be ordained priest.

With the downgrading of the laity, we began to see a shift in our terminology. In the early and patristic periods, the Body of Christ was understood to mean the church.[10] Now, with increased emphasis on the consecration, it was taken to mean the eucharistic species; so to say, as the Fathers did, that the priest was responsible for the Body of Christ was presumed to mean that his primary responsibility was the Eucharist.

The first eucharistic controversies of the church took place at this time, with Ratramnus further shifting the eucharistic focus to the exact manner of Christ's presence in the consecrated species. By the end of our period, Berengarius took too symbolic a position and was condemned and forced (in 1059) to accept that "The Body and Blood of Christ, not only in sacrament but physically and in reality, are grasped and broken by the hands of the priest, and chewed by the teeth of the faithful."[11] Officially as well as in popular piety it was felt that when the priest touched the host, he touched the very body of Christ. Priestly hands were, therefore, most sacred, and priestly life closer to the angels than that of ordinary men and women.

In the Eucharist the emphasis was less on the sacrifice of praise and thanks to God given by God's people, and more on the renewal of the sacrifice of the cross, an offering made through the exclusive mediation of the priest. When the Eucharistic Prayer was prayed silently, the central feature was that mysterious moment when the bread and wine were changed into the Body and Blood of Christ. The people no longer participated; they simply looked on.

Having split the sacrament off from jurisdiction and solid ecclesiology, eucharistic symbolism tended to turn into allegory instead. In the *De ecclesiasticis officiis* of Amalarius of Metz the liturgy of the Mass is explained down to its least detail as an allegory of the life of Christ. Although condemned by the Council of Quierzy in 838, it accurately reflects the ritualistic and almost magical spirituality of the Carolingian believer. People stopped receiving communion. But in the eleventh century the consecrated host was often buried in fields to insure a good harvest.

In this climate, religious life and practice were at an all time low at the end of the ninth and in the early tenth century. It must also be admitted that priestly life and virtue were equally low. Even the monasteries had become lax. Then the inevitable reaction set in. Cluny was founded in 909, soon followed by other abbeys, and monastic life began to flourish again. After 1000, a whole religious renewal had begun, to be capped with the reforms of Gregory VII at the end of the century.

It has been said that the Old Testament was the breeding ground of feudal spirituality (the New Testament only came to occupy a central position in the twelfth century). The monks felt themselves to be the firstfruits of the people of God. Those who lived in the world were regarded as second-class citizens. While this negative attitude toward the world is perhaps understandable given the rough and barbarian society of those days, there was a rebound effect in how one regarded the good gifts of creation.

Society was often seen as divided into three categories of people: those who prayed (*oratores*), those who waged war (*bellatores*), and those who worked (*laboratores*). While this may have been intended to emphasize the importance of prayer for a well-ordered feudal society, the priests were no longer regarded as men of prayer; this function was taken over by the monks—and those who adopted their form of life.

We end with a quote from Bernard Cooke, who notes that as laity became more and more isolated from activity in the Eucharist, the priest became mainly a dispenser of sacraments whose action was not meant to be particularly meaningful as long as it was causally effective.

> One thing may be of major importance in this regard: it is the unquestioned shift from the celebrant as the sign of Christ's presence to the consecrated elements as that sign, which indicates the other basic shift in Eucharistic understanding, from mystery action to real presence. By the twelfth century we begin to see quite clearly the view that the Eucharistic celebrant makes Christ present not by being there himself as a sacrament but by transforming the bread and wine.[12]

Summary

1. The period from the sixth century to the eleventh was one where the union of church and state became both the theoretical and practical ideal. The emperor not only thought it his duty to defend the church, he accepted canon law as the law of the state. But the relationship was too cozy. Most of the bishops came from the same social class and families as the nobility, and they played the same game by somewhat the same rules. It was a form of power politics, and it marked a change in the structures of the church.

2. With the advent of monasticism, priestly life and ministry took certain specifically different forms. The ideals and lifestyle of the monastery wielded enormous influence on the understanding and practice of all clerical life, eventually causing a change in its self-concept and practice. The monastery was the ideal of all Christian life. In fact, most of the outstanding churchmen of the day came from the monasteries.

The East even had the example of Gregory Nazianzen, who abandoned his bishopric to enter a monastery.

3. There was a subtle but important pastoral change in how one understood celebration of Eucharist during this period. Priests continued to act for the church, no less than in previous times. In earlier periods, however, "church" meant the priest was acting for the benefit of the present worshiping community. In effecting the Eucharist he was providing his community with a sign of the church whereby they could see themselves as part of the larger church and one with the mystery of Christ on which their life depended. Celebration helped them to become more deeply identified with and embodied in the church. In this period, however, the emphasis shifts to an abstract community. The priest now has the power to obtain the benefits of the sacrifice of Christ for those present (if there were any present), and for all living and dead for whom the Mass was offered.

4. At the beginning of this period, the local church was, to a surprising degree, autonomous, self-sufficient, and insular. It might have its own canon of Scripture, creed, and Eucharistic Prayers. Though there was a vivid awareness of the universal church, unity was expressed in faith rather than in organization or discipline. The local congregation had to look beyond itself only for the ordination of a new bishop. In such a house-church setting, the bishop was, in fact, a father, the patriarch of an extended family. Chosen by the people, he assumed a life-long familiar relationship with them. With the expansion of the church by the end of the first millennium, the intimate arrangement of the past had gone. Policy was now set in distant episcopal synods. Councils overrode local preferences. Whereas the bishop formerly represented the views of his church to the synod, he now begins to represent the synod to his people. The bishop had gone from being a leader to being an administrator.

5. Almost everywhere in the West by the tenth century, the diaconate had lost most of its meaning as an order, and was left only a limited liturgical role. The archdeacon survived, however, the forerunner of the chancellors or vicars general of today in a role that often rivaled the bishop for power.

6. In the West, the power of orders was divided in two, with the development of the idea of jurisdiction. This was church authorization to use the power of orders in certain places, or at certain times, and was an independent grant from that of ordination. Though it usually depended on ordination, one could have orders without jurisdiction, and even jurisdiction without orders. This effectively served to separate the

"power" of ordination from its rootedness in community, and make it an independent and autonomous grant from higher authority.

7. One of the ultimately more harmful effects of the monasticization of Christian life was the feeling that perfection was to be found not in the world but in a life of detachment, and in the spiritual exercises proper to the monastery. This "otherworldly" spirit left the world, literally, to go to the devil, while those seeking holiness turned to more spiritual pursuits. This led to a dichotomy between the world of the profane and the sacred, to the detriment of both.

8. With the union of church and state, the church soon became rich in land. Bishops thus became temporal as well as spiritual rulers. The foundations of the papal states were laid in this period. It would be only a short while before the pope would have his armies like any other ruler. To the extent that the church became politicized, it lost its spiritual leadership and had to rely more on the coercion of its law. Canonists soon justified the monarchical and authoritarian structure of the church rooted in the character of orders. The institution itself was supposed to mediate grace irrespective of the officeholders. Discipline replaced doctrine in importance.

9. In this period the understanding of Roman primacy changed to the more vertical understanding of all power flowing from the pope to the bishops to the priests to the people—a good feudal way of thinking. What it replaced, however, was the notion of the church as fundamentally collegial and co-responsible. Roman primacy was no longer situated within the episcopacy. Thus, we have the beginnings of the idea that bishops are simply the errand boys of the pope in various areas of the world.

10. The priests in this period fell into two groups. The first tended to be found in the cities, and were middle and upper class; they tended to be more educated, and had at least a moderate grasp of theology. In the countryside, however, priests were often ordained simply so someone could celebrate Mass. They might be practically illiterate and often had almost no theological training. They were only a cut or two above the peasants they served with sacramental ministry. They were there to provide sacramental service when called upon. As one empowered to act on behalf of the people, they had quasi-magical powers; as the channel of (sacramental) grace, they could mean the difference between heaven and hell.

11. Private Masses increased during this period, some priests being ordained only for this. This was partly due to seeing the Mass as a renewal of the sacrifice of the cross, with the implication that we were

pleasing God and benefiting ourselves each time with the infinite merits of the Son's sacrifice. Other factors were the cult of the saints and the desire to celebrate Mass on their relics. The ultimate result was to make the people unnecessary to the understanding of and celebration of Eucharist. There soon followed the priest reciting the canon in a low voice, celebrating with his back to the people, etc. Even in a cathedral, it was a private Mass!

12. With the East-West split, we lost for good any possibility of integrating the Eastern understanding of Eucharist and priesthood into Western theology. When the Fathers were rediscovered in the twelfth century, the West looked mainly to the Western Fathers for inspiration. In this period, however, the main difference between East and West was between a more spiritual versus a more institutional understanding of church. This continues to characterize the churches down to the present. Note the different theology and spirituality when there is little political power.

Discussion Questions

1. Was the monasticization of the church a blessing? How? In what ways might it have been a disadvantage? What ways can you think of now that the church is still affected?

2. Until 1965 it was official church teaching that union of church and state is the ideal. What are the pros and cons of this?

3. To what extent does the private Mass give a distorted picture of both ministry and Eucharist in the church?

Suggested Readings

Cooke, B. "Ministry in Medieval Culture," _Ministry to Word and Sacrament_, Chap. 4, pp. 113-122. Also Chap. 17, "Medieval Structures of Church Service," pp. 362-370.

Cowdrey, H. "Dissemination of St. Augustine's Doctrine of Holy Orders During the Later Patristic Age," _Journal of Theological Studies_, 20 (1969), 448-481.

Osborne, K., "Ministry in the Early Medieval Church, 600 to 1000 A.D.," _Priesthood_, Chap. 6, pp. 161-194.

Power, D., "Early Ordination Rites of Rome and Gaul," and "Changes in the Ordinal in the Middle Ages," *Ministers of Christ and His Church*, pp. 52-86, 87-105.

Schillebeeckx, E., "Organization and Spirituality of Ministry in the Course of Church History," *The Church with a Human Face*, Part 3, pp. 156-194.

Tavard, G., "Episcopacy and Apostolic Succession According to Hincmar of Rheims," *Theological Studies*, 34, 4 (December 1973), 594-623.

6

Ministry as Hierarchy

The dates above situate us roughly between the Gregorian reforms and one of papacy's lower moments—the time when it was split between competing popes. The entire period, however, is overshadowed by the final schism that split Eastern and Western Christianity. Though its roots go back as far as Chalcedon, July of the year 1054 saw what Martin Marty calls "the magnificent clash of two opinionated men": Pope Leo IX and the Patriarch Michael Cerularius mutually excommunicating each other, excommunications not lifted until 1965.

This final break with the East is one of the saddest periods of church history. Many sharply contested positions in theology and sacramental practice had led up to this over centuries. Caesaropapism, iconoclasm, Photianism, the filioque controversy were all hot issues simply waiting for a spark to set them off. The centuries of wrangling over rank and order of precedence were even more influential than theological differences. Most decisive of all were the political struggles of both sides, especially the head-on clashes during the mission to the Slavs and the crusades. After this, clerical narrow-mindedness simply cemented the break with ugly recriminations. (Though this book concerns itself mainly with Western theology and practice, it is good to at least be reminded that the history of the church is far larger and richer.)

This age was also punctuated by conflicts between the papacy and empire. If, in 1077, Pope Gregory VII could force Emperor Henry IV to crawl to Canossa to have the ban of excommunication lifted, and Boniface VIII (1294-1303) could claim superiority of the spiritual over the temporal sword, the power of the popes was nonetheless unsettled. The political machinations, the schism of 1159-1177, the Avignon popes, and the great Western Schism show a domineering yet impotent papacy. Popes like Boniface were motivated more by a need to advance their own power by means of the papacy than a desire to serve the church. This so weakened the church's credibility and authority that there were many calls for a council to make the church believable again.

The Avignon papacy removed the popes to French soil for 75 years, and when Gregory XI, the last of the Avignon popes, died in 1378 (he had, in fact, moved back to Rome), the church was faced with a successor whom the cardinals did not like and for whom they soon elected a substitute. Before this mess was over, it had dragged on for another 40 years (to 1417) and presented the church with a choice of three popes at the same time.

The competing hierarchical claims were finally settled (1414) by the Council of Constance. This explains the popularity of conciliarism, one of the suggestions (pushed especially by the University of Paris) made to avoid a similar situation in the future. There was a strongly felt need to be able to react as a church against gross incompetence, insanity, or anything else that might render the pope incapable of governing the church. Conciliarism died partly because of its own venality and ineptness. This theological area, however, has never really been fully explored or settled.

Compounding the woes of this period, the bubonic plague swept across Europe in the fourteenth century, wiping out practically one-third of the people. Many of the better priests and monks were affected, because they were out ministering to the sick. Thus, they were lost to the church at a time when they were most needed. For many reasons, this was a sad and low period in church history.

Despite this, the thirteenth and fourteenth centuries have often been called a period of renaissance. Church historian Walsh has even called the thirteenth "the greatest of centuries." In the history of Western culture it was a time of creativity whose influence is still felt in our own times. In no area was this more true than in religion. If the renaissance was anything, it was the expression of a widely accepted and vibrant faith at the grass-roots level, despite the poor example of many church leaders.

The Gregorian Reforms

If the previous period was stamped by the reforming spirit of Gregory the Great, this period is equally marked by the zeal of a monk: Hildebrand, Pope Gregory VII (1073-1085). Gregory came to office in one of those times that cry out for greatness, and he provided it. We have mentioned above his struggle with Henry IV. No other pope of the century would have been able to take on a ruler as powerful as Henry.

People could be excused for thinking that Rome was incapable of reform. But the impetus from Cluny began to touch even Rome, and Hildebrand pushed through a radical reform in the church, putting his stamp on the emergent medieval society as well.[1] Gregory's efforts were directed principally to freeing the church from lay investiture. However, as Cooke reminds us, the struggle to keep the secular power out of the sanctuary pushed Gregory to exalt the power and authority of the papacy.[2]

We may criticize Gregory today for claiming (and exercising) immediate jurisdiction over all Christians. But unless he had intervened in many a diocese, the needed reforms of the church would never have been possible. And, unlike a Boniface VIII, he seemed moved only with what he thought best for the church, not his own prestige or power. Theoretically, he was in line with Leo I, Gelasius, and Gregory I. But Hildebrand was able to implement their theory concretely.[3]

Hildebrand had enormous admiration for his predecessor, Gregory I (who styled himself *servus servorum Dei*); he also directed much of his effort to the moral and spiritual well-being of the clergy. He felt—rightly—that the spiritual level of the entire church depended on it. He was willing to depose or excommunicate bishops who clung to an evil way of life or who refused to enact his reforms for the clergy. Cooke reminds us that once papal claims to headship over all of Christian society, or at least its spiritual element, began to crystallize, this logically brought with it the conclusion that the bishop of Rome had not only the right but the responsibility to watch over the entirety of Christendom and to intervene in disputes that were threatening the faith or morality of Christians, if it seemed necessary.[4]

Priests were the first ones to feel the repercussions of the new spirituality. Some bishops even urged people to boycott Masses said by married priests. (To balance this, others laid penalties on people who did *not* want to come to a Eucharist presided over by a married priest!) The Gregorian reforms provided the final impetus for the law obliging priests to live celibately. To aid this, Gregory also tried to have them live in community, and bound to the divine office.

This same period saw the first general council to meet in over 250 years. And from 1123 to 1215, the Lateran councils met four times—

each time dealing with matters of church discipline. They made universal laws saying that laity could not own church property or make appointments to church offices. They prohibited church lands and offices from being hereditary. They established procedures for the election of the pope and qualifications for bishops and priests. They suspended clerics who violated church laws (especially celibacy) and tightened the accountability of priests to bishops and bishops to the pope.

The first Lateran Council (1123) had prohibited clerical marriages. The second Lateran Council, fifteen years later, made them not only illegal but invalid. Even though this law continued to be violated, it signaled the end of a married priesthood in the Roman church, and the imposition of the present discipline of celibacy for those in the Latin Rite of the church.

Many priests rebelled at this. Others opted for a form of canonical life, as Gregory VII had advocated. Although the requirement of community was partly motivated by the desire to withdraw clergy from the power of the feudal lords and bring them directly under episcopal control, it was also seen as a safeguard for celibacy. However, many found this too difficult, which ultimately led to the failure of the Gregorian reforms. Only a minority came to live together as "regular canons," eating and sleeping communally.

Overall, however, the Gregorian reforms produced much improvement in life and spirituality. One consequence, however, was that the laity were increasingly left in the cold, excluded from the sacral and intellectual world. Many turned to extreme forms of piety, the flagellants, for example, or those making difficult pilgrimages or painful penances. After all, holiness was to be found in the extraordinary and the heroic. This attitude would help fuel the crusades in the next century.

Ministerial Developments

As we saw in the previous chapter, monasticism had made a deep impact on Christendom. With the Gregorian reforms at the beginning of this period, we are still at a point where monasticism was being renewed, and fervor was high. It was the monks who reestablished and maintained many of the ministries that had once been performed by the people. They were the teachers, the prophets, and the ones who cared for the sick and the poor. And at this time zeal led to religious orders being founded to take care of temporal needs, even seemingly strange ones like the Knights Templar or the Trinitarians.

Most of these new developments took place in the twelfth and thirteenth centuries, though their roots lay in the reforms of the eleventh. If the reform of the monks had been motivated by spiritual reasons, that of the secular clergy had some political motivations as well. Legislation of the period is aimed at stopping lay investiture (not always successfully), the passing on of church lands and titles to members of one's own family, as well as the threat to the power of the bishop over his priests. As mentioned above, efforts made to secure the independence of bishops from the power of the nobles often chose the expedient of making them owe their allegiance even more directly to the pope.[5]

The eleventh and twelfth centuries saw a great increase in ecclesiastical organizations. The more organized the church became, the more the lines of authority eventually led to Rome. Canon laws were collected and classified by Gratian, and the papal curia (which doubled in size during this period) decided which ones applied not only to Rome but to the entire church. The presbytery of Roman pastors developed into the college of cardinals. It was obvious that all power seemed to flow from the pope through the bishops to the priests and laity.

The developments in Christian ministry during this period were reflected in the ordination ritual. The early church was content to use a simple laying on of hands; after the sixth century, they began to dress candidates in the insignia of office. In the feudal period, they were also given symbolic tokens of their responsibilities. Rulers were given crowns and scepters, porters received a key, lectors a book of the epistles, deacons a gospel lectionary, acolytes a candle, and priests the chalice and paten with the bread and wine. The prayers made it clear that priests were receiving the power to offer Mass and forgive sins.

One interesting sideline is that the multiplicity of rituals for ordination posed a problem for scholastic theologians. When was the exact moment when priesthood was conferred? Bonaventure held for the imposition of hands. Others, like Aquinas, felt that it must be the handing over of the instruments, since these more clearly signified the transmission of priestly powers. This, incidentally, became the common opinion until Pius XII told the church that it took place at the imposition of hands and the prayer of the bishop.

Another problem that arose was the nature of priesthood itself, of which more later. It should be mentioned, however, that scholastic theology was both a reflection *of* as well as a reflection *on* the priestly ministry as it existed in the Middle Ages. They brought their theological acumen to bear on what they inherited in the practice of the church. Reflecting on their own experience, they constructed a theology of priesthood that was consistent with that. Very few doubted that there were seven orders of priesthood (episcopacy was not considered a separate order) or that priestly ministry was essentially sacramental ministry.

Yet by this time clergy performed almost all the other ministries in the church as well. As bishops they ruled; as professors they taught in the universities; as canon lawyers they preserved order; as preachers they reminded Europe of its obligations to God. About the only non-ordained who served the church were the monks and nuns, but they were not regarded as laity, and their work was not regarded as ecclesiastical ministry. In almost every aspect of Christian life, priests were the primary mediators between the people and God. Their priesthood was seen almost entirely in terms of liturgical, cultic ministry. Other functions were thought of not in terms of priesthood, but of authority, office, and jurisdiction.

But if the theology of priesthood remained relatively unchanged throughout the Middle Ages, its practice did not. Broadly speaking, it got caught up in the decline of the fourteenth century and the power struggles of the fifteenth. After the plague swept over Europe, it was obvious that the cultural renaissance of the thirteenth century had affected very few. Priests outside the large cities were still poorly educated. The *ex opere operato* theories of the Scholastics were understood in an almost magical way, as enabling priests to get people to heaven simply by the multiplication of Masses. Many were ordained just to say Masses on privileged altars for the souls of the dead.

Then, of course, there was the disgraceful spectacle of papal power politics, and the venality of the curia. Cardinalates could be bought if one had enough money, and many clergy seemed more interested in wealth and power than in spiritual realities. In the early fourteenth century, the college of cardinals got packed with Frenchmen—the popes from 1309 to 1376 were all French—and the papacy decided it was safer to live in Avignon. On their return to Rome, there were two popes, then three, each backed by rival factions of cardinals.

Ministry as Hierarchy

"Medieval" is often used as a pejorative term, connoting an overpowering ecclesiastical control over life, and a faith that was more superstitious than genuine. No doubt church influence was all-pervasive in this period. We can trace the growth of *hierarchization*, in the sense that the structure of church offices tended to dominate. But it should not be forgotten that, for many of the common people, church life at this time was vital and thoroughly evangelical.

Much of this period was one of religious revival, when the gospel was heard afresh and inspired conversion, dedication, and heroism in many men and women. It produced a large number of Christianity's finest minds, mystics, and saintly persons. Surprisingly, despite the corruption of the age, there were popular movements of piety that kept the laity alive spiritually. The monastic culture was a biblically rooted one. So were the new religious orders, especially the Dominicans and Franciscans. They provided many preachers, theologians, and bishops to the high Middle Ages. Some other orders founded at this time were the Carthusians, Premonstratensians, Carmelites, and the Hermits of St. Augustine.

After centuries of chaos, the renaissance of the twelfth and thirteenth centuries brought order to society. Parallels were drawn between the cosmos and the structure of human society. Metaphysicians proclaimed that beauty, unity, and truth were one, while political philosophers saw the same harmony in social life. The philosophical source for the ecclesiology of the Middle Ages is the quasi-mythical Dionysius (Denis) the Areopagite, patron of Paris. He thought of reality in terms of hierarchy, which alone makes life intelligible and possible.[6]

Hierarchy became the structural model of public and ecclesiastical life at this time. Just as social classes made up the fabric of society, within the church there were the three orders of deacon, priest, and bishop. Add these to all the other offices, from popes to abbesses; ecclesial ministers manifested a public dignity and status in the wider social hierarchy. At the summit of the hierarchy was the bishop, the divine or angelic principle within the church. "Other ministries are silent before him because he illumines and vivifies them out of his being and grace."[7] The higher (bishop) illumines the lower ranks because such is the pattern coming from the Trinity.[8]

As medieval civilization evolved, cities, with the cathedral at their center, came into greater prominence. These at least had better preaching, liturgy, and a higher quality of Christian life. Sadly, the people in the countryside were not so well taken care of, since rural clergy were often ill equipped, hence the popularity of the parish missions as a means for nurturing and correcting the faith of the common people. These endured well into the twentieth century. This movement eventually led to the foundation of religious orders that specialized in this form of evangelization, such as the Redemptorists and the Vincentians.

One of the most significant developments in the evolution of ministry during the high Middle Ages may be the emergence of the theologian as a major force in the church's life. If the patristic period was a period of great bishops, the Middle Ages was a period of great theologians. This not only resulted in a systematization of the teachings of the faith, but it meant that non-bishops increasingly came into prominence in theology. (Though taught in the universities, professional theology was still generally limited to clerics.)

Most of the theologians with whom people today are familiar came from the twelfth and thirteenth centuries. In the late thirteenth and early fourteenth centuries, however, ecclesiastical faculties wielded enormous influence. They tended to ignore magisterial statements of the church, especially if they were not based on Scripture and reason. It was the beginning of a real tension. But at the Council of Constance, Gerson, speaking for major theological centers at the behest of the bishops, could have determining influence in guiding the council's conclusions.

Many bishops drifted away from regular preaching at this time. The Fourth Lateran Council, while insisting on their responsibility in this area, prudently legislated that they should at least see to it that competent men be appointed to this task. (This council realized that ordination did not confer theological insight; bishops used others because of their own *defectus scientiae*.) This same council also provided that each metropolitan church should have a theologian attached to it to explain to priests the Scriptures and things needed for the care of souls.

For bishops at this time, the organization of the local church underwent great development. Besides his supervisory and political roles, the bishop also had to rule a growing diocese. He used deaneries to help in this, and also gathered around himself a trusted group of advisors and helpers. Originally, this was the cathedral chapter, with an all-powerful archdeacon as head; from the twelfth century on, however, the chancery office began to assume greater importance in this regard.

Especially at the papal level, this was a period of intense and thorough ecclesiastical organization, culminating in the pontificates of Innocents III and IV. In these days of struggle for power and control, attempt was even made to control thought, with the establishment of the Inquisition in 1231. Before this sad chapter closed, many people were tortured and even killed in the cause of a questionable orthodoxy. Still with us, sad to say, are many of the attitudes that led to this.

As mentioned above, for the common people, despite the external turmoil, this was a period of deep devotion to the person of Christ (also the saints and angels). There was a sincere and touching affectivity, even a tenderness that characterized piety in this period, a good deal of which is due to men like Bernard of Clairvaux and Bonaventure. This piety was to lead to a rise in mysticism, and a desire for a deeper life of prayer. The best example is the German mystics Master Eckhart, John

Tauler, Henry Suso, and John van Rysbroeck. Though these men were all religious, the desire for mystical experiences soon spread beyond the monasteries.

The need for an extra-liturgical piety was due to the fact that liturgy was well nigh incomprehensible for most people. Instead, people found their spiritual nourishment in the cult of the saints, in adoration of the Blessed Sacrament (the feast of Corpus Christi was instituted in 1264), and other popular devotions. Mysticism was something substantial they could relate to, because it touched them at the affective level. In the fifteenth century, this would bear fruit in the _Devotio Moderna_, which offered people a spirituality they found meaningful.

As regards _cult_, the liturgical forms crystallized in the twelfth to the fourteenth centuries remained practically unchanged down to our own time. Canon law was one of the most important influences in achieving this stability. One of the basic reasons for the formalizing of ecclesiastical structures during this time, in fact, was precisely the flourishing state of legal studies. In sacramental theology, canonical influence drew attention especially to the role of the minister and the question of jurisdiction, giving rise to the impression that there is some sort of power of jurisdiction that is other than the power of orders.

With canon law's concern with the externals, the least liturgical action was given meaning. Exactness of conformity to ritual actions had the primacy, rather than insight into what was taking place. This attitude could lead to neglect of the inner meaning and spirit of the sacramental system in favor of the visible and the canonically measurable.

The discipline of penance affords a good example. The definitive shift from the ancient discipline of the first millennium took place in the twelfth century. By the end of that century there was little trace of the ancient practice of penance. Emphasis had shifted to confession of sins and priestly absolution. Internal contrition was seen as necessary, as was some sort of penance. But the theories of attrition and the rapid growth of indulgences began to detract from both contrition and penance. It sufficed to have an ordained priest and the proper form.

This caused an important shift in the activity of priests, since a much greater portion of their time was taken up with hearing confessions, especially when regularity in confession became a matter of law (1215). In their own self-image also, the power of forgiving sins and passing judgment on the guilt of their fellows was bound to have an effect. More than ever, the notion of the pastoral office as one of ridding people from their sins became predominant. One preached in order to exhort people to repent and leave their sins, and thus approach the sacrament of reconciliation. One celebrated Eucharist so that Christ's death might justify sinners.

The tendency to reduce the priestly role to hearing confessions and saying Mass was given an added boost by Pope Alexander III. At the Third Lateran Council in 1179 he reinterpreted the "Title" of ordination to say that it merely meant that a cleric should be assured of sufficient income to live on.[9] This was a vast difference from the radical attachment to a community meant by Chalcedon. A further step toward reinterpretation occurred around 1198 when Innocent II argued that even a presbyter ordained "absolutely" still possessed his "presbyteral quality." This meant, in effect, that the ritual of ordination was sufficient in itself to make one a minister—a point that would have been hotly denied at Chalcedon, and is still denied in the East.

Another development at this time was the increased ordination of monks. Since few of these could be considered pastors, they were, in effect, simply Mass-saying priests. Priesthood was being further divorced from the notion of pastoral care. Surprisingly, despite the flourishing of theology at this time, little of it focused directly on ministry or priesthood. At the end of the twelfth century, we have treatises on the sacraments that leave out orders. There were no systematic treatises on priesthood. This was left to the decretists (canon lawyers). Only from Peter Lombard onward do theologians discuss ministry and priesthood, usually in terms of commentaries on the *Decretals*, thus introducing a strong canonical flavor into the church's formal thinking much more than for the other sacraments.

Patristic thought had already used Old Testament categories as a means of explaining Christian priesthood. When canonical thinking got hold of this, the tendency was to embrace Levitical legislation as well. The result was a strong influence of Old Testament thinking on the development of our theology of worship, sacramental sanctification, and priestly ministry. The distinctive nature of Christ's priestly act of redemption was consistently mentioned, but generally the basis of the distinction was the difference between *type* and *fulfillment*.

Moreover, the ethico-religious ideal of Leviticus, with all its overtones of separation from the profane and the human need of professional mediators to approach God, became a common source for reflection on the sanctity expected of priests. It is interesting to note how often Leviticus is quoted in the campaign to impose and enforce clerical celibacy. Constant reference to Old Testament ideas of priesthood may have also been an influence in identifying cult as the primary purpose of Christian ministry.

Within the process of theology at this time, the understanding of the priesthood of Christ had the most critical influence for our subject of ministry. A fundamental Christian insight is that Jesus is the only priest, and that anything else that is called priesthood can be justifiably called that because it stands in some special relation to his unique priesthood. However, different thinkers and different periods have understood this relationship in different ways. And a wide divergence of views marked twelfth-century reflection on Christ's priesthood.

Anselm of Canterbury (d. 1109), whose influence was determinative in turning the theology of redemption toward the notion of satisfaction, says nothing about the priesthood of Christ.[10] In other words, he did not link Christ's redemption with his priesthood. Bernard of Clairvaux is another of a long line of theologians who see Christ as the one true priest acting in and through the visible minister of the sacraments. Though he never spells out how, there seems to be some idea of instrumental causality at work, Christ working invisibly through the priest.[11]

In the *Sentences*, Peter Lombard discusses Christ's role as mediator at length, but makes no explicit relation of this to priesthood. He does have one succinct remark about Christ as priest, victim, and the price of our reconciliation, but does not tie this in to his mediatorial function.[12]

Hugh of St. Victor, despite his rich insights into the sacramental life of the church, speaks of Christ acting as high priest at the supper and at Calvary, and of ordained ministers acting as priest in Eucharist and penance. But this is treated as a *continuation* in historical sequence only (i.e., priests do *now* what Christ did *then*, rather than a simultaneous action of Christ through the priest).[13]

Hugh also tried hard to bring together priest and bishop into one order, within which there might be several degrees. He used the order of deacons as a model, since there were regular deacons, archdeacons, etc. But he was not followed to any great extent here. Since Venerable Bede (d. 735), most commentators thought the bishop above the priest (as the Twelve were above the 72) in the administration of the Christian community, but in the administration of the sacraments they were equal. This led to seeing the bishops' role as being church administration, and the priests' as sacramental administration.

The Sacrament of Order

Peter Lombard seems to have been the first to give a definition of "order," saying it was a certain sign—that is, something sacred by which a spiritual power and office is given to the one ordained. The certain "sign" spoken of here indicated the external ritual by which the internal gift and spiritual power or office is given. Later theologians, however, changed Lombard's meaning of *sign*. Rather than the ritual, it was taken to mean the character that remained with the ordained person throughout his life.[14]

Albert the Great, Aquinas, Bonaventure, and Scotus all followed this pattern. None of them doubted that *order* was a sacrament. Some used the last supper as the occasion of its institution, but this was by no means common in the thirteenth century. However, the connection of *order* with Eucharist was almost unanimous. Alexander of Hales (d. 1236) who, in presenting Lombard's definition above, added, "*Order* is a sacrament of spiritual power for some office established in the church for the sacrament of communion."

In his *Summa*, Aquinas divided the material on this sacrament into five sections, the first dealing with "order in general." Thus, he begins with the church and asks whether there should be order in the church. He answers by pointing to the way in which God generally acts: creation and all God's works reflect what God is in Godself. This means beauty and, therefore, order. Only if one understands the church as an ordered society, reflecting an orderly God, will one understand the meaning of the sacrament of order in the church. It is worth noting that the emphasis in this approach is not ministry or service, or even priesthood, but *order* in a church as a (perfect) society. This at least gave their thought a strong ecclesiological base.

"Power," and "Eucharist" are recurrent ideas in the high scholastic approach to *order*. Aquinas' classic quote in the *Summa* indicates the general idea:

> Since the consecration conferred in the sacrament of orders is directed to the sacrament of the Eucharist, the principal act of each order is that whereby it is most closely directed to the sacrament of the Eucharist. In this respect, too, one order ranks above another in so far as one is more nearly directed to that same sacrament.[15]

This theory of a eucharistic priesthood has dominated the Western theology of priesthood down to the present time. It was pretty much taken for granted for the next eight centuries, until deliberately rejected by Vatican II. The three essential elements of the scholastic definition of priesthood were:[16]

- priesthood as geared to the Eucharist;

- priesthood as a power;
- priesthood culminating in the priest (not the bishop).

The notion that the priesthood focused essentially on the Eucharist created a liturgical, or sacral, understanding of the priest. Though this might seem rooted in good Christology, it was a rather narrow vision, one that limited the whole understanding of Christ's own priesthood to sacrifice.

Second, the idea that priesthood was essentially a *power* tended to move theological thought away from the earlier notion that ministry was essentially *service*. This can (and has) led to priesthood being seen as a sort of domination over the Christian people, and associated more with the power to rule than to serve. True for the scholastics, this was a sacred power to bring salvation to sinful humanity. However, it is also true that service, *diakonia*, is not central; rather, consecrating the bread and the wine and forgiving sins are the normal ways of expressing this power. But it remains a fact that *power* became the normal way of understanding the sacrament of order.

Finally, during this time, the bishops were definitively excluded from the sacrament of order. They were not ordained to their position, only *consecrated*. The episcopacy was a dignity and an office, not the "fullness of the priesthood." No one denied that the college of bishops succeeded to the college of apostles. But since this did not flow from orders, the collegiality implied here was seen more as coming from jurisdiction granted by the pope. For practically the entire first millennium, the bishop had been seen as the chief ecclesial minister. The priesthood of Jesus, the apostles, and the bishops were all somehow interconnected. Now the link with Jesus and the apostles had to be found elsewhere—in a dignity or in the administration of jurisdiction. This, combined with the centralizing tendencies of the papacy, all served to severely limit the collegiality of bishops.

Theories of Priesthood

The broad generalizations and summaries made in this book should not be taken to mean that the image of the priest was uniform in this period. Even the theological syntheses of the thirteenth century show considerable variance. Even the famous character, so associated with the scholastics, was seen by them as being essentially in continuity with the early church, as pointing to a visible link between ministry and church. Furthermore, a character was given at all ordinations, from sacristan to bishop. It remains true, however, that elements of the scholastic teaching have been absolutized to our own day. Let us attempt a summary.

Thomas Aquinas (d. 1274)

Though Albert the Great paved the way for seeing the priesthood of Christ in terms of Aristotelian categories of causality, the systematization of this insight was left for St. Thomas Aquinas. Taking mediation to be the heart of priesthood, he insisted that the action of mediating was essentially Christ's obedient acceptance of suffering and death. Thus Christ's true worship was his offering of himself as expiation, atonement, and source of justification for all humankind. Though short, the treatment of Christ's priesthood in the *Summa* is a sketch for the sacerdotal interpretation of the entire Christ-mystery.

Because of his great influence, much of later theology on priesthood consists of repetition or comment on Thomas's explanations. Even Trent, though not tied to a particular school, is very open to Thomistic interpretation. Aquinas accepted the notion that all the faithful shared in Christ's priesthood, but he also taught that the sacrament of orders gave individuals a special mode of sharing in this one priesthood that was *active* in its orientation, as opposed to the somewhat *passive* (or receptive) nature of the common priesthood. One was ordained to receiving sacraments; the other to giving them.

Because the key manifestation of Christ's own priesthood came in the supreme cultic act of his death and resurrection, the principal function of the priest is the celebration of the Eucharist. It is here that Christ's own priestly worship is made present in the midst of the worshiping community. The basic power involved in ordination was the power to confect the Eucharist. Subordinate to this supreme exercise of the ministerial office and the supreme moment of the church's existence are the other powers of the ordained: penance, preaching, and governing the community.

In the performance of the Christian ritual, the ordained minister (priest or bishop) acts as an instrument of Christ, who is the main agent of the sacraments. But the minister acts as a *human* instrument precisely as *minister Christi*, channeling and specifying the divine causative intentionality by his own understanding and intent. However, the eucharistic celebrant does not primarily give expression to his own intention, but to the communal faith and intent of the church, and beyond that to the redeeming intent of the head of the church itself: Christ.

Thus, one enters the hierarchical structure of the church to the extent that one has a relation to sacred things. The most sacred of all things, of course, is the Eucharist. Aquinas described priestly ministry in terms of its real, physical functions with the Eucharist. Aquinas does this despite the difficulties it causes him with the office of bishop; he finally emphasizes the bishops' teaching/preaching as a higher form of priesthood.

In the twelfth and thirteenth centuries increased attention began to be given to the idea of the character of the sacraments. If this is combined with the notion of ordination being essentially a ritual action, whether a candidate met other conditions made little difference for him to receive the permanent character of priesthood. Aquinas did not question this framework, though he refined it by defining the character as a spiritual power especially related to cult and to Eucharist. As regards ordination, Aquinas felt that even the minor orders gave a character; and the liturgical rite was the moment when it was bestowed. He felt it was so permanent that it survived even death.

Duns Scotus (d. 1308)

Bonaventure does not introduce the notion of priesthood into his extensive treatment of Christ as mediator and redeemer. Like him (and the rest of the Franciscan tradition) Duns Scotus is very Christocentric. Yet, there is a strongly juridical and moral character to his soteriology that leads him to stress merit and satisfaction when he discusses Christ's passion and death. Ultimately, Scotus distances Christ's priesthood from the church (and from the Eucharist) much more than Bonaventure, who speaks of the priest as being a spouse of the church, and of the character as configuration to Christ.

Scotus's position on the cultic reality of Christian priesthood may seem quite similar to that of Aquinas. Their similarity comes more at the level of the positive things that they taught rather than at the philosophical level; they have very different views of sacramental causality. With most of the rest of medieval theology, Scotus sees the essential power of the ordained priest as being his power to effect transubstantiation. Like Aquinas, he links this to the sacramental character given in ordination. But he sees the character as being more a title to divine concurrence than an intrinsic modification of one's intellectual power.

Scotus saw the role of the priest in the Eucharist very differently. For Aquinas, the action of the Mass is one where Christ is active and present, working through the one who presides *in persona Christi*. Scotus sees the minister acting rather *in persona ecclesiae*. Christ himself is not immediately present and actively offering the sacrifice; it is the will and intent of the church that is effective, with the priest as an instrument of this intention of the church. Thus, the way was open to seeing the Mass as the church's own sacrificial action, related to and drawing upon Christ's own action, yet distinct from it.

Gabriel Biel (d. 1495)

William of Ockham, the founder of Nominalism, paid no attention to Christ's priesthood. His treatment of Eucharist deals almost entirely with questions like the relation of substance and quantity in transubstantiation. Though a devoted follower of Ockham, Biel's notions of priesthood are closer to Scotus. He speaks of Christ mystically immolated on the altar, and how he acts in the Eucharist through the instrumentality of the ministers who are his vicars. Discussing the various meanings of "sacerdos," he lists three reasons why the ordained are called priests:

1. They administer or give sacred things (only priests have the power to administer the sacraments).
2. They say sacred things (preaching the word of God, reciting office, celebrating Mass).
3. They confect sacred things (the body and blood of Christ).

Not only does he distinguish the function of ministering to the word from that of the eucharistic ministration and transubstantiation, but he distinguishes the latter two from each other. Scotus and Bonaventure had already done this. It is iteresting that for Biel, pastoral administration of the Eucharist is not a function of *ministry* (thus it cannot be shared with deacons, who are also ministers), whereas confection of the Eucharist is seen as a cultic or strictly *priestly* act. Both are viewed as properly priestly. Among the priestly functions, confection of the Eucharist is preeminent. These distinctions would influence many Reformers.

However, in explaining the *manner* in which the eucharistic celebrant participates in transubstantiation, he follows the Scotistic concentration on the divine will. God has so determined it that when a proper celebrant performs the proper external acts with the proper intention, God's creative power will effect a change in the bread. Though his explanation of causality differs radically from that of Thomas Aquinas, he is one with all the scholastics in seeing priestly dignity as stemming from the power to consecrate.

One of the most interesting and important aspects of Biel's teaching on the efficacy (and reality) of the eucharistic action is his emphasis on the faith and intention of the church. Hence he could affirm the effectiveness of the sacraments performed by an unworthy minister; these stem from the power of the faith of the entire church.

It has been mentioned that medieval treatises on the sacrament of orders dealt almost exclusively with the *powers* of those ordained. This left practically untouched any theological explanation of the role of the episcopacy or presbyterate as a social force in the community. This was left to canonists, in the context of legal power and jurisdiction.

Because priestly powers were understood to stem from the permanent sacramental character, priesthood was forever. This position worked its way into official teaching. The Council of Florence first mentioned this permanent character in 1439 in its decree for the Armenians. And the Council of Trent reiterated it in its 23rd session (July 15, 1563). It gave it added importance by anathematizing anyone who contended that a priest could ever again be considered a layman.

This was a profound departure from earlier Christian understanding of ordination. Though importance was given to ordination in the early church, its significance went far beyond liturgical rites and indelible marks. And those whom the church rejected as ministers could no longer lay claim to the priesthood. The modern Latin understanding, however, has come to see the ordination ritual itself as being *the* determinative factor in the valid transmission of ministries, to the exclusion of virtually every other consideration. There are ecumenical difficulties caused by this stand, as it differs from that taken by the Eastern, as well as by some of the Protestant (e.g., Anglican) churches.

The later history of ordination in the West is thus one of increasing emphasis on the liturgical action, which, if validly celebrated by a competent minister, effects an ontological change in the ordinand. Given this view, it is not surprising that the priesthood of the ordained is said to differ *essentially* from that of the laity. With such an emphasis on the sacred powers that ordination bestows (the power to consecrate the Eucharist, to forgive sins, etc.), we can understand why one who is dispensed from priestly obligations is still regarded as possessing the indelible priestly character, even though he does not (or may not) exercise the office.

The whole of the thirteenth and following centuries thought of the sacramental character as a theological commonplace—though it was understood in very different ways. For Aquinas the character was equated with the power of priestly action. Others saw it as a relation of reason. For practically all theologians, however, the character was used as the key to explaining the efficacy of sacramental actions performed by an unworthy minister, as well as the root for the non-repetition of ordination.

Priest and Bishop

We have already said something about the theology of the relationship between bishop and priest. The general feeling was that the bishop is what a priest is—only a little more so (in the sense that he can ordain and his power of the keys extended even to excommunications). Since this was seen mainly as an exercise of jurisdiction, episcopacy was not seen as a distinct order.

We know that from the ninth century on, "presbyter" was essentially equivalent to "priest" (completing a process that had begun in the fourth century), though it was admitted that the term technically applied in the first instance to bishops. This conclusion followed logically from the fact that priests celebrated the Eucharist. Seeing the essential priestly power as being that of consecration, and given the fact that priests were primarily ordained to say Mass—and this was the common practice—there was surely little to distinguish priests and bishops.

A powerful boost for this way of thinking came from influential theologians like St. Peter Damian (d. 1072). In his *Liber Gratissimus*, written to Archbishop Henry of Ravenna, he argued vehemently against reordaining bishops who had been consecrated by simoniacs. His first reason was like Augustine, but the second insisted that the episcopate is not in itself a new "order" but only a more excellent rank within the order of *priesthood*. Defining priest as one who "offers sacrifice to God," especially in "the mystery of the Lord's body and blood," Damian clearly assumed that presbyter = priest.

Peter Damian's definition of priest—one who has the power to consecrate the Eucharist—became the standard one for medieval theology. This had two consequences. First, bishops were no longer an "ordo," but an excellence added to the order of priesthood. This was the position held by the school of St. Victor in the twelfth century, and by Aquinas in the thirteenth.

Second, bishops were not ordained to their ministry. In mentioning the election of Hildebrand (Gregory VII) to the papacy in 1073, we noted that, since he was only a deacon at the time of his election, he was first "ordained" priest before being "consecrated" bishop. This procedure was innovative, since in earlier centuries people were simply ordained bishops, without first being ordained presbyter. But if episcopacy was not a distinct order, this was the normal thing to do.

This was a logical conclusion flowing from the emphasis placed on the Eucharist as the changing of bread into Christ, and on the priestly power of effecting this change. Not that pastoral concerns vanished, but priesthood as a cultic reality had gradually gained center stage in preference to apostolic proclamation of the gospel. The relationship of the bishops to the apostles had by now become a polemical argument for jurisdiction, rather than for sacramentally making the apostolic tradition present.

Hence, by the twelfth century, the presbyter = priest equation was firmly entrenched. The priesthood was also defined primarily in reference to the "powers" given at ordination, chief among which was that of consecrating at Eucharist. This power was acquired independently of pastoral connection with a concrete community of Christians. By the end of the twelfth century, these powers were seen as a permanent possession of the ordained person, who was "indelibly marked" with the "character" of priesthood. Bishops were simply priests with greater dignity. Laity were passive recipients of sacramental ministration.

Order and Jurisdiction

If priesthood is the highest order in the church, and if it consists essentially in the power to consecrate the Eucharist, and if this power is shared alike by presbyter and bishop, how does one distinguish between these two ministries? The twelfth-century theologians solved this with the idea of ranks of dignity within one order. But this kind of distinction was not good enough for a canon lawyer, who wanted to be able to specify the exact status of each. The concern was intensified because there was also a struggle going on between state and church at that time. The issue was more than an ideological one, for many medieval writers thought that kings, anointed and consecrated as they were, were as much priests as any ordained cleric.

At any rate, canonists began to distinguish between the spiritual power that results from ordination itself (*potestas ordinis*), and the power to exercise ecclesiastical jurisdiction (*potestas jurisdictionis*). This distinction between orders and jurisdiction helped explain the notion of an indelible character attached to ordination, which remained even if the person was not allowed to exercise his power. Also, the growing fact of absolute ordinations allowed people to think that power independent of any ecclesial bond was conferred by the ritual. Thus, while the power of orders was permanent, the power of jurisdiction might be delegated, withheld, restricted, or withdrawn by competent authority.

This may sound like hair-splitting, but the distinction is still with us in church law, and the practical consequences were far reaching. For one thing, it meant a further split between the liturgical rite and the ancient significance of the "title" of ordination. For the ancients, the whole purpose of the liturgical rite was to give ritual expression of the mandate of the church to serve. Now, one could be a priest without this mandate. Today we still have titular bishops—having the power of orders, but without any specific people to serve (no jurisdiction). Likewise, one could be ordained without ever assuming the work of pastoral care and ministry.

We also had the interesting phenomenon of being able to possess orders without jurisdiction, and jurisdiction without orders. Popes gave some abbots (who were only priests) the right to ordain; and we had numerous "prince bishops" over the centuries who could exercise episcopal jurisdiction in a diocese without ever actually being ordained priest or bishop. Though this began in earlier centuries, it was the canonical legislation of this period that made it a permanent feature of the clerical landscape.[17]

Priestly Life

As can be imagined, priestly life was mainly cultic. As long as one could celebrate Mass, one achieved the purpose for which one was ordained. This cultic shift is illustrated in the 27th canon of the Fourth Lateran Council, which speaks of the formation of clergy:

> Since the care of souls is the art of arts, we strictly command that bishops, either personally or through others who are well fitted to the task, seriously instruct and train those who are to be advanced to the priesthood. Specifically, they should instruct them about liturgical celebrations and the church's sacraments, so that they can perform them correctly.

Here the ancient idea of the care of souls that characterized earlier periods was reduced to providing them sacraments. And it sufficed to perform the rituals correctly. Since the eucharistic action was essentially Christ's, the Eucharist enjoyed a basic freedom in its reality and effectiveness from the capabilities or sanctity of any celebrant. The fruitfulness of any celebration was unlimited.

It is interesting that despite the theology of character eliminating the question of the Eucharist depending on the sanctity of the minister, there is an enduring conviction during this period that somehow the Mass celebrated by a holy priest is better than one celebrated by one who was a sinner. Gregory VII and some of his successors even forbade people to attend the Masses of those who were known sinners.

Theoretically, exemplary lives were expected of priests and bishops. "Example" here meant good ethical behavior, especially in sexual matters. It was in the twelfth to the fourteenth centuries that a relatively universal effort was made to apply the rule of clerical celibacy. It was treated as the touchstone of clerical morality. The main thing missing here was a careful theological grounding for the discipline of celibacy, and there were many violations of it. Despite this, the rule reinforced the idea that the clergy was a higher state than that of the laity. In the medieval period we are considering here, the clergy were a world within a world, and there was a great gulf between the clergy and the life of the common people. There was a similar gap between the higher clergy and the majority of priests, who were often poorly educated and closer to the people in outlook.

A Final Word

If we have styled this period "Ministry as Hierarchy," it is because the Middle Ages gave rise to church institutions that were marvelous in their complexity. Yet, the more one looks, the more one senses that practically all this growth was organizational and administrative in nature. Essentially a proliferation of ecclesial bureaucracy, it enabled the popes to call crusades, to launch the Inquisition, and to extend their influence over the entire church. In this sense, there was nothing *new* added to previous centuries, but a greater centralization emerged.

The creative thrust of the church's life was happening elsewhere, such as in new religious communities, popular religious movements, theology, and the rise of mysticism. These currents did not bear the fruit they should have, however. The insularity and exclusive inwardness that had developed made the institutional church approach anything new rather negatively. There was a lurking fear of the dangers of new ideas and ways. Consequently, the theological and cultural promise of the twelfth and thirteenth centuries never bore the fruit we might have expected. Pluralism was suspect. So also was secularism, and anything involving women.

When Abelard tried a new approach to philosophy, he was bitterly attacked by Bernard of Clairvaux; when Aquinas tried to bring Aristotelian thought into theology, he was condemned by the University of Paris. The new approach was more experiential and willingly used modern science. Such naturalism in knowledge was suspect to those wedded to the neo-Platonic monastic spirit.

The trial of Joan of Arc might exemplify this, as well as a general suspicion of women that existed at this time. Not only did Joan break gender roles, she dared to claim that her religious instincts, rather than the fiat of ecclesiastical authority, were to be trusted. This was too much for masculine suspicions and the general negativity toward women at this time. Women were often suspected of being witches. By the end of this period, women were canonically relegated to a double second-class citizenship in the church. They were laity (neither priests nor religious), but they were not even lay*men*, something only remedied in the 1983 Code. In one sense, we might say that at this time, celibacy was the great symbol of clerical freedom from taint, either by the secular or by women.

Summary

1. Priesthood was defined almost exclusively in relation to sacramental ministry. This meant mainly the power to consecrate the bread and wine into the Body and Blood of Christ. Everything else revolved around this. *"Consecrare enim est principalis actus, ad quem sunt actus omnium ordinum,"* said Albert the Great. Other functions of the priest were seen as flowing from his jurisdiction, something that the authority structure of the medieval church understood well. This was so well reinforced by the rise of canon law that no one seemed to question it.

2. These centuries are celebrated for having been a time of renaissance. There is no doubt that theological knowledge and sophistication, to say nothing of the development of the natural sciences and of art, took an enormous leap during this period. Medieval cathedrals are a standing tribute to a deep faith. In retrospect, however, we can say that the theological discussions did not really influence the large mass of Christians. It is almost as if popular piety was divorced from the discussions of the schoolmen. From a practical point of view, however, this time signaled a renewed importance for the theologian in the church. Theologians also began to feel capable of passing judgment on the pronouncements of bishops and popes.

3. At the external level, the period was one of great organization and centralization. It was an age of strong bishops and even stronger popes. Rome was able to mount crusades against the East and against deviations from the true faith within Christianity. Canon lawyers made it possible for popes to extend the theoretical bases of their supremacy over both the church and secular rulers. But this was not a period we can look back to in pride. There was much corruption, and the example of Christian life given by the hierarchy, even in Rome, was positively scandalous. It was a good thing that communications in those days were not what they are today, for the majority of the people did not know the extent of these realities.

4. The increased organization and centralization of the church that

took place in this period meant the increased influence of Rome in the affairs of the rest of the church. The four major councils were all disciplinary in nature. There is no doubt that the hierarchy of the church was trying to insure good morals and clear lines of authority. After all, feudal society saw hierarchy and order as part of the divine plan for the entire world. All the more so in the church.

5. In the thirteenth century, great scholastic theologians dominated the theological landscape. The major theological centers wielded enormous influence in the church, both with their theology as well as their canon law. With the relative peace that the end of the previous period brought, the accumulated wisdom of the monastery libraries was gathered together into books that served as the source-books for students. Aquinas's *Summa* is an extended commentary on the *Sentences* (source-book) of Peter Lombard.

6. In the twelfth century the form of the sacrament of penance was shifted around to put major emphasis on the absolution of the priest. In 1215 it was mandated that people confess once a year. This resulted in a shift in the understanding of the role of the priest, forgiveness of sins being added to the power to celebrate the Eucharist. Removing the rootedness in a community insisted on by Chalcedon further reduced the pastoral role of the priest.

7. The theologians of the period may have thought of Jesus as priest, but very little theologizing was done on the topic. Much more thought was given to Jesus being the mediator between God and humankind. It remained for later men like Albert the Great and Thomas Aquinas to define Christ's priesthood. This they did mainly in terms of causality, though they differed from each other in the type of causality involved.

8. One less happy contribution of Aquinas to theology is his description of the ordained priesthood as active, and the common priesthood as passive. This helped cement the understanding that the people always received the blessings of the church from the priest. Justifying only a completely passive role for the laity abetted the tendency to discuss priesthood in terms of the powers of those ordained, and further distanced sacramental theology from sound ecclesiology.

9. In this period, the practical equation of priest and bishop was cemented theologically. After all, both could celebrate Mass and forgive sins. This constituted the essence of their priesthood. Specifically episcopal powers were seen as flowing from the power of jurisdiction, not the power of orders. Again, these powers were seen independently of any pastoral connection with a given community.

10. This was not a period, however, that welcomed new ideas. The

tenor of the age was a narrow self-righteousness and inward turn that tended to a very conservative understanding of religion. The crusades are only one example of how people could be marshaled to destroy others in order to honor Christ. Other examples were anti-Jewish legislation, the Inquisition, and the felt need to do everything possible to insure orthodoxy.

Discussion Questions

1. What are the advantages and disadvantages of having the pope appoints bishops directly? Will it affect the flock over which they preside? How does this contradict the practice of the earlier church? Is this good or bad?

2. Would it be possible to have a church without hierarchy and still be faithful to the mind of Christ? How would such a church maintain unity?

3. What were the main developments in terms of ministry in this period? Are these steps forward or backwards? Why?

4. What was the main contribution of the scholastics in regard to priestly ministry in the church? How do their views differ from those of the patristic church?

Suggested Readings

O'Malley, J., S.J., "Priesthood, Ministry and Religious Life: Some Historical and Historiographical Considerations," *Theological Studies*, 49, 2 (June 1988), 223-258.

Osborne, K., "Ministry in the Scholastic Period," *Priesthood*, Chap. 7, pp. 200-218.

Power, D., "Changes in the Ordinal in the Middle Ages," and "Scholastic Theology," *Ministers of Christ and His Church*, pp. 87-105, 115-126.

Ryan, S., "Episcopal Consecration: The Legacy of the Schoolmen," *Irish Theological Quarterly*, 33 (1966), 3-38.

7

The Reformation of Ministry

The great papal schism, though a significant low point in the church's history, is an admittedly arbitrary historical division. There is no doubt, however, about the demarcation of the period under study in this chapter: the rupture of Western Christendom. The challenge of Protestantism was finally met by the Council of Trent—monument of the Catholic (counter)reformation. Though often called for, a council had been long resisted because of papal fears of conciliarism, and what it might do to weaken papal power. Only the Reformation forced the church to face the moral decline of the church. Unfortunately, it came when there was no longer any possibility of reunion between Catholics and Protestants. Catholics could now only turn inward and look to their own house.

Twice in its history the church has been rent by schisms that split off huge sections of Christianity. The first was long in coming: the Eastern schism. The second seemed more abrupt, and came from within what was left of Latin Christianity. From the twelfth century on, the demand for a more believable church had become increasingly vehement and radical. People were losing hope that Rome could ever reform itself, let alone lead a general reform of the church. Between Constance and the Reformation, there were continuing cries for reform "in head and members."

With the waning of the Middle Ages, two problems still begged for resolution by the church. The first was the ecclesiological question of the primacy and universality of the pope. This had been given theoretical justification especially in the struggle against lay investiture in the previous centuries, and the effort to make the spiritual power triumph over the temporal. These papal claims, however, were clearly rejected by the reformers.

The second issue was theological and involved the sacramental system: the question of how grace was transmitted in the church. The reformers, reacting to the sterility and juridicism that characterized church life and practice, also rejected Catholic teaching in this area.

Externally, the church appeared rich and powerful. One had only to look beneath the surface, however, to see fragility and internal contradictions. If the papacy seemed a self-assured dominant power, the Avignon papacy and the long years of conflict between popes and antipopes, each excommunicating one another's followers, all served to lower papal prestige and influence, especially in Germany. Despite continued rumblings for change during the fifteenth and early sixteenth centuries, the history of the church continued to be one where greater interest was given to ecclesiastical power than to spiritual welfare. Decadence had set in.

However, this age of benefices, ecclesiastical patronage, increasing secularity and worldliness of the higher clergy, non-residence, and theological ignorance, is also the age of the *devotio moderna* and of many new religious orders. As might be expected, most of the impetus for renewal welled up from the faithful, rather than from the authority structure of the church itself. It came from below—a sign of the presence of the Holy Spirit in the entire assembly.

The modern (or *new*) devotion is attributed to Master Geert Grote of Deventer in Holland. His movement became relatively standardized by the beginning of the fifteenth century. Often living in common, its adherents had no intention of founding a new religious order. Rather, they made the free choice to live a genuinely Christian life together. Their frustration with the often sterile argumentation of the scholastics is captured well by the *Imitation of Christ*—a book second only to the Bible in the number of copies sold over the years.

> Of what use is it to discourse loftily on the Trinity, if you lack humility and hence displease the Trinity? Truly, lofty words do not make one holy and righteous, but a virtuous life makes one dear to God. (I,1,7)

This genuine grass-roots yearning for a more fervent piety also helps

explain the rise of movements like the Cathars, Albigensians, and Wal-
densians, or the Hussites and Wycliffites, basically all currents of
reform. Such movements were hard to put down. Individuals could be
silenced by the rack or the fires of the Inquisition, but the desires that
they left behind were still there to inspire others. This would account
for the popularity of Luther's teachings among many of the common
people in the sixteenth century.

Piet Fransen's depiction of the church in this period is provocative
enough to be worth quoting.

> The priesthood, implanted in a society issuing from the barbarian
> kingdom, having doubtlessly profited from its involvement in the
> world around it, began to display more and more clearly after the
> dawn of a new epoch (i.e., after the end of the 14th century) the
> profound defects of its accommodation with the barbarian world.
> It could even be maintained...that from this epoch onwards the
> history of the priesthood had been reduced—apart from some pe-
> riods of reform and intense renewal—to a slow process of detach-
> ment from a shell which was also a burden....
>
> Christian ministry was in process of losing its originality and
> becoming excessively similar to a pagan or Old Testament priest-
> hood. The ministers were so well integrated into the machinery of
> feudal society that they no longer had the strength to react against
> the pressure of dealing commercially in the sacral and ministerial.[1]

The question of ministry within the church was not the primary focus of the Reformation. When Martin Luther nailed his theses to the
door of the Wittenberg cathedral in 1517, the main theological issues
were: 1) the relationship of grace and good works, 2) the question of
justification, 3) the place of the Scriptures, 4) and the role of the pope.
Naturally, ministry is bound up with most of these. At root, however,
the Reformation was a religious protest against the localization of
God's activity in the human and the created. This went beyond any
pastoral program to renew the life of the local church.

Another factor was the continuing struggle of the church with the
secular state. In many ways, it can be said that if Protestantism succeeded, it was because it was aided and abetted by the state. The princes
were often moved not so much by religious motivation as by down-to-
earth considerations of political power. In discussing the downfall of
Catholicism in the Scandinavian countries, the Protestant historian Karl
Heussi remarks, "This reform arose not from the religious needs of the

people, but from the political needs of the princes who imposed their restructuring of the church on the people." The Church of England owes more to Henry VIII's marriage problems than to his piety.

The world was very different when Luther proclaimed his startling opinions about the church. For 500 years the Christians of Asia and Africa were no longer part of the Roman church. The church had become a European church, and it was a very small Europe at that. The Russians had joined the Eastern church; the Balkans and Spain were under the influence of Islam. Southern and central Europe itself was threatened. This heightened the seriousness of what was lost during the Reformation: the Scandinavian countries, England, Scotland, and Wales, as well as large sections of Germany, Switzerland, and Hungary.

At the same time, very important changes were taking place in the secular sphere. Explorations had opened up whole new sections of the world. Trade was booming. The whole image of the world and our knowledge of nature was being called into question. 1492 could well serve as a demarcation line between the Middle Ages and the modern world. And though it took 30 years for the pope to call a council to address the issues brought up by Protestantism, the quality of that response would also lead to a new era in church history. The Tridentine age was solidly founded; it lasted 400 years.

Protestantism

Unfortunately for our study, perhaps, there is no such thing as a uniform "Protestant" theology or practice. Although we can generalize to some extent, the Protestant camp soon split into various factions, many of which were almost as opposed to each other as they were to the church of Rome. There is no way we can do justice in these short pages to the diversity of views that characterized the reformers. Even Luther's writings were contradictory at times, or were repudiated by a later generation.

In general, most of the reformers rejected the medieval style of church ministry along with the scholastic theories supporting it. They discounted the notion that authority in the church was something funneled from Christ to the pope, and through him to the bishops and priests. Finding no scriptural evidence that ranks of orders existed in the early church, they objected to the way men were ordained to ministries that they never performed. Seeing no reason to believe that ordination made men better than other Christians, gave them supernatural powers, or made them ministers for life, they equally dismissed the idea of a sacramental character.

Likewise, they observed that the practice of celibacy was often a scandal in the church. Since they had abandoned the idea of the Mass as a priestly sacrifice, they saw no reason to apply Old Testament rules of purity to Christian ministers. They substituted a pastoral ministry of preaching and teaching in place of a priestly ministry of cult and sacrifice. After all, if salvation came as a result of faith in God's Word, that Word had to be heard. Thus, they also encouraged the translation of the Bible into the vernacular so that it could be read by the people.

The reformers were inspired by a New Testament vision of church and worked to renew ministry according to their understanding of that model. Their challenge to celibacy and monasticism was also aimed at eliminating the class system in the church and the passive role of the laity. Luther's preaching on the priesthood of all believers, in fact, went so far as to stress the dignity of every human occupation; the human kingdom should reflect the divine.

A call for a "return to the sources" was common at this time, a call espoused by Catholic reformers as well. Because of their relatively exclusive reliance on Scripture and downplaying the role of tradition, however, the Protestants drew more heavily on the Bible, and they reinstituted many external offices mentioned in the New Testament, such as elders.

While Catholics did not reach back to recover external structures the way Protestants did, they did develop a detailed argumentation from New Testament texts to show that ordained episcopacy and priesthood as it existed in the church was the sole legitimate successor of the primitive Christian ministry. Special stress was laid, of course, on the "divine institution" of the papal primacy and the hierarchical structure of the church.

One thing that both Catholics and Protestants assumed, however, was that somehow Christ had directly instituted the structures of the true church, hence the need of preserving these as being *de jure divino*. Most theologians today do not feel the need to imagine Jesus as leaving the church an exact blueprint for its future development.

To some extent, the Protestant success in breaking down the barrier between the sacred and the profane did the church a favor. One-sidedness in this regard, however, could (and sometimes did) lead to a new danger. Stressing secular vocations excessively can lose a certain transcendence. Ministry can seem no different from any other work. In its praise of the secular vocation, the Protestant church had difficulty distinguishing ministry from other professions. They wound up with a mixture of elements from the New Testament and the current medieval forms, which risked being too secular at times.

Even today, the furnishings of many Protestant churches are little different from those of a law court or a theater, the minister's suit no different from a banker's or an academic's. This lends a certain austere quality to Protestantism, but it can also rob it of the sacral and the personal.

Another side effect of the effort to bring back the period of New Testament charisms was pietism, all manner of fundamentalisms, charismatic and healing churches, and churches that shared things in common. Some of these have inspired great generosity. However, they sometimes lacked a bond to the wider church, past and present. Often they did not survive cultural changes, nor did they spread far. Beneath the narrowness and superficiality often found here, however, Protestant fundamentalism was an effort to reecho the New Testament view of ministry: a world of ordinary people expecting charisms, willing to serve their community and to change the world.

The reformers rejected ordination as a sacrament, though they differed in exactly how they understood the term "sacrament."[2] There tended to be a unanimity in seeing God as the source of designation for ministry, and in seeing the ceremony of ordination as a recognition of this divine calling. There was a felt need for some observable ceremony allowing men and women to minister in the church. Such designation could not be arbitrary or sheerly pragmatic. Two elements must be certified in a prospective minister: vocation by God and ability to perform the ministry in question.

Though ordination in some sense was commonly accepted (the rite was not considered *effective* in the Catholic sense, however), there is a notable absence of the idea that it put the individual on a special sacred level of existence. The reformers did stress the special example expected from the ones ordained, a fact that itself helped maintain a certain dichotomy. Practically, however, the sacrificing cultic priest was replaced in religious matters by the public functionary.

Basic to the differences between Catholic and Protestant understandings of priesthood is the attitude toward cult. The reformers rejected a cultic priesthood different from the common priesthood of all believers. The reason for this repudiation lay in their understanding of salvation by faith and not good works. They also could not see how the once-for-all efficacy of Christ's sacrifice as taught by Hebrews was not contradicted if priests were to continually renew the sacrifice of the cross.

As far as the reformers were concerned, the vast institution called the medieval church rested on two pillars: the priestly and the sacramental systems, both intimately related to each other. Both seemed to prevent people from having direct access to God. The clergy claimed a quasi-monopoly of the means of grace, especially because of their sole ability to offer the sacrifice of the Mass. This made them mediators between God and the people, seemingly to the detriment of Christ's own mediation. Let us look further at the positions of two of the main reformers.

Martin Luther (d. 1546)

Lutherans themselves will admit that the doctrine of ministry in Lutheranism is still unclear, uncertain, and subject to dispute. This is because so many of the ecclesiological issues dear to the hearts of the reformers converged and intersected at this point. It might be good to remember that at the time of the Reformation there was a substantial distinction between clergy and laity. Priests existed in an order apart, because of the special "character" that made their priesthood essentially different from that of the laity. This was bound up with the key Reformation questions of how God judges a sinful person, and how God, in Christ Jesus, saves the sinner.[3]

This led to the emphasis on justifying faith, the priesthood of all believers, and the centrality of the gospel.[4] One result was to break down the wall (or at least lower it a bit) between clergy and laity. In one sense, the problem of the reformers was the opposite of ours today. Because priesthood seemed the only church calling, the only real vocation, and priests occupied a privileged status in society, Luther asserted the sacredness of all callings, thus removing claims for uniqueness on the part of the clergy. Perhaps today, when many see nothing special about ordained church ministry because of a more secular view of vocation, there is more need to show what is unique to the ministry.

We tend to associate Luther's protest against a clerical priesthood with his teaching about the priesthood of all believers. Though surely popularized by Luther, this teaching in itself is not new; it was a commonplace with the Fathers, and is based on 1 Peter 2:5–9. However, the operative understanding of this fundamental baptismal reality had been obscured for many centuries by the claim of the ordained that they alone were the *sacerdotium*. Long before the sixteenth century, *priest* had become a proper name for the presbyters and bishops in the church.

The early Luther could make statements like "We are all equally priests, i.e., we have the same power in respect to the Word and the sacraments."[5] While Luther denied any essential difference between clergy and laity, however, he did not deny the need for a special ministerial group in the church, especially for the sake of public order. There were two basic dimensions of ministry: the first, a common ministry proper to all, based on baptism; the second, a special ministry of Word and sacrament that included both priests and bishops.

Though not totally consistent in his views, it seems that Luther never really equated the two priesthoods. In his commentary on Psalm 82, he says, "It is true that all Christians are priests, but they are not all pastors. Over and above what he is as a Christian and priest, he must also have an office and a field of work that has been committed to his charge." Thus, while some may be entrusted with official tasks, they are only doing what each Christian has the radical power to do, since all Christians are basically equal in terms of their Christian dignity, spiritual capabilities, and evangelical responsibilities. It might be added that the issues raised by stressing the universal priesthood as well as the need for an ordained ministry have never been fully agreed on by Luther's ecclesiastical heirs.[6]

Luther's view of office was shaped by the two doctrines of *sola fide* and of the Word as the means to faith.[7] Furthermore, he realized a need for someone to preach the Word, and saw this ministry as coming essentially from God. Though it was perhaps mediated by and rooted in the community, the call came from God. This has led to the classical Lutheran teaching that people are set apart for ministry for the preaching of the Word and the right administration of the sacraments. Any other ministerial offices are important only to the extent that they also, even indirectly, serve the Word.[8]

Luther's position can perhaps be clarified by recalling a distinction between offering sacrifice and administering sacraments that had been developing in medieval theology since the thirteenth century. In general this corresponds to a distinction between cultic and pastoral functions. As applied to the Mass, when the celebrant is seen as offering the Eucharist in worship of God, he is "priestly"; when he is seen as giving communion, or even in performing the actions of the Mass so that the merits of Christ's passion and death can be applied to the people, he is "ministerial" in his activity. "Christ bids Peter to pasture the sheep, that is to preach the Word or govern the church with the Word."[9] Luther considered this a pastoral function.

Luther (and most of the reformers) used this distinction to reject the cultic aspect of Eucharist and any distinctive "priestliness" of the ordained person, while retaining official ministerial functions regarding the sacraments. Luther rejected the idea of the Eucharist as worship because this made it seem like grace could be mediated by this "work," and not by faith. He insisted that the ministry of the sacrament was an aspect of the ministry of the Word, thus a form of prophetic proclamation. The cleavage between Word and sacrament that occurred in later Protestant thought is unfair to his basic insights here.

It is in this connection that Luther rejected the sacrificial character of the Mass, perhaps the most divisive issue separating Lutherans and Catholics. It was linked with the question of the gratuity of grace over good works and the full efficacy of the sacrifice of Jesus. Thus the differences are more Christological than sacramental.[10]

Lindbeck summarizes the Lutheran position as follows:

From the three premises that 1) justification is by faith alone, and 2) faith comes by means of the "external" Word in preaching and the sacraments, and 3) the office of minister of the Word is therefore necessary,

Four conclusions follow: 1) the ministry of the Word [and sacrament][11] is of divine origin, but 2) only so far as it in truth serves the Word. 3) It alone is *de jure divino;* 4) the other ministries are important to the extent that they also serve the Word.

Corollary: The priesthood of all believers and the ascription of the same "powers" to lay persons as the clergy protect against erroneous views of the office, but they are not the basis for the positive content of the ministry. This is founded on the need for a special office with special functions. Ordination is for the community, and is not normally repeated.[12]

We might note in closing that Luther returned to the practice of the early church as regards absolute ordinations. Those to be ordained were to receive a call from a specific community of faith, usually a local congregation or a representative of the community. He defended the congregation as the primary calling agency especially because he felt the people of God could not exist without someone to preach the gospel.[13]

John Calvin (d. 1564)

It is relatively easy to know Calvin's views on ministry, for the simple reason that he wrote logically and clearly. In his *Institutes of the Christian Religion* he treats the matter at length, giving a solid Christological and ecclesiological basis to his thought. He takes pains to ground everything in Scripture, along with a historical interpretation of the first five centuries. Calvin's teaching on the ministry rests solidly on his ecclesiology, which is explained in detail in Book IV of the *Institutes*. This section of his work is pretty much the key to his whole thought, and it grew over the years in subsequent editions of his work. His ecclesiology, in fact, is more a treatise on the ministry of the church, an expression that he uses often.

Like Luther, Calvin sees the church as truly existent wherever there is authentic preaching of the gospel and genuine celebration of the sacrament; he also places the dynamism and efficacy of the sacrament within the operation of the Word. But his understanding of these realities differs from Luther's.[14] For one thing, there is a greater emphasis on the spiritual character of Christian worship, not only as regards the psychological element of human faith, but in the action of the Holy Spirit. Today he might characterize that church as a *servant church*, although the metaphor he prefers is that of a kind mother.[15] This conception is close to that presented in Colossians and Ephesians.

For Calvin, ministry in the church is meant to be *diakonia*, a disinterested service of God and the church. In fact, whenever he treats of ministry in general, he constantly appeals to the example of St. Paul, and says nothing about priesthood since this is not mentioned in the New Testament.[16] He stresses the Pauline notion of gifts and charisms, all within the structure of a collegial service. This desire to have a truly ministerial church led him to set up a training program for ministers that could well have been emulated by Catholics.

In terms of his treatment of priesthood, his thought is so dominated by the unique and transcendent priesthood of Christ that he sees no way in which we can participate in that priesthood, whether really or nominally. Seeing Jesus as the sole mediator between God and humanity, he felt little need for any human priesthood. Whenever he does use the term priest for those who minister the Word, he does so strictly analogically.

In this Calvin is a bit illogical with himself. For when he treats of the Levitical priesthood as a prefiguration of Christ's, he stresses their teaching and sacrificial roles as both leading up to and participating in the grace of Christ's own priesthood. He often uses them as models of true gospel ministry. However, in the time of the church, he seems careful to avoid any mention of the sacrificial aspect of church ministry.[17] The paradox is that while he extols the ministerial priesthood of the Old Testament, despite the richer gifts of the New Testament, there is no longer any sacrificial aspect to the ministry of the church.[18]

Calvin also speaks of the idea of the common priesthood of all believers. But even here, in the later editions of the *Institutes* he eliminates Luther's statement that "we are all priests" and stresses the need for a ministerial priesthood within the church. Coming a generation after Luther, he wanted to avoid the rank democracy of the Anabaptists. He even agreed with the second session of Trent, which condemned those who held that anyone in the church could administer the sacraments in view of their common priesthood.[19]

Calvin allowed the church to choose its own ministers, although he wanted to guard against arbitrariness in this matter. Thus, in practice, the choice was made by those already in the pastoral ministry along with the elders. The people's role was one of approbation only. There is no doubt that he saw the pastoral ministry as being of divine origin. It did not stem from the common priesthood. Continuity of ministry in the church was always the result of a constant intervention on the part of God, who gave the vocation.

Those chosen were ordained by a laying on of hands (though he did not call this a sacrament like baptism and Eucharist). Once ordained, a man was bound in servitude to God and the church, and should lead a life worthy of his calling. Calvin is very strong in denouncing the unworthy ministers he sees in the papal church.

He was willing to accept priests and deacons (and even bishops) provided they were ordained by legitimate church officials, as he finds all of these somehow in the New Testament. He reveres church ministry and sees it as an essential part of the church from the beginning. Since they are chosen by God, the pastors exercise their ministry by the power of God. Whether they preach or celebrate the sacraments, it is God who is acting through them. Ministers, however, do not so much *possess* power by reason of ordination; they exercise powers that come from God.

Calvin insisted that the institution of official ministry neither grows out of the priesthood of all believers nor depends on it; rather, all ordained ministry comes from God. Effective because the Spirit works through it, it was meant as a service to the universal priesthood of all believers. Choosing a man for ordination is essentially a recognition of the gifts already bestowed by the Spirit. Thus, the authority that attaches to official ministry comes from the power of the Word and Spirit working through it. Office, or personal dignity, did not enter in.[20]

Calvin stressed four basic tasks in his positive teaching on church ministry. People were ordained to be teachers, pastors, rulers, and servants (deacons). He saw nothing scriptural in the way the Catholic church was structured in the sixteenth century. He writes that our Lord provided for four offices in the church, "pastors, teachers, elders, and deacons."[21] He saw teaching as the most basic task of the minister, who is also the principle of unity for the church. In helping to achieve this, he is servant both of the Lord and of the community.

If Luther's views of priesthood depended on his theology of justification, grace, and good works, Calvin's depends more on his understanding of the Mass. For him, the Catholic position of the Mass as a sacrifice posed two major problems: the sufficiency of Jesus' own expiation on the cross, and the relationship between grace and good works.[22] He bases himself on a solid soteriology, and rejects as false any understanding of priesthood that would have the priest performing a "good work" in order to merit grace, or which would endanger the once-and-for-all aspect of Jesus' redemptive sufferings.

Calvin carried on more controversies with Luther and Zwingli than with Catholicism.[23] He rejected any excessive realism regarding Christ's presence, though he did accept a real presence in the celebration of the Lord's Supper that made it possible for the believer to enter into communion with Christ.[24] He also rejected transubstantiation. For him, the Lord's Supper is a profession of faith and an act of worship, because it is essentially God's action of promise—a true proclamation of the gospel.

Calvin's main divergences from Catholic teaching involve his rejection of a sacrificial priesthood. Though abandoning the Roman theology of the Mass as sacrifice, he accepted that it could rightly be called sacrificial. He also did not regard ordained ministry as being a sacrament. Like Luther, he attributed the efficacy of the Eucharist to the power of the Word. His understanding of "*sola Scriptura*" not only gave it pride of place within the church; it placed it *above* and even anterior to the church inasmuch as it comes from God's eternal Word.

Calvin's thought, however, also contains similarities with which we can resonate. He stressed the church as the Body of Christ, and as a visible and caring mother—this in spite of his teaching on God's utter transcendence, a conviction that led him to minimize somewhat the incarnational principle and attribute all to God. He stressed the "service" character of the ministry, something that has always been taught in the church, although too often neglected in practice. And though he denied strict sacramental value to ordination, he did see the various ministries as sacred functions.

The Cultic Focus of Ministry

The Catholic understanding of priesthood at the time of the Reformation would be as follows: Because of ordination the priest had special powers that enabled him to perform his vocational work of "saving souls" effectively. The most important and basic of these powers was that of consecrating the eucharistic bread and wine. Next was the power of absolution. These powers were possessed "absolutely," i.e., regardless of one's attachment to any given church community. Ordination and proper performance of the ritual guaranteed the effectiveness of the sacraments needed by the faithful. Far more emphasis was given to providing correct performers of church ritual than to preaching or pastoral care.

Seeing priesthood in terms of power, however, risked absolutizing the powers themselves. One result, at least for priesthood, was that the relationship between *ministerium* and *ecclesia* shifted to a relationship between *potestas* and *eucharistia*. The ecclesiological dimension faded into the background.

The powers of the priest also led to his being thought separate from the ordinary or profane realm. Chaucer makes it clear that even though clerics were often perceived to be immoral or lazy, people (even men like Thomas More) still accepted the superior status of the clergy within the structured life of the church. Popular belief also emphasized other sacred "powers" of the priest: to bless people, animals, and things; to heal or avert harm. God listened (only?) to priests.

The (mis)understanding of the idea of power was historically intelligible. Feudalism had led to a church that became the pawn of secular rulers. The fight for superiority between church and state was often based on an understanding of power that was hardly biblical. At the end of the thirteenth century, Vincent of Beauvais uttered the famous remark: "*quodque principi placuit, legis habet vigorem*" (whatever pleases the prince has the force of law). Keep this in mind when thinking of the "fullness of power" claimed by the church; power or authority begins to be seen as a reality in itself apart from the community in both civil and ecclesiastical spheres.

Thus, many non-theological factors made the medieval theological shift possible. For example, when Christians were a minority, talk of the "spirit of Christ" and the "spirit of the world" could easily be applied to all those in the church vs. all those in the world. But when everyone belonged to the church, the boundary began to apply to those who had received "second baptism" (vows) vs. the rest of the church. Monks and priests began to typify the "ideal" Christian and be seen more as a special state of life.

This stratification of the church into realms of sacred and profane, into "agents" and "those acted upon" had been established by centuries of legal precedent and theological justification. Until the Protestants came along, those desiring reform did not question the validity of the lay-clergy dichotomy; they simply sought to lead the ordained to a better fulfillment of their vocational ideal.

As we have seen, the later history of ordination in the West was one of increasing emphasis on the liturgical action which, if validly celebrated by a competent minister, effected an ontological change in the ordinand.[25] The sacred powers that ordination bestows—to consecrate the Eucharist, to forgive sins, etc.—flow from this change. This also explains why one who is dispensed from its obligations is still regarded as possessing the indelible priestly character.

One of the most widely held Protestant theological positions is that ordination does not confer a *character*. It confers a function or office of ministry. But no new power is required to do this beyond what we receive through baptism. The question arises as to whether the reformers, with their strongly functional views on ministry, would have rejected an understanding of character that was more dynamic and ecclesial and less tied to hierarchical rank and to transubstantiation.[26]

Earlier, Aquinas and the great Scholastics understood sacramental character more in continuity with the early church; that is, it helped them describe the link between ministry and church. They even thought that some proper character was given in ordinations to any order. By the 1500s, however, the character was seen as bringing about an ontological change in the one ordained. As mentioned above, the first official mention of this permanent character was made in 1439 by the Council of Florence, and the Council of Trent reiterated it in its 23rd session (July 15, 1563).[27] It also anathematized anyone who contended that a priest could ever again be considered a layman.

This was a departure from an earlier understanding of ordination. Though importance was given to ordination in the early church, its significance went far beyond liturgical rites and indelible marks. And those whom the church rejected as ministers could no longer lay claim to the priesthood. The modern Latin understanding, however, has come to see the ordination ritual itself as being *the* determinative factor in the valid transmission of ministries, to the exclusion of virtually every other consideration. Again, there are ecumenical difficulties caused by this stand, as it differs from both Eastern as well as most Protestant churches.

A critical difference in soteriology, however, lies behind the Protestant move away from a cultic emphasis in ministry. Whereas the Catholic church stressed the *ex opere operato* effectiveness of sacramental ritual, the Protestants stressed the process of *faith being aroused* and nurtured by the communication of God's Word. Thus, we are dealing with the manner in which salvation and justification is mediated through the action of the church and its ministers.

Both Luther and Calvin raised substantive issues regarding church ministry. It would seem, however, that one can best respond to them via the Christological bases that served as the foundation of their views. Trent, unfortunately, did not see the question in this light, as we will now note.

The Council of Trent

Catholicism was ill-prepared for the challenge of the Reformation. The council that eventually met at Trent had a long and checkered history (sessions = 1545-1547; 1551-1552; 1562-1563). Nevertheless, when all is said and done, Trent did serve to unify the church. Both in the establishment of doctrinal unity, and in the initiation of genuine institutional reform, the influence of Trent on subsequent Catholicism can scarcely be exaggerated. Only with Vatican II did the official church suggest that there was any other way of being Catholic than the Tridentine model.

Trent suffered from two main limitations. The first stems from the very historical circumstances that necessitated the council. The work of Catholic reformers was difficult enough before the Reformation broke out. Thereafter, however, the success of Protestantism made internal criticism and reform more difficult than ever. To censure abuses—even the most flagrant ones—was to make one suspect of Lutheranism. Protestant printing presses were ever ready to publish Catholic self-criticism in support of their cause.

Furthermore, the avowed purpose of most of the dogmatic conciliar decrees was to counter what was being denied by the Protestants. There was no effort to give a complete or balanced teaching on the various subjects treated. Unfortunately for subsequent theology, however, Trent was usually taken as the last and only word on any topic, leading to a rather static theological sterility.

Trent repudiated the Reformation on every important doctrinal issue. Against justification by faith, the council reaffirmed the traditional view that faith manifested by works saved people. Against *scriptura sola* it upheld two sources of church authority. It reiterated the belief that the Mass was a repetition of Christ's sacrifice, and that the bread and wine became the transubstantiated body and blood of Christ. Purgatory, indulgences, the veneration of the saints and relics were given a new endorsement. Also reaffirmed were the seven sacraments against the Protestant reduction to two. And so on.

Trent's positions on ministry are not only found in the decree on Orders; the doctrinal decrees on the sacraments in general and on the sacrifice of the Mass are equally significant. Trent would probably also have considered the disciplinary decree on clerical reform important. All of these give us an understanding of the council's view on the nature and function of Christian ministry. Together, all have had lasting consequences.

Unfortunately, Catholic theology was particularly unprepared to understand the fundamental issues raised by the reformers concerning ministry, priesthood, and worship, as well as the more central areas of justification, ecclesiastical authority, and the criteria for faith. The deeper implications of these questions and the religious need to confront them openly were not really recognized. The Protestants, on the other hand, surely appreciated the religious need, but without always adequately seeing the theological issues involved. Thus, the issue was never really joined at the same level of discourse.

Though faced with serious and radical questioning of its traditional understandings of priesthood and ministry, the Council of Trent did little more than insist on viewpoints that had been in existence for centuries. Lacking creativity in meeting the Protestant challenge, its doctrinal decree on Orders was content to synthesize one narrow aspect of scholastic teaching. For all practical purposes, there is no advance in Catholic theology at Trent beyond the positions of the Middle Ages.

Perhaps because the Catholic theologians at the council were skilled theological debaters, their very competence as apologists worked against grasping the deeper issues and underlying suppositions of Reformation thought. It also prevented them from developing an imaginative and constructive approach to understanding Christian ministry. In fact, the counterattack against the reformers may even have diverted attention from some of the better theological reflection of the time and directed it to less important or even specious issues.

Simply speaking, the Council of Trent set out to remedy a crisis that it considered a disorder. It was seeking to insure that hirelings within and wolves without would no longer threaten the church. To effect this, the council had recourse to as clear and traditional a theology as possible (the scholastic theology and framework), as well as to disciplinary measures. Trent, it has been said, "rethought the sacrament of order to restore order in the church." It did this job so well that for 400 years practically no change took place and, unfortunately, no new response was given to the new challenges and questions that society was posing. How did this happen?

Ganoczy feels that the problem lay in Trent's not having a true *theology of the Word*. This would have given it a hermeneutic principle for its teaching on ministry, as well as an ability to continually reinterpret it to meet changing conditions.[28] Protestants stressed *verbum solum*. We did not enter into dialogue with them on this point until Vatican II. Realistically, however, it was perhaps impossible for Trent to do otherwise.

Trent began to consider the sacrament of ordination in December of 1551. Decrees on justification and the sacraments in general had already been issued in 1547, and these issues were not taken up again. In fact, the main issue that underlay many of the discussions was the relation of pope to bishops. This was more a question of power and jurisdiction. The papal position was that only the bishop of Rome was instituted by divine right.

There follow some important aspects of the Tridentine teaching on ministry. We will also mention some of the causes as well as consequences of these positions.[29]

1. *The sacramentality of order*. Trent wanted to draw a clear distinction between the ordained priesthood and the common priesthood. This would have met no objection from reformers like Calvin. But Trent did so by returning to the scholastic theory of an indelible character that makes it impossible to ever become a layperson again. With "reductions to the lay state" a reality in our time, we might look once again to the Protestant idea that the sacrament creates ministers of the Word and not sacrificers. Is ordination an ontological consecration of the priest, or more a deputation to the functional service of the Word in the form of preaching and sacrament?

Two issues are at stake here (and often very confused). There is the distinction between the priesthood possessed by all Christians and that possessed by the ordained. Then there is the question about the nature of priesthood itself. Is it evangelical or sacramental? The tendency at the council was to safeguard the sacramental principle and the preeminence of the ordained clergy by attributing genuine sacramental activity to them alone.

Eck, for example, though he insisted that the priest offered sacrifice "*sicut minister Christianae ecclesiae*," was not thinking of the entire community (i.e., the body of Christ) entering into Christ's own offering of himself to the Father. In fact, he reduces the priesthood of the faithful to a purely spiritual reality, sharply distinguished from the sacramental priesthood of the ordained. Had he argued that Christ, working through the instrumentality of the priestly community that is his body, constantly exercised his priesthood in the eucharistic sacrifice, this more profound understanding would have confronted better the real issues being raised by Luther and others, and be in less danger of separating the church's eucharistic sacrifice from Christ's own sacrifice.

At the time of the council there were some that held this position, e.g., Eck's contemporary Schatzgeyer, (whom Eck himself cites), and Bishop Michael Helding. He held that ordination gives a man the power to function *"in persona Christi,"* thus to offer his sacrifice. But when he does so, he functions as a servant of the entire church, for the celebration is the action of the entire community. Christ's priesthood thus finds expression in the entire church, though with special sacramentality in the ordained minister. Helding was able to admit with Luther the basic importance of the universal priesthood, but he also preserved a genuine sacramental role, not just an evangelical one, for both laity and priests.

A much less conciliatory attitude toward Luther's teaching was taken by Bishop John Fisher. He taught that ordination was of divine origin, gave the ordained a special measure of grace, and clearly set them apart from the laity. They are the rulers; laity are the ruled; they are the tillers of the Lord's field; the laity are the field. Christ himself was anointed by the Spirit to evangelize; only ordained pastors of the church share in this anointing. For him, one can only speak of a priesthood of all believers if one immediately adds that there is a distinctive priesthood and ministry that belongs only to the ordained.

This negative attitude toward the priesthood of all believers is reflected in the fact that council says so very little about it. Trent was trying at all costs to avoid saying that the church was initially congregational, and only later a hierarchical society. The initial structures of the church were always differentiated, according to the council.

2. In regard to the *authority of the priest*, prevailing opinion based it on the power of ordination alone. In other words, the ritual itself conferred authority even apart from personal gifts and charisms. Though the council did insist on basic theological and spiritual competence (and there were many debates on the matter), it did little to provide effective implementation. By this time, however, many Protestants had founded colleges that succeeded very well in preparing ministers for pastoral work. Calvin's Academy was outstanding in this regard.

Unfortunately, the cost factor prevented most council fathers from seeing the deep underlying need. Decrees 13, 14, and 18 were weak requests demanding only a bare minimum of knowledge. Nothing was said about the significance and importance of what was decreed, nor were normative structures set up. The real renewal in training was the work of an active minority after the council.

The council not only did not give extended theological treatment to the sacrament of orders, it focused most of the discussion on episcopal prerogatives, the extent of episcopal superiority over priests, and the dependence or independence of bishops vis-à-vis the papacy as regards jurisdiction. The classic distinction between *potestas ordinis* and *potestas jurisdictionis* was the unchallenged foundation of this lengthy argument. Jurisdiction was a hot issue, some arguing that it came from God, others that it was from the pope.

In 1563 the council took up this issue again, but it could not agree among the conflicting medieval opinions, and did not reach a definitive decision about the precise sacramentality of episcopal office. Somewhere along the line the questions raised by Reformation theology got lost in the power struggle between the papacy and episcopacy—a struggle, incidentally, that threatened to disrupt the council, until a compromise formulation (avoiding the phrase "*de jure divino*" in regard to the origin of episcopal power) was accepted by both sides.[30]

As a result, we were left with a view of ministry based on a model of personal power rather than on pastoral service. But by insisting that jurisdiction was needed for the exercise of that power, the canonists kept alive what was earlier required when the church insisted that ordinations be for a specific community.

In the background of the medieval discussions of priesthood, orders, and jurisdiction, lies the question of sacrament. We are so used to thinking of orders as a sacrament that it comes as somewhat of a surprise to realize that this was not generally accepted as such until the twelfth century. It was first affirmed only at the Council of Florence (1439). The meaning of "sacrament" also underwent a long development. Florence finally defined the sacrament of orders as one that is permanently effective and that imprints a character. Exactly how priests and bishops were related or distinguished was not clearly defined here or at Trent. This would have to wait for Vatican II.

3. The Council accepted the *explicit sacerdotalization of ministry* that was then current. In their haste to condemn Protestant errors, the council fathers did not develop any constructive concern in regard to the distinction between *sacerdotium* and *ministerium*. The *Doctrina de sacramento ordinis* of 1563 makes no reference to the unique sacrifice of Christ (referred to in the 1562 *de Missae sacrificio* as well as in the 1546 *Decretum super lectione et praedicatione*, which tried to define the proper

relationship between preaching and sacrament). No holistic picture of priesthood was attempted beyond defending the power of consecrating and absolving.

Theologically, the beginning of the decree takes it for granted that ministry is to be considered under the notion of priesthood, and that this priesthood/ministry is primarily characterized by its ordination to sacrifice. Nothing is said about the ministry of the Word, except in the jurisdiction framework of canon seven, where it is stated that only those who have been ordained and commissioned by recognized church authorities are legitimate ministers of word and sacraments.

There is no further clarification of the sacrificial role of the priest, neither in the decree of Orders nor in that on the sacrifice of the Mass. One is simply left with the task of drawing out the various implications of the following statements:

•The action of the Mass is truly a propitiatory sacrifice, for Christ himself is the offered and the offerer through the ministry of the ordained priest.

•The ordained priest truly offers the body and blood of Christ, in commemoration and representation of his once-for-all sacrifice on the cross.

•Even when he celebrates Eucharist privately, i.e., with no other Christians sharing in the action, the priest performs an act that is effective of salvation, since he is acting as a public minister of the church.

•Only the ordained possess this priestly character, which distinguishes them intrinsically from the laity.

•What he does in the Eucharist, the priest does in virtue of the power given him in ordination, power that comes from the sacramental character that is permanently impressed on him and remains a source of effective sacramental action even when he lapses from grace.

•Any notion of the common priesthood of the laity that denies the essentially hierarchical structure of the church is to be rejected.

•Only those who have been ordained by proper ecclesiastical authority can legitimately function as ministers of sacrament.

Remember that Trent itself only wanted to express "what had been denied by the Reformation." Besides this admitted one-sidedness, there is a further problem in that Trent did not necessarily have a good idea of what the reformers were really saying. At best, their positions are counter-positions. Thus, for example, in stressing the priests' cultic role because it was being denied by the reformers, the council said nothing about the role of preaching and teaching, as these were hardly being denied. In many ways, too, the church was not attempting to canonize any particular structure, as much as insist that it had a right to define its own church order.[31]

4. *The principle of functionality*. The reformers never ceased to castigate the Roman practice of conferring an order on someone who would never exercise it, either because he was incapable or because the order no longer corresponded to a real ministry (e.g., the minor orders). Though some of the council fathers made suggestions for reform here, Trent did nothing except declare the minor orders to be stages on the ascent to priesthood. A good theology of the Word would have allowed them to drop those that had become obsolete and add new ones to meet needs, just as the early church had done.

Another aspect of functionality was expressed at the council: the intention of the minister in the exercise of his mission. On this point Trent claimed that the action of the church is more important than the intellectual or moral quality of the agent. Whether saint or sinner, the priest acts in the name of God and the church as long as he is serious about the purpose of his actions. In this case, the sanctifying value of the Word makes up for individual differences, or for any individualism that is harmful to true community.

Moreover, the council was able to take disciplinary steps to make the clergy better witnesses of God's grace. In terms of bishops, the most important thing legislated was in regard to *residence*. Bishops were to reside in their proper dioceses, and the accumulation of more than one benefice was forbidden. Penalties were invoked against those who neglected their people, including loss of benefice. It was also decreed that when they were given episcopal jurisdiction, they had to be ordained within three months or forfeit their benefice (10-20 years delay was not unknown at this time!). The bishop was also to conduct parish visitations, have a diocesan synod every year, preach regularly, and insure the quality of preaching in his diocese.

Regarding priests, the same requirement of residence was insisted on. They were not to be absent more than two months a year. Rules were made to eliminate the *vagi* (wandering priests). Seminaries were also decided on, though they were neither mandated nor funded. Examinations were to be given before promotion to orders or being allowed to hear confessions. Diocesan priests were also put into soutanas at this time (religious already wore the habit as a matter or course).

5. The council did tackle a *theology of the Word*, to some extent, though its record is mixed. In 1546 it issued the *Decretum super lectione et praedicatione*, which tried to define the proper relationship between preaching and sacrament. The council followed the Thomist tradition, whereby the Eucharist forms the center of priestly activity, and preaching is only a remote preparation for this.

Prior to the council there was pressure to upgrade the importance of the Word and the fundamental place of the Scriptures in the life of the church. Not only the Protestants, but the Council of Cologne (1536) decreed that every administration of the sacraments should be accompanied by preaching. (Trent eventually incorporated this requirement in 1563. But the stress given this by the Protestants prevented it from really taking root.)

A considerable number of fathers had reservations about the priority of preaching. It seemed too Protestant! The 1546 decree was eventually given a juridical cast, and penalties were threatened to those who neglected the sacred books. The whole matter was put in terms of handing on everything one has to know in order to be saved. The one decisive result was that the preaching of the gospel was made the *primary* function of bishops.

Unfortunately, subsequent work at the council was marked by a series of retreats on this point. Some were more interested in condemning the Lutheran teaching that ministry consists *only* of the power of preaching than they were in recalling the duty of bishops (and priests) to preach and teach. For fear of appearing too Protestant, the council refused to develop the dogmatic content of its disciplinary decree of 1546.

Indirectly, at least, these retreats had two consequences: a lack of clarity on the triple ministry of bishops (teaching, sacraments, discipline), and an excessive sacerdotalization of the ministry of priests.

6. *Exeunt the laity*. Lacking a deep theology of the Word, the council did not understand the church as a people of God gathered together. The layperson is seen more as a non-cleric. The priest is not seen as arising from or representing the people but rather as descending into them. There is no mention of gifts and charismata that fit one for ministry.

The extent of mention given the laity at the council was to oblige them to Mass on Sundays and days of obligation. Dueling was forbidden, and the minimum age for marriage fixed. Should we be surprised that no single session of this long council was devoted to the laity? No picture was sketched of what the faithful Christian, inspired by the spirit of Trent, should be like. Perhaps it was felt that the catechism of the council would provide the laity with all the necessary rules and answers that they needed in order to be saved.

The understanding of laity at this time was still largely negative, and theirs was a passive role in the church. It was considered that they would be holy if their priests were holy. But none of the requests of the Protestants—for example, giving the people the chalice, reciting the Eucharistic Prayer out loud, the vernacular—were granted.[32] The sacraments, remember, worked *ex opere operato*!

Summary

1. On the ministerial level, the most visible and serious attack made by the Protestants against the structures of Catholic ministry was to deny the cultic nature of the ministry. They did this by using a well accepted scholastic distinction between the cultic and ministerial functions of the ministry, and putting all the emphasis on the latter. This was both an attack on ministry and a theological statement about the nature of the Eucharist. They did not see how it could be a sacrifice because of the statements in Hebrews about Jesus' sacrifice being "once for all." But their logic extended also to those who ministered the Eucharist.

2. The Protestant emphasis was an effort to root ministry once more in the church. Hence, they deplored ordaining people to non-existent ministries, or in seeing ordinations as empowering people "absolutely." Those whom they chose as ministers were deputed by the community for the community, and derived their priestly "powers" from baptism—the common priesthood of all believers. Calvinists, however, saw priestly power as coming from God, not the community.

3. The Protestants denied any indelible character given a person at ordination, rejected clerical celibacy, and exalted the notion of the common priesthood of all the baptized. There were also psychological roots to this. The reformers wanted to break down the class distinction between clergy and laity, and to remove from it all the developments or accretions that could not be shown to be required by the New Testament. They also wanted to make the laity active members of the church once more.

4. Both Catholics and Protestants appealed to the authority of Scripture. Protestants tended to read it in terms of reproducing or renewing structures found in the New Testament. Catholics tended to use it to justify the developments found in the current hierarchical arrangement of the church. On the one hand we have authoritarian popes, called "the whore of Babylon" by some Protestants. On the other, we have the

Protestant minister going about in a business suit and a severe de-emphasis on form and ceremony. No one found the middle road!

5. Luther's denial of any essential difference between clergy and laity did not lead to his denying the need for a special ministerial group within the church. He did not feel that any individual could take it upon himself to do this, either. He had to be called by God, a call mediated by those responsible for the community. (In case of need, however, anyone else could fill in.) Although he stressed the importance of preaching the Word, he also emphasized the importance of the sacrament of the Eucharist. The distinguishing feature here is that he saw it as a *ministerial* and not a *sacrificial* reality.

Luther insisted that two elements were required to have an authentic Christian community: genuine preaching of the Word, and authentic celebration of the sacrament. He taught that the main function of the ordained is the pastoral preaching of the gospel, to which is linked administration of the sacraments. These were the primary vehicles mediating God's free gift of grace.

6. Calvin's position was more subtle than Luther's in terms of the nature of the Eucharist and the ministry. Key to understanding his thought is the action of the Holy Spirit. The effectiveness of the ministry lies not in the fact that it comes from an approved office-holder (the grace of state), but from the fact that he acts as a mediator of God's word and Spirit.

7. The main problem with Trent (this view comes essentially from hindsight) is that while it made no effort to give a complete theology of the sacraments, wanting only to answer the objections raised by the reformers, their positions have determined the emphasis in our theology to this day. Trent did not understand or really face the basic issues the Protestants were bringing up. The canonical mentality, the issues of power, etc., prevented the council fathers from giving an in-depth analysis to the underlying theological issues about the nature of the church, soteriology, and the sacramental system itself.

8. In wanting to emphasize that there was a distinction between the common priesthood of all baptized and the ordained priesthood, the council felt that it was necessary to defend the reality of the sacramental character. The character grounded this solidly, it was felt. Fortunately, the council did not define what this character was. But they did want to state that we are dealing with something real here; they stated this in terms of a real change that bestows powers that guarantee the effectiveness of the priest's ministry.

9. The cultic and sacrificial nature of priesthood—what we have called sacerdotalization—was hardened by this council. Jesus' own

ministry as the source of all ministry was never mentioned or used as a basis of understanding the priestly role. This effectively put the emphasis on the priest's cultic role as worship leader, and tended to downplay the ministerial role and the real importance of the ministry of God's word. In fact, scriptural studies went into decline after this, to recover only after Vatican II.

10. Putting the emphasis on the powers of consecration and the power to forgive sins resulted in three things that have hurt the church over the years. First of all, it deepened and perpetuated the split between clergy and laity, between the sacred and the profane. Second, by focusing on personal power inherent in having received the special character of ordination, the sacrament itself loses its ecclesiological basis. Instead of being rooted deeply in the church, it resides in the person of the ordained. Third, absolutizing the powers of the priest also ignores pneumatology. Sanctification in the church does not happen by magic, however. Trent was unable to show us how these three are related to each other.

11. The council did make provisions for the moral reform of the clergy, from the pope on down. Only exhortations were given the pope, but there were legal requirements laid on the cardinals, bishops, and priests to help make their lives a better witness of Christian values. The council also encouraged seminaries, which did more than anything else to standardize the training of priests around the world, and to considerably upgrade the competence of the presbyterate into modern times.

12. Exemplary lives were asked of priests and bishops. "Example" here meant good ethical behavior, especially in sexual matters. Since mandatory celibacy in the twelfth century, this was treated as the touchstone of clerical morality. Because there had been no really careful theological grounding for the discipline of celibacy, there were many violations of it. The French School would later try to remedy this.

13. The relationship between bishops and pope was not resolved. With the council refusing to say that their authority came from God, bishops were made to seem dependent on the pope, and collegiality was again weakened. Vatican II tried to solve this.

14. The laity fared poorly at this council. They were still regarded as passive members of the church. Because of its espousal by Luther, the council never explored the ramifications of the universal priesthood. The people were at the bottom of the feudal order and they were treated like little children needing to be protected by the leaders of the church against heretical ideas by proper catechisms, the Index of Forbidden Books, even the Inquisition, so that they might "save their souls."

Discussion Questions

1. From the knowledge we have now, how could the split between Catholic and Protestant have been avoided in terms of the theological issues? the practical questions?

2. How can the theology of the sacramental "character" be explained in such a way as to be acceptable to all?

3. What basic Protestant positions have proven correct in the light of Vatican II and current practice? On what other disciplinary issues might they prove prophetic? How? and Why?

4. Is the cultic understanding of priesthood really essential to Catholic theology? Can it be explained in such a way as to be acceptable to our separated brethren?

5. List what you consider to be the three most serious issues at the time of the Protestant Reformation. Justify your answer with reference to both history and Catholic tradition.

Suggested Readings

Fisher, L. "Another Look at Luther's Doctrine of the Ministry," *The Lutheran Quarterly*, 18 (1966), 260-271.

Ganoczy, A., "'Splendours and Miseries' of the Tridentine Doctrine on Ministries," *Concilium* 10 (1972), 75-86.

Gerrish, B., "Luther on Priesthood and Ministry," *Church History*, 34 (1965), 404-422.

Green, L., "Change in Luther's Doctrine of the Ministry, *The Lutheran Quarterly*, 18 (1966), 173-183.

Legrand, H.-M., "Indelible Character and the Theology of Orders," *Concilium*, 74 (1972), 54-62.

Lindbeck, G., "The Lutheran Doctrine of the Ministry: Catholic and Reformed," *Theological Studies*, 30 (1969), 588-612.

Osborne, K., "Ministry in the Theology of the Reformers," *Priesthood*, Chap. 8, pp. 161-194.

_____. "The Sacrament of Order and the Council of Trent," *Priesthood*, Chap. 9, pp. 248-278.

Reumann, J., "The Doctrine of Ministry in the Confessions," *The Lutheran Quarterly*, 15 (1963), 118-129.

_____, "Ordained Minister and Layman in Lutheranism," *Eucharist and Ministry*, from *Lutherans and Catholics in Dialogue*, vol. IV, pp. 227-282.

_____, "Ordained Minister and Layman in Lutheranism," *Eucharist and Ministry*, New York: U.S. National Committee of the Lutheran World Federation, 1970, pp. 228ff.

8

Ministry as Cult

Following the Council of Trent, the church went through a profound renewal and change that has lasted down to our day. Unfortunately, the theology of that council had been defensive and apologetic, and its positions were to be repeated over and over again against the Protestants. It was a time of orthodoxy and suspicion of innovations ("modernism" was considered a heresy). Ecumenism was a bad word.

That Trent was able to accomplish anything at all was due to a number of factors. It benefited from some theological investigations, a great deal of genuine holiness, and painful groping on the part of many. Without that council the church could never have reformed itself to the extent that it did. In a church as centralized as ours, renewal has a difficult time affecting the entire body solely on the strength of initiatives from below. The hierarchy and pope have to support it.

This chapter looks at the period between the Council of Trent and Vatican Council II. The great missionary efforts throughout the world that took place in this period testify to a depth of faith and zeal throughout the church. At the same time, on the world stage despite (or perhaps, because of) the reforms instituted by Trent, it was a period when the church became increasingly turned in on itself and irrelevant in the world.

The Reformation had left Christianity totally fractured. This meant not only the church, but the fabric of society itself. The synthesis of the Middle Ages, with its union of church and state, would never again be possible. But its ideal tended to dominate the minds of most church-men, so that the Enlightenment and the new political realities ushered in by the American and French revolutions were either misunderstood or opposed by a church that found itself with little new to say to the world. In the nineteenth century, the church of Pius IX condemned practically every development in the previous 300 years.

It was an age when European Christendom was racked by wars of religion that went on for decades, offering the scandalous spectacle of religious division and naked ambition painted in blood and tears. The church, which so often presented itself to humanity only with its dog-mas and stern moral code, inevitably ran up against either the knife of public criticism or polite scorn, but tended to focus only inward.

The Counter-Reformation organized ministry along the lines of what O'Meara calls a baroque papacy and spirituality, along with a romanti-cization of the ministry and an exaltation of cult in the nineteenth cen-tury. As a player on the world scene, however, the church exhibited little real understanding of the profound changes that were affecting humanity in the West. It consequently had little influence on the vari-ous movements that have gone to make up the modern world.

Ecclesially, the efforts to marshal forces against Protestantism led the church to speak with one voice (usually that of the pope) during the Counter-Reformation. This thrust collegiality into an obscurity from which it took four centuries to emerge. After Trent the church was gov-erned in a more and more autocratic fashion. The expanded system of nunciatures, which exercised a supervisory role over bishops, promot-ed curial directives and stifled innovation. A mystique of authority per-meated the church. This mystique may be characterized as the notion of a complete identification of the will of God with institutionalized au-thority; in the latter it is God's voice we hear and heed. The papacy benefited from this. As Congar put it:

> The pope is really the *episcopus universalis*. Each individual Catho-lic has a more immediate relationship with him than with his own bishop, as far as the general pattern of his life is concerned. The encyclicals tell him what he should think, the liturgy is regulated by Roman documents, as are also fasting, canonical preparation for marriage, the Ratio Studiorum for seminaries and canonically erected faculties. The saints we venerate are those canonized by Rome; religious congregations ask Rome for the authorization of their rule....Rome intervenes directly in the question of adapting apostolic methods to the needs of the times. She keeps a sharp eye

on publications, books, reviews, even catechisms and, on occasion, orders their suppression. In short, the exercise of authority in the modern Catholic church is largely that of its central and supreme seat in Rome.[1]

The Tridentine Church

From fragile beginnings and uncertain hopes, the Counter-Reformation became a major force in the church, shaping the worldview of its members. During this period the theology of ministry had two main poles: the organization of church life in detail around the papacy, and the designation of the interior life of grace as the basic object of Christian ministry. The purpose of life was to save one's soul, and the priest was there to show one how to do it. The focus on worship and prayer was a definite improvement on the past and helped recapture a sense of the sacred.

That Catholicism could renew itself at all is a tribute to the power and action of the Holy Spirit. Despite the limitations of Trent, we can point to the lives of thousands of people caught up in a new spirituality and missionary spirit. Protestant spiritualities tended to keep God and humanity apart and were not attractive to a Catholic mind geared to sacramentality. Mediterranean cultures, especially, found Protestantism's sober secularity unappealing. The inwardness and Catholic style and spirituality that resulted has been called "baroque." We developed and embellished our own fortress.

Intent upon renewal, the fortress church took organization seriously. The church would be an expression of the body of Christ, but seen as a rational, efficient "perfect society" centered in the Vatican. Just as medieval theology introduced the idea of the pope as vicar not only of Peter but also of Christ, and therefore head of the church, this period increased the centralization in Rome with a whole set of curial offices for evangelism, religious orders, seminaries, etc. The ministries of the local churches were to be well guided and controlled.[2]

Protestantism, with its emphasis on charisms and its fairly independent churches, seemed not only divisive but schismatic. The Tridentine answer was to look for pastoral bishops and a regime where Rome was the center and summit. The liturgy was frozen and local variations were discouraged. The Roman curia was the basic organizing principle, and found diversity in new religious orders and curial offices, not in ministries. It is no surprise that the many new religious orders founded during this period took as their purpose some precise work of the church, not monastic contemplation or the general goal of the friars.

The new emphasis in religious orders on personal conversion and method in prayer led many to ministry through the religious life. For most people, being holy meant joining a religious congregation. Francis de Sales is perhaps the only one at this time who provided a means of holiness in the world that was not a watered-down version of the religious life (a form of monasticization). The secular priesthood was brought under control by the introduction of seminaries and the spirituality of the French school, where the priest was formed in a perennial theology and spiritual lifestyle.

In many ways the task Rome set itself was an impossible one: to incarnate itself in hundreds of cultures. The weight of cultural incarnation was avoided, however, by clothing the gospel in a single "universal" language, law, and theology—that of Rome. In the fourth to the ninth centuries the world was evangelized through local churches with their admirable bishops. In this period, the faith was propagated by the clergy as an extension of Rome.

There were successes as well as tragedies in this approach. In 1614 there were 300,000 Catholics in Japan, but fewer than 100 native priests. Celibacy and other requirements saw to this. Thus, when persecution came, it easily eliminated the ministry and most of the church with it. China was also a flourishing mission, but was almost completely eliminated by squabbles between the nations and religious orders, which Rome solved by forbidding the use of the Chinese rites.

During this time the outer world was evaluated as being secular and pagan. It was seen as a place of darkness, dominated by Calvinism or the Enlightenment. It was evil and the realm of Satan. Grace was seen not as a service to this world and a force to build God's reign, but as an aid to the interior life. The spiritual was separated from the public, the believer from the secular citizen. The fulfillment of baptism was not ministry to God's reign, but an inner call to save one's soul by persevering in a life of prayer.

If monastic schools influenced the education of priests and bishops in the Middle Ages, now the task was performed by the Jesuits, whose educational expertise was widely admired and copied by the numerous religious orders that were patterned after their active style.

A secondary influence was that bishops began to comport themselves toward their fellow Christians in the ministry much like a Jesuit superior. The Jesuit rector had far more control over his subjects than the abbot or prior, and their theology of obedience tended to identify the superior's will with the will of God. In this ecclesiastical atmosphere, a Christian exercising a charism or ministry had no rights, no question, no insight or appeal. This transformation of the bishop from one who coordinated the ministries of the diocese into an authoritarian superior is the final stage of episcopalization.

Authority did not stop at diocesan boundaries; with the ultramontane movement of these years, it ended in Rome. In the nineteenth century, Rome (and most of the church in general) tended to conservatism. In 1864, in his "Syllabus of Errors," Pope Pius IX condemned most of the prevailing movements of the day, from the liceity of withdrawing obedience from unjust rulers to "liberalism, progress, and recent civilization." By the time of Vatican I and its definition of papal infallibility, the idea was firmly planted that the church was a monarchy, and that this structure came from Christ himself.

The church of these centuries saw itself as embattled and on the defensive. Its efforts to maintain the purity of the gospel, however, were not always enlightened or helpful. From the Inquisition to the campaign against modernism at the beginning of the twentieth century, great fear and prudence were engendered; by the time of Vatican II the church was far behind most of the Protestants in scriptural and historical understanding.

This look at post-Tridentine trends may seem one-sided. There is no desire to minimize the many good things that happened during this period—for example, the rise of many religious orders, especially those of women. The fact remains, however, that the individualistic piety of the time did not equip Catholics to influence or change the world. The church was unable to challenge either the hostility or the impersonality of the secular state. It did not lead to a Christian politics with insights into the nature of socialization, or of war, at a time when these were desperately needed.

At the beginning of the Italian state, for example, any Catholic voting in elections was excommunicated. Statesmanship was left to masons and free-thinkers. Catholics became a fortress church, one that added little to the major trends that have shaped modern society. It took Vatican Council II to take the world seriously and begin the dialogue that made them better able to read the signs of the times.

Characteristics of Post-Tridentine Theology

Despite the complexity, it is possible to point to certain basic approaches to ministry and priesthood that followed Trent, approaches that still control Catholic theology and practice to a large extent.

During the immediate post-Reformation period, Catholicism saw the Reformation, rather than modern rationalism, as the enemy. Theology in this time of religious wars was polemic. As regards priesthood, the church contented itself with using texts from St. Thomas to buttress the statements of Trent. But Trent had based itself largely on the previous Council of Florence, especially its Decree for the Armenians, which was itself based on Thomas's *Opusculum de fidei articulis et septem sacramentis*. Relatively little new was added. In fact, the main developments came not so much from formal theology, as from the various schools of spirituality.

All too often Protestantism drove Catholics not to new depths of understanding, but to the unprofitable tendency to seek justification for perpetuating practices and viewpoints of the past. Thus, for example, the French School hung on to the clericalized notion of priesthood and simply emphasized the need for holiness in the ordained and the value of reciting the breviary and celebrating Mass; in other words, glorifying and enhancing the lofty dignity of the clerical state.

Another trend saw the emphasis on jurisdiction further developed in the ecclesiologies of a Bellarmine or Suarez. An important extension of this came in the seventeenth century in F. Hallier's treatise, *De sacris electionibus et ordinationibus, ex antiquo et novo Ecclesiae usu*. Here great stress was placed on the legal and canonical aspects of the sacrament of orders.

In the long run, the false presuppositions accepted by both Catholics and Protestants as the basis for their dispute did more harm to Catholicism than did the desire to defend what the Reformation attacked. In the matter of the ministry and priesthood, there were two crucial areas of false problematic: the sacrificial character of the Eucharist and the nature of sacramental causality. Neither Protestants nor Catholics questioned the simple identification of Christ's sacrifice with his death on Calvary. The resultant identification of sacrifice with some form of giving up or immolation caused everyone problems. The Protestant solution was to deny the sacrificial character of the Mass. Meanwhile, Catholic theologians devoted their efforts to devising various theories of mystic oblation or unbloody sacrifice.

Obviously, such views affected the idea one had of the minister's role in Christian worship. For Catholics, the effort to explain how the priest at the consecration was an instrument of symbolic immolation pushed any study of the evangelical, prophetic, or personally charismatic elements of his functions into the background. Linked with this were philosophical presuppositions about the nature and effectiveness of sacraments. Instead of picking up some of the more profound twelfth- and thirteenth-century probings into the functioning of symbols, the effort was made to explain causality as either physical (thus classifying priests as instrumental causes) or moral (linking the effectiveness of the priesthood to legalistic theories of extrinsic denomination).

Continuation of these lines of thought into modern times cut off the consideration of faith's role in sacraments, and hindered a genuine understanding of sacramental symbolism. The result was a false opposition between evangelical and sacramental approaches to Eucharist and its ministry. This period left the basic question about the nature of Christ's own priestly ministry—and, therefore, the resultant questions about ordained ministry within the church—unresolved.

It might be worthwhile to mention three of the key theologians of the Counter-Reformation whose formulations have influenced the long line of texts that were used in the seminaries. Until Vatican II, there had been little change in these areas. These Tridentine men have provided the basic methods, the essential content, and the common arguments that characterized discussion for centuries.

Thomas Stapleton (d. 1598)

Contemporary with Trent, Stapleton was an Englishman who spent most of his life in exile in the Low Countries. He correctly saw the issue of justification as being at the root of the controversies between Protestants and Catholics. What Stapleton contributed to continuing polemics was his insistence on the illegitimacy of ordinations in the Protestant churches because they lacked true apostolic succession. He also stressed the illegitimacy of their teaching, since they have not been properly sent by Christ through succession from the apostles. This extends to sacramental acts as well.

Not surprisingly, Stapleton sees *potestas ordinis* and *potestas jurisdictionis* as being very closely linked; indeed, they are two aspects of one office. For him an ordained minister's activity is effective if and because he is authorized. In this regard he saw the reformers' opposition to the Catholics as being not a choice *for* the Scriptures, but one *against* the teaching authority of Rome. Because they have rejected the authority of the true church of Christ, neither their teaching nor their other ministerial acts can bear true witness to Christ.

Robert Bellarmine (d. 1621)

Though his role is both praised and criticized, there is no doubt that Bellarmine was the most influential theologian in the latter part of the sixteenth century. He especially influenced views on *de ecclesia*, and his understanding of priesthood and ministry became the model for the Catholic view on priesthood for the next three centuries. His work is characterized by laudatory use of Scripture and early church tradition, as he attempted to meet the Protestant reformers on their own ground. Church practice in his time was presented as the true interpretation of New Testament data.

Following the common understanding of his day, he identifies the "order" with the ordination ceremony and gives numerous scriptural "proofs" that it is a sacrament. The ministry to which ordination is directed is sacramental; the power that is given the ordinand is *potestas conficiendi et ministrandi sacramenta*. He identifies the power of ordination with the character (he is generally Thomistic), but does not see it as an intrinsic modification, a power to act. Rather, he views it as a covenanted assurance of God's concurrent activity in sacramental actions.

Bellarmine makes his own the view of Hugh of St. Victor that priesthood has two grades: presbyter and bishop. The bishop is the *summus sacerdos*, or the *primus sacerdos*. Their sacramental character is said to be greater "extensively" than that of priests. Interestingly, he states that if the episcopacy were to be conferred on someone who had not been previously ordained priest, ordination to episcopacy directly would also contain ordination to priesthood (unlike the situation in Hildebrand's time).

Conscious that denial of the character was a cardinal trait of the reformers, Bellarmine insisted that ordination conferred a spiritual power that permanently distinguished the ordained from the laity. Ministry is, therefore, more than a simple function that can be given one day and taken away the next. From a practical point of view, he also insisted that the priest is to function *humanly*; he is not to multiply mechanical sacramental signs working with some sort of *ex opere operato* impersonal force. Nor is his role as agent of Christ and of the church one of rigidly performing an external rite.

Francis Suarez (d. 1617)
When reading Bellarmine, one gets the impression that he was on the verge of discovering what we now call the ecclesial dimension of the sacraments. Suarez, who was a contemporary and fellow Jesuit, represents the world of Spanish theology (as opposed to Rome and Louvain), and has quite a different spirit. There is a strong influence coming from political models of thought. His is a law and order mentality. All structures of reality are ontologically monarchical; all truth and life and grace come down to us in a chain of causes from the top.

As applied to priesthood, Suarez relates it to Christ, for he is mediator of all created reality and all grace by reason of his high priesthood. Suarez follows Aquinas's treatment of Christ's priesthood, and places almost exclusive emphasis on the notion of offering sacrifice. He also stresses the identity of the sacrifice of the cross and Christ's sacrificial offering in the Eucharist. But Suarez then shifts his attention to the *monarchical* power of the high priesthood, and ends with the statement that royal dignity and power belong to the very notion of priesthood, at least as this is found in Christ's priesthood and in his vicar on earth.

Suarez sees only the pope as entering fully into this possession of monarchical spiritual authority; this perspective definitely controls his notion of how other ordained ministers function. The ordained offer sacrifice as ministers of Christ, through his power, and in terms of applying the merits of Christ's sacrifice to those who need it. The primary role of the priest is to worship God by offering sacrifice in the name of the whole people. Second, he must prepare and lead the faithful to worship God and to save their souls. He does this by teaching, governing, and judging.

In the Eucharist, Christ himself is the principal agent. The ordained person acts *in persona Christi*. Because he alone possesses the sacramental character of ordination, only the priest has the power to consecrate and offer sacrifice. If one understands it correctly, one may call the entire people priestly and say that they all offer sacrifice. This means that the priest acts officially and publicly in their name; it is presumed that each Christian joins his own intention to that of the celebrant who represents him. A layperson can increase his participation by intensifying his own interior consent to the act (or by giving a stipend), but this does not mean that he or she becomes an immediate principal in the sacrificial action, something reserved to the priest.

Spirituality of the Counter-Reformation

The spiritual leaders of the Counter-Reformation without exception turned back zealously to the sacramental system that the Reformation had done so much to undermine. They stressed more frequent confession and communion for devout laity, and the ideal of a daily celebration of Mass for priests eventually also became the common wisdom. Along with this came the insistence on regular examination of conscience and meditation, and the science of spiritual combat.

Confession, for example, held an entirely different place in Catholic religious life in 1650 than it did in 1400. The same is true for eucharistic practice. The Middle Ages may have adored the host at Mass, but paid little attention to it outside of it. It was surely not the center of devotions. Benediction, Forty Hours, visits to the Blessed Sacrament, however, are very much a Counter-Reformation phenomenon. Forty Hours, for example, first began in Milan in 1527 to invoke divine aid during a time of plague, but afterward achieved popularity as it got caught up in the growth of devotion to the Blessed Sacrament that is a feature of modern Catholicism.

Frequent communion was the rule, not the exception at first. From the beginning, for example, Jesuit scholastics were counseled to communicate two or three times weekly; this was probably the norm for unordained clerics in the mid-sixteenth century. Laypeople might be restricted to once a month, or perhaps weekly. This lessened later in the seventeenth century under the influence of Jansenism, but it retained its mystique and importance. It can be said that the three poles on which Tridentine piety rested were: a revival of sacramental life, the spread and development of eucharistic devotions and techniques of mental prayer, and an urge to good works and outward activity as a factor in personal sanctification.

The parishes had the Sunday Mass and sacramental life as their framework. Regular catechism was added, based especially on the catechism of the council. Parish missions were also used to great effect to deepen the religious life of the common people, especially under new congregations like the Oratorians and Vincentians. St. John Baptist de la Salle set up a number of schools for poor children, and his congregation pioneered a new way of life: dedication without priesthood. The Ursulines and others extended education for girls. Religious education was a priority of many.

This spirituality had distinctive traits. Broadly speaking, its genius stressed individual rather than corporate or liturgical expression. It was not biblical (in the Protestant sense of basing oneself on the direct reading of the Word of God). The humanity of Christ became the object of increased veneration, and there was a heroic effort at self-control, self-improvement, and good works. There was also a much greater concentration on apostolate than on contemplation (witness the rise of the active orders typified by the Jesuits). Camillus de Lellis, for example, required his clerks regular to take a fourth vow: to serve the sick and plague-ridden (and in Naples in 1657, 96 out of 100 of his priests died of the plague!).

Indeed, the sixteenth and seventeenth centuries saw the emergence of many Christian heroes. From Ignatius, Charles Borromeo, and Vincent de Paul, to Jane de Chantal leaving her children to enter religious life, a whole generation was aflame for mortification, the rejection of the world, and the rigors of the spiritual life. St. Teresa gave a lasting impulse to contemplation, but not without, as John of the Cross reminded us, stifling in herself all appetite for what is not God. Thousands entered the religious life during this period, and many thousands went to the missions of Asia or the Americas. It was a time of deep personal love of Jesus; the devotion to the Sacred Heart is but one example.

The one religious congregation that typified all that was new about the post-Tridentine church, however, was the Company of Jesus. It is difficult for us to imagine today how revolutionary—how modernist— the institution of the Jesuits must have appeared in 1540. The abandonment of the common recitation of the Office seemed so heretical to many that the popes twice forced them to put it into their rule. For the Jesuits, however, community prayers were kept at a minimum, as were liturgical functions. Action was prayer, and prayer led to action. This worked, incidentally, because the spirituality of the Jesuit was intensely personal. All the "traditional" asceticisms were also frowned on. Jesuits were encouraged not to mortify their bodies to excess by fasting, scourging, or denial of sleep so that their studies or work on behalf of others be not impeded. They were to embody the spirit and strength of the Counter-Reformation. They had enormous influence on other orders, and on the approach that was taken to church life during this era.

The French School

One of the most important influences in the reform of the clergy following the Council of Trent originated in France during the seventeenth century. Thanks to the work of men like Cardinal Pierre de Berulle and Jean-Jacques Olier, a phenomenon known as the French School shaped priestly self-understanding. Having spread to other countries because of groups like the Oratory, Saint Sulpice, and the Vincentians, their influence touches us yet. Their understanding of the priest forms the background of all clerical literature down to Vatican II.

Berulle, founder of the French School of spirituality, was the moving spirit behind many seventeenth-century efforts to foster the sanctity of the diocesan clergy. He did this by stressing an exalted notion of the priestly office. Some of his disciples—Vincent de Paul, Jean-Jacques Olier, and Jean Eudes—founded communities of priests that have been in the forefront of seminary education for the past three centuries. Hence their views have had tremendous historical influence.

Some of the seminal ideas used by Berulle were formulated earlier by Josse Clichtove (d. 1543). His own deep spirituality in a decidedly unspiritual age, combined with his biblical, patristic, and medieval ideas, led him to see the priest as being detached from the world (even the world of Christian laity). This notion of being taken out of the world completely determined his image of the priest. Levitical laws of purity, along with celibacy and monastic ideals, all figured in because priesthood was defined essentially by its relationship to cult (and not with the community); the priest was set apart entirely for this.

Clichtove was concerned to work out a special priestly spirituality for the large number of ordained at the beginning of the century who had not been given any pastoral responsibility. The basis of this was the priestly "grace of state." Priesthood is less an office than a state of life, grounded in cultic activity. His desire to reform the clergy, unfortunately, rested on very narrow theological grounds. Clichtove's importance is that his views influenced the fathers at Trent as well as French School spirituality. The ideal of the priest as solitary sayer of Masses owes much to him.

In Berulle's view, priesthood had two objectives: to worship God, and to produce Christ in souls. Thus, cult and spiritual direction play a dominant role in priestly ministry. Their understanding of these two functions is controlled by their worldview, a view that focuses primarily on the Incarnation, and specifically on the priestly aspect of God becoming man (a view grounded in the Pseudo-Dionysian view of a world and church ordered in strict hierarchical fashion). All creation exists to manifest and pay witness to the grandeur of God; in this process Christ is *the* mediator. He is the unique adorer of the Father, the great sacrament of religion.

Thus, the mysteries of Christ's life must become the object of meditation and interior imitation. This finds paramount expression in the mysteries of the liturgical cycle. And, since Jesus' own mission as unique mediator and adorer of the Father came to focus in his redeeming sacrifice, the self-immolation of Jesus continues in the eucharistic action in which he continues to empty himself for the sake of his Father and all humankind.

Berulle's understanding of sacrifice is central to his notion of Christian spirituality as well as ordained ministry, since the ordained are to live out the Christian ideal of life in superior fashion. Christ's own adoration of the Father, especially his act of sacrifice, consists in utter self-emptying. This is the essence of his priestly function of worship. So, also, are priests to act: to be living sacrifices, emptying themselves utterly so that Christ can completely take over in them, letting nothing hinder the work of the Spirit.

This attitude should be especially realized when the priest stands at the altar to celebrate the most sacred of sacrificial actions. In a sense, he is to lose his own identity so that Jesus and the entire church can work though him in offering Christ to the Father. Eucharist and life are one unbroken process of sacrifice, of self-denial in a most radical sense. When one is completely empty of self, Christ can take over and rule the whole course of one's activity by the power of the Holy Spirit.

Though this ideal of sacrifice is to find more perfect expression in the ordained, it is also the basic law of perfection for all Christians. For this reason, the object of a priest's pastoral care is to form Christ in the hearts of people. This he does by spiritual direction, by preaching the gospel, but most of all by his own life of prayer. As St. Gregory the Great said, the care of souls is *ars artium* and it is essentially letting God work through one's ministry. The wisdom connected with this art is no ordinary kind of human knowing, but enlightenment that comes only from prayer.

In this way, the French School developed a refined synthesis of cult and pastoral ministry. One of its good characteristics was to place a contemplative life at the heart of ministerial activity. On the other hand, the theological basis for much of it is suspect, inasmuch as it roots Christ's priesthood in his divinity, rather than his humanity. Through priesthood, then, the ordained share in a very mysterious, highly mystical power. They are other mediators between God and humankind. This could (and did) lead to an exalted view of priesthood somewhat out of line with its origins and purpose.

The ideas of the French School were made a permanent part of the priestly landscape because of the influence of the Sulpicians in the work of seminary formation. They were founded by Jean-Jacques Olier (d. 1657). The influential book *Treatise on Holy Orders* was attributed to him until recently, when it was discovered to have been written by a disciple of his, Pierre Tronson. Tronson has a much more cultic (and less apostolic) view than Olier, and these views were largely responsible for forming the clerical and cultic views of the fortress church.

Olier understood that "the entire missionary life of the church was a true and living sacrament of the universal salvation of Christ." Tronson limited this vision of sacramentality to priests alone and makes of priesthood a sort of religious, cultic state. Likewise, Olier saw mystical life as flowing from baptism for all Christians; Tronson stressed far more the denial aspect of spirituality that was necessary if one wished to enjoy spiritual gifts. This led to an otherworldly (and world-denying) type of attitude. Jansenism would take this to its ultimate conclusions in the next century.

Also, Olier understood the bishop as the fullness of the priesthood, though he explained this in a very mystical way. For him the theology of the bishop is essentially a theology of grace, not of office and jurisdiction. Tronson does not stress this. In a sense, Olier was much closer to the ideas of priesthood of Vatican II; it is a shame that it was Tronson's ideas and not those of Olier that prevailed.

Critique of This Period

The Council of Trent attempted to defend the priesthood by defining what has come to be known as the sacramental character. Most of the subsequent studies on this character have focused on the sacrament of orders, although baptism and confirmation are also included among the sacraments having an indelible character. This paradox shows very well the true nature of the problem. The primary and exclusive preoccupation of Trent was not a thesis of sacramental theology; it was a search for justification of a theology of the priestly office.[3] Let us examine what our theology says on this point.

The notion of a sacramental character is anathema to the Protestants as well as the Eastern churches. These latter have been able to hold to permanency in the ministry without the need of an intrinsic character. Objections are increasingly raised against using the idea of a "character" as the axis for a theology of priesthood even by Catholics, i.e., in the classic sense that what makes a person a priest is some individually possessed power, with no intrinsic reference to any given community.

Over the years the controversy has oscillated between two poles: One begins with the character (ontologism), the other with the community (functionalism). Each one minimizes the other. In recent years theology tends to favor an approach that begins with the priestly, missioned community within which all ministry is exercised. Those favoring this approach tend to minimize or ignore the idea of a character, or to treat it only in terms of the actual *functions* of ministry.

Luther rejected the idea of the character in his *de Captivitate Babylonica* because his first concern was for the community. For him the notion of character, as it was then used, was "the most proficient instrument for consolidating all the deformities introduced into the church...the way by which Christian brotherhood has been lost."[4]

For their part, the defenders of the character did not hesitate to make it fundamental to a truly Catholic understanding of the priesthood (this is something like making limbo the decisive element in baptism). By ignoring the ecclesiological dimension of the problem, many proponents were content to opt for a doctrine that suited their case. Today, many see in the debate the fear that requests for laicization will increase if the character is thrown out—which makes it easy for them to charge the hierarchy with using character as a means of repression.[5]

Since Trent's definition of the existence of a character is the issue here, let us pose two questions:
- What was actually defined?
- Were these definitions of faith?

Vatican II, which reaffirmed the existence of a sacramental character, was only echoing Trent; we have to go there to find out what was intended. Trent's motivation was clear. It wished to counter the Lutheran denial of character, in the belief that it was tantamount to a denial of the belief of the church in the unrepeatablity of ordination.[6] Council documents show that:

1. Trent merely affirmed the existence of a character, as had already been mentioned in the Decree for the Armenians in 1459. It expressly renounced any affirmation as to its nature. In a detailed study, Jean Galot has shown the many contrasting medieval views on this question.[7] The ontological interpretation of the sacramental character was far from unanimous. Others saw it effecting only a relation of reason, or a juridical relationship.

2. Trent avoided going into detail about the connection of the sacrament with the non-repeatability of the character. A first draft explained the character as the reason *why* the sacraments could not be repeated, but they rejected this in favor of a weaker and vaguer *unde*, which was already in the Armenian decree. The council thus wanted to record the practice of non-repetition, or to link the existence of the character with the fact of non-repeatability. It did *not* wish to affirm a consequential link between the impression of a character and the impossibility of a priest becoming a layman again.[8]

3. Trent makes no distinction between the character of order and that of baptism/confirmation. It made no effort whatever to understand the character of orders in functional terms while that of baptism and confirmation would be ontological. This problem is alien to Trent, since it does not exclude the possibility that the character is only a relation of reason.

To sum up: Just as someone who has been confirmed can no longer be considered as never having been confirmed, so one who has been ordained. The ordination produces a permanent result. In connection with this fact (not necessarily *because of* this fact) one cannot be ordained again. This sums up Catholic teaching on the subject. It is quite clear, and very narrow.[9]

Even knowing what the council intended to teach, there still remains the question of whether this is a definition of faith. This depends on how we understand the intention and value of the Tridentine *anathema sit* that closes their definition. Here are the facts:

Trent's intention was to reaffirm the doctrine of the decree for the Armenians. They reproduced this without adding anything to it. This decree itself did not have the value of a doctrinal analysis, since it did not include binding definitions. It has yet to be proven that Trent wished to go beyond this level of affirmation.

The presence of an anathema is *not*, according to the experts, a certain and sure sign of the intention to issue a definition of faith. Decisions of the papal magisterium also confirm this.[10]

The teaching of Trent, therefore, seems to represent an ordinary teaching of the Latin church from the fifteenth to the twentieth centuries. The doctrine of character was unknown in East or West for the first 1000 years, and was never accepted by the Eastern church.

Final conclusion: It is *not* dogma! The church has always taught that only what the church expressly wishes to define can be considered *de fide*.[11]

What can we conclude from this? The dogmatic "content" of character really seems too inadequate to serve as a valid basis for developing a theology of ministry. Unfortunately, this has been done since the thirteenth century, and especially since Trent. We can summarize the results of such a choice here; it was both the result and the cause of the rupture between ministry and the community.[12]

1. Since the notion of character focused attention on the person of the minister, it made it more difficult to see the *object* of the ministry. When we begin with the notion of character, we no longer stress *ministry* as service to God's people, but put the emphasis on a theology of cult: that is, on the priest as the one who is personally empowered to offer the Eucharist. This perspective, which goes along with absolute ordinations and private Masses, puts the person of the priest at the forefront of consideration, to the detriment of ministry itself.[13]

Serious imbalances can result from this—and have. The ecclesiological determinations of presbyteral ministry are replaced by the "ontological" qualifications of the priest. The indelibility of the character reinforces this removal of ministry from its proper location. Consequently, the person of the minister becomes more determinative than the choice of the community or the charism of the Spirit.[14]

We know how much the question of the permanence of ministry depends on this mentality. If the will of the ordinand counts for more than the will of the community and the action of the Holy Spirit, it is clear that priests will leave the ministry for reasons other than unsuitability. The idea of ordination for a limited time derives from the same mentality. And it runs the risk of delaying the urgently required reform of orders.[15]

2. The character has accentuated the difference between clergy and laity. The "character" is used to prove the superiority of the clerical over the lay state. It is also the basis for a special clerical way of life. This has split the unity of the church. It has also made all ministry dependent on the hierarchy.[16]

3. By emphasizing the notion of power, character has devalued that of service. As Joseph Lecuyer says, "All the Thomist theology of order centers on the idea of a transmitted power, and not primarily on that of a gift of the Holy Spirit in view of a particular ministry within the church, as during the patristic period."[17]

We might well ask how a doctrine that is so weak dogmatically has played such a considerable (though often questionable) ecclesiological role through the years. We must also ask if there is any possible resolution of the issue. Perhaps only by interpreting character in the scriptural sense of charism will we be able to satisfy the theological, pastoral, and ecumenical demands that face us today.

The 1971 Synod of Bishops tried to describe the idea behind the character as a charism of the Holy Spirit. It has been described theologically by Pope John Paul II as a participation in "the charism of the Good Shepherd." This is oriented to a pastoral ministry that expresses a self-giving even unto death. It can also be seen as a charism ordered to the unity of the community—a charism operative within the network of human relationships and gifts that constitute the reality of the congregation.

This avoids the reductionist solution of interpreting character to mean only that an ordination took place, which obviously minimizes its implications. Ordination, of course, affects the individual, but how, other than in the form of charism as described in 2 Timothy 1:6? Within this necessarily ecclesiological and pneumatological framework, the charism would seem to be conferred in view of the ministry in the diversity of services that constitute the community. In this way priests would know that their trustworthiness does not depend on them alone; through ordination they have received a lasting gift from God. Isn't this the point of the doctrine of character to which Catholics (and Protestants) are really committed?[18]

General Understanding of Ministry

Let us take a brief look at the church at the end of this period, as it existed before Vatican II. For all practical purposes, this marks the end of
the second millennium regarding the development of ministry. After
the council, the church was set on a new path, with a definite tangent
away from the mentality and practice of Trent.

1. If we examine the church from the point of view of building community, the Tridentine church represents a monumental failure of
Christian ministry. If the primary purpose of ministry is to foster community within the church so that the church can then be an instrument
of unity within the world, the individualism that developed during this
period was counter-productive. Efforts at unity in the world at large
depended on force, either of arms or of the Inquisition. When this
failed, a sort of "tolerance" of the deviants developed. This was due to
political pragmatism more than to religious insight, however. And
within the church, repression of dangerous thought was the main
weapon.

As mentioned already, this period stressed individualism in religious practice. To a certain extent this was good, inasmuch as it made
the person responsible for his or her own religious practice. But by
stressing individual responsibility to such an extent, the community dimension of Christianity was lost. The sacraments became personal
channels of grace for individuals rather than corporate actions of the
Christian community.

Thus, the church saw itself as increasingly beleaguered in a hostile
world and, within the church itself, lost sight of the communitarian nature of Christianity (Vatican II would bring it back with its notion of
the "People of God"). As the catechism of Trent put it, the purpose of
our creation was that each of us "save our souls." This narcissism reduced religion to not breaking commandments and indicated a shocking lack of a sense of social justice. Eucharist was not to make us just,
but to gain grace and give glory to God.

Ecumenism is a case in point. It was only in the twentieth century
that this was given any attention worth speaking of, first among the
Protestants and, eventually, with grudging participation on the part of
Catholics. It really took the council to change our attitude completely in
this regard. It is probably true to say, however, that a good deal of the
impetus for change here came from a deeper understanding of Scripture and a deepening of historical and theological research.

2. As regards the story-telling aspect of Christianity, it would be
easy to stereotype (as for any of these areas). In the seventeenth centu-

ry, after Trent, preaching was taken seriously by both Protestants and Catholics. Vincent de Paul's "Little Method" helped train seminarians for two centuries. And Fenelon's *Dialogues on Eloquence* published in 1717 continued this emphasis in France. Treatises on preaching abounded in the seventeenth century, all advocating a return to a simple and earnest preaching style. The content was usually ethical, however, and Scripture did not form the springboard for understanding; it tended to be used in "proof text" fashion.

Sharing the Word of God in missionary efforts was great from the seventeenth to the twentieth century. Europe (and later America) sent thousands of missionaries to bring the good news of Christ to all the newly discovered areas of the world. The pastoral practice that followed this, however, tended to reflect the country of origin and the increasing centralization of the church.

Schools were extensively used by the church in this period and succeeded in educating generations of Catholics. They served in extending a uniform understanding of church. Perhaps the fear of "modernism" in the early part of this century shows better than anything else the essentially defensive nature of Catholic education. Efforts were made to prevent the changes taking place in society from affecting the church. It took World War II to shock people into realizing how impotent much of our teaching and preaching had become.

Theologians were seen as having the role of defending the teachings of the church (read: hierarchy). They were to demonstrate the truth of the views held by the church and prove false the views of those opposed to the church. No one saw the theologian as having a separate ministry. Even seminary education was a sort of high-level catechetics, a deep indoctrination.

3. Prophesying was one of the weaker aspects of church life in this period. It has been mentioned several times that the church grew inwardly in this period. It was aloof from the great developments of the age. From the condemnation of Galileo, its antagonism to the Enlightenment, its lack of influence during the Industrial Revolution, the bitter struggle between the church and the French Revolution (and others), and the petulance over the loss of the papal states, the church exercised little influence over the development of modern society.

While this was happening, the lack of prophetic spirit and foresight caused the church to lose many of its members. The working class was lost in Europe, and only belatedly did Leo XIII issue *Rerum Novarum*. It remained a dead letter in most places. The church lost the men, especially in Latin countries, and the intellectual class, especially as typified by the scientific community. By the time of the Second Vatican Council, very few countries could boast of having the majority of Catholics active either in the church or in society specifically as Catholic. Catholicism had become privatized and lost its prophetic edge.

4. Nurturing was better attended to in this period. Of course, for most this meant having access to the sacraments. This was done. And in the twentieth century, at least, the corporal works of mercy were a prominent and impressive aspect of Catholic life. Indeed, it is only recently that modern states have begun to provide some of the social services that until now had been provided by various church ministries.

The main criticisms that can be mentioned here (and they have the benefit of hindsight) are that these social services were excessively controlled by the hierarchy, which did not serve to develop a deep social concern among the broad mass of people. Also, in many cases, social programs addressed only the results of societal ills, and made no sustained effort at eliminating the structures that caused the misery in the first place.

It is probably fair to say that most analyses of the church on the eve of the Second Vatican Council would have pointed with pride to the heroic efforts in the field of education, healing, and other social concerns. The very organizational structure of the church made it possible to extend these over the world. If it seemed monolithic at times, it impressed by that very reason, and most Catholics thought there was no better way; this was what God had intended, and they were proud of what their labors had produced.

5. As regards missioning, it can be stated that for the most part the laity had little role to play in the ministry of the church. In the hierarchical mentality that ruled after Trent, the proper role of the laity was seen as obeying the teachings of their duly appointed pastors.

During this period, as regards the papacy, Rome's exercise of ecclesiastical jurisdiction reached unprecedented levels, culminating in Vatican I's definition of infallibility. Ultramontanism also effectively killed local churches in the nineteenth century. The pope emerged as the supreme pastor of the flock, supreme judge, the last court of appeals in all ecclesiastical matters, and subject to the judgment of no one in the church. This was not only embodied in the 1917 Code of Canon Law, but was previously given a dogmatic basis at Vatican I.

As the supreme officeholder within the church, the pope had the authority and responsibility of controlling institutional life at all levels and could pass judgment on any member of the church. This has led to a watchdog mentality, the widespread use of condemnations and silencings to maintain a sometimes questionable orthodoxy. Even though only one use has been made of the infallibility spoken of in Vatican I, an aura of infallibility hovers over most papal pronouncements, which began to be given in practically all areas. This effectively canonized a clearly hierarchical perception of church, where the pope was above the bishops, the bishops above the priests, and the priests above the people.

Correspondingly, the role of bishops had been neglected by Vatican I. (It should be remembered that the council was brought to an early end by the Franco-Prussian War.) The council never got around to discussing the theology of the episcopacy. If episcopacy was not a priestly reality, it served to reduce bishops to delegates of the pope. Despite the seeming ascendancy of some national hierarchies in the seventeenth and eighteenth centuries, the aftermath of the French Revolution considerably weakened the local churches and the general role of bishops in the church. The appointment of nuncios or apostolic delegates to countries served to keep a Vatican watchdog on the scene, and to give to the pope the key power of appointing bishops. This was an almost universal fact by the time of Vatican II.

Vatican I was able to go much further than Trent, which contented itself with insisting on residence, on parish visitations, and on not having multiple benefices. It is interesting that Trent mandated regular synods—a nod, at least, to some form of collegiality. This was not new, however, but went back to the earliest ages of the church. What was new was the erection of seminaries. Not every diocese complied with this requirement, although the vast majority of priests came from seminaries by the twentieth century. In the United States some 90 percent of diocesan priests even came from the *minor* seminary system. What has not been sufficiently examined is the type of education imparted in these seminaries, and why it did not necessarily prepare priests to face the needs of the modern world they were called to serve.

If the authority-power relationship between pope and bishop shifted, so also did that between bishop and *priest*. In general, there was a pattern of increasing episcopal control. Each bishop was a little monarch in his own diocese. By virtue of the promise of obedience given bishops at ordination, compliance with the bishop's demands was made a matter of moral obligation. Because of his need for "faculties" within each diocese, a priest depended on episcopal approval in order to preach or act as sacramental celebrant. Canonical regulations made this even affect the validity of marriages.

Most of the day-to-day conduct of church life was controlled at the local level by the pastor. He was seen as the delegate of the bishop. The faithful were taught that his authority, since it was divinely established, must be accepted as an act of religious obedience. And though there was no official claim made for monarchical powers, some pastors could (and did) dictate the policies of conduct for practically everything in the parish. Few were the pastors who shared authority or decision making with the laity. At least it can be said that priests at this time were considerably more spiritual than in previous centuries.

In all fairness to the criticism that the laity were left out of the larger picture of the church, it is a fact that the "simple faithful" were for the most part just that. Very few were educated, and, as one bishop wrote to Vincent de Paul, "In truth, the greater part of those called Catholics are Catholics only in name, because their fathers were Catholics before them, and not because they know what it means to be called Catholic." In one town south of Rome a visiting priest was amazed to find that "the majority do not even know the Our Father or the Creed, let alone the other things necessary for salvation." Thus, the effort for education and for preaching afforded people a chance to hear a bit of Christian doctrine and teaching.

Women throughout this period were still regarded as minors, and were severely restricted in their activity by the church. St. Angela Merici in Italy, Mary Ward in England, St. Jane Frances de Chantal and Louise de Marillac in France all tried to found groups of active laywomen in the sixteenth and seventeenth centuries, but were forced into habits and cloisters.

Clearly, the time for the empowerment of the laity would have to wait, at least for its theoretical justification, until after Vatican II. This work, and indeed much of the work of the council, were prepared for in the first half of the twentieth century by serious historical studies and the rise of social consciousness. These served to undergird the work of the council and to make its work relevant in a pluralistic age.

Summary

1. The success of the Tridentine reforms in bringing about a qualitative religious change after the Reformation owes much to the great desire for such a change among the grass-roots Christians. There were also some very remarkable churchmen at the time who were able to give institutional teeth to the disciplinary decrees of the council.

2. In terms of our relationships with Protestants, the first hundred or so years of the period was characterized by internecine religious wars. Conversion to truth was at the point of a gun or because of fear of the

fires of the Inquisition. Thus, the basic thrust was not to convince the other by means of rational arguments, but to see each other as opponents in a debate. It was the tendency of both sides to use Scripture or tradition to defend already established positions or ways of acting. In this sense, it prevented any real rethinking of our practices or deepening of our theological understanding. It was as if all truth had been fixed by the council and all that was needed in the present was a better understanding of how it applied to today.

3. Several areas of dispute were based on a false problematic. One was the nature of the sacrifice of the Mass (which required a cultic priesthood, naturally). The other was the nature of sacramental causality and the character of the sacrament of orders. Focusing on notions of instrumental causality or the sacramental character put all the emphasis on the person of the minister, not on the action of God or the needed acts of the recipients of the sacraments. Sacraments became objectified and "received" in a passive manner. Symbolism and the centrality of the Word were consequently neglected.

4. There was (if possible) an increase in the notion of jurisdiction as an essential component of ministry in the church. This was helped by the work of theologians like Stapleton, Bellarmine, and Suarez. By stressing the nature of the church as a perfect society, or as a monarchical organization, order and obedience came to be seen as the chief virtues.

5. The spirituality of the Counter-Reformation was strongly sacramental. Mass and communion were stressed as the surest path to sanctity. The people learned to expect the sacraments from their priests; Sunday Mass and regular prayer were offered to the laity as the universal paths to holiness. The opposition here was sacraments as opposed to the Word. Because of the Protestant emphasis, there was less stress on the Scriptures and more on the sacramental aspects of church life within the Catholic church.

6. All priests were influenced by the spirituality of the French School, which did much to foster an effective spirituality of the clergy. However, because one of the chief emphases was on the priesthood of Christ, which they rooted in his divinity rather than his humanity, they wound up with a correspondingly exalted notion of ordained priesthood. The main view of the priesthood was cultic. After celebrating Mass, the priests' most noble task was to form Christ in others, something accomplished through spiritual direction.

7. The French School also taught prayer not only as the indispensable means to direct others spiritually, but as the means of being able to

reproduce in oneself the various states of Christ's life. This meant especially his state of immolation on the cross that the Mass represented. This ideal of self-denial was further aided by acts of mortification and penance aimed at self-mastery and flight from the (evil) world.

8. One of the strengths as well as weaknesses of the Tridentine reforms is their tendency to foster religious individualism. From the point of view of strengthening personal virtue and relationship with Christ, this was a very strong factor. To the extent that it lost sight of the idea of church as community, it was a definite weakness. It reduced the task of Christian living to saving one's soul.

9. One of the main ways that Trent's strong emphasis on ordained priesthood has come down to us is in the Tridentine teaching on the sacramental character. This does not seem to be the best way to ground a theology of ministry, however. Not the least problem here is that it tends to make the issue a question of either/or: Does ordination confer something ontological, or is it merely a function within the church? This leads to minimalism. It has also led to widening the split between clergy and laity and relegating all ministry to the ordained. It is also the underpinning for the priesthood as a superior state of life over the lay "state."

10. Today, we can make the following statements: a) Trent deliberately did not define the nature of the sacramental character. This means we may choose between seeing it as either bringing about some strict ontological change in the one ordained, or seeing the character as simply a relation of reason. b) Trent also avoided stating the exact relation between the character and the non-repeatability of the sacrament, which was the main thing it wanted to safeguard. c) Canonists assure us that the anathema does not imply by itself that Trent intended to issue a dogmatic definition; since the character is unknown in the East (and in the West for the first 1000 years) it is not a defined truth of the faith. d) The best approach is to restore the ecclesial sense that was common in the patristic period and to see ordination as one of the charisms of the Spirit that mark a man permanently; his ministry does not issue from him but from a work of the Holy Spirit.

11. The church community turned itself into a fortress during this period, and was extremely intolerant of new ideas or any suspected deviancy from the "truth," especially the errors of the Protestants and those of the secular world. Despite the strong face shown the world, the spirituality of the church in this period was one of religious individualism. This may have helped people to see the purpose of life as "saving one's soul," but it did nothing to develop a sacramental sense based on

the nature of the church as the new people of God, and committed to be leaven for the transformation of the world.

12. There were heroic efforts during this period to spread the Word of God, especially through missionary efforts throughout the world, which served to take the church into the "whole world." The main danger here was of exporting a Western version of the faith and thinking of it as the only possible expression of the will of Christ. Thus, questions of indigenization or acculturation had to wait until the period after Vatican II.

The controlled and inbred attitude engendered during this period led to using Scripture to prove positions already stated by the magisterium, rather than appreciating Scripture in its own right, and in reducing theologians to defenders of the positions adopted by the hierarchy. The basic attitude during this period was a defensive one.

13. Perhaps the weakest element of church life was the prophetic one. This was an age when huge sections of the world were lost to Catholicism, and many of those remaining in the church were lost to religious practice. The defensive mentality engendered by the Reformation led the church to fight most of the major developments of the age; consequently, it lost to a great extent the ability to affect the development of the modern world.

14. Nurturing the people within its fold was one of the glories of this period. Schools, hospitals, and social welfare agencies are characteristic of the church of this period. There was, however, little effort to address the root causes of human misery, and even less success in developing an enlightened social conscience among those who were "practicing Catholics."

15. As regards missioning, the laity were effectively excluded from any real role in ministry. Pius XI did allow them to "share in the apostolate of the hierarchy," but the church on the eve of Vatican II was a strongly hierarchical one. Ultimately all went back to the pope, who was seen as the supreme pastor of the church. His role was strongly reinforced at Vatican I with the definition of his infallibility. This led today to what is called "creeping infallibility," the tendency to invest all statements of the pope as somehow sharing in this charism.

16. The model of the church as a hierarchical institution was not only widely taught, it was widely practiced. The seminary system, which accounted for almost every single ordination in the church at the beginning of Vatican II, is partly responsible for this. So also was the mystique of obedience, which was elevated to the chief virtue in the church.

Discussion Questions

1. Assess the general strengths and weaknesses of the Tridentine period.

2. This chapter has stressed many of the limitations of the period as regards ministry. Is there any one root cause for the weaknesses of the period? Why do you think so?

3. Given the historical period we had emerged from, was it possible for the church to have reacted in any other way during the Tridentine period?

4. What can we learn from the successes of the period? What aspects should be retained in the church today?

Suggested Readings

Berulle and French School: Selected Writings, Mahwah, N.J.: Paulist Press, 1986.

Cooke, B., "Ministry in the Modern Church," *Ministry to Word and Sacrament*, Chap. 6, pp. 160-181.

Legrand, H.-M., "The 'Indelible' Character and the Theology of Ministry," *Concilium: The Plurality of Ministries*, eds. Hans Küng and Walter Kasper, New York: Herder and Herder, 1972, pp. 54-62.

Osborne, K., "The Sacrament of Order in Counter-Reformation Theology," *Priesthood*, Chap. 10, pp. 280-306.

Schillebeeckx, E., "The Nucleus of the post-Tridentine View of Ministry," *The Church with a Human Face*, pp. 202-203.

9

The Reappraisal of Ministry

If other councils were called to answer particular needs in the church, and can therefore be seen as somewhat defensive against outside threats, the Second Vatican Council was called in the midst of a period of relative calm. It took the church by surprise; there had been no great clamor for a council. Many questioned its necessity and wondered what could possibly justify its being called. It was Pope John XXIII, no doubt inspired by the Spirit, who realized the need for what he called "aggiornamento." He wanted to drag the church into the modern world.

As we look back on that period now, it is obvious that the world itself was at a turning point in its development. The period of Western domination was coming to an end. At the close of World War II, there were 57 nation-states in the world, and 51 of them became part of the United Nations. Most of these were from the northern hemisphere: the developed world.

That world was soon to come to an end. The United Nations is now close to 200 member states. We no longer automatically think of Europe when speaking of the world or even of the church. And our world seemed split at the time between what President Reagan was later to term "the evil empire" (the Communist world), and the "forces of light" that made up the rest of the world. All of that is now gone.

Though we have concerned ourselves mainly with western Europe in this book, we were on the verge of a new age when Pope John called the council to "open the windows of the church." Even had we included Eastern church developments, of necessity we would have left out vast sections of Asia, Africa, Latin America, and more. The pendulum is shifting, however. By the year 2000, 70 percent of the world's Catholics will be in the third world. We are no longer a "Western" religion. Pope John could sense this. It is still not clear to many.

It was only during the pontificate of Paul VI that the actual shift in the ecclesiological center of gravity took place. This has continued under John Paul II. In Asia now, more than 95 percent of the bishops are indigenous. The same is true of Latin America. Africa has more than 80 percent who are local in origin. Yet, as of now many areas continue to see themselves largely as "missions," carbon copies of the parent church. The time is coming for them to have their full say within the framework of the entire church. Vatican II has given them the responsibility of doing so.

The Vatican Council also opened a dialogue with the rest of the world, a world that until that time had been classified as the "enemy." Thus, ecumenism has taken new and enormous steps. We have come to accept the world of science and to take political pluralism for granted. With Vatican II, we stopped being a fortress church.

When will the period of aggiornamento end? At least one Roman document[1] began with the ominous phrase, "Now that the period of experimentation is over...." Updating, however, is a never-ending process. In life, the only things that no longer change are already dead. It is safe to say that the same is also true of the church. Aggiornamento is necessary if we want to keep alive and healthy.

Vatican II and Ministry

When the council gathered, only a few people in the church were aware of the historical facts regarding the development of ministerial structures through the ages. Surely almost nothing of it surfaced in the first schema of its Constitution on the Church. This constitution now begins with the words *Lumen gentium*. But the light of the nations it is referring to is not the church itself; it is Christ. In thus giving a solidly Christocentric basis to its theology, Vatican II relativized our understanding of the church. Only when the church reflects Jesus is it truly the church.

It is the Christological understanding of Jesus as teacher, sanctifier, and leader that led the council to see the church in the same way. This provided the ecclesiological basis for any specialized church ministry. Two great documents of Vatican II deal directly with the church: *Lumen gentium* and *Gaudium et spes*. Roughly, the first deals with the inner nature of the church (*ad intra*), and the other with the mission of the church (*ad extra*). Let us say a word about the latter first.

Gaudium et spes is notable for having reversed hundreds of years of flight from the world, from seeing the world as the place of evil. Pius X, we are told in the Breviary, exercised "constant warfare against the errors of the age"; half a century later *Gaudium et spes* asserts that the church is open to and exists on behalf of the world. In fact, the world sets the agenda for the church. She is not only *in* the world, she *is* the world, that community of people who have heard the Word of God. The very purpose for the existence of the church is in service to a world in need of salvation.

Since the church is mission, a Christian is essentially a missionary. One is not saved by withdrawing from the world and concentrating on saving one's soul; it is by living in the world and committing oneself to saving others. We can no longer simply identify the Kingdom of God with the church. The church exists in the service of the Kingdom. This aspect of mission is the most important aspect of ecclesiology, and dwarfs the discussion of the nature and internal structure of the church. The church is and should be structured to better carry out its mission.

This is a work in which both hierarchy and laity can and must collaborate for a ministry of service. As *Gaudium et spes* puts it, "With the help of the Holy Spirit, it is the task of the entire people of God, especially pastors and theologians, to hear, distinguish, and interpret the many voices of our age, and to judge them in the light of the divine Word."[2]

In some ways the council sent out mixed signals regarding church ministry. Though general principles were laid down in *Lumen gentium*, priests were mentioned only in passing (a fact later remedied by devoting a separate document to presbyteral life and ministry). And Article 43 of *Gaudium et spes* seems to remove priests from any active role in the life of the world. This was conceded to the layperson. Even here, while the council did not achieve full emancipation for the laity, it did stress the importance of lay activity and involvement.

The Ecclesiology of Vatican II

The council devoted its only dogmatic constitution to the nature of the church itself. Successive drafts of this constitution strikingly reveal the tremendous development that took place in the self-understanding of the church. As Avery Dulles noted, of all the documents of Vatican II, none underwent more drastic revision between the first schema and the final text.[3]

Surprisingly, in *Lumen gentium*, the church, for the first time in its history, refused to attempt a definition of itself, and was content to say that the church is a *mystery*.[4] The church is the mystery of Christ who lives on in the world. This not only implies that its essence can never be fully captured in any human theology, but that its form can never be structured according to the organizational ideas of any given age. There is a difference between a perfect society and a mystery. This mystery, furthermore, is a mystery of communion.

In the more biblical turn that characterized the council, *Lumen gentium* then went on to speak of the church as people of God. This chapter was deliberately put ahead of the one on the hierarchy, which is consistently spoken of as "servants of the people of God," nothing more. The hierarchy are not the owners of the church, diocese, parish, or community. Nor are they masters, to be served and glorified. There was quite a good deal of reaction to the triumphalistic clericalism that characterized the fortress church from the very first session of the council. It was the reason the first and second drafts of *Lumen gentium* were shelved in favor of the current text.

Chapter 1 brings out the fundamental unity of church members and that baptism is our foundational sacrament, the source of our dignity and ministry. It is only after this common foundation has been laid that we can begin to speak of differences. Baptism grounds our common priesthood. It also enables us to see ministry as a sort of second stage, an aspect of service within, and either for or on behalf of the community.

Thus, baptism becomes an ordination into that apostolic, charismatic, and sacrificial body we call the church. However we interpret a subsequent ordained ministry, we should not lose sight of the once-for-all, life-long ordination of baptism, which provides our primary identification. Every ordained minister in the church, from pope to priest, remains a baptized person.

Having begun with the people of God, the council only then speaks of the hierarchy, especially the bishops. The exact nature of the episcopal state had been left hanging at Trent, and Vatican I could not consider it because its sessions were interrupted by the Franco-Prussian War. *Lumen gentium* stresses the properly priestly role of the bishop as brought about by sacramental ordination. For years bishops had been considered as empowered by the pope, as his branch managers in their own little kingdoms. Now they were told that they were pastors of the local church in their own right and, further, that the local church was the prime manifestation of church.

Instead of being seen as priests who had been given greater jurisdiction by the pope, their office was now seen as primary; it is not something non-sacramental added on to priesthood. And the council spoke of collegiality as a fact of church life from the beginning. Thus, the pyramidical structure of the church was somewhat flattened out, and the sharp lines of authority were softened in the light of a new emphasis on cooperation rather than obedience.

After Trent and Vatican I, the Catholic church had come to appear more and more as one big diocese: the pope's. As reflected in his title "Pastor of the Universal Church," the bishops were seen mainly as his administrative assistants. They had been treated this way also, especially since Vatican I. One of the amusing incidents at the council came from an intervention by Maximos IV, the Melchite Patriarch:

> Some of the "faculties" which it is proposed to "delegate" to the bishops make one wonder...the faculty to allow priests to say two or three masses a day, or to allow one's nuns to wash corporals, purificators and palls....Really, if a successor of the apostles cannot on his own authority allow nuns to wash purificators, what can he do?[5]

Now, thanks to Vatican II, Rome no longer has an official monopoly on initiative. Here is where the council introduced something very new into the discussion, for the council spoke of bishops as teachers, sanctifiers, and leaders in a collegial, not individualistic, way.[6] Decisions are supposed to be made in consultation with other churches. Even though much still has to be done in practice, collegiality has become official church teaching.

But the key change is that the episcopacy is not merely an office or dignity beyond the priesthood, but the fullness of priesthood itself. Furthermore, priesthood can only be understood in and through its relationship to episcopal ministry.

Further, both episcopal and presbyteral ministry can be understood only in their apostolic dimension and relationship, which means that all ministry is based on the life and ministry of Christ. The council saw Christ's ministry as threefold: teaching, sanctifying, and leading. Thus, Jesus' ministry becomes the source as well as the model for all church ministry. All ministry will have this threefold characteristic.

The council added new emphasis to the role of priests in speaking of a *fraternal* relationship between priests and their bishops. Preaching and teaching were not something simply added to their ministry, but an essential part of it. They were to foster a spirit of Christian community in their parishes, and to entrust laity with responsibilities enabling them to play a more active role in the church. This will be discussed further on.

The council defined hierarchical ministry in more pastoral terms and took steps to include more people in the ministry of the church. Laity also were told that they were an active rather than passive part of the church. Apostolic laity were no longer simply participating in an apostolate that belonged by right to the hierarchy. The decree of the "Apostolate of the Laity" was issued to underscore this.

The council's teaching, in fact, was grounded not only in ecclesiology, but in a better Christology and appreciation of the continuing role of the Holy Spirit. These are precisely those aspects of sacramental theology that were lost in the last millennium, when we began to develop an independent theology of sacramental power and jurisdiction. Unfortunately, perhaps, having given us an improved perspective in this area, the council did not draw out neatly all the implications of what it said.

The People of God

The council was careful to insist that the church was the people of God before speaking of the various groups that make up the church: hierarchy, laity, and religious. In fact, had the council eliminated chapter four, it might have been a better document, for laity are there described only negatively, as being neither priests nor religious. And as the chapter states explicitly, "Everything said so far concerning the people of God applies equally to the laity, clergy and religious."[7] There is a richness and potential in chapter two that is diluted here.

Though section 31 of the Constitution may seem to relegate the laity simply to worldly affairs, they are twice said to have a special vocation to Christianize their world. Thus, to understand laity the way this council did, it should be linked with the idea of vocation, a special call from God. Not to live this vocation is to empty one's life of any specifically Christian character. God's people have the duty (divine call) to "seek the kingdom of God by ordering temporal affairs according to his plan."[8]

The laity are told that their apostolate "is a participation in the saving mission of the church"[9]—a statement that was agreed on only after some discussion, as it explicitly abandons the idea of lay apostolate as a participation of the laity in the apostolate of the hierarchy. Apostolate does not belong exclusively to the ordained members of the community.

In its resurrection of the doctrine of the common priesthood, the council retained the triple "priestly, prophetic, and kingly" roles that are predicated of Christ. These are applied to the laity as well as to the clergy. Here we will limit ourselves to a few thoughts on the royal and prophetic aspects mentioned by the council.[10] In a key council text we read:

> Christ, the great Prophet, who proclaimed the Kingdom of his Father by the testimony of his life and the power of his words, fulfills his prophetic office until his full glory is revealed. He does this not only through the hierarchy who teach in his name and with his authority, but also through the laity. For that very purpose he made them his witnesses and gave them understanding of the faith and the grace of speech, so that the power of the gospel might shine forth in their daily social and family life.[11]

We are told here that "he gave them knowledge of the faith." This is not simply the act of faith in God's Word as guarded and infallibly taught by the teaching authority of the church. It is that sense of faith found in all, from the bishops to the least of the laity, aroused and sustained as it is by the Holy Spirit.[12]

In distinguishing between the action of the Holy Spirit exercised in the sacraments and ministries, and that exercised through charisms, the council is stating that there can be (and is) divine action that is not bound up with the sacraments. The Holy Spirit is not the private preserve of any special group in the church. The council would later remind pastors of their duty of "acknowledging with joy and fostering with diligence the various humble and exalted charisms of the laity."[13]

The council then goes on to state how all the faithful share in the kingly role of Christ, devoting all of section 36, on the transformation of society, to that purpose. Human work and human culture must be harmonized with moral values. A Christian conscience cannot be put away in a drawer somewhere; there is no human activity in secular affairs that can be withdrawn from the dominion of God. The laity are said to possess special competence here by reason of their secular calling and education.

The council states that it may also be necessary to order the church for the sake of the Kingdom. According to the knowledge and competence of each, lay persons have the right and even, at times, the duty of "expressing their opinion on things which concern the good of the church."[14] They are to do this "in truth, in courage, and in prudence." The words "in courage" were kept in despite the objections of a number of bishops. This section goes on to seriously urge church leaders to make use of the talents of the laity, and to promote their activity.

We have mentioned in passing that the conciliar teachings on the people of God and the common priesthood were important foundations for understanding the church as well as Christian vocation. If we opt for a model of church based of the idea of our being a community of disciples, as was suggested by Avery Dulles, and try to understand the vocation that we all share by reason of baptism, this antedates any division into groups such as cleric or lay in the church. This notion is basic to understanding the call to ministry that belongs to all in the church.

Dulles, in his widely-read book *Models of the Church*, has shown several ways the council allows us to understand the church, now that the institutional model has been demoted.[15] He has been puzzled in recent years as to why none of them has really caught the popular imagination. In the early 1980s he suggested yet another model, which he called "Community of Disciples."[16] This deserves to become a paradigm for our understanding.

This model picks up several conciliar themes, especially that of the church as a pilgrim people—a much more modest concept than that of the church as a perfect society.[17] It reminds us that we are all still on the way together. All in the church must struggle to be faithful each day and to grow in fidelity to their call. Life in the church is not a static condition, but a continual movement toward the fullness of the Kingdom. The eucharistic rhythm suggested here is that of people who are gathered together at Jesus' call, challenged, and nourished to go forth and participate actively in mission and ministry.

This concept of discipleship also makes it clear that each member is under personal obligation to appropriate the Spirit of Jesus. If church membership is seen in this way, it is neither passive acceptance of a list of doctrines, nor abject submission to the precepts of authority, but an adventure of following Jesus on a difficult challenge in ever new and changing situations. The church is a group of disciples who support one another in this task. Because of the community we have the help of the Scriptures, the sacraments, and countless other means of aid.

Also, discipleship suggests a response to the call of Jesus that is personal and demanding. This allows more consideration for the needs of personal piety for a deep relationship with the Lord. By requiring all to truly live their Christianity, it banishes the split-level attitude that allows so many to divorce religion from life. It helps take the "magic" out of religion and allows the sacred and profane to interact with each other so that religion is the expression of life. Following Jesus is not just with the mind, but with the heart, so that we become *doers*, and not just hearers, of the Word.

This restores the prophetic element that had gone out of Christianity, allowing people to challenge the assumptions of the age in which we live by measuring them against the values of Christ. The church was intended by Jesus to be the leaven of society. The baptized are to grow to full Christian maturity because they have been equipped to do this by the church. Further, the church cannot exist except through a living chain of discipleship and an active assumption of what it means to be "church."

For most Christians, the term vocation still applies only to those who have been called to the priestly or religious life. In this sense, one is born a Catholic, but only a chosen few "have a vocation" to special commitment. The others are thereby reduced to a sort of second-rate citizenship, and lesser responsibility than the elite. This process began as early as the Middle Ages, and has been reinforced by scholastic theology and the ecclesiology of Trent.

With the monasticization of the church in the Middle Ages, popular opinion passed into common teaching. The religious life, from the scholastic period on, has even been called a "state of perfection." The progression seems to be that all are born laypersons, but some choose to enter other states that imply a higher degree of virtue or of heroism. There seems little choice about being a layperson. One is born such whether one likes it or not. And if the religious life is a state of perfection, then the lay state is, almost by definition, less perfect. Hence, there is little reason why one could not be contented with half-hearted performance there, to simply drifting through life.

Suffice it to say here that, though the new Canon Law still refers to laity as "neither priests nor religious," it has abandoned the "states of perfection" terminology. Hence, there is no longer any need to make comparisons between one state of life or another. This should also make it possible to find a proper spirituality for all the different states of life in the church.

Up to now, the spirituality of monasticism and the religious life has influenced all other states of life in the church. In the first place, it has affected the priesthood (at least in the Latin church) by the ideal of celibacy, the recitation of the divine office, and a spirituality that emphasizes practices that may be more proper to a monastic state than to the active life of a parish priest. In the same way, it has affected the laity. Many books on spirituality make an attempt to devise some watered-down variation of religious piety for the laity's use.

More happened at Vatican II, however, than simply allowing the laity to exercise the apostolate of the church. The lay state itself was regarded far more positively than ever before. The normal state of most laity—marriage—is also viewed more positively. If before some regarded marriage as a concession for the weak, and if sexual pleasure was seen as unseemly (if not at least a venial sin), there is a new appreciation of marriage as a form of Christian perfection. These ideas, one may be sure, did not emerge as part of the great celibacy debate![18]

What all this comes down to is that all Christians are enabled to pursue perfection by the mere fact of consecration as a member of God's people. The various ways in which they do this can and will vary depending on the particular state of life they have chosen (or—more properly—God has called them to). All, however, are called to holiness of life, no matter which state they happen to be called to. Holiness is not a special prerogative of only a few individuals in the church.

Keep in mind that when dealing with lay apostolate or the mission of the laity, we are not simply doing so because of the shortage of priests, or the conciliar idea of co-responsibility, or even greater democratization. These are all external factors. The inner basis of all apostolate lies in a deeper awareness of the church itself and its mission in today's world.

The council made it clear that every Christian is called to be an active, responsible member of the church. All are sealed with the Spirit. All are church. All have a role to play in the building up of the church and for the salvation of the world, since both are linked.

The rediscovery of the laity's theological mission is an important part of the church's rebirth in our century. The ecclesiology of Vatican II emphasized unity in a diversity of charisms, offices, and ministries.[19] Though Vatican II did not attempt to eliminate the distinction between clergy and lay, it did state everyone's common responsibility.

The council repeated that an "essential" distinction existed between the ordained priesthood and the common priesthood. Ordination is not simply an intensification of the common priesthood; were that so, the clergy would be better or more complete Christians, and this is obviously untrue. The common and the ordained priesthoods are not different on the level of being Christian. Rather, within the communion of all Christians, the distinction has to do with ministries.

The council did not give a theological definition of the laity. It has been argued by some that its negative phraseology had a positive orientation—that is, that a secular quality is proper and special to the laity.[20] We have often been reminded in recent years that laity exercise their mission in the midst of the world. This is fine as a descriptive definition or expectation, but it is theologically suspect as an attempt to restrict roles.

At the root of this is the question of the relationship between what is seen as *salvation service* and *secular service*. As we have hinted above, there has been a historic "problem" in the relationship between the church and the world. Are Christians only *in* the world, or do they have a mission *to* the world? The council did insist that the service of the laity in the world is not purely secular service; it is salvation service that is at the same time ecclesial service, for it shares in the church's sacramental/symbolic nature as universal sacrament of salvation.

A second question concerns the new offices of the laity within the church itself. While these might be important in carrying out the church's pastoral mission, efforts to upgrade the role of the laity should not focus chiefly on the church's internal life as much as the church's mission. (This is not to deny that there is need of more laity in the internal structure of the church in roles that have been usurped by the clergy over the years.) The various offices and roles that the laity may now exercise are not concessions due to need only; they are grounded in baptism and confirmation. They should also be continuing reminders that secular service and salvation service are not two hermetically separated and different missions.

A third question concerns the place of women in the church. The council only hinted at the problem. Since then its importance has exploded. It cannot be dismissed as simply the concern of a few radicals in America; it remains a universal problem, and one that will continue to grow. The American bishops have worked long on a pastoral letter on this subject, and the pope has recently issued a letter on it, which is at least an acknowledgment of its seriousness. If this is not faced honestly soon, we may be in danger of losing a whole class of people to the church. Right now women make up at least two-thirds of our churchgoing population.

This goes beyond the question of the ordination of women, which cannot concern us here. Canon law now says that women have equality with men (can. 230); yet they cannot serve Mass, or be installed as lectors or acolytes. They are seldom given any positions of responsibility within the diocesan church structures. Is this simply a legitimate differentiation of roles, or is it based on misogynistic and patriarchal concepts that are now outmoded? It is certain that the answers that have been given so far do not satisfy, and have caused women much pain and disaffection from the church.

As far back as 1955, Karl Rahner published his thoughts on the subject of lay apostolate. At that time he argued that if the layperson were the Christian who remains in the world, he or she should have a specific task in the world that determines one's station not merely in secular life, but also in the *church*. From that point of view, the "layperson" does not mean "a Christian who has practically nothing to say in the church, and is only the passive recipient of efforts of salvation on the part of the church (= clergy), and *therefore* busies himself with profane and worldly things." A man is not supposed to busy himself with secular things as if they were devoid of religious signification, as he would do if he were not a Christian. His work has relevance to his Christianity.

Rahner argued that when engaging in Catholic Action, the layperson, in a sense, ceased being lay, and became simply an extension of the hierarchy. Without going into Rahner's theory (which is dated), one valuable consequence is that laypersons do not have to think in terms of joining a church group or activity in order to be holy. One's life can and should be one's apostolate. This is more than simply "giving good example." This implies deep personal motivation and an understanding of self that is grounded in the spirituality of the church, along with an active ministry to and for the world in which we live.

Though Vatican II has provided more directions than answers, it has redirected the church and asked for ecclesial conversion in three major areas. In the years immediately after the council, the church came to see itself as a community; then as a community living in the heart of the world; finally as a community in the heart of the world in order to minister to the world. Community, incarnation, and ministry are three conciliar insights that were applied to *all* the baptized. All were called to be sacrament of the world in the circumstances of their own lives.

The council told us that the layperson was "a living instrument of the mission of the church herself."[21] This instrumentality can be exercised individually or as a member of some group. One's charismatic gifts ought to be used. These principles have opened new avenues of involvement for the laity in evangelization, family ministries, social development, world transformation, and internal church life.

We have noted that lay ministry goes beyond simply witnessing by leading a good life. It also goes beyond volunteer work taken on as an extra. (This seems to divide the committed layperson from the mediocre.) Rather than speak of part-time ministry, it would be better to speak of a permanent commitment to ministry that results from and is inspired by one's baptism, which commitment is exercised in either full- or part-time service, depending on one's circumstances.

What is the role of church leadership in all this? It is always the tendency to institutionalize the charism—to provide some form of authorization and public approval to various types of ministry or service. However, the question must be asked: Is church leadership meant to assist, or to regulate? To cooperate or to delegate? Too often, ecclesial acceptance has been confused with ecclesiastical acceptance. The former is always necessary; the latter is not.[22]

It is the usual tendency to think of lay ministry as meaning the full-time services of some professional or paraprofessional to the church, whether paid or unpaid. Some even suggest a sort of quasi-ordination of these people as a step toward declericalizing ministries. But, like lectorate and acolytate, this simply seems to put added rungs on the clerical ladder. Furthermore, such a full-time apostolate would always involve only a minority within the church, and tend to imply that the work done *ad intra* was more valuable than that done *ad extra*.

In regard to the work done *ad extra*, some of this can be done as individuals, or it can be done as part of some organization committed to that particular apostolate. There are a number of associations committed to the social welfare that have varied degrees of relationship to the church. Many of these would also have a spirituality (or a general philosophy of life) that would form the basis for one's own spirituality and involvement.

Today, especially in areas of social justice, these groups might well be ecumenical, or inspired by people outside the institutional church. Thus, for example, we have members of the people of God working in the field of education or in different cultural spheres. They may be found in any of the healing ministries or in social service work. We also find them in political life, and in the communications field. They are in various industrial fields, and spread throughout the workplace. Though the hierarchy is not responsible for any of these areas, all need to be touched by the grace of Christ. This is the responsibility of those with competence in these fields. Though some fields may seem to have little social relevance, *all* work can be an occasion for spreading the gospel and for holiness.

If baptism makes us all stewards of the mysteries of God, we must truly live our Christian faith. Our vision of Christ and church, as nourished by Scripture and the liturgy, should make us more aware of opportunities—either alone or in collaboration with others sharing our vision—to build the Kingdom for which Jesus lived and died. We might list various ways in which this ministry to the world might take place through members of the people of God.

1. *Christian presence in the world.* This refers to the ministry being performed by those who are responding to the universal call to holiness, and thus influencing the particular world they live and work in as authentic Christians. They celebrate the presence of God, create community, serve the suffering world, and proclaim the good news in countless ordinary actions of life.

2. *Ministry and service of non-professionals.* The backbone of any parish or organization is those who generously give their time and service to the accomplishments of the group's objectives. They are often unpaid and unsung—the volunteers without whom any group could not function. There is a need for these to see that their contribution is significant and appreciated and is, indeed, ministry.

3. *Professional ministry.* Within the church, many tasks formerly performed by priests are being taken over by the non-ordained. Many of these have or are receiving professional training for their new roles. We must encourage this as well as the underlying spirituality sustaining all ministry—faith in the Lord and love for his church.

4. *Ordained ministry.* At this time in the church's history, the priest is perhaps the most crucial enabler of ministry of others. He can open doors for others or keep them shut tight. As the one who presides over the community, his chief role should be to enable others to use their giftedness in the service of the Lord. The specificity and role of the priesthood of the ordained is an issue that is still being clarified since the council. As we grow in our self-understanding as church, there will be significant shifts in theology and practice, until we reach the stage of genuinely mutual collaboration of all in the church.

Requirements for a Ministry of World Transformation

The renewal of church and society that we are talking about requires being clear about the mission of the church and organizing resources for the pursuit of that mission. These resources include people who must be allowed to share in the process of defining the mission and establishing the goals if they are to be effective.

In our own minds, we must try to achieve a clear vision of what God is calling us to do and be. In the first place this requires what the Vatican Council, following Pope John XXIII, called "reading the signs of the times." We need to become more aware of the social environment in which we live to see how we may respond to current needs for gospel values. We also need a knowledge of ourselves, of our own gifts and talents so that we might use these as best we can in our particular environment.

In recent years, the church's social teaching has been enshrined in a number of magisterial statements—from Pope John XXIII's *Pacem in terris* and the council's *Gaudium et spes* to John Paul II's *Sollicitudo rei socialis*. These have come back time and time again to several major themes or principles that should be integrated into an ecclesial spirituality to help provide the broad agenda needed if one is to carry out the mission of the church effectively today. We might note eight basic themes in urgent need of Christian attention:

1. *Link of the religious and social dimensions of life.* The "social" is not secular, in the sense of being outside God's plan. Faith and justice are necessarily linked closely together. Today, this would include not only the bonding of human beings who recognize that they are on a shared journey together to God, but also a bonding of human beings to Earth in a new appreciation of its holiness. We need to eliminate the dichotomy between life and religion.

2. *Dignity of the human person.* Made in the image and likeness of God, men and women have a preeminent place in the social order, with inalienable rights that need respect and defense. In fact, all of creation carries a dignity that can mirror the divine for us. The church has spoken eloquently of the dignity of people in the world; we still need a practical realization of the same right within the church.

3. *Option for the poor.* A preferential love should be shown the poor, whose needs and rights are given special attention by Jesus. This has been achieved most conspicuously by the emergence of basic ecclesial communities in many third world countries, and this is perhaps one of the most exciting developments in ecclesiology today. We are fighting, unfortunately, the fact that the poverty of peoples and the degradation of the environment often go hand-in-hand. The desire for profits results in both the rape of the land and oppression of peoples. This cannot continue.

4. *Promotion of the common good.* The common good is the sum total of all those conditions of social living—economic, political, cultural—that make it possible for women and men to achieve the perfection of their humanity. Today this also implies a greater awareness of the environment in which people live and its ability to enhance human life. The church must see (or continue to see) its role as extending beyond its

own borders to all the needy.

5. *Stewardship*. All property has a "social mortgage." All people are to be respected and given their fair share of the resources of Earth. We know too little how to steward the earth; we have become too used to recklessly intervening in the life systems of Earth in a way that exploits and pollutes them.

6. *Global solidarity*. We belong to one human family and as such have mutual obligations to promote the development and well-being of peoples across the world. Perhaps what is needed is a greater respect not only for peoples, but for Earth on which we live. It is one way, and an important one, of acknowledging our common dependence on God. The old colonialism and the new nationalism tend to be narrowly individualistic—and un-Christian.

7. *Political participation*. Participation in decision making and allowing people to have a say in their own destiny is one of the best ways of respecting the dignity and liberty of peoples. The way to respect the dignity of all the members of the total Earth community is to provide mechanisms whereby they can participate in decisions affecting their lives. We should become more and more aware of those who tend to be exploited and disenfranchised: women, minorities, laity in the church, and many others.

8. *Promotion of peace*. Peace is the fruit of justice and is dependent upon right order among human beings and among nations. Cooperation and coordination are the qualities that build the world, not competition and exploitation. Guns and bullets do not promote a positive solution to anything, but only increase the levels of violence that plague our world. We have not yet evolved a consistent ethic of life or of peace, both of which the world sadly needs.

Each of these areas needs a deeper theology as well as committed members of the people of God. They propose a global awareness showing how gospel values can be integrated into a holistic spirituality. They help shape understanding of how to apply the vision of the Kingdom to the everyday world in which people live and breathe and spend most of their time. Christianity must be put to work in the workplace.

People spend most of their time working. Christianity can treat this portion of life in three possible ways. a) Work is of no real importance. We reserve religion for the church; in the marketplace we behave like those around us. Thus, values of honesty, integrity, justice, seldom come into play, especially if they go against the prevailing mores. b) It has some importance. People feel called to be honest in business dealings, to give their employers a good day's work for their pay, to be friendly with the people they are working with. c) It is everything. Is full Christian life simply not cheating one's employer, or being nice? No. It is about ordinary people becoming partners with God in the transformation of the world. This partnership is in the whole of life, not just in "churchy" things.

This can be more difficult for those who have repetitive, mechanical jobs. There may seem to be little socially redemptive about what they are doing, especially when they have no direct contact with the final product, or its quality or usefulness, and have no real influence on work conditions.

Perhaps the question that needs to be asked is whether or not one has sufficiently appreciated the talents God has given. How can they be better used to make the world a bit more humane? These are all questions about Christian ministry. In this largely uncharted field, there is a need for maturity and a sense of stewardship, not to mention greater attention on the part of the church to providing more help and guidance.

Summary

1. As regards the theology of ministry, the greatest change at Vatican II was to shift the emphasis from the top to the bottom. Bishops were spoken of as receiving their ministry and authority from Christ (not from the pope) as leaders of the local church for which they were ordained. Their office was primary. At the same time, the council spoke of collegiality as the "style" that should characterize the church in our day.

2. At the same time, the office of bishop was seen as *primary*, i.e., the priesthood shared somehow in the office of the bishop, not vice versa. For over 1000 years it had become customary to see the bishops as sort of "maxi-priests." This came from seeing the essential part of office as the ability to consecrate. At the council they were seen as having the fullness of the priesthood and not simply as priests with jurisdiction.

3. Because the council also downgraded the institutional model of church in preference for the idea of church as "People of God," this implies a like shift in how the laity are understood. A major part of this shift lies in seeing them as active members of the church, not simply as passive recipients of grace. Also, their ministry is more than a form of participation in an apostolate that belongs properly to the hierarchy.

4. Vatican II gave a solidly Christocentric basis for ecclesiology, and also reversed the tradition of flight from the world, which had led to seeing the world as an evil place. At the council, the church defined its

mission in terms of service to the world, a world that sets the agenda for the church. It is by living and working in the world for its salvation that we come to realize our own mission as church and how we, as individual members of that church, come to "save our souls."

5. In speaking of the church as a "mystery," the council effectively said that its essence can never be captured in human language or models. It also implied that its form is not immutable, but at the service of its mission, which will always remain the primary consideration. Thus, the particular organization of the church in various places can vary according to the needs of those places in the service of others.

6. The council's treatment of the "laity" is ambivalent. On the one hand they are a sort of non-group in the church, being defined as "neither priests, nor religious." On the other hand, by being the largest number of the people of God, they are said to have both a special vocation and call from God to advance the coming of the Kingdom. They are also reminded that this implies that they also have a call to holiness. They are no longer the "imperfect" members of the church.

7. Chapter 2 of *Lumen gentium*, in resurrecting the theology of the common priesthood, retains the traditional mode of speaking in terms of "priestly, prophetic, and kingly" functions of that priesthood. This remains one of the areas that is in need of extensive treatment today. In speaking of the prophetic vocation of the laity, however, the council spoke of the sense of faith that is found in all the believers. It recognized that the Holy Spirit could be and was active in the individual members apart from the actions of the hierarchy. It also urged priests and pastors to rejoice in this development and to foster it with diligence.

8. The kingly role of God's people is twofold. In the first place it is to transform human society so that there remains no aspect of human life that is withdrawn from the action of God's grace. It is also affirmed that it gives people the right to be active in expressing "with courage" their opinions in what concerns the good of the church.

9. Thus, the increased activity of the laity after the council was (and is) due not primarily to the shortage of priests, but to a deeper understanding of the dignity of all the baptized. This led to a much more positive evaluation of the lay state itself. (It would have been better to drop the very term "laity" in favor of the more unifying concept of "People of God," or "disciples.") The weakness of the council here lay in not giving a positive or a theological definition of laity. It also left several areas of continuing tension in regard to the scope of their ministry, new offices within the church, the place of women, etc.

10. It is obvious that the larger part of the ministry of the laity will be "in the world." This is not to be understood as a theological specification of roles, but as a sociological observation. We have no right to restrict the roles of the ordained to the church, and the role of the other members of the people of God to the secular realm. All are responsible for the entire mission of the church.

11. The approach of the council has led to the search for a specifically "ecclesial" spirituality, as opposed to using monastic spirituality as the model for everyone in the church. All are called to perfection and holiness of life, and to be active members of the church in accord with the charisms of each.

12. It would seem that the chief role that should be emphasized today would be in line with the social teaching of the church in the last 100 years. Especially since Pope John XXIII's *Pacem in terris*, recent popes have stressed more and more a morality based on social issues that beg for Christian presence today. This is the task that should occupy all in the church either directly or as an aspect of the work that is one's primary consideration.

13. Ultimately, the task of the church is to become relevant once again. Either Christ is important in the marketplace, or he is irrelevant. Christianity claims to have a message that is supposed to transform society. We are called to prepare for the coming of the Kingdom. All of this is part of the stewardship that God has given us over the work of his hands.

Discussion Questions

1. What practical ways can you think of in which the conciliar teaching on the church can be applied to the role of laity in the church today? How can this be done smoothly and with a minimum of friction?

2. What practical consequences can the changed role of the bishop have for the life of the church today? Does this depend on their good will and willingness, or are there other factors involved?

3. The council preferred to stress the community, rather than the institutional, dimensions of church. How can this be taught or preached so that people have a greater awareness of their call to holiness and to ministry? Is there a good model of church that is appealing to people?

4. What do you consider to be the major developments in the theology of the "laity" in the church today? Why? What are the areas you feel still need development?

5. What would be the qualities and characteristics of an apostolate based on the social teaching of the church today? What do you consider the most important social needs in North America? Why?

Suggested Readings

Doohan, L., _The Lay-Centered Church_, Minneapolis: Winston Press, 1984.

Kloppenburg, B., _The Ecclesiology of Vatican II_, trans. M.J. O'Connell, Chicag: Franciscan Herald Press, 1974. Esp. Chap. 2, "The Nature of the Church," pp. 12-80; Chap. 6, "Papal Primacy and Its Limits," pp. 169-204; and Chap. 8, "The New Theological Portrait of the Bishop," pp. 218-262.

Kroeger, J., "The Signs of the Times: A 30-Year Panorama,_EAPR_,26, 2 (1989), 191-196.

O'Meara, T., "Ministry and Ministers," _Theology of Ministry_, Chap. 5, pp. 134-175.

Osborne, K., "Ministry in the Documents of Vatican II," _Priesthood_, Chap. 11, pp. 307-342.

Power, D. N., "Vatican II: The Presbyterate According to the Constitution on the Church," _Ministers of Christ and His Church_, pp. 127-140.

10

Reappraising Presbyteral Ministry

As we have traced the development of priesthood in the church, we have seen it pass through several clearly defined stages. In the first two centuries, no one was considered a priest save Christ alone. It was only during the third century that the term began to be timidly applied to the bishops. The group whom we now so cavalierly call priests were never so called at this time. Rather, they went by the name of presbyters and, as a collegial body in the church, their responsibilities were not liturgical but advisory to the bishop.

In the fourth century, however, due to the press of the many who flocked to the newly legitimized religion, the bishops began to depute their presbyters to celebrate the church's mysteries in outlying areas, because the entire church could no longer gather in the same place at the same time. As this practice became more common, the presbyters lost their collegial status and even their name.

From then on they were not only called the church's priests, but ordination began to be seen as the ritual that made them the equals of the bishops, since it deputed both groups to celebrate the church's liturgy. Bishops had greater jurisdiction, to be sure, but they were identical in terms of the Mass and the ability to consecrate the body and blood of the Lord. Both were equally empowered to change the bread and wine.

This eucharistic equation soon defined the common understanding of the priesthood. There were several unfortunate consequences that followed this, however. One was that as people began to think of priests as men who had the power to consecrate, these powers were seen as residing in the person as person rather than as head of the ecclesial community. In addition, as these powers became private prerogatives, the role of the Holy Spirit in mediating the blessings of the Lord and in sanctifying began to be forgotten and not made part of the theological understanding of how priestly powers were transmitted or functioned.

As crass as the popular understanding of priestly powers may have been, the Council of Trent etched it even deeper into Catholic theology because of the pressure of Protestants, who were denying the sacrificial nature of the Mass and any right of the ordained to be considered priests. From the seventeenth century, the spirituality of the priesthood was based almost exclusively on their powers of consecration, which set them apart from the church's laity, making them sacred ministers and giving them exalted status in the hierarchy of the church.

Vatican II was to take this long history, specifically the scholastic formulation that had been used by Trent, and find it wanting. For the first time in its history, a council was to give a relatively complete and balanced theology of the church and its ministry. In the previous chapter, we looked at the changed ecclesiology that came from Vatican II, and sketched the consequences of that theology within the church for the laity as well as bishops.

The very first document the council considered was *Lumen gentium.* This document went a long way toward redefining the role of the "laity," or the non-ordained part of the people of God. It was precisely the clarity of the council's teaching on the laity and its redefinition of bishops that caused many of the council fathers to be dissatisfied with the marginal treatment given priesthood.

For many, the theology of the laity seemed to have put a question mark behind the theology of the priesthood. With the upgrading of bishops to the highest rank of orders, and the equal promotion of the laity to active roles in the church—to the same dignity, a like call to holiness—what was left for the ordained ministry? Though the common priesthood of all believers was said to differ "in essence" from the ordained priesthood, we were never told convincingly what this essential difference was.

This resulted in a new document being drafted that eventually became *Presbyterorum ordinis.* From the various commentaries on the documents of Vatican II, we know that this document had an interesting history. Originally entitled *De clericis,* a second schema saw the title changed to *De sacerdotibus.* This became *De vita et ministeria sacerdotali* in the next session. Final revisions also brought a decisive title change to *De ministeria et vita presbyterorum.*

The title changes are significant. Note that the final document preferred to call its ordained ministers *presbyters* rather than priests.[1] Further, the earlier drafts had begun by discussing the life of priests almost in the abstract. The final document consciously chose to speak first of the *ministry* of the ordained. The particular lifestyle or spirituality appropriate to them would be a consequence of the ministry that was theirs.

Thus, *Presbyterorum ordinis* goes beyond *Lumen gentium* in its treatment of ordination. Those places where it differs are an indication of further thought and development.[2]

The Theology of the Presbyterate

Historians will argue for decades about why, despite the council's best efforts, the years following the council saw so many thousands leave the ministry. In an amazing reversal of trends, the number of those entering the seminaries in many Western countries dropped precipitously, and is now nowhere near sufficient to offset those retiring or dying. Practically all countries have a serious priest shortage these days.

Even Paul VI, in one of his more pessimistic moments, said to the lenten preachers in Rome in February 1968:

> Violent waves of questions, doubts, denials and open-ended new ideas are crashing against the ministerial priesthood. Problems are being raised about its true nature and primary function, about its proper place, and about its original, authentic reality. Assailed by these doubts, the priest begins to wonder about his vocation. He begins to question the canonical form of the Catholic priesthood. He fears that he has made a poor choice in his life's work. He no longer sees celibacy as a free offering of sacrifice and love, but as an unnatural burden. Having withdrawn from the world in order to know, evangelize and serve it better, he now looks back on it, not with apostolic love, but with worldly nostalgia. All too easily he can delude himself that he could redeem it better, or at least balance his own inner anxiety, by immersing himself in its temporal and social dimensions.[3]

As we have seen, the tradition coming from the scholastic era regarded the priest as a man of sacrifice and defined him in terms of his relationship to the Eucharist. It was precisely this approach that enabled the scholastics to see bishops as being little more than priests with jurisdiction, because their paramount power—over the Eucharist—was the same: "The whole fullness of the sacrament is to be found in one order, namely priesthood; the other degrees represent participations in the sacrament."[4]

Trent itself had made no effort to teach the sacramentality of the episcopate. And it spoke of priesthood in terms of a single function: celebrating Eucharist. The commission that worked on *Presbyterorum Ordinis*, however, called this "the scholastic definition of priesthood," and abandoned it once and for all. In presenting the Decree in its final form, Bishop Francois Marty strove expressly to make this position clear:

> The chief and controlling idea in this draft is this: since priests are, in the sacrament of orders, consecrated by the anointing of the Holy Spirit, and made like to Christ the Priest, they are servants of Christ the Head in his church, and deputed to serve the People of God. Therefore, in the ministry which they exercise, they act in the person of Christ himself, who through them continues to carry out the mission he received from his Father. The Eucharist is consequently the source and center of the priests' whole ministry. But this ministry must be more adequately defined, and that in light of the apostolic mission on which it depends. If the apostolic ministry itself is viewed in a rounded way and if the doctrine of the New Testament and especially of the Pauline letters is kept in mind, the two ways in which presbyteral priesthood has been explained here at the Council can be readily harmonized. For a genuine apostolate and an authentic adoration of the Father are closely connected, indeed are inseparable one from the other, so the two aspects must be found in the life of every priest. St. Paul himself declares that by preaching the gospel he is adoring God, for by confessing the Lord to the Gentiles, he sings praise to the Lord's name (Romans 1:9).[5]

When modifications to the text were being made, a group of council fathers attempted to reintroduce the idea that the essence of priesthood is derived from its relationship to the Eucharist, but the commission simply rejected it, explaining:

> The majority of the Fathers, as is clear from comments made in the Council hall and from written comments handed in to the commission, want it shown that the priestly office of the presbyter

derives, as it were, from the episcopal office and is connected with the latter. Now the functions of a bishop embrace much more than his eucharistic functions, though the latter is the crown of his whole work; his total function is properly described as "apostolic," and LG, ch 3, and the Decree on the Bishops' Pastoral Office in the Church make this clear. We must keep these documents in mind, as the commission constantly did. The priesthood of presbyters must be seen as being in the same line as the priesthood of bishops, with the necessary allowances.[6]

Here we have a clear statement of the intention and mind of the council regarding the nature of the presbyterate—and the council clearly prefers this name to priesthood. Though increasing the emphasis it gave the Eucharist to please those who wanted the old scholastic definition, the council held firm to situating the presbyterate in a broader framework. Like the bishops, their responsibility extends to the whole mission of the church.

Let us look more closely at *Presbyterorum ordinis*. It has only three chapters. The first is more dogmatic, and deals with the presbyterate in the church's mission. Chapter two goes on to deal with the ministry of presbyters, and Chapter three with the life that flows from it.

From the start, the council teaches that the anointing and mission of Christ are shared by the whole church: "There is no member who does not have a part in the mission of the whole body."[7] This Christological and ecclesiological vision, which also summarizes *Lumen gentium* and Decree on the Apostolate of the Laity (*Apostolicam actuositatem*), officially provides a new theological starting point for ministry: one of equal dignity of all in the people of God.

The next paragraph goes on to say that within this people, in which all are priests and apostles and have equal dignity, Christ has established a certain number of ministers with sacred power to foster unity, offer sacrifice, forgive sins, and exercise the priestly office publicly in his name, for the sake of all. The word "publicly" here was the subject of some controversy. It was retained with the explanation that it was a technical expression calculated to distinguish the personal, private priesthood common to all the faithful from the priesthood proper to ministers.[8]

This is the closest the council comes to a definition of priestly ministry. The distinctive elements are: 1) the exercise of a sacred power, 2) for the sake of men (and women), 3) in a public way, 4) in the name of the church and of Christ, 5) in order to join the faithful together into one body. Maintaining and fostering community is at the heart of all ministry. It has pleased God to save us not as individuals but as a community. All other functions are to be seen in the light of this primary purpose. Service to the community is *the* function of the ordained.

The third of these elements is especially significant. The fact of ordained ministry being an official public service is perhaps the main feature distinguishing it from the ministry of laity in the church. This maintains Trent's insistence that ordained priesthood differs essentially from that of the laity. Trent wanted to reject the idea that anyone without distinction (*promiscue*) could do anything in the church. Vatican II also wanted things done in decent order, without reducing one priesthood to the other. The notion of official public service in the name of the community does this.[9]

The council typology proceeds from Christ, sent by the Father, in his turn sending the apostles in order to make present and operative his mission as head of the church. The apostles in their turn sanctified and sent the bishops. The nature of all ordained ministry must be found in this consecration and sending of bishops. Unity in one and the same ministry comes from the common source of both in the gospel message.

All of this had been stated in the decree on the bishops, and is now taken up in relation to presbyters as well. In this nuanced way is priesthood said to be "established" by the Lord.[10] The idea is that Christ remains present in his church, ceaselessly leading and nourishing his people. It is Christ himself who continues to guide the church *through* the pope, bishops, presbyters, etc. And if the bishop is the living sign of Christ, so also presbyters, "so that they might be the co-workers of the episcopal order in the proper fulfillment of the apostolic mission entrusted to the latter order by Christ."[11]

At this point a significant modification was made in the proposed text, which originally read, "The bishops have legitimately communicated their ministerial role to presbyters, though in a limited degree."[12] The problem here is the origin of the "priesthood" from the "presbyterate." The council decided to sidestep the historical question by stating only: "This ministerial role has been handed down to presbyters in a limited degree."[13]

In linking presbyters organically to the episcopate as the fullness of ministry, the council rejects the presbyteralism of St. Jerome, while affirming that (like the bishops) presbyters are "the living instruments of Christ the eternal priest" (section 12/2). Bishops and presbyters are almost mirror images. God equips both for their mission in a way that affects them radically. This is not a juridical arrangement. It is ministry in the name and person of Christ. Presbyters represent the glorified Lord because they are sent by him.[14]

This points to another important change made by the council. Ministerial priesthood was related to the entire mission of Christ; it is not simply specified by its eucharistic role. Presbyteral representation of Christ is in terms of his entire public ministry, not only its cultic dimension. In all that they do as presbyters, the ordained ought to be a sign (a living instrument) of Christ the head. Presbyters share in the authority of Christ himself, not in that of the bishop. "Through the ministry of the bishop, *God* consecrates presbyters."[15]

Ordained powers, then, come only from God. Strictly speaking, it is inexact to say that the presbyter is a minister of the church. One of the modifications proposed for the text of *Presbyterorum ordinis* wanted to use just this expression. It was rejected with the explanation that while it was possible to say that presbyters acted in the name of the church, they act as ministers of Christ.[16]

It is equally erroneous theologically to say that the presbyter as such acts "in the name of the bishop" or that he represents the bishop. It is more exact to say that he sanctifies and governs under the bishop's authority that part of God's flock entrusted to him. Presbyters always act "in the person of Christ," not "in the person of the bishop." In the same way, it is incorrect to say that a presbyter depends on the bishop for his power. The power comes directly from Christ, not from the bishop. This does not deny, however, that presbyters are dependent on the bishop *for the exercise of* their power.[17]

This is sufficient to show that it is not a question here of the bishop passing on to presbyters a part of his own priesthood. In the early draft of *Lumen gentium* 28 it was said that the bishops "communicated grace from their paternal fullness of it" (words taken from the preface of ordination). This drew enough opposition that the final statement read, "The sole source of presbyteral priesthood is the priesthood of Christ."[18]

This also shows the relationship between presbyters and bishops. If presbyters received all they had from the bishop, there would be a good theological foundation for stressing the paternal role of the bishop: he is the father; priests are his sons. But this basis has vanished. Presbyters are now related immediately to Christ. The council goes on to say, some sixteen times, however, that presbyters are "co-workers of the episcopal order." They are not autonomous. This relationship is called "hierarchical communion." "The very unity of their consecration and mission requires their hierarchical communion with the order of bishops."[19]

Presbyters, then, as in the first centuries, should be the natural advisors of the bishop, who should treat them as "brothers and friends" rather than "sons and subjects."[20] In the third century, Cyprian was an excellent example of this ability to work with his college of presbyters, whom he called "fellow priests." This was more than a polite or politically astute way of speaking. The very nature of the church as communion required it.

Let us now look a little closer at the question of the specific ministry of the presbyter. Older theology tended to focus on the special powers of the presbyter, an emphasis the Protestants rejected. As during the Reformation, there were two tendencies at the council. Some felt the priest was essentially a cultic person; others an evangelizer. The impasse was broken by starting from Romans 15:16, where Paul asserts that he has become a minister of Christ Jesus with the priestly duty of proclaiming the gospel of God. Granting that presbyters are in the apostolic ministry, then what Paul says about himself holds for them as well. They receive from God (through the sacrament) the grace of being ministers of Christ among the nations and carrying out the sacred service of preaching the gospel, so that the peoples may become a pleasing sacrifice that the Holy Spirit consecrates.[21]

When *Presbyterorum ordinis* speaks of priestly power, it means especially presbyteral authority to build up the flock in truth and holiness. There is nothing magical or automatic about this, inasmuch as this is authority for service, not magic or domination. Those possessing it have, strictly speaking, only one power and right: to be adequate signs and living instruments of Christ the teacher, priest, and shepherd, and to exercise this office publicly in the name of Christ. The presbyter is to be a man of God's Word, of the sacraments, and a leader of God's people. We might schematize his functions as follows.

1. *To lead the people to maturity,* so that each member of God's people might be led to the full development of their gifts and vocation.[22] "Presbyters exercise the office of Christ the Head and the Shepherd. Thus they gather God's family together as a family of living unity, and lead it through Christ and in the Spirit to God the Father."[23] The two chief ways in which this leadership is accomplished are through:

2. *Preaching.* "The People of God finds its unity first of all through the Word of the living God, which is quite properly sought from the lips of priests."[24] In a note on this passage, we are told that everything said about bishops proclaiming the Word applies equally to the presbyters. The Word of God, said the council, "is one of the most significant elements or endowments which together go to build up the church."[25]

3. *Presiding at the liturgy* to perfect and complete the worship of the people in the sacrifice of Christ. "Through the ministry of presbyters, the spiritual sacrifice of the faithful is made perfect in union with the sacrifice of Christ, the sole mediator. Through the hands of presbyters, and in the name of the whole church, the Lord's sacrifice is offered in the Eucharist in an unbloody and sacramental manner until he himself returns."[26]

Section 5 of *Presbyterorum ordinis* stresses the sanctifying role and sacramental ministry of presbyters and points out that it culminates in the celebration of the Eucharist. "For their ministry, which takes its start from the gospel message, derives its power and force from the sacrifice of Christ."[27] The council goes out of its way to emphasize the role of the Eucharist in the church. "The office of pastor is not confined to the care of the faithful as individuals, but is also properly extended to the formation of a genuine Christian community....No Christian community, however, can be built up unless it has as its basis and center the celebration of the most holy Eucharist."[28]

Presbyterorum ordinis suggests that both presbyteral mission and adoration of the Father should be reflected in the life of the presbyter. Life and spirituality flow from mission. Here again the Pauline principle holds true: The preaching of the gospel is a form of worship; it glorifies God (Romans 1:9), and is the exercise of a sacred service (Romans 15:16). The ministry and life of presbyters have but one finality: "the glory of God the Father as it is to be achieved in Christ."[29] God's glory is shown when humanity, in a free, conscious, and thankful way, accepts the work that God has accomplished so perfectly in Christ.

A final question we should consider is when presbyteral ministry may have been instituted by Christ. As we know, many Protestants refused to consider orders a sacrament because it is not clearly attested in the Scriptures. Catholics, on the other hand, have tended to associate its institution with Christ's words, "Do this in memory of me." Trent, in fact, went out of its way to pinpoint the exact moment of institution by anathematizing anyone who said it was not done at the Last Supper.

Vatican II, however, has broadened the vision of Trent. Consistent with its preference for the terms "ministry," or "ministerial priesthood," it cannot see the Last Supper as the *sole* moment of institution of the apostolic ministry, and hence of the presbyterate. Rather, the founding time (if we must use that concept) extends throughout the public ministry. It ranges from the time when Christ chose his disciples, formed them, and sent them forth to preach and heal in his name, to forgive sins, etc.[30]

Given this brief description of presbyteral ministry and life as found in *Presbyterorum ordinis*, it can be seen that there are rather wide differences in emphasis between Trent and Vatican II on a number of points. Less polemical, Vatican II wanted to give a more balanced and holistic picture needed by the church today. Let us schematize these as follows:[31]

1. Point of departure: celebration of the Eucharist (Trent) vs. mission of the church (Vatican II).

2. Institution: the Last Supper (Trent) vs. the establishment of the totality of the apostolate (Vatican II).

3. Specifying element: power over the eucharistic body (Trent) vs. over the Body of Christ [church] (Vatican II).

4. Regarding the content of priestly ministry: cultic priest (Trent) vs. apostolic minister (Vatican II).

5. How to understand the ministry and life of presbyters: theocentrism of worship (Trent) vs. theocentrism of the priest's whole life and ministry (Vatican II).

At Trent we had primarily a theology of priesthood as correlated to sacrifice. In Vatican II we have a theology of the presbyterate in relation to the whole mission of the church.[32] In a sense, the Tridentine definitions were not absolute, inasmuch as Vatican II introduced far broader perspectives. The real mistake of the fortress church was to take the partial doctrine of Trent as exclusive and complete. Insufficient heed was given to the historical and doctrinal context in which Trent took place and the basic intention of that council.

The climate was different at Vatican II. There was no longer the preoccupation with defending the sacramental order, and a far greater sensitivity and understanding of the Protestant positions. Also, at Vatican II the priority went to pastoral preoccupations.

The essential continuity between the two councils is that both taught that ordination is a true sacrament that confers a special grace and "character."[33] In this there is a lesson and example for the future. Our attitude to the teaching authority of the church cannot and ought not be one of simple acceptance, repetition, and fixation of what was said. There must always be room for amplification and homogeneous development. Councils have not always decided every matter definitively or in the best possible way. Theology, then, must be more than passively and subserviently repeating dogmatic formulas of the past. Vatican II provides many proofs of this that should be models for the future.

The Meaning of Ordination

Basing ourselves on the teaching of Vatican II as well as the history of
the church, let us try to sketch an understanding of ordination that is
based more on the patristic tradition (especially the Eastern tradition
that we have largely ignored). Understanding this viewpoint can give
us a better perspective from which to view the teachings of Vatican II,
and to integrate these into a total theology of church, without ignoring
the Holy Spirit—always a Western tendency.

From everything said so far, it should be clear that it is impossible to
treat ordination as an autonomous subject. It is part of Christology as
well as ecclesiology. But if we deal with ecclesiology and Christology,
we are also dealing with the action of the Holy Spirit, so that pneumatology is also involved. And all this is in the service of mission: Thus
the cosmic and eschatological aspect is also part of the total picture.[34]

This means that we should look at the question of ordination from
the angle of the concrete community of the church before we come to
consider it from the point of view of the ordained persons themselves.

Let us recall here two principles that go back to the early church, and
that (in theory, at least) characterized the first millennium: 1) No ordination takes place outside the eucharistic assembly of the local church;
and 2) no ordination can be "absolute," i.e., without binding a person
to a concrete community.

The first theological implication of this tradition is that ordination is
not to be understood in terms of an objectified and transmitted grace or
power, but as an act whereby the Holy Spirit establishes particular relationships within the community of the church. These are not just abstract and logical relationships, but deeply existential and soteriological
ones.[35]

Another fundamental implication is that ordination cannot be understood simply in terms of *causality* (in other words, in terms of "validly
ordained bishops" acting as God's instruments having power to automatically bring about the character and grace of state whenever they
ordain). It represents a divine act realized through the eucharistic community. In ancient days, the bishop was ordained precisely as head of a
particular community, and not as an individual. Had he been empowered to act individually, he could perform ordinations at whim in his
living room![36]

Note that attaching importance to the community does not imply
that the community has some sort of logical or temporal precedence.
The charismata do not follow the existence of the body of Christ; they
are constitutive of it. Ordination is a primordial and constitutive act of

the Christian community. Each ordination constitutes the church anew in a pneumatological way. It comes into being here and now as the Body of Christ in this place.[37]

Describing the difference between the ordained and the rest of the people of God in terms of relationship avoids reducing ordination to something purely functional. This avoids the old dilemma that tried to force a choice between an ontological or a functional understanding of ministry—a problem not resolved since the Reformation.

Saying that ministry belongs to the community places the ordination problematic outside the dilemma where we must choose between whether ordination bestows something indelible on the one ordained, or merely empowers one to function for a certain purpose. Understanding ordination existentially shows this distinction to be misleading, since no one possesses a charism of the Spirit simply as an individual. The Holy Spirit, it is clear, always acts for the good of the church, for the community.

The point to remember is that theologically, any ontology that can be conceived of without its relational character contradicts pneumatology, where everything is dependent on communion. Furthermore, ministerial functions with no ontological content would be purely utilitarian. While this might apply to a secular group, it becomes almost blasphemous when used of the church, which is the communion of the Holy Spirit.

Instead of understanding what is effected in a person by reason of ordination only in ontological or functional terms, it should be seen in *personal* terms. Personhood is different from individuality; it is a relational category that conditions one's being existentially. The early fathers spoke in this sense. Any grace the presbyter receives is "for those who need it," and as part of the eucharistic community.

The fact that ordinations were always incorporated into the eucharistic liturgy is of great importance in helping us to understand how the early Christians did not see the creation of orders or classes in the church as being divisive. Besides coming from a personalist culture, they knew that there could be no ministry *outside* or parallel to the community; all ministry was identical with the church body. In her being the Body of Christ, the church existed as a manifestation of Jesus' own ministry in the world.

Another fundamental implication is that ministry should not be understood as some form of representation or delegation of authority by the community to certain individuals. This is a juridical perspective, and eventually leads to a separation of the ordained person from the community. Anyone acting *on behalf of* the community somehow stands *outside* the community, because he is thought to act in its stead or on its behalf. Understanding ministry communally is to affirm that there is no ministry that can stand outside or above the community.

Ordination to the ministry in eucharistic communion implies that the seal of the Holy Spirit cannot exist outside the receiver's essential relationship with the community. Its indelible character can best be compared to that which is possessed or given by love. It is bound to die outside this existential bond with the community, just as the Spirit who gives this charism constantly sustains it only for the good of the community.

Understanding this allows us to transcend the divisions created by the variety of ministries. The early church grasped this when it decreed that all ordinations were always on behalf of a specific community. The bishop's exclusive right to ordain was only within his own community, i.e., in relation to his role as the one who offered that entire community in Eucharist to God. His whole existence as bishop made no sense apart from his role as the one through whom all divisions (including those of orders) are transcended. His primary function was to make the catholicity of the church reveal itself in a certain place. There is no ministry in the church that can exist absolutely, apart from a community.

The above reflections might seem abstract, or a form of "high" spirituality. Actually, using the conciliar teaching on the people of God as well as the primacy of the local church, they simply try to situate the question of ordination in biblical or patristic terms rather than in the juridical categories that have shaped our thought for the past 800 years.

To ask the question about how ministry originates and is transmitted in the church from a juridical perspective implies an understanding of ordination as a transmission of powers, with or without the transmission or bestowal of a charism or grace. Here, grace is objectified and understood as some *thing* that can be possessed by an individual, or transmitted from one individual to another in a sort of unbroken line.

This then leads to the notion of sacramental causality. As seen by medieval theology, the main problem was trying to understand what kind of causality was involved. Since then, practically speaking, we broke down into two main camps, as we felt forced to choose between the transmission of the ministerial power 1) through an ordaining minister as part of the linear historical line of apostolic succession, or 2) through the community, understood as possessing charismatic life or as delegating authority. Catholics have tended to opt for the first, Protestants for the second.

The revival of biblical studies has been pushing theology toward the second position. However, the sources only give answers to the questions we pose. It may be that the dilemma is a false one to begin with. For one thing, the dilemma still operates with the notion of causality; this itself may be part of the problem.

Let us begin by asking whether there is anything that may be seen as preceding and causing ordination in the church. What is the source of ministry? Is there a generic principle of the ministry (be it the power of the ordaining bishop or the "priestly" nature of the community)? In other words, how does ministry come about?

1. In the first place, it should be noted that for most of the Fathers, there are no "non-ordained" persons in the church. Baptism and confirmation are essentially an ordination to taking one's proper place in the eucharistic assembly. A person does not simply become a Christian, he becomes a member of a particular community and has a particular "ordo" within the church. When we forget this, we can easily think and speak of the "laity" as unordained, and eventually make them an unnecessary element in the eucharistic community.[38]

Furthermore, ordination—that is, assignment to a particular "ordo" in the community—paradoxically appears to be not something that *follows* a preexisting community,[39] but an act *constitutive* of the community. An individualistic ontology makes it difficult for us to think of a community that does not exist first and *then* produce or sustain ministry. It is easier to imagine a community existing first as a unity, and then of a diversity of ministries.

This, however, leaves the Holy Spirit out of the picture. If our ontology is pneumatologically conditioned, the fact is that the Spirit unites while dividing (1 Corinthians 12:11). Ordination, like baptism, is an act that creates the community as the existential locus of the convergence of the various charismata of the Spirit.

2. If ordination is approached in this way, ministry ceases to be understood in terms of *what it gives* to the ordained, and becomes describable only in terms of *the particular relationship* into which it places the ordained person. If ordination is understood as constitutive of the community (and if the community as the *koinonia* of the Spirit is essentially a relational entity), ministry as a whole is a complexity of relationships within the church and in its relation to the world. In fact, without the notion of relationship, ministry loses its character as a charism of the Spirit and as service. Relationship here is not just a relationship of reason; it has a deeply ontological reality.[40]

This is reflected in the Pauline text, "Stir into flame the gift God bestowed when my hands were laid on you" (2 Timothy 1:6). This implies that a pastoral charism is given for the sake of the church. It derives from the purpose of ordination to ministry. Thus, one's priestliness is not one's own thing. It is a gift (charism) for the church. With ordination, through the mediation of the church itself, presbyters receive a special gift from God: a continuing promise of the Spirit's presence and action in their ministry for the proper ordering of the church's life.

An interesting corollary suggests itself here: *The presbyter is still a lay person.* The problem with the clergy/lay dichotomy is precisely that it is thought of as being disjunctive. That is, one is either a priest or a lay person. The Code defines laity as being "neither priests nor religious," something like being either married or unmarried. In terms of ordained ministry, however, Vatican II has made clear that this is not true. The ordained person does not cease being a member of the people of God. As Augustine said in one of his sermons some 1400 years ago:

> What I should be for you fills me with anguish; what I can be with you is my consolation. Because for you I am a bishop, but with you a Christian. The first points to my duty, the second to grace. The first shows the danger, the other salvation.[41]

The Presbyteral Role in the Church

The council highlighted public or official leadership within the Christian community as a key aspect of presbyteral ministry. Other functions were seen as flowing from this, and were the ways in which one exercised leadership ministry. Borrowing from the understanding of the early church, we might note that the presbyter presides over the celebration of Eucharist because he is first called to preside over the life of the Christian community. As noted in the introduction, presiding has five major expressions.

1. Presiding over the Church as Community

The chief role of the presbyter is fostering community. Leadership and service of the community is *the* function of the ordained. It has pleased God to save us by making us part of the new covenant community, and it is this community that is to become the sign and reality of salvation to the world. All other priestly functions, including the sacramental ones, are to be seen in the light of this primary purpose of joining the faithful together into one body.[42]

Thus, the gathering of God's people for the eucharistic celebration is a sacramental expression of what is supposed to characterize the Christian church itself: a community where there is no longer Jew nor Greek, slave nor free, male nor female, but where all are one in Christ Jesus (Galatians 3:28). Presbyteral ministry aims at making this united community a reality. Thus, Vatican II gave us a broader theology that puts the presbyterate in relation to the entire mission of the church. The presbyter is charged with continuing Christ's own threefold role of sanctifying, teaching, and leading his people.

2. Presiding over a Community Formed by the Word of God

Although it identifies presbyteral ministry with the entire public ministry of Christ,[43] the council notes that the chief way this is carried out is through preaching the Word of God. Starting from Romans 15:16, where Paul speaks of having been given the grace to be a minister of Christ Jesus with the priestly duty of preaching the gospel, what the apostle says about himself is applied to presbyters as well. They receive from God the grace of being ministers of Christ, carrying out the sacred service of preaching the gospel so that the people may become a pleasing sacrifice that the Holy Spirit consecrates.

The council has made it clear that without the Scriptures the community cannot be built up. "The people of God is formed into one by the Word of the living God, which is quite rightly sought from the mouth of priests....It is the foremost task of presbyters...to preach the gospel to all....This is of paramount importance in the case of the Liturgy of the Word within the celebration of Mass."[44] The Word of God, according to the council, "is one of the most significant elements or endowments that go to build up the church."[45]

The importance of preaching and teaching was affirmed with startling insistence and emphasis by the council. It was consistently ranked first. The high importance given the Eucharist (as the center of the assembly over which the presbyter presides) is said to flow from the fact that it is the source and summit of all preaching of the gospel.[46] It should be noted that the Word of God reaches its highest power in the Eucharistic Prayer, as Christ is once again made present in his community through the action of the Holy Spirit. It is also one of the main ways in which the presbyter helps the growth of the community.

In stressing the importance of the Eucharist for the church, the council called it the "source and summit of Christian life." They even spoke of a right of the people to Eucharist. *Lumen gentium* says, "The laity have the *right*, as do all Christians, to receive in abundance from their...pastors the spiritual goods of the church."[47] Furthermore, "no Christian community can be built up unless it has its basis and center in the celebration of the most holy Eucharist. Here all education in the spirit of community must originate."[48]

Thus, it is insufficient to feed the faithful with the Word of God, and not offer them the Bread of Life. The council affirms, in fact, "The eucharistic celebration is the center of the assembly of the faithful over which the presbyter presides."[49] The proclamation of God's Word is meant to culminate in the eucharistic celebration.

3. Presiding over a Prophetic Community

The Word the presbyter preaches is not simply informative or consoling. It is also meant to be *challenging*. The presbyter-priest is called to lead the people to Christian maturity, so that each member of God's people might be led to the full development of his or her own gifts and vocation. "Very little good will be achieved by ceremonies, however beautiful, or societies however flourishing, if they be not directed toward educating people to reach Christian maturity."[50]

The council defines the mission of the church as both bringing the message and grace of Christ to people, and penetrating and perfecting the temporal sphere with the spirit of the gospel.[51] Priestly ministry is not an "otherworldly" reality. Evangelization and development go hand in hand for, as the Synod of 1971 pointed out, "Action on behalf of justice and participation in the transformation of the world fully appear to us to be a constitutive dimension of the preaching of the gospel or, in other words, of the church's mission for the redemption of the human race and its liberation from every oppressive situation."

It is because of this that theologians speak of a "basic option for the poor." Unless the social dimension of the church's message is heard, we can reduce priestly ministry to the sacristy or sanctuary and never take it into the marketplace. *Evangelii nuntiandi* tells us: "[The church] is not willing to restrict her mission to the religious field and disassociate herself from temporal problems."[52]

The church thus has a role in the moral, spiritual, and religious dimensions of all economic, social, and political matters. Ever solicitous of the temporal needs of people, the Word of God itself impels the church to act on behalf of justice and the transformation of the world. The light of the gospel must be shed on human problems, to clarify them, to proclaim justice, and to inspire all people to pursue the temporal good, condemning whatever is unjust and oppressive.

4. Presiding over a Eucharistic Community

Celebrating the Eucharist does not make a eucharistic community.

Everything that Eucharist is and symbolizes must characterize the life of the community as well. Because of the community dimension of the church as well as of the eucharistic celebration, our communion at the Lord's table is meant to go beyond a narrow one-way reception of the Lord. Jesus shares himself with us so that we can learn to share him with others. We are nurtured so that we can become a nurturing community.

The council notes that "Through the ministry of presbyters, the spiritual sacrifice of the faithful is made perfect in union with the sacrifice of Christ, the sole mediator."[53] A Christ-like life, one of self-giving and concern for others, is the fruit of Eucharist, hence the emphasis through the years on care for the poor, education, and works of mercy of various kinds.

The council stressed the nurturing aspect of priesthood in its insistence that the ministry of the presbyter is rooted in the entire ministry of Christ and not in the Last Supper alone.[54] His healing, feeding of the multitudes, the compassion that characterized his dealing with others are all foundational moments showing us the full implications of the presbyteral role.

5. Presiding over a Ministerial Community

In speaking of the common priesthood of all baptized, the council affirmed the laity's equal dignity, equal call to holiness, and equal responsibility for the mission of Christ. The ordained and common priesthood are ordered to one another. The presbyter's ministry is performed within the priestly community "publicly, in Christ's name, for the sake of others." Ordination gives him an official deputation on behalf of the community to coordinate, guide, and inspire the faithful so that they take their rightful role in the church.

Paul spoke of the church as a body where each part had a specific job and function. The leadership role needed from presbyters at this time is to rouse the laity from the apathy that has been induced after so many centuries of inactivity—because of the hyperactivity of the hierarchy. It is not the function of the clergy to *dominate* the laity, but to be their servants in the cause of salvation and for the sake of the kingdom. In its rescuing of the laity from utter passivity, the council made it obvious that the laity's contribution to the work of the church is to be welcomed and fostered. Presbyteral ministry should make the faithful more aware of their proper Christian ministry.

Recapitulation

The major change of orientation made by the Vatican council was to shift the emphasis from the sacral or cultic model of ministry to a more presbyteral or ministerial one. This shift was consciously intended as a correction of what it believed to be the unbalanced emphasis of the previous scholastic approach. Doing this subordinated the presbyter's cultic functions to his ministerial role; that is, the sacramental functions were seen as being in service of building up and preserving the church in unity and love. This concern for the total welfare of the community is at the heart of presbyteral ministry.

In many ways the orientation of Vatican II manifested a return to the teaching of the early church, especially in the idea of understanding priesthood as a continuation of the whole of Jesus' public ministry in the world today. In linking the presbyterate with Christ's "headship," it made it a function of leadership and guidance of the community, seeing liturgical leadership as only part of this more general task.

Stating that the council tried to correct centuries of popular thought and piety is not to say it was reinventing priesthood. With a better knowledge of both the Bible and of church history, we are able to have a clearer picture of how our ancestors in the faith understood the church and its ministry. These insights into primal ministry can be used by us as a guide for our present practice in order to provide us ever better ways to serve God's people.

It is important to note that one of the church's continuing convictions is that the Holy Spirit is always there to guide and, in a sense, preside over the development of church structures and practices. Structures are not the same as doctrines, but are ways in which the church adapts itself to meet the needs of any given age. Very few structures can be traced back as directly willed or instituted by Christ.

The unfinished task is perhaps to elaborate structures that are more effective or more in touch with modern needs. Despite the changed emphasis of Vatican II and the crying need for more priests, no major changes in structures have been made since the council. Seminaries are still run much as they were 100 years ago. All presbyters have to undergo a long scholastic training along the ideal of the Tridentine model. Ministry is still conducted more along the lines of the old sacramental model than, for example, along the lines suggested by the basic ecclesial communities. Churches are encouraged to share priests with other parts of the world to make up for the gross inequality in numbers and inadequacy of presbyters in many places, rather than finding new ways to build up leadership in the local churches.

A church that simply decrees that presbyters should pray more, dress better, be less authoritarian, poorer, and more celibate, solves very little unless there are structural changes to facilitate the desired behavior or outcomes. Despite the criticisms that have been made of priests, it should be borne in mind that priestly service is probably better now than it has been at any previous period in the last 1000 years. Simply looking for ways to do the same old things "better" may be shortsighted.

Talk of a "sacerdotal character" has been a bone of contention in the past. Church councils have described this as a charism of the Holy Spirit (cf. Synod of Bishops, Rome 1971). It has been described theologically by John Paul II as a participation in "the charism of the Good Shepherd." This is oriented to a pastoral ministry that expresses a self-giving even unto death. It can also be seen as a charism ordered to the unity of the community—a charism operative within the network of human relationships and gifts that constitute the reality of the congregation.

Thus, to speak of a permanent character is to recall the permanent covenant God establishes with God's people in baptism. Christian ministry exists to remind the church that its preaching, sacraments, and service are *God's* work, not its own. There is a permanent need for word, sacrament, and service; ministry responds to this. Ordained leadership also involves discerning God's presence in the texture of human history.

Summary

1. Since Vatican II the priesthood has been seen, rightly or wrongly, as having been demoted. The entire people of God celebrates the Eucharist; the presbyter only presides. The people are now recognized as having equal dignity and a like call to fostering the mission of the church. The role of bishops has been upgraded. Loosening the clear linking of priesthood to a sacrificial understanding of Eucharist seems to make priesthood less important. Vatican II, however, gave us the principles whereby we can outline a new theology of ministry that is both clear and compelling.

2. There is no doubt that the council deliberately abandoned the Tridentine identification of priesthood exclusively with cult. They rejected what they called "the scholastic definition of priesthood." Their approach was to link presbyteral ministry more closely to the entire public ministry of Jesus. They affirmed that priests shared in the "apostolic" ministry. Further, they stated that this ministry was how we adored the Father as he wished to be honored and worshiped.

3. The council did not wish to downplay the Eucharist. But a deeper understanding of the ministry did require that it not be restricted to only

one function. Since presbyters were seen as sharing in the same ministry as that exercised by the bishops, this, by definition, involves a broader concept of mission and relation to the community than simply presiding at the table of the Eucharist. Eucharist is part of a larger reality.

4. The council also found distinctive the fact that presbyteral ministry is exercised in a public manner, and that it is at the service of communion. Other charisms within the church are exercised privately and do not have the same power to move and mold the community into the true body of Christ.

5. Vatican II broadened the Tridentine idea that priesthood was instituted at the Last Supper to state that it was instituted throughout Jesus' public life. His calling disciples, his forming them and giving them power over unclean spirits, power to teach and heal, to forgive sins, etc., all indicate that he wished his community to be able to carry on all of his work and mission. This is what has been transmitted to presbyters today. The council was prudent enough to skirt all the historical issues and left its wording broad enough to allow for change and development in the present structure of orders.

6. The council also rejected the idea that priesthood was the basic sacrament and bishops were just presbyters with more power or jurisdiction. Episcopacy was seen as the basic or highest degree of orders. Presbyters share somehow in the priesthood of the bishops—but not by the bishops sharing some of their powers with them. This comes directly from God.

7. Priests are not people who act "as ministers of the church." They are ministers of Christ, acting in the name of the church. We must avoid any theology that takes the presbyter *out* of the church. Ordination confers a new relationship within the Christian community. Presbyters are also co-workers with the bishops within their community.

8. The two main functions of presbyteral ministry today are the preaching of the Word and the celebration of Eucharist. Both are seen as constitutive elements on which the Christian community is built and maintained. This combines to give perfect praise and worship to God the Father. It also makes presbyters living instruments of Christ, teacher, priest, and shepherd.

9. There are five major differences between Vatican II and Trent—in regard to the basic point of departure, the institution, the specifying element, the content of presbyteral ministry, and the presbyter's relation to the worship of God. In each of these Vatican II broadened and gave a new perspective to the views of Trent, which help give us a more balanced picture of presbyteral ministry today.

10. One of the reasons for our theological impasses in the past was that we tended to look at the question of ordination and what it bestows as an abstract question apart from the community that one was being ordained for. We cannot understand ordination properly unless we see it ecclesially and as a gift of the Holy Spirit to and for the church.

11. Ordination is an act whereby the Holy Spirit establishes particular salvific relationships within the community. This takes the issue of ordination out of the ontological/functional dilemma by suggesting instead that no charism exists for an individual, but for the good of the church. We should substitute the word "personal" for individual when thinking about ordination, since personhood is essentially relational. Ordination forms relationships that are real and that perdure.

12. A problem Vatican II did not solve is whether ordination results from the transmission of powers through bishops having a linear connection with the early church, or whether apostolic succession mainly implies fidelity to the faith of the church. The linear theory focuses attention on presbyteral powers in ways that are historically questionable, and as if they would be irreparably lost if anything happened to break the line of transmission.

13. The five-fold aspects of presbyteral (indeed, of church) ministry are amply supported by the council. Clearly, ministry is proper to all the faithful, not only to the ordained. It is the proper role of the presbyter to inspire and encourage the other faithful by his own life and example and to so preside over the community's life that they live their Christianity more fully. His is a role of leadership and service, that the reign of God might come.

Discussion Questions

1. What are the advantages and disadvantages of the Vatican II treatment of priesthood? Are there any ways in which the disadvantages might be minimized?

2. How might the new teaching about the nature of priesthood be integrated in our seminary training today? What aspects of the Tridentine seminary have become outdated? Why?

3. What might be done to acquaint older presbyters with the new theology of priesthood today? Is there any contradiction between the old and the new as far as pastoral practice? As regards lifestyle? What might this be?

Suggested Readings

Crehan, J., "Ministerial Priesthood: A Summary of Work Since the Council," *Theological Studies,* 32, 3 (September 1971), 489-499.

Haight, R., "Mission: Symbol for Understanding the Church Today," *Theological Studies,* 37, 4 (December 1976), 620-649.

Kloppenburg, B., "The Theology of the Priesthood," *The Ecclesiology of Vatican II,* pp. 263-293.

McBrien, R., "Church and Ministry: The Achievement of Yves Congar," *Theology Digest,* 32, 3 (1985), 203-211.

Mitchell, N., "A Theology of Holy Orders," *Mission and Ministry* Chap. 5, pp. 260-313.

O'Meara, T., "Sources of Ministry," *Theology of Ministry,* Chap. 6, pp. 176-207.

Power, D. N., "Vatican II: The Presbyterate According to the Decrees on the Pastoral Office of Bishops and the Ministry and Life of Presbyters," *Ministers of Christ and His Church,* London: Chapman, 1969, pp. 141-162.

Schillebeeckx, E., "The Catholic Understanding of Office in the Church," *Theological Studies,* 37 (1969), 567-587.

_____. "Listening to the Complaints of the People," *The Church with a Human Face,* Part 4, pp. 209-258.

11

Unresolved Problems in Ministry

This survey of ministry in the church has taken us from the ministry of Jesus himself, through its various stages of development, to the present. We have noted the various changes of direction that have taken place over the centuries, stressing how the teaching of Vatican II in many ways veers away from medieval and Tridentine thought. While only scratching the surface, we have also tried to show how historical developments so often affected the church's ministry.

Theologically, in many ways the entire period may be divided into three. The first period corresponds to the first millennium, and is characterized by a much closer relationship between ministry and ecclesiology. Because ordination implied a relationship to a particular community, "absolute" ordinations were contrary to church practice in those days. Ministry was always on behalf of a church.

The next period corresponds roughly to the second millennium, which came to an end with Vatican Council II. During this period the church became much more hierarchical, scholastic theology and the influence of canon law made itself felt, and priesthood was understood in terms of personal powers bestowed on a person at ordination. The entire purpose of ordination was seen as being an empowerment to confect the Eucharist and to forgive sins. This canonically inspired theology was accepted at Trent, and passed down relatively unchanged to our own day.

The third period was launched by Vatican II. Thus, we are only at the beginning of a new era in the church. That means that, in one sense, we are the architects of the future. It is important to keep in mind the demographic shifts that underlie this. In another ten years, more than 75 percent of all Catholics will be in the third world. In the Asian sphere, especially, there is a need to take leadership to insure that the church truly becomes catholic in fact as well as in name. The effectiveness of ministry there can be an object lesson for the rest of Christianity.

Despite the Vatican Council (or, perhaps, because of it), we are still left with many problems regarding ministry. This chapter will touch on a few of them, but, unfortunately, not in any lengthy or definitive way. But perhaps we can at least raise the issues and show what the *status quaestionis* is. These are areas that will need further thought and study over the years if the church is to grow and to flourish.

The Celibacy Question

In Chapter 4 we noted the historical circumstances that led to the requirement of celibacy in the Latin church. Since this question is only one of church law, there has been much discussion of it since Vatican II (open discussion on this point was not allowed at the council). From a phenomenological point of view, thousands of priests have left the ministry to marry. In many places there is a shortage of priests because of the celibacy requirement. And many priests who have married would like to continue in the ministry. Yet, there has been a remarkable reluctance to change that law despite the need for priests throughout the world (with the possible exception of Poland). Why?

Paul VI provided several reasons in his 1967 encyclical on priestly celibacy, *Sacerdotalis coelibatus*. His arguments can be summarized in four points: the tradition of the Western church; the Christological significance of celibacy, since the priest stands "in the person of Christ"; the ecclesiological significance, particularly the freedom for ministry and the close bonding to the church that celibacy provides; and the eschatological witness to values that are beyond the values of the world.[1] John Paul II condensed these even further in his 1979 "Letter to Priests," speaking of celibacy as a gift of the Spirit providing freedom for pastoral service.

Significantly, the "official" justification has avoided the somewhat questionable bases for celibacy, such as the cultic approach of the Middle Ages, as well as the sexual taboos that led to the law in the first place. Regarding freedom for service, there is no doubt that the celibate is bonded in an unusual way to the church, for celibacy reaches down to the most intimate aspects of his personal life. And it does make him free to go wherever he may be sent, as an icon of total availability. Some people charge, however, that because the presbyter is now fully an "organization man," celibacy now remains the clearest evidence of domination, having become the primary consideration in the canonical understanding of official ministry.

By admitting that the charism of celibacy is not intrinsically tied to priesthood, that its Christological dimension is only an argument from fittingness, and that it is not essential for eschatological witness, recent popes have highlighted the ecclesiological or disciplinary importance of celibacy for the present structuring of ministry. Pope John Paul's resolve on the matter was stated clearly in his letter: Celibacy was "a characteristic, a peculiarity and a heritage of the Latin Catholic Church, a tradition to which she is resolved to persevere, in spite of all the difficulties to which such fidelity could be exposed."

Presumably, this means it will be retained despite the shortage of priests, or the scandal given the faithful by priests who violate celibacy or leave the priesthood in order to marry. It also seems to exclude any consideration of the question of a right to Eucharist by the faithful.

We should note from the outset that the church has a right to set requirements for its ministers. This is not the issue. However, from the inhibition of discussions at the Vatican council and at the 1971 Synod of Bishops, as well as from the letter of Pope John Paul II, it seems clear that there is a fear that any relaxation of the celibacy law would result in the loss of this charism in the church.

The problem here is that the open discussion of celibacy often takes place in the newspapers and magazines, rather than on official levels, where this still remains very much a taboo subject. Twenty years ago when _Concilium_ magazine asked for reaction from various countries, many refused out of fear of their bishops. In the Philippines priests were suspended or relieved from their posts for daring to contribute.

Nevertheless, should celibacy be mandatory?

Of the arguments given, total availability is undoubtedly enhanced in one who is unmarried. If the ministry is to be considered full-time service, many marriages might suffer if pitted against the demands of ministry. The question remains as to whether all presbyteral ministry need be full-time. Is the example of the Eastern or Protestant churches such that married people have proven to be ineffective ministers?

Some aspects of the official reasoning cause problems, however. Earlier it was generally assumed that there was some sort of competition between love of God and married love. This can no longer be justified theologically. For this reason Vatican II explicitly rejected a prepared text that said that "undivided love" and "dedication to God alone" must be seen as the real characteristics of religious celibacy. The final text reads, "That precious gift of divine grace which the Father gives to some...so that by virginity or celibacy they can more easily devote their lives to God alone with undivided heart."[2]

After all, total and undivided dedication to God is required of all Christians. Celibacy simply makes it easier for *some* to achieve this. We also need to avoid the old comparison of the celibate and married states, making celibacy the "higher" one. Again Vatican II disposed of this argument in its treatment of marriage. And, in a reversal of the usual argumentation, it was admitted that there can also be an affinity between marriage and ministry, especially in regard to parents.[3]

We might question the wisdom of a *universal* law of celibacy, that is, one for the whole church, or even for all presbyters. Despite the new face Vatican II tried to place on it, celibacy remains a statutory obligation that must be taken in order to get ordained; only mental gymnastics will get people to accept the reasoning that the Latin church simply chooses its priests from among those who have voluntarily embraced celibacy.

Many who argue for the detachment of priesthood and celibacy do so on the basis of human rights. This is (to my mind) a weak argument. Anyone can renounce his or her rights. Furthermore, no one can claim a right to ordination. We have to be careful not to confuse our human notion of "rights" with gospel values.

I would tend to agree with Schillebeeckx, however, that there are two basic reasons why celibacy should be reconsidered. The first is the credibility of the charism of celibacy. This goes beyond saying that celibacy should be well lived. Rather, until it is freely chosen, presbyters are constantly under the suspicion of either being gay or effeminate, or of wanting to marry but not being allowed to. And it is a well-known fact that in some countries many priests do not live up to the ideals of the celibate state, yet continue to function. This causes scandal among the people and weakens the ability to preach effectively.

Second, insisting on celibacy puts all the attention on presbyters themselves, and not on the people they are supposed to be serving. Instead of beginning with the requirements of ministry in any given community, we start with abstract qualities of the ones who are allowed to minister. Why must celibacy be a universal norm for every country in the world, despite its dubious sign value in many places?

Some argue from the theology of the church that the Christian faithful have a right to ministry, especially to the celebration of the Eucharist, but they must do without because of a lack of priests. This argument will be treated more at length in the next section.

The Right of the People to Eucharist

Schillebeeckx and others bring up the question of the right of God's People to celebrate the Eucharist.[4] De facto, at present many people are able to celebrate only infrequently because of lack of priests. That is especially true in third world countries. But as priests age more and more in the first world, it is becoming a factor there as well.[5] The official policy now for our numerous priestless parishes is that on Sundays they gather for some form of the Liturgy of the Word. If possible, some eucharistic minister brings hosts consecrated by the priest in the local parish (which may be miles away) so that there can also be a communion service. For many people this is the regular form of worship that they know; the priest gets to them for Mass only three or four times a year, if that often.

Another form of parish organization, especially in areas where already existent parishes are now left priestless, is that "pastorship" is given juridically to a non-ordained member of the community. In some cases these are religious sisters or brothers; in others laypeople are appointed to oversee the parish and assure the education and pastoral care that most parishes expect. A priest comes to celebrate Mass and hear confessions whenever possible. Thus, we are beginning to see a clear disjunction between leadership and priesthood—a clear departure from the practice of the first centuries, which linked leadership with presidency of the Eucharist.

Are our interim solutions sufficient? The general principle stated by the council was that the Eucharist was the source and summit of Christian life. The patristic principle was that the Eucharist makes the church and the church makes the Eucharist. What happens when people have to go without Eucharist for months because church authorities are unwilling to ordain married men to serve in a priestly capacity? Are we not in fact Protestantizing the church? Can we be content with occasional communion or simply with adoration of the Blessed Sacrament?

This notion of a *right* to the Eucharist is even mentioned by the council: "The laity have the right, as do all Christians, to receive in abundance from their sacred pastors the spiritual goods of the church."[6] Further, "participation [in liturgical celebrations]...is their right and duty by reason of baptism."

Yet there are some countries in Africa, for example, where there are no native priests; the people are served entirely by foreign missionaries.

Why? Because not marrying is seen by the people as an act of impiety toward the ancestors, who will be denied descendants to pray for them. How long can this last?

Many of the areas lacking priests are in the third world. The faith is kept alive there in many instances by the basic ecclesial communities. Can we say that there are no good people, no Christians in these Christian communities who would be worthy of being ordained, and who would make excellent priests?

The question remains: How can these communities of the baptized, *who have a divine right to the Eucharist,* be deprived of it for human or ecclesiastical reasons? Which "right" has the priority? The "right" seems to run up against at least three laws. One is the law of celibacy. That has been treated above. Another is a question of our ordaining only men (we will treat this later). The third would be our present structures of ministry with their requirement of many years of study.

There is a cultural barrier between the classic Western-educated type priest and the third world poor. Most priests today are somewhat like middle-class bureaucrats who have assimilated the culture and education of the dominant class. Is this the kind of priest who will function well among the mass of people today?

The complaint made at the meeting of Rectors of Asian Seminaries in 1988 was that most vocations, although they come from the poorer classes, soon become middle class and unable to relate well to the very people they come from. The more the priest studies, the broader the gap becomes between him and the people. They seem to belong to two different worlds. [7]

It would seem that identification with the people requires a person who can 1) live permanently among them; 2) understand their mentality and appreciate their religious needs; 3) communicate an intelligible religious message; 4) be a leader of or in the community. This is psychologically difficult for the kind of clergy we have at present.

This raises the question of whether or not we might diversify the type of priests we have at present, and invent a new canonical form. Mature men who have already given ample proof of their dedication and stability could be presented for ordination without having to undergo the complete education now required by the *Ratio Studiorum.* This was in fact proposed by the Conference for the 1990 Synod of (Philippine) Bishops. It has been proposed several times by the Indonesian bishops as well.

This could well mean a sort of part-time priest. Would St. Paul have approved? This issue is being raised increasingly by the basic ecclesial communities. This does not mean that we would no longer have the present type of priest. But their main function would be to work with the bishop in helping form the college of presbyters throughout the diocese.

We might add that this would bring back one aspect of ministry that was taken for granted in the early church. Each community was responsible for its own ministry and choosing its own leaders, who were then ordained without the benefit of seminary training.

Second, it is important that we not reduce people like this to simply "Mass-saying" presbyters. This was a problem in the Middle Ages that we do not have to repeat today. The Vatican II understanding of the presbyter as an evangelical person, a leader of the Word, and otherwise committed to a total concern for the community would have to prevail. This would imply some minimum of education and continuing formation.

Structures of Ministry

This brings up the larger question of the structures of ministry today. How can we evaluate and change (if necessary) even existing structures so that they are more effective? As things now stand in the church, the official ministry is to be found in the triple structure of deacon, priest, and bishop. The Vatican Council felt free to abandon the medieval pattern of various minor orders and sub-diaconate. With the reintroduction of the permanent diaconate, it tried to make the structure of church ministry actual and more meaningful. Recently the lectorate and acolytate were added, giving Christians a share in the ministry by right of baptism (but it was restricted to men).

If we are to solve confusions about the nature of the Christian community and move into the twenty-first century revitalized, the question must be faced: What is lacking in our present structures of ministry? This would affect not only the possibility of new ministries, but a reappraisal of the old ones as well.

In these pages there has been a stress on the role of the community. Perhaps the main area where we should be concentrating attention is precisely in that of empowering the laity to take their rightful place as baptized members of the community. Our theology tells us that baptism should lead all Christians to some ministerial activity. Most of our attention up to now has been given to those tasks that we might term professional ministries—professional in the sense that they exist after a serious call and long preparation, and that require essentially full-time or even lifetime commitments.

The distinction between professional ministers and other ministries should be based on the significance of these ministries to the continuing life of the community, and not on arbitrary distinctions between groups of Christians or on any theology of ordination that neglects the dignity of baptism.

Other ministries needed by the church may vary in different times and places. Some churches may need specialized ministries—for justice or for peace, for example. There are different ways in which churches will find other ministries. Some might try reintroducing ministries spoken of in the New Testament. Others might look to local needs and decide to concentrate in other areas. Here, charisms and service are directed toward a specific service of the Kingdom, or of the church, or of the human race.

Bernard Cooke argues for more open classes of ministries. He sees five fundamental areas of church life, and has organized his whole book *Ministry to Word and Sacrament* around them. They are: the formation of community; ministry of the Word; ministry to human needs; ministry of God's judgment; ministry of sacraments. Some of these categories overlap. Nevertheless, they correspond roughly to the five basic aspects of ministry often spoken of in this book. Each of them is also capable of many realizations.

There are two dangers here. The first is that of clericalizing the various ministries of the community if these are given official recognition by some form of church liturgy. The second danger is where to stop. We may easily think of ministries that are exercised by some people as being less important than those that are officially recognized. We canonize far more teachers or religious than we do politicians. Yet these latter have the potential for far greater influence than most people.

What will ultimately emerge will be some sort of concentric circles of various types of ministry. In the center will be the ministry of leadership exercised now by bishops and priests. In an adjoining circle will be other full-time or lengthy types of service that need preparation—for example, teaching, social work, counseling, peace and justice work, etc. These may well be gathered together into pastoral teams. A third circle would include more part-time ministries. Here the intensity of commitment would vary, as would the amount of preparation needed. Again, these might be within the church or service of the community. We can easily think of service by retired people or other professionals after having raised their families.

What should be realized within the church at this time, however, is that mission is the task of the entire church. Pope John Paul II's recent encyclical, *Redemptoris missio,* was written precisely to remind all Catholics of the centrality of mission to the Christian gospel.

Many of the non-Catholic churches have already been using the year 2000 as a means of stirring up greater mission awareness and zeal among the faithful. Even if we do not carry the gospel message across frontiers, there is no excuse for not witnessing in those areas in which we find ourselves. It is a question of remaining faithful to the injunction that we are to teach all nations whatever Christ himself has taught us. No one is exempt from this charge. How have we structured the church to facilitate and enable its being carried out?

Women in the Church

As far back as 1971, a group of Catholic women in Ottawa met with the Canadian Bishops' Conference and asked the bishops for five things:

1. To declare clearly and unequivocally that women are full and equal members of the church, with the same rights, privileges, and responsibilities as men.

2. To make strong and immediate representation to the forthcoming synod of bishops, asking that all discriminatory barriers in church law be removed.

3. To ordain qualified women for ministry.

4. By whatever means deemed appropriate, to encourage the presence of qualified women on all bodies dealing with matters that concern all church members.

5. To take all practical measures to insure that the attitude of the clergy towards women, sexuality, and marriage respect the inherent dignity of women.

With the single exception of the auxiliary bishop of the Ukrainian eparchy (who thought women's place was in the home), all the bishops accepted these recommendations, and were willing to raise these questions at the 1971 Synod. This was but one example of the growing dissatisfaction of women with their subordinate place in the church.[8]

Yet, more than twenty years later, not much has changed. Even aside from the ordination question itself, there seem to be a number of maddening ways in which women are reminded of their inferior status. From their exclusion from the installed ministries of lector and acolyte, to the prohibition from washing their feet on Holy Thursday, to the continued use of sexist language in the liturgy, women are told in countless ways that they are not equal, no matter what the new Code of Canon Law states.[9]

Meanwhile, in society as a whole, women have made enormous strides. They can vote and hold the highest of offices. In North America, the discontent at the disparity that exists has led to the formation of groups like "Womenchurch" to accuse the church of patriarchal and male chauvinist ideas and practices. The Womenchurch group is trying to build a sense of sisterhood with women throughout the world. Elisabeth Schüssler Fiorenza expresses some of the discontent of women in these words:

> For the first time in Christian history we women no longer seek to express our experience of God's Spirit within the framework of an androcentric spirituality. We attempt to articulate that we have found God in our soul in such a way that this experience of her presence can transform and break through the traditional framework and androcentric theology and patriarchal church.[10]

The discontent of women is no longer simply a complaint; it is a sharp accusation of our practice. As long as they are excluded from all decision-making positions, there can be no question of true liberation within the church. Since the root of the major discontent comes from the question of ordination, there is not much any of us can do. We can, however, be aware of the problem and at least do nothing in our own attitudes and practices to further the alienation women already feel.

Thus, *Baptism, Eucharist and Ministry* made the following rather cautious statement in 1982:

> 18. Where Christ is present, human barriers are being broken. The church is called to convey to the world the image of a new humanity. There is in Christ no male or female (Gal 3:28). Both women and men must discover together their contributions to the service of Christ in the church. The church must discover the ministry which can be provided by women as well as that which can be provided by men. A deeper understanding of the comprehensiveness of ministry which reflects the interdependence of men and women needs to be more widely manifested in the life of the church.

> Though they agree on this need, the churches draw different conclusions as to the admission of women to the ordained ministry. An increasing number of churches have decided that there is no biblical or theological reason against ordaining women, and many of them have subsequently proceeded to do so. Yet many

churches hold that the tradition of the church in this regard must not be changed.

The hopes of women on the ordination question in the Catholic church had already been dealt a severe blow in 1976 when the Congregation for the Defense of the Faith (CDF) issued a statement saying that they could not be ordained. This seemed doubly insulting to them because the Pontifical Biblical Commission had said only a few months previously that there was nothing in the Scriptures that could be used to prove that women could not be ordained. This was not referred to in the CDF statement.

One of the main arguments used by the CDF—that of tradition—has always been a strong argument for Catholics. It was claimed that since the church had not ordained women in 2000 years, the presumption was that this was indicative of the will of Christ. This argument has recently been dented by the research of Dr. Giorgio Otranto, an Italian scholar. Citing papal letters and inscriptions on graves, he argues that women actually *were* ordained during the first millennium.

One letter came from Pope Gelasius (494 C.E.). The pope wrote that "divine affairs have come to such a state that women are encouraged to officiate at sacred altars and to take part in all matters imputed to the offices of the male sex, to which they do not belong."[11] Obviously, this can be interpreted two ways. But the very fact of papal disapproval shows that the practice was common enough (in Sicily and southern Italy) to merit comment. As in the case of frequent confession, a practice is forbidden only when it has become accepted. It might be more prudent not to argue that we cannot ordain women because we have never before done so.

Aside from the long recent tradition of not ordaining women, the CDF also argued that since Jesus was male, those who function *in persona Christi* must also be male. I remember a satirical piece on TV that same week, when the "news announcer" said the following: "Last Wednesday the Vatican announced that women could not be ordained priests in the Roman Catholic Church since they did not resemble Jesus; since that announcement, Colonel Sanders has also announced that only people looking like chickens could work in any of his franchises."

This somewhat un-theological remark is included here only as a warning of how our argumentation can often make us look ridiculous to others. It is safe to say that this has been the one point most bitterly attacked by theologians and others in the last dozen years. Commentators point out that Jesus redeemed us because he was human, not because he was male. If redemption depended on his maleness, women would be excluded.[12]

Mention should be made of Sara Butler's contribution to the voluminous literature on this issue. As head of the Catholic Theological Society of America task force studying the women's ordination question, she was very committed to the women's position. Recent years, however, have at least helped her to understand the CDF position, something many of its critics do not always manage to do.[13]

Butler found herself in a position of having to present the CDF arguments to a non-Catholic audience, and it struck her that so many of the arguments used to "refute" the CDF have not addressed the deeper points the document was trying to make. This is inevitable if one does not understand the mind-set of the authors. In regard to the central argument of the CDF, she notes:

1. The argument that women could not image Christ is *not* what the Declaration states; it argues rather that as eucharistic leader (and only in that capacity) is woman not an apt *symbol*. Symbolism is the issue here, not function. Women are obviously capable of doing what priests *do* (which is why exclusion from ordination is so painful for them). The priest is not a God-symbol, but a Christ-symbol—Christ the priest and mediator between God and humanity. It is in his humanity that Christ came among us as mediator, and that humanity was male.

2. The crux of the problem is that it is the *incarnate* Word who offers this sacrifice, and the particular form of humanity he chose was male. This is a more significant factor than eye color, size, or any other factors that do not specify one's humanity. The cluster of symbols used by the Declaration seem to depend heavily on the above understanding.

3. It is not only the fact that Christ was and remains a *man* that is said to establish maleness as a requirement for one who would preside at Eucharist. Priesthood is seen as linked with other essential symbols of the economy of salvation: Adam, the nuptial expression of God's covenantal love, the sacrifice of the cross, and the image of Christ as bridegroom.[14]

4. What we are really dealing with is the quest for a holistic theological *anthropology*. How do we understand our embodiment as male or female, accepting the way that embodiment conditions and shapes our experience and simultaneously underscores personal freedom to choose and define social roles? Sexuality is both biological and personal. We are conditioned by our biological sex, and yet free to determine within that horizon which roles are appropriate expressions

of our personhood. Our humanity, individuality, and sexuality are integrally related; one would not be the same as a member of the opposite sex.[15]

5. This may help explain the intention of "equality is in no way identity," the phrase used by the Declaration to explain why there is no injustice in excluding women from ordination. It goes beyond non-interchangeable and mutually exclusive social roles. We may not find the reasoning of the CDF probative, but we must at least try to understand the anthropology that consistently informs Vatican documents, as well as Pope John Paul II's "theology of the body."

That having been said, there is much left to criticize in the Vatican position. And it would be easier to accept their sincerity if other roles not dependent on ordination were open to women. When they come from seemingly closed minds and lack pastoral sensitivity, even the best arguments fail. Furthermore, many women are voting with their feet because the present discipline seems arbitrary, and because Vatican reasoning seems irrelevant to the larger issues of justice and equality. Do we really want to lose the women in the church?

The Mutual Recognition of Ministries

Ecumenism is perhaps the most exciting new development in the last half of the twentieth century. Though the Protestant churches had joined together in the World Council of Churches earlier in the century, it was only with the participation of the Catholic church after the Vatican Council that there seemed any real possibility of healing the splits that were brought about since the Reformation. Mutual acceptance of the validity of ministry in the other churches is one of the key questions that arises when the question of ministry in the various churches is discussed.

It is not only a question of different stresses and emphases that other churches have given to the practice of ministry. What is at stake is whether or not they possess a "valid" ministerial structure or priesthood. Vulgarly speaking, can a Protestant minister consecrate the Eucharist? Can we receive communion in their churches? Do their Masses "count"?[16]

This issue was given extended treatment in the relatively brief Lima Statement on Ministry, an indication of its seriousness and importance. As Schillebeeckx points out, this document is a (not *the*) legitimate and ecclesially responsible starting point for discussion of this question among the churches.[17]

There are several ways to approach this complex topic. Before the

Vatican council, it seemed clear that for Roman Catholics, the criteria for valid orders were the following:

1. The intention of doing what the church does.

2. The use of a sufficiently sacramental form with the laying on of hands as the visible sign or matter (general standards here have never really been established).

3. Possession of the requisite "character," i.e., the minister of orders must be in apostolic succession and able to trace his descent back (in theory) to the apostles.

In cases where one or more of these conditions are not found, the church was unable to recognize the ordination as a valid one.

Even these criteria have often been questioned, and the issue remained moot at the time of Vatican II. As we know, however, this council did several things to change our understanding of this entire general question.

1. We now have a broader notion of church. *Lumen gentium* rejected the idea that other Christian churches are "outside the church";[18] this provides the basis for the dramatic new teaching on ecumenism that was spelled out in *Unitatis redintegratio* (UR). It is also laden with implications for the validity of orders. If the mainline Protestants are not "outside the church," then the guidelines of Cyprian[19] (cf. chapter three) would imply that their orders are valid. The argument can be summarized by saying that if they have a true church, they must have valid orders.

2. Furthermore, according to Vatican II, a "defect of orders" does not necessarily mean there is no Eucharist at all.

The ecclesial communities separated from us lack that fullness of unity with us which should flow from baptism, and we believe that especially because of the lack of the sacrament of orders they have not preserved the genuine and total reality of the eucharistic mystery. Nevertheless when they commemorate the Lord's death and resurrection in the Holy Supper, they profess that it signifies life in communion with Christ and await his coming in glory.[20]

Two things can be noted here. The decree does not call Protestant orders null and void. It says simply that there is a "defect of orders" (not a *lack*). Second, it does not say that because of this their Eucharists are invalid, as 152 bishops wanted the text to say. The explanation given is that what was lacking to the Eucharist was not the presence of the body and blood of Christ, but something else that is integral to the eucharistic mystery, the expression of church unity by one who stands in an ordered relationship to a bishop.

3. This question has been the subject of much reflection in the ecumenical dialogues that have taken place since the council. There is a general consensus that has emerged in recent historical and theological scholarship:

a. There is consensus that New Testament evidence shows that the primitive church had pluriform structures of ministry. While ordination has its roots in the New Testament, there is no evidence that only the apostles or ordained persons presided at the Eucharist.

b. Historical research has shown that while ordination by bishops was the universal norm before the Reformation, there are examples of unordained "charismatic" leaders of the Eucharist, especially in the early church, and certain examples of ordinations by priests over a period of many centuries.

c. There is a growing consensus that apostolic succession is not confined to episcopal succession. Instead of being seen as coextensive with apostolic succession, the historical episcopate is being seen as an ancient and continuingly viable and effective sign of the apostolic succession of the whole church in the apostolic faith, life, teaching, mission, and witness. (The immediate implication of this more historically defensible position is that ordinations that take place outside the pattern are not ipso facto invalid.)

d. Virtually all the dialogues point out that ordination, like all sacraments, is a sacrament of the church. This new emphasis on the ecclesial context has important implications. It avoids the ontological argument and looks rather for manifestations of true ecclesiality. And because the council has stressed that the church is made present in the local church, the question should be studied there first of all.

e. The term "validity" itself may not be the best. It is a relative latecomer to Christian vocabulary, having only been officially accepted by Pope Benedict XIV (d. 1758). To equate this with earlier language can (and has) led to distortion of the original intention of the earlier texts. Furthermore, it is ambiguous and leads to the implication that in every case it represents the way God sees things.

f. The historical character of the church is another point. Since we now see ourselves as a pilgrim people (and not as a perfect society), none of the existent churches can identify with the perfect church. Further, canon law is not meant to be applied with severity, but as a law of grace. The counterpart to this in our history is the idea of *oikonomia* in the Eastern church and the notion of *ecclesia supplet* in the Latin church.

As Catholics, we have placed much emphasis on the linear understanding of apostolic succession. Yves Congar has shown, however, that until the late Middle Ages the idea was primarily one of succession in apostolic faith and love (belief and practice). A succession of laying on of hands was no more than a sign, which lost its power as soon as the one holding office lost faith by apostasy. The imposition of hands is therefore only a sign that the office-bearer is in communion with the apostolic church.

The change from the earlier theology to one based on rather extrinsic criteria of validity came as a result of the changes that sacramental theology underwent in the second millennium. After the first 1000 years, interest shifted from the activity of God made present in the office of the church. Analytically-minded theologians of the scholastic period, influenced by the rise of canon law, were instead more interested in the inner structure of the abstract sacramental rites. Thus they gave more prominence to the task of establishing criteria for validity. This emphasis focused on the observable, visible elements of the rite rather than on the role and action of the Holy Spirit. The result was something new: an emphasis on matter and form, not only of the church itself, but of its theology of office.

Today we can argue that if office in the church is a true expression of the gospel in and for the community, and if it serves to build up the church, there would seem to be no theological objection to a mutual recognition of offices.

Priestly Spirituality

This last point is included because of its importance and because of our need to find an alternate for the French School spirituality that has dominated the church since the seventeenth century. The burn-out experienced by so many priests in recent years might have been avoided if they had had a spirituality more attuned to the age in which we live. The image of priesthood sketched by Vatican II requires a corresponding priestly spirituality today.

The difficulties we face here come from one main source. It was customary in the past to think and speak of priesthood as a special *state*. Priests belonged to this state no matter what their duties might be. We still find traces of this mentality at the Vatican council.

Presybterorum ordinis (8), for example, tries to address this issue, but nothing said there takes a fresh look at the needs of priests today. Chapter III deals with presbyteral life, and has three sections. The first deals with the priestly call to perfection (sections 12-14), goes on to speak of the special spiritual needs of the priestly life (sections 15-17), and ends with the means of support for priestly life (sections 18-21). Basically, this is a rehash of the concepts and theological categories of the past.

Thus, section 12 tells us that priests "take on the likeness of Christ" and therefore "have a special obligation to acquire perfection" inasmuch as they were "consecrated afresh to God when they were ordained." They have been made "living instruments of Christ," and the council urges them "to use every means the church recommends...to attain an ever greater personal holiness" so that they will become "more fitting instruments in the service of the whole People of God."

In going on to discuss priestly holiness, the Decree takes it for granted that there *is* a distinctive brand of priestly holiness. In this area, the council did not face up to some of the consequences of its own theology. In section 14, the Christian community is once again seen as the flock committed to the care of the priest (an old and basic misconception that takes the priest out of the community). This approach prevents anyone from seeing the necessity of asking them to work in communion with their fellow Christians. They are asked to work in communion with their fellow priests, however, which is good; but this has always been found in books dealing with priestly holiness.

No room is provided for the possibility of disagreeing with "those whom God has appointed visible rulers of the church" (section 15). Indeed, the basic spirituality is imitating Christ's humility and obedience "responsibly and gladly given [to] those who are principally responsible for ruling the church of God." A parallel is set up between Christ's obedience to the Father and the priest's obedience to the will of his superiors. There are at least four theological difficulties here:

> 1. In many of these statements we find that the determining factor is Jesus Christ, the priest, or God. But we do not find a well-articulated Christology, or any advertence to the fact that priests must operate in a fast changing world far different from first-century Israel.

2. When the question arises, how priestly spirituality is to work itself out concretely, the answer is usually the same: The guiding norms are regular pious exercises and a specific pattern of external conduct. This can easily lead to the misconception that priestly spirituality is something we can measure, learn, and make comparisons about, based on the amount of prayer or other externals.

3. It is presumed from the start that there is a distinctive priestly spirituality over and against "lay" spirituality. If any attempt is made to justify this, it is all too often based on differences in function within the church, ecclesiastical office, or differences in state of life.

4. If the relationship between spirituality and the Christian ethos is pondered at all, the usual response is that priestly spirituality is a special instance of the over-all Christian spirituality. We are told over and over again that true perfection can only be found when this special spirituality is sought after, but little proof is offered to back up this assertion.

Hans Urs von Balthasar once defined spirituality as, in general, a person's basic existential attitude and approach to life. It is the product and the expression of one's religious or ethical outlook, of one's own commitment as a person. The distinctive nature of Christian spirituality, then, must be sought in the nature and purpose of Christian commitment.

Thinking of spirituality as the style of a person's response to Christ before the challenge of everyday life in any given cultural environment captures both the personal dimension of call and response, as well as the environmental factors of time and place that will necessarily affect that same call and response. Vocation is God calling us anew each day to be faithful in the circumstances of time and place. Thus, we need the ability to read the signs of the times.

This understanding of spirituality allows for evolution in our understanding of God, faith, commitment, sin, etc. The yardstick is not a set of rules, but fidelity to a relationship both to Christ and to his people. It is something tailored to the gifts and vocation of each. There will always be a tension between the spirituality of one generation and another, and what it should be today and tomorrow. Vatican II's attitude and approach is a perfect example, inasmuch as it invites a whole new look at this reality we call church and religion. Many of those who have rejected the council have done so because they saw it as a betrayal of the past rather than as an invitation to grow into the fullness of Christ.

As to how we grow and express our commitment, it is not sufficient to answer this by simply pointing to Jesus, or Christ the priest, or the "will of God." For one thing, Jesus does not represent some transcendent, otherworldly spirituality that we struggle to reach with our frail human efforts. Jesus is the great historical happening where we encounter God's definitive yes to humanity and to our world (cf. 2 Corinthians 1:19).

"Jesus Christ" means that human nature has a beginning and a future ordained by God from all eternity, and inseparable from him. It would seem that the authentic basis of Christian spirituality (and *a fortiori* that of the priest) is *life*, insofar as it is the embodiment of the grace that has been given to us and its dimensions and future prospects are revealed to us in Christ.

Thus, Christian spirituality begins when we grasp our given human situation as a real opportunity, and we commit ourselves to the human race that God loved so much that he sent his only-begotten Son (John 3:16). There is no other "will of God" for us. The ultimate orientation of spirituality is laid out for all in the gospel, where God has identified himself with humankind.

The gospel represents an opportunity and an open-ended future as we try to make God's will for humanity a reality. Our having been claimed for Christ through baptism is already a promise of God's fidelity and willingness to empower us by his Spirit. The spirit here is that of Paul in Romans 8:18-25, when he sees all of creation groaning to be brought to the perfection willed for it by God. Our commitment to this means that there is only *one* Christian spirituality. Any particular spiritual works, pious practices, or good deeds are secondary.

This is important, because the tendency in the past has been to identify spirituality with external practices, whether they are prayers, acts of mortification, or any other pious deeds. There has also been a tendency to see holiness as belonging only to priests and religious, with the consequent downplaying of the spirituality that should be proper to the entire people of God.

Thus, there is only one spirituality. We are justified in speaking of a "special" spirituality of the priest only in the sense that he forms part of a group that has made a special public commitment to serve as a servant of Christ Jesus and his gospel. What we have is essentially a servant spirituality. That being the case, we can speak about its spirit, as well as its goal. The *spirit* of this servant spirituality can be found in numerous places in the gospels. Some of the basic attitudes would be:

Humility. Priests have been called by God; they have not chosen him, he has chosen them. Their task is gift. This rules out pride, vanity, and class consciousness. At the same time, all God's servants have been given the same opportunities, the same grandeur, and the same reward (Matthew 20:1–16). There is no place for a spiritual hierarchy, for all are unprofitable servants (Luke 17:10) who must have the mind of Christ Jesus (Philippians 2:6ff).

Mercy would be another characteristic. The gospel servants have a strict and unconditional duty to be merciful, because mercy has been shown them (Matthew 18:23–35). They are not to measure, judge, or condemn (Luke 6:37ff). They are physicians, not judges. God can take care of the weeds at judgment day.

Fidelity, combined with *efficiency* and *productivity* are also involved. Knowing God's will, priests will be punished for carousing in God's absence (Luke 12:45–48). Whatever is entrusted to them (and it is the gospel) is not to be buried in the ground for safekeeping. It is to bear fruit for God (Luke 19:12–27; Matthew 25:14–30). Their ability to read the signs of the times will help them note opportunities to serve better day by day.

As regards the *goal* of spirituality, the implication is that priests— like all the baptized—be fully committed to building a better world. In this sense, the areas of social justice mentioned in Chapter 9, on the *aggiornamento* of Vatican II, are appropriate. This is the only thing that will keep them from having a spirituality so otherworldly that it bears little relation to the real world in which they live and work.

Several authors have addressed the issue of spirituality in the last decade. Ancilli, a professor in Rome, suggests that these trends characterize our age: a sense of community, a longing for the absolute, a return to the sources, and an opening and commitment to the world. This harmonizes well with what we have said above.[21]

As one reviews developments today, it seems that there are four major trends, or thrusts, in spirituality.[22] 1) Spirituality today is *ecclesial.* This thrust includes everything that emphasizes a sense of church, community awareness, the prayer and life of the people of God, and attitudes or styles of living that portray the group dimension of the church.

Recent years have witnessed a growing awareness of what it means to be church along with a commitment to fostering community growth. Numerous forms of renewal since the council emphasize conversion and renewal as an ecclesial experience. Some dioceses have directed their renewal efforts to setting up basic ecclesial communities. The most visible characteristics of the majority of these movements are sharing in faith, witness of mutual charity, and the community or ecclesial thrust of the members' lives. Even in prayer groups and charismatic groups the most visible feature is usually the common prayer and praise of a believing people.

All of this requires support groups and structures to facilitate co-responsibility, a sense of solidarity, dialogue, mutual appreciation, and fidelity and perseverance in each one's commitment to the other. In other words, many of today's trends, such as prayer movements and prayer groups, require group forms of asceticism or spiritual commitment. Almost all of these have added a community aspect to individual prayer and have reemphasized active participation in liturgies.

This community element has overflowed into a wider community awareness on a civic, national, and international level—an awareness that has led to a sense of brotherhood and sisterhood, a need to share, and a feeling of responsibility for world needs. It has also led to the development of movements supporting minority rights in civil society and church.

2. Spirituality today is *incarnational*. This thrust includes contemporary movements that foster a positive appreciation of the world, that call for dialogue between church and organizations, between corporate structures and science, and that lead to an integration of the spiritual and the temporal. As the previous trend reflected a new and willing cooperation with one another and with God, so this one reflects a new attitude to the world in which the church exists.

The church now not only sees the world positively but also envisions its own role as one of self-insertion into world realities. Christians are called to commit themselves to the temporal, though using it with detachment; to heal, animate, and transform the world; to consecrate the world to God in Christ. In this the influence of *Gaudium et spes* is evident.

Incarnational spirituality is a spirituality of influential presence. It implies a positive appreciation of the world and a self-insertion into that world to sanctify and redeem it. Of the four major thrusts referred to, this one has received most attention in the last fifty years. Possibly Matthew Fox and those who have shown increased interest in the health of our planet express this trend best. Theirs is a creation-centered spirituality for today, not the fall/redemption spirituality of previous eras.

Bound up with an incarnational emphasis in spirituality is a healthy appreciation of the world—an appreciation that leads, for example, to ecological concerns and to non-possessiveness in one's own life. In addition, many of today's trends in leisure, exercise, health foods, and so on are not just fads, but have a religious basis. Today, too, our concept of "neighbor" has undergone a dramatic change as we examine our world. Some authors, reflecting on Jesus' command, suggest that "neighbor" is not just the person one meets but also foreign cultures, nations, organizations, and so on. In fact, we have come to understand that our treatment of the world is part of our very journey to God.

3. The third major thrust is toward *service to the world*; it includes all forms of the ministry of all the baptized in the world. Not only are we more clearly aware of who we are as church and more fully appreciative of the world in which we live, but we see service to that world as an integral part of our spirituality. While many forms of ecclesial ministry for all the baptized have developed in recent years, the major thrust in spirituality has been for ministries to the world. Just as the incarnational thrust was an extension of the ecclesial, so this service-oriented thrust is basically a deeper commitment to the incarnational dimension.

The concept of "servant church" is not explicitly used in the documents of Vatican II, but it certainly permeates many sections of the documents, notably numbers 40 to 44 of the Pastoral Constitution. Here the church is seen as serving the world by being a leaven and soul for human society, by giving meaning and value to everyday human activity, and by having "a healing and elevating impact on the dignity of the person."[23]

The church teaches the meaning of human existence, anchors "the dignity of human nature against all tides of opinion,"[24] proclaims the dignity of conscience and freedom of choice, advises all the baptized to use their talents for God's service and the world's, and protects human rights. On a social level the church serves the world by insisting on family unity, by aiding the needy, and by being a sign and instrument of universality.

4. The fourth major thrust, which has many varieties, is itself a development of the third but has become so pronounced and extensive that it deserves specific consideration. Spirituality today is *liberational*; to be authentic it must move from liberation and justice in oneself to others, including instrumental structures, whether civil or ecclesiastical. The world is also seen from an ecological perspective.

This fourth trend in spirituality is related to the others in that it is an intensification of, or a particular aspect of, serving the world and responding to its cry for fullness of life. Since the council, an acute awareness of social, structural, and cosmic sin has developed among Christians; an appreciation that we are all victims dying from a lack of compassion—hence a concrete commitment at all levels to liberating ourselves, others, and the world from this generation's oppressions. The conviction is growing daily that spirituality is not simply individual but must be authenticated in a dedication to social justice. This liberational thrust of spirituality tends to manifest itself in three ways.

a. The first is through healing. On a personal level this is directed against compulsiveness, competitiveness, and possessiveness, and it is turning many to a life of simplicity in which Christians de-emphasize luxuries and the consumer mentality and live in simple ways, using all superfluous wealth to help others in need. On a group level we have seen a whole spirituality of healing shared in workshops that provoke new attitudes to self and others and lead to a sharing of life with others who are no longer seen so much as "less fortunate" but as unfortunate, as we all are in our individual ways. L'Arche communities are an example of this attitude and life sharing.

b. The second way that the liberational thrust of spirituality tends to manifest itself is through a prophetic challenge to society. This challenge—sometimes called contestation—is a personal or organized struggle against the injustices of structured society, whether civil or ecclesiastical. The passivity of former spirituality has hindered the development of this dimension, and we still need to educate both clergy and laity to genuine evangelical contestation. Many have become involved in social justice issues. Just salaries, rights of minorities, defeat of sexist positions, justice for political prisoners, opposition to unlawful governments, challenge to abuse of position, and correcting legal injustices have all been the focus of challenge. Others have challenged the way we all abuse the environment, and the way multinational corporations have selfishly exploited it.

c. In addition to the emphasis on healing and prophetic challenge to society, a third approach within the liberational thrust has been the adoption and development of new attitudes of creativity, imagination, and hope. If we are to resolve world problems, we must challenge them in new ways and offer new solutions and alternatives. Organizations, whether civil or ecclesiastical, seem dedicated above all to self-preservation, and structured injustices will remain unless the prophetic Christian can propose new and creative solutions. Prophets today, dedicated to liberation, must have imagination and vision, facilitated by leisure and contemplation of the Word.

This long explanation is to show why today's spirituality has a political and social dimension. Involvement in social justice issues is seen as a dimension of faith and of the will of God. The major trends in today's spirituality also show a clear return to values found in the lives of all the baptized. The emphases are ecclesial, not ecclesiastical; incarnational, not flight from the world; oriented toward service to the world, not to hierarchical ministry; liberational, not exclusively sacramental. These never exclude their alternatives, but complement them. They also form the basis of all spirituality in the church—priestly as well as lay.

Discussion Questions

1. If celibacy is retained as a discipline in the church, what can be done to make it a better witness in the world? What obstacles on the part of people might make optional celibacy rather difficult? Is the removal of the celibacy requirement a cure-all for the vocation crisis?

2. What can local churches do to respond more effectively to the ministerial crisis in the church at large? How can the talents of women be better used? How can communities be made more responsible for raising up their own ministers?

3. What ministerial structures could well be changed today? Why? Are there examples of different forms of ministry from other Christian groups that might be helpful? What are they?

4. What might be done to prevent the further alienation of women from the church today? What might be done at the parish level now?

Suggested Readings

Burrows, W. R. New Ministries: The Global Context, Maryknoll, N.Y.: Orbis Books, 1981.

Butler, S., "Second Thoughts on Ordaining Women," Worship, 63, 2, (March 1989), 157-165.

Clarkson, Shannon, "Steps Towards Unity—A Mutual Recognition of Ordained Ministries," J.E.S., 23 (1986) 489-521.

Gaine, M., "State of the Priesthood," Modern Catholicism: Vatican II and After, New York: Oxford University Press, 1991, pp. 246-255.

Hendrickx, H., "The People of God in Holy Scripture," EAPR, 23 (1986), 210-230.

Küng, H. and W. Kasper, The Plurality of Ministries, Concilium, 74, 1972.

Rademacher, W., "Women in the Church," Lay Ministry, New York: Crossroad, 1991, pp. 145-168.

Reumann, J.H.P. Ministries Examined: Laity, Clergy, Women and Bishops in a Time of Change, Minneapolis: Augsburg, 1987.

12

Toward an Evangelical Ministry

This survey has provided a rather cursory trip through 2000 years of Christian history. Though tomes can be (and have been) written about any one of these periods, it is hoped that this survey has at least made the point that the current theology of ministry is the end result of a long process of development. The real question that now faces us is how we can use the past to help us face the future. What lessons are there that might be normative for us today?

It bears repeating once again that few changes were consciously planned. (Vatican II is one of the rare exceptions.) Most resulted from the need to adapt to changing historical circumstances. They were responses to need and appeared to people at that time as the best way to be faithful to the mission of Christ. Thus, it becomes important to ask *why* certain shifts and changes took place. Hindsight may show them to be understandable at the time, but regrettable in long-term consequences.

Looking for some sort of pattern in our past, we might note once again that there seems to be a general shift of theology in the second millennium from what obtained in the first. This went beyond simple changes of practice; it involved major theological shifts as well. These have been alluded to in the text. As we stand at the threshold of our third millennium, however, with the scriptural and historical knowledge that is now ours, and with the Vatican Council as a guide, we can appreciate more the new guiding principles of church ministry. These will be the real achievement of Vatican II.

Principles of Church Ministry

It has been customary to speak of ordained ministry mainly in terms of priesthood. In the decree *Presbyterorum ordinis*, Vatican II tried to distance us from this by avoiding the use of the word "priest" (except for Christ), using *presbyter* instead and speaking of *presbyteral ministry*. These words are seldom heard today, however. Even thirty years after the council, everything seems to come back to priesthood. How can we update its meaning?

The following are the basic assumptions that seem to flow from the council and from historical awareness of our past. They should underlie any theology of ministry today.

1. Christ is the origin of all priesthood. This is not restating the obvious. Because of our longstanding preoccupation with the notion of jurisdiction, priestly ministry was thought by some to come from the bishop. Even the bishops' authority was seen as coming from the pope. And the link that we did retain with Christ was deficient in two main ways.

First, we developed what many have called a "Christo-monistic" theology of ministry. Ministry was related directly to Christ in such a way that we ignored both the reality of the church itself and the Holy Spirit who is the very life of that church. With the hierarchization of ministry in the second millennium, priesthood became an abstract entity unto itself, and ordination was reduced to the transmission of powers from individual to individual, almost apart from any relationship to the community that they were ordained to serve. We will say more about this later.

One of the major insights of the New Testament—though found only in the Letter to the Hebrews—is that Christ was a priest. He is, in fact, the ultimate example of all priesthood, his perfection being such that it exhausts the category. Likewise his sacrifice is so perfect that by a single offering he has for all time perfected those who have been sanctified (Hebrews 10:14). He is the one sacrifice, the one mediator (Hebrews 9:15).

Hebrews begins with the insight that all cultic attempts to reconcile ourselves to God are useless and futile human works. In the first place, God has no need of anything we could ever sacrifice (the whole world belongs to God). Second, nothing sacrificed can ever substitute adequately for the adoration and submission to God expressed by our "Yes," our total gift of self to God. Handing ourselves over to God completely constitutes the only genuine worship.

Only one person alone has ever managed to do this perfectly: Jesus.

This is why he is the only one who deserves the title of "priest." The blood that he offered (Hebrews 9:12) is not some*thing*, one of many things that he might give; he offered him*self* completely. In a gesture of total love, he offered the totality of his human existence to the Father. Though his entire life was lived out in the "profane" sphere—his execution as a public criminal was a very profane action—his complete dedication to God is the only true liturgy. In breaking down the dichotomy between sacred and profane, Jesus shows us what true worship is.

This is why, at the same time that it speaks of Jesus as the one true priest, Hebrews makes it clear that it is attempting to redefine what priesthood is all about. The barrier of sin has been destroyed because of Christ's total commitment to the Father, and we can now approach God with trust and confidence. Jesus is the only one to possess this priesthood, and his sacrifice is said to be "once and for all." His death manifests the holiness of the apparently profane, and the non-holiness of the apparently religious.

Raymond Brown has noted how this implies a radical obedience to Christ, who is the source of all priesthood and authority in the church.[1] Vatican II insisted that priest/presbyters get their authority directly from Christ, not the bishop. Allegiance is primarily to him, not the institution. The priest is not just a religious functionary, an agent of the bishop, any more than the bishop is meant to be an agent of the pope.

Hebrews, however, makes another point that is often lost (the spirituality of the French School being a prime example): Christ's priesthood is based on his humanity, not his divinity. It is because he was like us in everything but sin that his total obedience to God enabled him to offer a perfect sacrifice (Hebrews 4:15; 5:7–8).

This is why the council was careful to relate priestly ministry to the entire public ministry of Christ. Again, as Brown points out, priests may vie to celebrate the Eucharist, and see this as the prime reason for their priesthood, but they are not so eager to wash one another's feet.[2] The council offers a valuable corrective here for true presbyteral ministry. Priesthood is not a question of power or glory, of having an exalted state of life above that of other Christians; it is the ability to incarnate Christ's own compassion and concern for people along with his wholehearted love and obedience to his Father.

2. *Christ's priesthood is shared by the entire church.* The only other priesthood mentioned in the New Testament, besides that of Christ, is the common priesthood of all believers. Jesus instituted a structured community which is, as an entirety, holy, priestly, prophetic, missionary, and apostolic. Charisms and ministries are at the heart of the life of

the church, all freely raised up by the Spirit. Some of these are recognized and linked by ordination to the special mission of the Twelve. But baptism remains the foundational sacrament. It is constitutive of all Christian dignity, the principle of missionary awareness as well as the principle of Christian responsibility in the world.[3]

The church is a community built up by a great number of modes of service. It was within the original community of disciples that Jesus chose the Twelve. It is from this same community that the ordained ministries now come. This has been schematized through the years in various ways. The basic schema most people are familiar with is the strictly linear one, where everything passes from Christ, through the pope, the bishops, priests down to the laity. This was so crass that council explicitly jettisoned it.

According to Congar, the council schema imagines a simultaneous but separate action of Christ and the Holy Spirit on both the community as a whole as well as on the ordained ministers. Moreover, there is also a reciprocity of action between this people of God and its ministers.

Congar himself, however, prefers a somewhat different schema. He envisages the church as a whole, like a circle. Both Christ and the Holy Spirit act directly on this community within which the various ministries exist. Here again, there is reciprocity between the community and the ministries. No ministries exist outside the community.

In older times, for example, this was expressed by the election of pastors by the faithful. Then the charism of a person would be recognized by the community and that person called (sometimes even against his wishes). Election by the community was part of an organic process that culminated in ordination.[4] This is far from the current understanding of vocation where one feels a personal attraction that is verified by superiors and subsequently effected by ordination.

By the second and third centuries the community understanding of church resulted in the dictum that the one who presides over the Christian community also presides over its prayer or liturgy. Presidency over the Eucharist flowed from leadership and care of the community, not vice versa. For most of the first millennium, in fact, the link between the minister (bishop or priest) and community was so close that ordination was not to take place outside the eucharistic assembly of the local church; furthermore, no ordination could be "absolute," i.e., without binding a person to a concrete community. Absolute ordinations were forbidden in the church until the twelfth century.

Neither could bishops or priests move from church to church, because they were ordained for the service of a specific community and were, in a sense, wedded to that same community. There is much that can be learned from this regarding concern for the flock, as well as the pastoral style that enables presbyteral ministry to be a collegial effort to build up God's people that all might reach the maturity of Christ Jesus.

There is another important ecclesial consequence here in terms of apostolicity, which goes far beyond the idea of apostolic succession. Apostolicity here is one of faith which, according to Vatican II, adheres to the whole church (cf. *Dei verbum*, section 10). Congar's own growth has led him to give priority and decisive importance to this faith, which is a property of the whole church. Because of it the council could insist that the whole church was apostolic. This is the unifying principle allowing bishops and faithful to be joined in one common effort.

Any theology of ordained ministry should derive from a solid ecclesiology, not vice versa. The danger of thinking of priesthood in ontological categories (as we did in the past) or in terms of the character imparted at ordination is that it results in a Platonic mindset whereby we think in terms of powers and status quite apart from any specific community.[5] It should be the other way around, for ministry is derived from the church and exists for its sake.

3. Ordained priesthood is for the community. For those accustomed to a cultic understanding of ordained ministry, it comes as a shock to realize that nowhere in the New Testament is priestly vocabulary attributed to the Twelve or to any of Jesus' disciples. These were given (secular) names that expressed the notion of ministry or service, or positions of responsibility within the community.

Despite no mention of ordained priesthood anywhere in the New Testament, there is no need to consider it a distortion of our New Testament foundations. The council carefully avoided the historical problems here. Instead of linking the ordained ministry only to the Last Supper, it spoke instead of Christ having instituted ministry throughout his public life. The ordained are heirs to this.

In the past we were led to over-sacralize the priesthood by reverting to the Old Testament models of Melchisedek and the levitical priesthood. This starting point can still lead to interpreting the conciliar statements that by ordination presbyters share in the ministry of Christ the *head* as a legitimation of power and domination. This effectively takes ministry out of the community and sets it over and against it, whether in judgment or in controlling the means of grace.

We need to reexamine our older understanding of the priest. The Catholic priest has long been understood—not only in rhetorical exaggeration, but in the liturgical and theological tradition—as the liturgist, as the one who performs the eucharistic celebration. How do things now stand? Was that understanding false? Should this function now be eliminated?

There is no need either to perform such radical surgery or to assume that there is really little need for ordained ministry in the church. In our renewed understanding of the New Testament concept of ministerial office, the sacramental—and specifically eucharistic functions—are not eliminated but embedded more clearly in the context in which they belong: a ministry that is a complete and total imitation of Christ's life of service.

4. *The church is a spiritual communion.* Western theology in general has been less aware of the Holy Spirit than has the Eastern. This was especially evident in how sacraments were understood. The Western Eucharistic Prayer never even bothered to include an invocation of the Holy Spirit. No one worried about this until Vatican II. We did invoke the Holy Spirit in our ecclesiology, but mainly to assure the rectitude of the acts of the ecclesial institution and the efficacy of the sacraments or, in modern times, to guarantee pronouncements of the Magisterium.

Congar notes that a truly pneumatological view of the church can be spelled out in five points. Three are especially pertinent to our subject.[6]

a. The church is never complete or fully made, but is constantly being molded by the Spirit. There is always room for people to make their personal contributions and exercise their creativity.

b. The fullness of the Spirit in the church comprises the sum total of all the gifts with which the members are endowed. The church is not a pyramid with the people spread out passively at the bottom receiving everything from the top. Further, the church is catholic precisely by virtue of its embracing all the particular and varied gifts that each church has received.

c. Realizing the importance of the Spirit helps us to conceive a Trinitarian model of ecclesiology. Such a model would help us understand the church as a communion of persons, a diversity of situations, and the necessity of mutual communication and exchange. The hierarchy must not get tied up in itself and think that it has a monopoly of the Spirit.

It is precisely pneumatology that enables us to see ordained ministry not so much in terms of metaphysical changes being wrought in the one ordained, but in terms of the new relationship brought about with the community. Ordination is an act whereby the Holy Spirit does establish particular relationships within the community of the church—not just abstract and logical relationships, but deeply existential and soteriological ones. Describing the difference between the ordained and the rest of the people of God in terms of relationship avoids reducing ordination to something purely functional.

Saying that ministry belongs to the community places the ordination problematic outside the dilemma of choosing between an ontological or a functional understanding (i.e., whether ordination bestows something indelible on the one ordained, or merely empowers one to function for a certain purpose). After all, no charism of the Spirit is possessed simply as individuals. The Holy Spirit always acts for the good of the church.

As we noted in Chapter 9, attaching importance to the community does not imply that it has some sort of logical or temporal precedence. *Charismata* do not follow the existence of the body of Christ, they are constitutive of it. Ordination is a primordial and constitutive act of the Christian community. Each ordination constitutes the church anew in a pneumatological way as the Body of Christ in this place.

5. Priestly ministry is a call. The beginning of Mark's gospel (3:13–19) prefixes his account of the calling of the Twelve with the statement, "and he called to himself those whom he desired." These words fix the origin of New Testament ministry, as well as where and how it takes shape. According to Mark, ministry is above all a response to this call and acceptance of Christ's will. Jesus calls those whom he desires. His will is manifested by the times and circumstances, and our ability to read accurately the "signs of the times."

It is the moments of response to a call and acceptance of God's will that are constitutive of ministry in the New Testament. They also ground the priest's personal relationship with Jesus, whose instrument he tries to be. As far as the New Testament is concerned, it is the entire public ministry of Jesus that sets the scope for all subsequent ministry. The ordained are called to incarnate Christ's own compassion and concern for the flock. They are far more than simply celebrators of the sacraments.

We have in this call a lasting and fundamental determination of what constitutes spiritual office in the church. It rests on the existential posture of the servant who has learned how to allot second place to his own will in favor of the will of the person to whom he belongs. Priests belong to Christ, but especially to his body which is the church.

6. Church ministry is prophetic. Of course, the New Testament passages dealing with the call of the Twelve, whose ministry priests now share, are not to be taken historically. They are cast in the Old Testament mold portraying those who have received a prophetic calling from God. It is extremely significant that the ministry of the Twelve is described within the parameters of a prophetic call and not, for example, within the traditions of Leviticus, or of Temple priesthood. This surely means that the servants of Christ are claimed in the deeply personal fashion characteristic of prophetic ministry.[7]

So can priests today be said to be called to preside over a prophetic community. For Jesus sent out the Twelve "to preach and to have authority...." They are sent for the purpose of preaching, in order to preside over a community that is truly formed by God's Word. In carrying out Christ's deeds of power, his destruction of the domination of evil, in being messengers of the kingdom that is to come, we can see the significance and constitution of Christian ministry.

It is in this context that the eucharistic celebration takes place, for Eucharist is the fully empowered proclamation of the death and resurrection of the Lord, a proclamation of such force that it brings about the actual presence of this saving event. It is in this way that the liturgy is the manifestation of the community that is the church. And it is through the empowering and presence-creating proclamation of the saving deeds of Jesus that the risen Lord comes among us to form us into the one body that is the church.

The liturgical aspects of presbyteral ministry flow from the prophetic or "missionary" understanding of the priest. Not only is there no opposition between them, they mutually support and interpret one another. While the New Testament itself is silent as to who presided over the Eucharist in the early days, we know from the *Didache*, a work contemporaneous with the gospels, that the prophets and apostles (missionaries) were the ones who ordinarily presided. If we understand the Eucharist as the highest expression of the power of the prophetic Word, this would be only natural. This also explains the insistence and priority the council gave to the proclamation of the Word.

Our lack of detailed information of church structures in New Testament times, coupled with a realization of their diversity in different places, contains a precious lesson: The early church relied on no fixed blueprint in their efforts to respond to the needs of their communities. The various churches struggled to find structures that would enable them to respond better to the needs of people, and make them more effective in building the kingdom for which Jesus lived and died. We need to do the same.

7. *Priestly office is representative.* An expression that the Vatican Coun-

cil preferred not to use was calling the priest *alter Christus*—another Christ. This nuance was also based on New Testament considerations. A fundamental element in the New Testament understanding of ministerial office is that such office is representational in character, a being-there on behalf of another, Jesus Christ. The priest is not himself another Christ; he only acts in his name.

This further differentiates New Testament ministry from every other form of priesthood. In other religions, individuals are independent bearers of their office; a priest is himself brahman, priest, mediator between God and humanity. The Christian priest, however, is never an independent mediator. Whatever title he may have, he remains ever a vicar, a representative.

Although the New Testament uses a number of images to clarify what is really implied by this representative character of priestly office, we might note simply one: the oft-repeated warning that authority in the church is for service and not for power. Luke goes so far as to insert the argument over greatness on the part of the Twelve into the discourse after the Last Supper (Luke 22:24–28), leaving us with the reminder that the Son of Man came not to be served but to serve, and to give his life for others.

Matthew also issues a hard warning to the servants of Christ (24:45–51). They are not to play the role of lords during his apparent absence, but to remain his servants. Mention is made of the steward appointed by the lord to manage his household in his absence. When the lord finally returns, the one who has managed well is contrasted with the one who mishandled his fellow servants and lived the life of the high and mighty. Such a man, we are told, has earned himself a place among the hypocrites—a term that usually refers to the scribes and Pharisees, the enemies of Christ.

Linking the ordained to the concept of fellow-servants faithfully representing their Master emphasizes the proper relationship they have with Christ. It also points to the deepest meaning of what the council was trying to express anew with the concept of *collegiality*. The ministry is a collaborative task, in which each—bishops with fellow bishops and priests, priests with laity—should help and support the other in simplicity and total dependence and trust in God who is ever faithful.

Summary Conclusion

Perhaps the most distinguishing characteristic of ministry in the early church is the fact that it deals with various aspects of service, or pastoral care. In New Testament times the emphasis was on building up the community and on various forms of service to that community. Paul, as can be noted in 1 Corinthians 12, makes it clear that the gifts and charisms that each have received by reason of baptism are expected to be used for building up the body of Christ. The most prized ministries seem to be those of apostles, prophets, and teachers.

These are only a few of the lessons we can gain from our past. But as we try to inform present ordained ministry with the breath of the Spirit as found in the New Testament, we will find it becoming more responsive to the needs of the people, more focused on the preaching of God's Word, and more deeply related to Christ who calls us anew to be faithful each day.

Discussion Questions

1. What principles from the ancient church might serve to help us rethink ministry in the church today?

2. How can the Eucharist become a more vital force for church growth and renewal? Can the roles of the faithful be enhanced to bring out the community dimension of the church?

3. How can parishes focus more effectively on the five basic tasks of ministry? Does a deeper understanding of the role of the Holy Spirit help solve any of the tensions found in the church? How can this be effectively preached?

4. Reread the questions of Chapter 1 (p. 10). Are your answers any different now as a result of having read this book? Discuss these differences.

Suggested Readings

Brown, R., "Rethinking the Church Biblically for All," *The Critical Meaning of the Bible*, Mahwah, N.J.: Paulist Press, 1981, pp. 96-106.

Congar, Y., "My Path-Findings in the Theology of Laity and Ministries," *Jurist*, 32, 2 (Spring 1972), 169-188.

Mitchell, N., "Ministry Today: Problems and Prospects," *Worship*, 48, 6 (1974), 336-346.

13

Reintegrating the Laity

Today most people think it natural that there is a priesthood in the church. But it is restricted to the ordained. We take for granted the distinction between priests and laity. People assume that this has been predetermined by Christ. Thus it always was and ever will be.

Biblical Background
The situation was quite different in the first centuries, however. The New Testament, for example, is remarkably reticent about calling any of its members *priests*. The Letter to the Hebrews does apply this term *(hiereus/archiereus)* to Jesus, but in such a way as to make it clear that he is such in a way that is totally different from the priesthood of the Old Testament. No other member of the church is ever given this title.

The only usage of the concept for anyone other than Christ is found in two New Testament writings which call the entire church "priestly." These passages seem to take for granted what they explicitly state, namely, that Christ's priesthood is shared in common by the entire people of God. In Revelation and 1 Peter the terms *hiereus* and *hierateuma* are used of the community of the faithful as a whole. The texts are:

> You too are living stones, built as an edifice of spirit, into a holy priesthood, offering spiritual sacrifices acceptable to God through Jesus Christ....You, however, are a chosen race, a royal priesthood,

a holy nation, a people he claims for his own to proclaim the glorious works of the One who called you from darkness into his marvelous light (1 Peter 2:5,9).

To him who loves us and freed us from our sins by his own blood, who has made us a royal nation of priests in the service of God and Father—to him be glory and power forever and ever! Amen (Revelation 1:5b-6).

With your blood you purchased for God men of every race and tongue, of every people and nation. You made of them a kingdom and priests to serve our God, and they shall reign on the earth (Revelation 5:9b-10).

Happy and holy are they who share in the first resurrection! The second death will have no claim on them; they shall serve God and Christ as priests, and shall reign with him for a thousand years (Revelation 20:6).

These texts so dear to the Reformation in evolving their teaching on the common priesthood of all believers were also highlighted by Vatican II. The pivotal chapter two of *Lumen gentium* which deals with the church as People of God, goes on to remind us that all baptized members share in the priesthood of Christ Jesus. Never before in church documents has the magisterium spoken so explicitly and positively of this common priesthood.

Alluding to the covenant nature of church, chapter two speaks of the radical equality that all enjoy by reason of baptism. This sacrament makes of us members of Christ's covenant community. "Established by Christ as a fellowship of life, charity and truth, it [the church] is also used by him also as an instrument for the redemption of all, and is sent forth into the whole world as the light of the world and the salt of the earth."[1] The chapter then returns to the ancient doctrine of the common priesthood of all believers, and notes that "The faithful join in the offering of the Eucharist by virtue of their royal priesthood....They likewise exercise that priesthood...by the witness of a holy life, and by self-denial and active charity."[2]

The document states that the Holy Spirit allots his gifts as he will. "He distributes special graces among the faithful of every rank. By these gifts he makes them fit and ready to undertake the various tasks or offices advantageous for the renewal and upbuilding of the church."[3]

As we envisage renewal in our understanding of ministry, along with whatever ecclesial restructuring this might imply, we should ponder well the implications of the doctrine of the common priesthood. The starting point for reflection is that the prime priestly reality in the church, after that of Christ, is the priesthood of the faithful that all receive in baptism. Church life and ministry develop from this common priesthood, rooted as it is in our common baptism.

One consequence as regards ministry in the church is that apostolate belongs to the laity by right, without need of further mandate or authorization from church leaders. Unlike the model of ministry implied in the theology of Catholic Action, all ministry does not belong by right to the hierarchy, to be exercised by the laity only at their behest and under their direction. Consequently, groupings of laity according to areas of professional involvement or interest in order to Christianize the environment is now seen as an exercise of the common priesthood.

Where does the ordained or ministerial priesthood fit in this scheme of things? In this model, ministerial priesthood is understood as service to the common priesthood, and it needs to be rethought accordingly. The leadership exercised by the presbyterate in the church is to encourage and make possible the activity of the laity. This is a work of liberation that is long overdue. All should rejoice in being able to reverse having kept the laity as a passive flock for so long in favor of their active involvement in the work of Christ.

Though not familiar to many people today, the doctrine of the common priesthood of all believers did not originate with Luther. Nor is it a "Protestant" notion. It was often used by the Fathers of the church, reflecting the fact of its obvious scriptural warrant. It deserves more serious attention than it has been getting. We might take at least a brief glance at 1 Peter to see how this idea was used in the New Testament itself. Then we can suggest some interesting possibilities for modern application.

1 Peter, where we find the first application of the originally Old Testament title to the Christian community, is a beautiful letter. Its tone comes close to that of *Gaudium et spes* at the council: optimistic and enthusiastic. Even though it refers to suffering more than any other New Testament book, it is a startling blend of suffering and joy. Few New Testament books match it in its sense of cosmic optimism and its evident enthusiasm for life.

The letter seems to have been written from Rome in the 80s or 90s, by a Petrine disciple. Interestingly, in 5:1, Peter identifies himself as a presbyter speaking to fellow presbyters about their supervision of the flock, yet there is no resort to presbyteral or other authority structure to encourage an audience undergoing a fiery trial (4:12).

Its concentration on Christ's sufferings is the key to its message. For the author, this becomes the pattern for all Christian existence (even for all human existence). He begins by constructing his vision of Christian life, blending vivid biblical metaphors to remind his fellow Christians of their awesome dignity as God's chosen ones, despite their trials.

The presentation of Christian basics that we have in this letter is heavily influenced by the Old Testament. The themes of the exodus, desert wandering, and promised land are taken over to show that the Christians are now God's people, heir to all the promises made of old. The author applies to the Christian community the same titles of election enjoyed by the Jewish people. 1 Peter is the first to use the texts in this way to encourage and stimulate his readers.

Thus we are reminded that we have been born anew with God as our Father, that we are a spiritual temple, a holy priesthood, a chosen race, that we were called out of darkness into light. Having done this, 1 Peter comes to the point of its message: the task of faithful discipleship is not to flee the world, but to participate in it. We are not called to condemn the world, but to lead it to the praise of God. There is no hint of a ghetto mentality here! We have instead a bold missionary thrust.

Two basic principles undergird Christian vocation for the author:

1. All are called to be active participants in the structures of the world. In other words, we are not called to flee the evil world, or to withdraw from it, even in the midst of conflict. Slaves are told to stay with cruel masters, and wives are enjoined to remain with hostile and unbelieving husbands. This is not out of a love for suffering, but out of the sense that though innocent suffering is not good in itself, it can be the cause of conversion for others. The author fully expects the example of the faithful slaves and wives to result in the conversion of the non-believers. Only by living the Christian life fully in the midst of the world can we further the work of God, who is working in and though us to move the world to its destiny, which is the fullness of redemption brought by Christ.

2. Christians must develop "inner freedom" (2:11, 16) in order to live with integrity and in strength. It is for this reason that destructive passions must be let go, and our eyes be kept fixed on Christ who has loved us and given his life for us. Ultimately, we must have the courage to live the vocation to which each of us is called.

What we have here is a *witness* spirituality. Interestingly, it is Christian example, rather than the Word, which is seen as being fruitful. The love and service that builds the community is the most powerful message we can give a world starved for meaning. Thus, the force that will change the world is the example of a truly Christian life. This is the fundamental Christian vocation. The letter was written to remind the baptized that they are basically God's people, and that they had acquired something better than their previous ties. They were united in baptism in order to exercise discipleship in the midst of the world.

Taking the whole of the New Testament into consideration, what is significant is that mediating power and efficacy are attributed only to Christ's offering. He is the one true priest. The priesthood attributed to the people of God is analogous only. By it their offerings and lives are brought into relation with the one authentic offering of the Lord.

Likewise, when 1 Peter speaks of "spiritual" sacrifices, this is not to distinguish them from the "real" sacrifice of Christ. That is, the contrast is not between a sacrifice that is wholly authentic and others that are symbolic, at best. The word *pneumatikos* serves to distinguish them from the sacrifices of the Temple and those of pagans. It is also taken in the light of the contrast between *sarx* and *pneuma* so often used by St. Paul. Every sacrifice that is pleasing to God is spiritual and utterly real (cf. Romans 12:1). As St. Augustine put it, "The true offering consists of every act we make with the intention of uniting with God in a holy and living communion."[4]

To offer up these real sacrifices is a task imposed on all the baptized. The common priesthood is a gift bestowed on all, laity as well as clergy within the church. The priest does not offer up the "true" sacrifice of Christ, while all the laity can do is join in offering up spiritual (i.e., "unreal") sacrifices. The function of the priest is not in the area of offering up any sacrifice different from that of the faithful.

The message of Revelation is the same. Stated in more liturgical terms, we are reminded that the reign of God means victory over the world of sin. We are not subjects, but rulers together with Christ. John looks to the eschatological fulfillment of the Kingdom for which Jesus lived and died. More than 1 Peter, he sketches a vision of a eucharistic community gathered together for the praise and glory of God, aware of its dignity and living up to its privileges and responsibilities.

This common priesthood of the entire community is given practical expression throughout the New Testament, though the term itself is not used. The whole church is charged with preaching the word, with liturgy: "When you are all prophesying and an unbeliever or uninitiated person comes in, he will find himself analyzed and judged by *everyone*...he will fall on his face and worship God, declaring that God is among you indeed" (1 Corinthians 14:24). Worship is thus credible only when all witness to the word.

In the Jerusalem community we are told that "all proclaimed the word of God boldly" (Acts 4:31). When Paul is in prison and unable to preach, "most of the brothers have taken courage in the Lord from these chains of mine, and are getting more and more daring in the proclamation of the message without fear" (Philippians 1:12-18). There are many other examples.

In the New Testament, Christian life is presented as a liturgy, a participation in the unique priesthood of Jesus. Paul considers the faith of the people as a "sacrifice and oblation" (Philippians 2:17). The financial aid he receives from people is "a fragrant perfume, an acceptable sacrifice pleasing to God" (Philippians 4:18). All of life is a priestly act; he invites Christians to offer their bodies "as a living victim, holy, agreeable to God: this is the spiritual worship you have to offer" (Romans 12:1; cf. Philippians 3:3; Hebrews 9:14; 12:28).

This worship consists as much in praise of the Lord as in charitableness and sharing goods in common (Hebrews 13:15). The ministerial priesthood is never spoken of; it is surely not seen as a privileged caste within the church, since all share the same common priesthood. As depicted in the New Testament, ministry is always ordered toward the service of others.

The cult, too, was performed by the whole community. Christ's command to "do this in memory" of him was understood as addressed to the whole church. When Paul writes to the Corinthians to reprimand them for their eucharistic celebrations, he addresses himself to the entire community, not to selected officials. Likewise, he gave the whole church the mandate and dignity of "offering to God a living, holy and acceptable sacrifice of spiritual worship" through her very being (Romans 12:1). "Through Christ let us offer God an unending sacrifice of praise, that is, the fruit of lips which acknowledge his name. Do not neglect good works and generosity; God is pleased by sacrifices of that kind" (Hebrews 13:15).

In the church of the New Testament, the "laity" also played their part in church order, as in preaching and liturgy. A chapter in St. Matthew, which has rightly been called the oldest example of church order, shows how the entire community has its role to play in correcting and admonishing others (18:15ff). Paul exhorts the community to settle problems "when you are spiritually assembled in the name of the Lord Jesus, and I am spiritually present with you" (1 Corinthians 5:4).

Early Church Teaching

If the New Testament taught the common priesthood, the Fathers likewise knew and taught of the priestly dignity of the whole church. Although providing for a hierarchical church, they stressed the unity of all in the church; e.g., "the bishop is in the church and the church in the bishop."[5] The bishop is not the church; he only represents it, just as the people are represented in the bishop.

Augustine says, "We call all Christians priests because they are members of the one priest, Christ, just as we call them all anointed because of the mysterious unction; hence the apostle Peter addresses them as "a holy people and royal priesthood."[6] Likewise, in his commentary on Matthew 16:18, he says, "It is not Peter alone who looses, but the whole church binds and looses the bonds of sin....You too bind, you too loose. For whoever is bound is separated from your community, and whoever is separated from your community is bound by you; and when the sinner is reconciled, he is loosed by you, because you, too, pray to God for him."[7]

They knew that Christ's ministry was not summed up by his *priestly* role. He was also prophet and teacher, shepherd and king of his people. Similarly, it is too narrow a conception to think of the common priesthood as concerning itself mainly with cult. It embraces the whole range of Christian activities. Christians share in the entire ministry of Christ; all share in the responsibility of proclaiming the good news. All are called to bear witness, to sing the praises of the One who has called us out of darkness into God's own wonderful light.

There is also a royal task to perform. 1 Peter mentions a royal priesthood, but the implication is that in Christ's kingdom ruling and serving are identical. The servant is not inferior to the master. All are integral parts of the one body of Christ.

Lumen gentium in its third chapter splits Christ's priesthood into these three basic functions when it treats the special ministry of the hierarchy. Chapter four, however, also applies this triple division to the lives of the faithful.[8] This takes current theology much further than the encyclical *Mystici corporis*, which first introduced the concept to Catholics, but applied the three functions exclusively to the special ministry of the clergy. Vatican II wanted to give the term "common priesthood" its fullest and richest meaning. This went further than section LG 10 as well, which treated the notion of the common priesthood almost exclusively in its priestly aspect.

We might note in passing that today summing up Christian mission in this tripartite division is increasingly challenged by ecclesiologists in favor of more mission-oriented categories. These three facets of Christ's ministry were never all mentioned together by the Fathers. This came only with the Reformation, a schematization, however, that was accepted by Vatican II.

These are all significant developments. Since the Middle Ages, the hierarchical structure of the church and the functions of the special ministry have been emphasized to such an extent that the concept of the common priesthood of all believers was hardly a living reality. Stress on the Eucharist as a sacrifice, especially in the hands of minor theologians and popular piety, led to making the Eucharist too independent, even adding a touch of magic to it.

All this secured for the cultic priesthood a very prominent place in the church. With the solution of the investiture crisis and the theology of the church as a perfect society, the clergy became the dominant ecclesiastical and social caste. Its power over the people lay not only in governing, but in cutting itself off from the life of the community at large with its own rites and customs. The clericalizing of the Eucharist eventually made it an action of the priest primarily rather than of the Christian community.

Later Teaching

Protestant reaction against centuries of clericalism in theology and practice came at a time of weak scriptural theology and spirituality. Luther's stress on the common priesthood must have seemed novel, much more radical and far less orthodox than it was in actual fact. The church saw it as an onslaught on the special ministry of the clergy; common priesthood was seen as antithetical to it (which it was on the practical level at that time). Neither side succeeded in harmonizing the facts. Though Trent never explicitly rejected Luther's theories on the common priesthood, it naturally spent most of its time in defending the sacramental nature of the special ministry and the right of the church to determine its own structures.[9]

The danger seen in using the term "common priesthood" comes from the fact that it was used by most Reformers precisely to deny any idea of priestly representation and mediation. Now that it has been fully accepted by the church, we have a different problem. The expression will make sense and begin to bear fruit only when all the faithful begin to truly believe it and exercise their rights and duties as a priestly people.

Unfortunately, it was not easy to appreciate this in the bitterness of the Counter-Reformation. Post-Tridentine writings, when they did not ignore the idea of the common priesthood, often went out of their way to deride it. For example:

> The so-called common priesthood, that hobby-horse of the pseu-do-mystics of every age, which is today being used again to batter the rock on which the church is founded does not differ from the special priesthood in rank only, but also in nature. It is a projection of the latter, and presupposes it, just as a shadow points to the body by which it is projected, and on which it is dependent.[10]
>
> A priesthood of the laity is a concept that cannot be seriously entertained by anybody. It shows very poor taste and exegetical confusion to deduce anything like it from 1 Peter 2:5,9.[11]

This is the concept that is now so much taken for granted that Paul VI could declare in his encyclical *Ecclesiam suam*: "The Christian realizes with joy that he is endowed with the dignity of the common priesthood, the characteristic of the people of God."

It must be recognized that *Lumen gentium*, despite having resurrected this doctrine and likewise upgraded the laity, has still given us no uniform notion or positive definition of laity. The council alternates between a single or double-pole description of their not being clergy, or neither clergy nor religious. That is somewhat like defining a Filipino as one who is neither a Spaniard nor an American. It does tell us something of value, but it hardly gets at the heart of the matter, since the basis of the definition, the pole of reference, is outside the reality defined.

There are a number of positive ideas found in the council documents, however. The chief one is that laity, as part of the People of God, have the fullness of Christian life, dignity, and mission. They are not second-class citizens, people to be held only to a lower level of holiness or participation, but fully members of the church. This notion, found especially in chapter two, surpasses in theological depth most of the rest of the document. As a principle it is unassailable. In practice, however, it is not always realized, nor are all the structures of the church geared so as to facilitate the implementation of this truth. The seed has been planted, however, and the implications are still being discovered.

Another positive idea is that there is a diversity of gifts, and that these are allocated to all in the church—not only to those in the clerical ranks. In line with this is the presentation of the truth that the lay state itself is a vocation. Lay people are not simply those who were left over after others chose the religious life or priesthood. Their vocation is to live out what it means to be part of God's pilgrim people, and there is no lower standard set because they are "only lay people."

A third positive note is that the laity are reminded that they have an active role in the church, not simply a passive one. Their gifts are to be used for the good of all. Thus they are called on to exercise initiative and generosity. The building of the Kingdom is the responsibility of all in the church, not only those in leadership positions.

A fourth point is that there should be cooperation and an active exchange between clergy and laity. Power in the church is not a one-way street. Rather, the gifts of all the members are mutually beneficial. Since all are responsible for the work of salvation by reason of the common priesthood which we share by reason of baptism, there should be a realization that we all learn from one another, and must be open as to how the Spirit speaks through even the weakest member of the community.

One conclusion from all this is that because it belongs to *all* God's people, not only the laity, we cannot deduce a special "lay" spirituality from conciliar teaching. It surely lends support for a more active lay role in the church today, but not to any characteristic manner of being lay as distinct from being a minister or priest. In fact, we would be much better served if people thought in terms of an ecclesiology of ministries in the church rather than using the old distinction of clergy/ laity. Likewise would "lay" spirituality be a spirituality of church.

This is also why a study of ordained ministry must necessarily include a discussion of the common priesthood. It is the basic category of God's people; the special ministry is posterior and is concerned with a specific role or function within the community. "The power of being the child of God and the right to receive grace is greater—even if also more general—than the power of making the sign of this grace present with the ministerial guarantee of authenticity" (K. Rahner). Strictly speaking, it is only by virtue of the common priesthood that the church's minister can call himself in any true sense a priest, together with all his fellow Christians.

Modern Possibilities

From the foregoing, let us now try to apply the theology of the common priesthood to five basic areas in which the faithful might rightly exercise more responsibility as members of the priestly people.[12] Vatican II is there to remind us that this all flows from baptism itself, and not some concession of the church.

1. *Direct access to God.* In pagan and Jewish worship, only the

priests had access to God. They alone could enter the temple and mediate between the God who was holy and the profane people outside. Hebrews has shown us that Jesus replaced all this by reason of his own death and resurrection. In faith, all the baptized have access through Christ to God and to grace, for baptism is a share in his life (cf. Romans 6:1-11; Hebrews 10:22).

The decisive reality in our new situation is not the barrier that once divided humanity from God, but the fellowship that links us to God through Christ. No human or ecclesiastical authority can take this away from us. It is the source of our ultimate freedom and responsibility.

2. *Spiritual sacrifices.* The unique sacrifice of Christ fulfills all sacrifices; there is nothing we can add here. We noted above, however, that the Christian is called upon to offer "spiritual sacrifices pleasing to God." These are utterly real and based on our having been transformed by the Spirit. It is not simply a marginal theology found in 1 Peter. As Paul says in Romans 12:1, we are to offer our lives as a living sacrifice, holy and acceptable to God: our spiritual worship. Philippians 4:18 speaks of the service of love as "a fragrant offering, a sacrifice pleasing and acceptable to God." Baptism has moral obligations.

Paul and other New Testament writers also put a number of ministries under this rubric: preaching (Romans 15:16; Philippians 2:17); the service of love of one's fellow men and women and praise of God (Hebrews 13:15); the offering of one's life (2 Timothy 4:6); the prayers of the saints (Revelation 8:3). All these are made possible by the Lord working in us through his Spirit. It should be clear here that this priesthood of all believers is not a matter of sacralization. These offerings are not part of worship in any temple, but worship in the world, in the midst of everyday life. It breaks down the distinction between sacred and profane that has kept so many as passive members of the church.

3. *The preaching of the Word.* The New Testament envisages that Christians witness not only by deeds, but by their words. We are called to "declare the wonderful deeds of him who called us out of darkness into his own wonderful light" (1 Peter 2:9). There are a number of different words in the New Testament that describe this activity: preach, proclaim, announce, teach, explain, speak, say, testify, persuade, confess, charge, admonish, etc. Ultimately, all can do this in one way or another. This variety should allow each to make his or her own contribution!

If all are to pray "that the word of the Lord may speed on and triumph, as it did among you" (2 Thessalonians 3:1), Paul is not simply asking for prayers for missionaries. All are called to live and proclaim, according to the charism given each: "When you assemble [for Euchar-ist] each one has a hymn, a lesson, a revelation, a tongue, an inter-pretation. Let all things be done for edification" (1 Corinthians 14:26).

The Christian message spread with such speed because it was pro-claimed by all, not simply a few with a special commission: all were filled with the Holy Spirit and spoke the word of God with boldness (Acts 4:31; cf. 8:4; 11:19). Every Christian is called to be a preacher of the word in the widest sense of the term, even though, because of the variety of gifts, not everyone can do everything! At the very least, all are called to preach by personal witness, without necessarily having to preach in the narrow sense of the word, or to be theologians.

Since Vatican II, the legal basis for liturgical preaching has shifted from jurisdiction to baptism, by which all the baptized participate in Christ's *munus docendi*.[13] Further, all the baptized are encouraged—indeed they have the responsibility and mission—to proclaim the gos-pel in the world.[14]

In early Christianity, preaching in the liturgical assembly was de-termined more by the charismatic structure of the community. Those who had the ability were encouraged to use it. By the second century, it was beginning to be restricted to office holders, although educated laity were invited at times to preach homilies. Origen preached as a layman in the third century. John Chrysostom only reluctantly allowed even presbyters to preach in the fourth, using Origen's argument that "it is one thing to carry out the functions of the priesthood, and another to be well instructed and perfect in everything."[15]

Leo I and some medieval synods forbade lay preaching (Tours in 813; Aachen in 836)—indirect proof that it was still going on, and was approved by some.

In the twelfth century, with the mendicant orders, especially the Franciscans, lay preaching again became common. It was the Council of Trent that decided that sermons in the strict sense should be given by bishops and their assistants. The present Code of Canon Law main-tains this (while calling specifically clerical preaching *homilies*), but al-lows more freedom than the 1917 Code.[16]

While lay preaching was stifled at an early date, lay theology lasted much longer. In the Eastern churches to this day the more prominent theologians are all lay. Their decline in the Western church owes more to the barbarian invasions than to the theology of a special episcopal magisterium.

This raises the question of whether the restrictions now placed on preaching by the non-ordained, not to mention the increasing emphasis on the magisterium of the church as the repository of all truth, does not need to be reappraised today. The distinction between the *ecclesia docens* and the *ecclesia discens* is almost useless today unless it is remembered that the entire church needs to learn constantly if it is to teach properly. In this, all have a role to play. Learning and teaching are two functions that should characterize all in the church.

4. *The administering of baptism, Eucharist, and the forgiveness of sins.* The question here is whether the gospel commands to perform these actions were restricted to a small group, or were meant for the entire church. This is an area little investigated. However, we are willing to admit that every Christian can baptize, and interpret Matthew's great commission (28:19) in a universal sense. Forgiving sins was also a charge laid on the whole church.[17]

As for the Eucharist, we also know that non-ordained persons presided over this action of the community where there were no bishops or priests at least up till the fifth century. What are the implications of this if taken in conjunction with the statement of Vatican II that "Mother Church earnestly desires that all the faithful be led to that full, conscious, and active participation in liturgical celebrations which is determined by the very nature of the liturgy. Such participation by the Christian people as a 'chosen race, a royal priesthood, a holy nation' is their *right* and *duty* by reason of their baptism."[18]

The very least we should conclude from this is that the sacramental life of the church should be an active one. It is too easy to think of the sacraments as the private preserve of the ordained, and ignore the role that the entire Christian community is called upon to play. If sacramental actions are to truly be community celebrations, all need to see them in a more active light. There is no need to say that anyone can do anything in the church. Everything must be done in order. Clearly, all are called to mission, and to be a forgiving and eucharistic people.

5. *Mediating functions.* This is the necessary, but often neglected, component of service to the world. It is the function of the priesthood to mediate between God and the world: "First of all, then, I urge that supplications, prayers, intercessions, and thanksgiving be made for all men [and women" 1 Timothy 2:1). Each is called to be responsible for his fellow men and women, called to share in their struggles and difficulties. "Bear one another's burdens, and so fulfill the law of Christ" (Galatians 6:2).

Have we taken the idea of our common priesthood sufficiently seriously that we appreciate that neglect in this area means that whole parts of our world will be neglected? The work of Christ was never meant to be left entirely to church professionals. Christians cannot take a passive attitude to life as if Christ expected nothing more. We are called upon to be our brother and sister's keeper.

It must be admitted that a developed theology of the common priesthood has not yet been done. For obvious reasons, there is resistance to the implications of some of these ideas. Rome is quick to insist that the common priesthood and the ministry differ essentially.[19] But what this essential difference is has never been specified. Nevertheless, we have here the seeds of a real blossoming in the understanding of the role and responsibilities of all baptized members of the community.

We may have to wait until the church is less clericalized than it is at present to have any significant and practical changes in this area. The laity have been on the receiving end of clerical ministrations for so long that seeing themselves as fully responsible members of the community does not come easily. In the 1917 Code of Canon Law, laity were even treated as minors. (Fortunately, this has been changed in the new Code!)

The theological error to avoid is seeing the common priesthood as deriving from the special priesthood, or in thinking that they are comparable on the same level. There is still a tendency to think in such hierarchical terms that all grace is imagined as flowing from Christ through the chain of ministers to the laity.

Even *Lumen gentium*, in the chapter on the laity, states, "...the supreme and eternal priest, Christ Jesus, wills to continue his witness and serve through the laity too...."[20] While we can rejoice that the council has resurrected the theology of the common priesthood, that little word "too" that found its way into the document is a reminder that the traditional clerical mind-set has not completely disappeared. The common priesthood, however, is a primary participation in that of Christ, not a secondary one (i.e., after the ordained priesthood).

Our belief in the presence of the Holy Spirit in his church can be a reason for gratitude, however, that this theology has been presented to us at all during the council. Like many tiny seeds, it is destined to bear much fruit.

Discussion Questions

1. What, in your opinion, is the main conclusion we can draw from the doctrine of the common priesthood? What change does this imply for ecclesiology? How can both the common and ordained priesthood minister to each other?

2. Is the perspective of 1 Peter still valid today? Which of its insights

might be particularly appropriate (or inappropriate)?

3. What applications can you think of that would be modern expressions of the idea of the common priesthood of all the baptized? What prevents us from doing some of these things right now?

Suggested Readings

Drilling, P., "Common and Ministerial Priesthood: LG 10," *Irish Theological Quarterly*, 53, 2 (1987), 81-99.

Fink, P., S.J., "The Priesthood of Jesus Christ and Life of the Ordained," *Priests: Identity and Ministry*, ed. by Robert Wister, Wilmington, Del.: Glazier, 1990, pp. 71-91.

Küng, H., "The Priesthood of All Believers," *The Church*, London: Burns & Oates, 1968, pp. 363-387.

Ryan, L., "Vatican II and the Priesthood of the Laity," *Irish Theological Quarterly*, 32 (1985), 93-116.

Schillebeeckx, E., "The Right of Every Christian to Speak in the Light of Evangelical Experience 'In the Midst of Brothers and Sisters,'" *Preaching and the Non-Ordained*, Collegeville, Minn.: Liturgical Press, 1983, pp. 11-39.

Vanhoye, A., "A Priestly People," *Old Testament Priests and the New Priest*, Petersham, Mass.: St. Bede, 1987, pp. 239-318.

Notes

Abbreviations of sources used in these notes:

AA (*Apostolicam actuositatem*): Decree on the Apostolate of the Laity, 1965
GS (*Gaudium et Spes*): Pastoral Constitution on the Church in the ModernWorld, 1965
LG (*Lumen gentium*): Dogmatic Constitution on the Church, 1964
PO (*Presbyterorum ordinis*): Decree on the Ministry and Life of Priests, 1965
SC (*Sacrosanctum concilium*): Constitution on the Sacred Liturgy, 1962
TDNT:*Theological Dictionary of the New Testament*, 10 vols., ed. by G. Kittel and
    G. Friedrich, Grand Rapids, Mich.: Eerdmans, 1964-1976
UR (*Unitatis redintegratio*): Decree on Ecumenism, 1964

Introduction

1. Thomas O'Meara, *Theology of Ministry* (Mahwah, N.J.: Paulist Press, 1983), p. 15. This opening section is heavily indebted to O'Meara, especially the beginning of his opening chapter, pp. 3ff.

2. *Ibid.*, pp. 16-24. O'Meara has an excellent section here on the church in both history and culture.

3. Gregory Baum, "Ministry in the Church," *Women and Orders,,* ed. Robert Heyer (Mahwah, N.J.: Paulist Press, 1974), p. 61.

4. *Ibid.*, p. 58.

5. This is a theme developed in many places by Walbert Bühlmann. See his *The Church of the Future: A Model for the Year 2001* (Maryknoll, N.Y.: Orbis Books, 1988). Especially pertinent is Chap. 1, "From Western Church to World Church," pp. 3-11.

6. Edward Schillebeeckx,*The Church with a Human Face: A New and Expanded Theology of Ministry* (London: SCM Press, 1985), p. 81. O'Meara also has a section in his book entitled "Toward a Definition" (pp. 136-143), where he considers this question at length.

7. Richard McBrien, *Ministry: A Theological, Pastoral Handbook* (San Francisco: Harper & Row, 1987), p. 11.

8. LG, 5/3. For ease of reference, when using the Vatican Council documents, we will also refer to the specific paragraphs within each section according to the Abbott translation. I hope these will not cause any difficulty for those using Flannery or the original Latin, which often has no paragraphs at all.

9. GS, 45/1.

10. GS, 39/4.

Chapter 1 The Foundations of Ministry

1. Bernard Cooke, *Ministry to Word and Sacrament: History and Theology* (Philadelphia: Fortress Press, 1976), pp. 35-36, 187-191. This massive book is one of the major sources detailing the historical development of the church's ministry. His approach is different from most, inasmuch as he takes one concept, e.g., "Ministry as the Formation of Community," and traces its development throughout the whole 2000 years of Christian existence. He then returns to the starting point and does the same with another theme, viz., "Ministry to God's Word," "Service," etc. Though my approach is more horizontal, Cooke is an indispensable source throughout.

2. Gunther Bornkamm, "Presbyteros," *TDNT*, vol. 6, pp. 651-683.

3. Karl Rengstorf, *TDNT, vol.*. 2, pp. 157-159.

4. Friedrich Baumgartel, *TDNT*, vol. 7, pp. 849ff.

5. Raymond Brown, *Priest and Bishop* (Mahwah, N.J.: Paulist Press, 1980), pp. 52-55.

6. For a more extended treatment of this whole matter, see the excellent book of Jerome Murphy-O'Connor, *Becoming Human Together* (Wilmington, Del.: Michael Glazier, 1981).

7. O'Meara, *op. cit.* pp. 87-90.

Chapter 2 Ministry as Charism

1. Although the exact date of the Jewish Council of Jamnia (as well as what it did) is disputed, there is no doubt that by the early 80s the Pharisees had taken over control of Judaism, and they managed to hold it together by enforcing a strict orthodoxy that found no place for Christians.

2. Raymond Brown, *The Churches the Apostles Left Behind* (Mahwah, N.J.: Paulist Press, 1984). This section relies heavily on Brown's analysis, and is a sort of summary of some of the material found in his book.

3. Schillebeeckx, *op. cit.*, pp. 94-99. Schillebeeckx accepts Brown's conclusions, but gives his own summary here.

4. *Ibid.*, 99-103. Interesting for the pastoral conclusions he draws.

5. Raymond Brown, *The Community of the Beloved Disciple* (Mahwah, N.J.: Paulist Press, 1984), pp. 52-53.

6. *Ibid.*, p. 17.

7. This is the opinion of Bernard Cooke, p. 61, and also of Douglas Powell; cf. "Ordo Prebyterii," *Journal of Theological Studies*, 26 (1975), 290-328. It is also endorsed by Nathan Mitchell in *Mission and Ministry*, pp. 154ff. All of these authors do a fine job of summarizing the material and discussion on the subject.

8. Powell, *op. cit.*, pp. 321ff.

9. André Lemaire, *Les ministères aux origines de l'Eglise* (Paris: Editions du Cerf, 1971), pp. 96-103.

10. Nathan Mitchell, *Mission and Ministry* (Wilmington, Del.: Michael Glazier, 1982), pp. 158-167. Mitchell's presentation here as well as for the first three centuries is excellent, and I have generally followed his development. Unfortunately for the purposes of this book, he does not concern himself to any extent with later historical development.

11. Edward Kilmartin, "Ministère et ordination dans l'Eglise chrétienne primitive," *Maison-Dieu*, 138 (1979), 62-63.

12. Mitchell, *op. cit.*, p. 167.

13. For a good explanation of this question, see the article by Herve-Marie Legrand, O.P., "The Presidency of the Eucharist According to Ancient Tradition," *Worship*, 53 (September 1979), 367-391.

Chapter 3 From Ministry to Bishop

1. Mitchell, *op. cit.*, pp. 178-180. For a slightly different presentation of this matter, see Mitchell's synthesis.

2. *Schillebeeckx, op. cit.*, p. 127.

3. Mitchell, *op. cit.*, 180f. I follow Mitchell closely in this section.

4. *Ibid.*, pp. 189-191. The schema is from Mitchell.

5. James Mohler,*The Origin and Evolution of the Priesthood* (New York: Alba House, 1970), p. 56. Though we sometimes differ in details, Mohler gives a good and detailed presentation of the first four centuries as regards the development of priesthood.

6. Dom Gregory Dix discusses the significance of this in *The Shape of the Liturgy* (New York: Seabury Press, 1982), pp. 33-35, showing how terminology eventually shifted to leave out the priestly people, thus turning them into a passive audience.

7. Maurice Bevenot, "Tertullian's Thought about the Christian Priesthood," (Bruges: *Corona Gratiarum I*, 1975).

8. In his letter 5, he advises presbyters to celebrate in prison for the confessors there.

9. Maurice Bevenot, "'Sacerdos' as Understood by Cyprian," *Journal of Theological Studies*, 30 (October 1979), 414.

10. This is still a controverted point, however. See Kilmartin, *op. cit.*, pp. 87-89.

11. Cyril Vogel, "Ordinations Inconsistantes et Caractère Inamissible" (Turin: Bottega d'Erasmo, 1978), p. 113. Quoted by Mitchell.

12. *Ibid.* Translation as quoted by Mitchell, *op. cit.*, p. 177.

13. Mitchell, *op. cit.*, pp. 231-233. The outline is from Mitchell.

14. In this there is a sharp contrast between Cyprian and his fellow African, Augustine, a century later. Cyprian did not recognize (considered "invalid") sacraments administered outside the church. He taught that Christ gave the sacraments to the church, which was the vehicle of the Holy Spirit here on Earth. Whoever abandoned the church, or was abandoned by it, lacked the Spirit and had no part in the dispensation of God's grace. Hence he insisted on rebaptizing or reordaining anyone who had received these sacraments in schismatic or heretical groups.

15. Pierre Van Beneden, "Aux origines d'une terminologie sacramentelle" (Louvain: Spicilegium Sacrum Lovaniense, 1974), pp. 53-62.

16. Cyril Vogel, "Laicus communione contentus: le rétour du presbytre aux rangs des laics," *Revue des Sciences Religieuses*, 47 (1973), 56-122.

17. Herve-Marie Legrand, *Worship*, 53 (September 1979), 413-438.

Chapter 4 Priesthood as Ministry

1. Mohler, *op. cit.*, pp. 76-77. The title of this section is also from Mohler.

2. *Ibid.*, pp. 77-78. The quote is taken from Mohler.

3. *Epist 146, Ad evangelium.* This is surely also the position of Chrysostom, who said that "by the act of extending their hand alone are they superior, by this alone do they seem to surpass the presbyters" (Epist. 1 ad Tim., Hom 11). Jerome's position is perhaps more nuanced than is usually noted. Though recognizing the episcopal domination of his day, he was quick to note that it was not always so. He looked back to the primitive church, where a collegial presbyterate was the pattern (cf. Cooke, p. 80).

4. *Apostolic Constitutions*, 8,24,2.

5. See the book edited by Roger Gryson, *The Ministry of Women in the Early Church* (Collegeville, Minn.: Liturgical Press, 1976). Especially pertinent here is Chap. 9, "The Latin Canonical Sources of the Fourth to the Sixth Century."

6. *Liturgical Homilies of Narsai*, Homily 32.

7. Mitchell, *op. cit.*, pp. 233-239. This section is largely dependent on Mitchell's fine summary.

8. Though these distinctions succeeded in settling the Donatist question, they seemed to have little influence outside of Africa. In Rome and other areas, re-ordination continued to be practiced. It was only when the Augustinian revival began eight centuries later that the implications of his teaching led to the idea of there being an indelible character that resulted from ordination, making any re-ordination useless.

9. Jean-Paul Audet, *Structures of Church Ministry* (London: Sheed & Ward, 1967). The whole first section of his work is entitled "Home and Marriage in the Service of the Community." Chapters 3 and 4 are especially pertinent here, pp. 53-122.

10. *Ibid.*, pp. 93-100.

11. *Ibid.*

12. *Demonstratio evangelica*, 1,9.

13. *De officiis ministrorum*, 1, 50 (248). The quote and translation are in Audet, pp. 142-143.

Chapter 5 The Monastery as Minister

1. "Dionysius" is one of the major sources for the ecclesiology of the Middle Ages. He was even commented on by St. Thomas. His influence was vastly greater than his neo-Platonic writings would warrant because it was assumed at this time, as well as in the late Middle Ages, that he was the person converted by St. Paul in Athens (cf. Acts 13:33ff). In actuality he was a Syrian monk of the 6th century who wrote three mystical treatises: *The Divine Names, The Celestial Hierarchy,* and *The Ecclesiastical Hierarchy.* As can be seen from the titles, his thought form was hierarchy, and he lent authority to this aspect of church thought for centuries. See here O'Meara, *op. cit.*, p. 110. Also Cooke, *op. cit.*, pp. 265-266, 356-357.

2. Kenan Osborne, *Priesthood* (Mahwah, N.J.: Paulist Press, 1988), p. 163. The material in this paragraph is developed at length by him in his sixth chapter,

"Ministry in the Early Medieval Church."

3. Mitchell, *op. cit.*, pp. 246-250. Mitchell has a concise summary of this question. See also Cooke, *op. cit.*, pp. 516-520.

4. Cooke, *op. cit.*, pp. 432-435.

5. This was the secret prayer for the ninth Sunday after Pentecost (7th after Trinity Sunday for the Dominicans). It was quoted as *exercetur* by St. Thomas in the Summa, 3a, 83, 1. On this matter, see the article by Joseph Crehan, "Priesthood, Kingship and Prophecy," *Theological Studies*, 42, #2 (June 1981), 222.

6. Vatican II used this text of Leo in #3 of *Lumen gentium*, but in its original sense and wording.

7. Robert Taft, "The Frequency of the Eucharist Throughout History," in *Concilium*, "Can We Always Celebrate the Eucharist?" ed. by Mary Collins and David Power (New York: Crossroad, 1982), p. 14.

8. In Benedict's day, none of the monks were ordained, and the abbots were lay. Monks went to church like everyone else. The ordination of the abbot, and then a good number of the monks, was a later development.

9. At first the expression "private mass" meant what used to be called a "low mass," i.e., one without the normal solemnity and not considered the celebration of the entire community. Only later in the period did it come to mean masses celebrated by the priest alone.

10. See Schillebeeckx, *op. cit.*, pp.193-194. Schillebeeckx notes that the matter is treated more at length in de Lubac's *Corpus Mysticum: L'Eucharistie et l'Eglise au moyen âge*, esp. chapter 5; also Congar's *L'Eglise de saint Augustin à l'époque moderne*.

11. Denziger, 690.

12. Cooke, *op. cit.*, p. 564.

Chapter 6 Ministry as Hierarchy

1. Cooke, *op. cit.*, p. 91.

2. *Ibid.*, p. 92.

3. Gregory was no innovator as regards papal power. The same cannot be said of Innocent III (d. 1216), who would follow him. An extremely able administrator, diplomat, and jurist, he brought to a fairly final form the juridical theology of the papacy. See Cooke, p. 465.

4. *Ibid.*, p. 442.

5. Bernard of Clairvaux, having no personal or vested interest, and widely regarded as a saint, was one whose advocacy of practically unlimited power for the papacy did much to shape twelfth-century thought, and secure the pope's influence in practical affairs. He seems to have been responsible for the use of the term *Vicar of Christ* for the pope. Cooke comments that this shows the extent to which the pope was seen less as bishop of Rome, and more as "head of the church" (p. 465).

6. See note 1 of chapter 5.

7. St. Thomas, 4 Sent. 24,3,2, q. 2, ad 2.

8. We might note that the Trinitarian model used was that coming from Augus-

tine via Pseudo-Dionysius. This stressed more the unity of the godhead. The Eastern understanding of the Trinity, by stressing more the operation of the divine persons, allowed for more independence for the local churches.

9. Though the intention of this regulation was laudable, it never would have become necessary if priests had not ceased being regarded as related to a specific Christian community. Thus, instead of ordination establishing a special relationship between a person and a church community, it was seen essentially as giving special powers to the individuals ordained.

10. Cooke, *op. cit.*, p. 577. Anselm's *Cur Deus Homo* was one of the most influential books of the Middle Ages, as well as of the Reformation.

11. *Ibid.*, p. 578.

12. *Ibid.*, p. 578.

13. *Ibid.*, p. 578.

14. It is only in the twelfth century that *order* was regarded as a sacrament. Indeed, only in the thirteenth century was it finally agreed that there were only seven sacraments. Before Lombard, some thought there might be as many as 40.

15. *Summa*, III, q. 38, a. 4

16. Osborne, *op. cit.*, p. 208.

17. See Mitchell, *op. cit.*, pp. 246-250. Occasionally this medieval distinction was applied in strange ways. We have a fifteenth-century rescript, for example, from Pope Boniface IX to an abbot of the community of St. Osithae in London granting him the right to ordain even to the priesthood. Here episcopal jurisdiction was clearly granted one who was not a bishop.

Chapter 7 TheReformation of Ministry

1. Piet Fransen, "Orders and Ordination," *Sacramentum Mundi*, IV (London: Burns & Oates, 1969), pp. 313, 367.

2. Most Reformers used the term "sacrament" only for what could be properly justified from the Scriptures. Since baptism and Eucharist are so clearly attested, these became the major sacraments of the Reformation.

3. For a quick summary of Lutheran teaching on ministry, three articles have been especially helpful. The first is an article by George Lindbeck, "The Lutheran Doctrine of the Ministry, Catholic and Reformed," *Theological Studies*, 30 (December 1969), 588-612. Then there is an article in *The Lutheran Quarterly* by Robert H. Fisher, "Another Look at Luther's Doctrine of the Ministry," [18 (August 1966), 260-271] in which he seeks to correct the views of Brian Gerrish, "Luther on Priesthood and Ministry," *Church History*, 34 (December 1965), 404-422, and Lowell Green, "Change in Luther's Doctrine of the Ministry," *The Lutheran Quarterly*, 18 (May 1966), 173-183. Finally, there is a more recent article by Kurt Hendel, "The Doctrine of the Ministry: The Reformation Heritage," *The Lutheran Quarterly*, 44 (January 1992), 23-33.

4. In 1539, in "On the Councils and the Church," Luther insists that the holy catholic church is present wherever the Word of God is preached, "for God's word cannot be without God's people, and conversely, God's people cannot be without God's word." Luther viewed ministers as instruments of salvation only because they were instruments of the Word and sacraments.

5. Luther's teaching on this subject is found especially in two works, both written in 1520: *To the Christian Nobility* and *The Babylonian Captivity of the Church*.

6. Luther wrote "There is no true, basic difference between laymen and priests, princes and bishops, between religious and secular, except for the sake of office and work, but not for the sake of status. They are all of the spiritual estate, all are truly priests, bishops and popes. But they do not all have the same work to do" (*Works* 40:22-34). Hendel notes that Luther makes two crucial points here. He asserts that laity and clergy do not differ as regards to status, only in office. Second, he defines the ordained ministry essentially in terms of an office, that is, in functional terms. The specific vocation or work of the clergy is to exercise the priestly functions *publicly*. This public nature of priesthood was also stressed by Vatican II.

7. Lindbeck, *op. cit.*, p. 590. It is important to remember that though Luther stressed the importance of faith, this itself was dependent on grace, which was a pure gift. Thus, perhaps we should stress *sola gratia* as much as *sola fide*.

8. *Ibid.*, p. 591.

9. Luther, Tract 30.

10. Osborne, *op. cit.*, p. 226. Osborne treats Luther and Calvin at much greater length, and is well worth reading.

11. Luther himself seldom separated the sacrament from the Word. He considered both necessary, almost as an organic whole, as the chief means whereby God's grace was mediated to his creation.

12. Lindbeck, p. 589. Lindbeck's position reflects the understanding of the basic Lutheran Confessional Statements, and not specifically the exact teaching of Luther himself.

13. This is a variation of the same argument used by Schillebeeckx and others. In the Catholic context this comes down to the right of the Christian people to Eucharist.

14. Calvin is much less sacramental than Luther who, in general, was closer to the Catholic position in sacramental understanding.

15. Alexandre Ganoczy, *Calvin, Théologien de l'Eglise et du Ministère* (Paris: Editions du Cerf, 1964), p. 221.

16. *Ibid.*, p. 243.

17. *Ibid.*, p. 256.

18. *Ibid.*, p. 257.

19. *Ibid.*, p. 245. The reference is to the 10th canon of session seven. Calvin notes, "No one of sound judgment can make all Christians equal as regards the task of administering the Word or the sacraments....we have the express command of Christ that these be provided by special ministers" [quoted in Ganoczy, p. 297].

20. Cooke, *op. cit.*, p. 604. For Luther, ordination conferred on a man an office of ministry, but no new power was required to carry out this office, for the necessary power was possessed by every Christian by reason of baptism. Calvin based the efficacy of ministerial activity not in some already inherent power, but on the concurrent activity of the Holy Spirit.

21. Quoted in Ganoczy, p. 299. He also notes that many Calvinist scholars feel that Calvin was not insisting so much on the number of offices in the church as much as the functions exercised by church ministers. They cite the example of

church police, or even Calvin's openness to some sort of episcopacy. This is still a debated point.

22. Osborne, *op. cit.*, p. 245.

23. Cooke, *op. cit.*, p. 598.

24. *Ibid.*, p. 598. It seems that Calvin preferred a more dynamic understanding of presence than Luther, whose views he found rather static and too spatial.

25. Even today, Vatican II (LG, 10) insists that the ordained priesthood differs *essentially* from the priesthood of all believers flowing from baptism.

26. Cooke, *op. cit.*, p. 604.

27. Note that neither Florence nor Trent defined what they understood by character. They left open whether this was an ontological reality or not.

28. Alexandre Ganoczy, "'Splendours and Miseries' of the Tridentine Teaching on Ministries," (*Concilium*, 10, 1972, ed. by B. Van Iersel), p. 76.

29. *Ibid.*, pp. 75-86. Ganoczy schematizes the work of Trent under six headings. In general I have used five of his six sections, though the order has been changed and other material used.

30. Leopold Willaert, "La Restauration Catholique," Fliche-Martin, *Histoire de l'Eglise depuis les origines jusqu' à nos jours* (Paris: Bloud et Gay, 1960), vol. 18, pp. 336-440.

31. It is much easier for us to see this today, and it is an accepted ecumenical principle. Rome was insisting that it had a right to define its own church order, and that what was in place at the time of the council was a legitimate development and not a deviation from NT principles.

32. The council actually did allow individual bishops to decide whether or not to give the chalice to the laity. The fact remains that very few ever did so, and little was done to make the liturgy truly the "work of the people."

Chapter 8 Ministry as Cult

1. Yves Congar, "The Historical Development of Authority in the Church," *Problems of Authority*, ed. John M. Todd (Baltimore: Helicon Press, 1962), pp. 144-148.

2. Though this sounds harshly critical, it should be remembered that given the extent of the need for renewal in the church, unless there had been a strong papacy, there is doubt that anything at all could have been accomplished.

3. Herve-Marie Legrand, "The 'Indelible' Character of the Theology of Ministry," *The Plurality of Ministries*, eds. Hans Küng and Walter Kasper (New York: Herder & Herder, 1972), p. 55. This section on the sacramental character is based on his analysis.

4. *Ibid.*, p. 56.

5. *Ibid.*, p. 57.

6. *Ibid.*, p. 58.

7. J. Galot, *La nature du caractère sacramentel. Etude de théologie médievale* (Bruges: Gembloux, 1956).

8. Legrand, *op. cit.*, p. 58.

9. *Ibid.*, p. 59.

10. *Ibid.*, p. 60.

11. *Ibid.*, p. 60.

12. *Ibid.*, p. 61.

13. *Ibid.*, p. 61.

14. *Ibid.*, p. 61.

15. *Ibid.*, p. 61.

16. *Ibid.*, p. 61.

17. Quoted by Legrand, *ibid.*, p. 62.

18. *Ibid.*, p. 61.

Chapter 9 The Reappraisal of Ministry

1. The document had to do with renewal in religious life.

2. GS, 44/4.

3. Avery Dulles, Introduction to the Abbott edition of the council documents, p. 10.

4. This statement came only after much labor and three years of work at eliminating the triumphalistic view of church that permeated the first drafts of the document.

5. 62nd general meeting, November 7, 1963.

6. LG, 6/2, 21/274; PO, 12/1.

7. LG, 30/1.

8. LG, 31/3.

9. LG, 33/2.

10. We might note that this triple division is not found in the NT or in the Fathers. It originated with John Calvin. A more missionary framework might be more appropriate today.

11. LG, 35/1.

12. LG, 12/1 speaks of the faithful as a whole, anointed by the Spirit, as not erring in matters of faith.

13. PO, 9/4.

14. LG, 37/1.

15. Dulles here outlines four other models: The church as Mystical Communion, as Sacrament, as Herald, and as Servant.

16. Avery Dulles, "Imaging the Church for the 80s," *A Church to Believe In* (New York: Crossroad, 1982), pp. 1-18. Dulles is concerned that there seems to be no powerful guiding vision for the church that would facilitate, indeed compel, participation in the life of the church.

17. *Ibid.*, pp. 7-9.

18. The council called the family the "domestic church." AA, 11/4. Families are the first and most vital cell in church and society.

19. LG, 31, 34-36; AA, 3.

20. LG, 31/2.

21. LG, 31/2; AA, 16/1.

22. Leonard Doohan, *The Lay-Centered Church* (Minneapolis: Winston, 1984), pp. 44-47. The entire book can be recommended as a short presentation of the theology and spirituality of the laity.

Chapter 10 Reappraising Presbyteral Ministry

1. PO consistently uses "presbyter" rather than "priest." Only nine times is the word *sacerdos* used, and then always in the plural. The Abbott translation of PO, which I have used in this chapter, always translates presbyter as "priest." I have changed this to presbyter whenever the Latin so warrants.

2. In our analysis, we assume that places where PO differs from LG ordinarily represents an advance in thinking. The secretary for the commission that did all the work on PO was Alvaro Portillo, now head of *Opus Dei*. And many efforts were made to retain as much of the scholastic understanding as possible. Despite the need for compromises, the vision of PO does represent an effort to rethink ordained ministry within the church.

3. Quoted by Bonaventura Kloppenburg, O.F.M., in *The Ecclesiology of Vatican II*, trans. by Matthew O'Connell (Chicago: Franciscan Herald Press, 1974), p. 264. Chapter 9 of this book is entitled "The Theology of Priesthood" and forms the basis of this section of my presentation.

4. Quotation attributed to St. Albert the Great.

5. Quotation translated by Kloppenburg, *op. cit.*, p. 267.

6. *Ibid.*, p. 268.

7. PO, 2/1.

8. *Ibid.*, p. 269.

9. It might be noted that this distinction would have been most welcome at the time of the Reformation.

10. PO, 2/3.

11. PO, 2/3.

12. Kloppenburg, *op. cit.*, p. 271. This formulation was taken bodily from LG, 28, where it probably slipped in as a reflection of the older theology.

13. PO, 2/3. The council here shows awareness of the many imponderables of history and confined its focus to the nature and scope of the ministry. The historical exposition given LG states this intention explicitly: "We are [simply] asserting that the divinely instituted ministry is exercised by various orders of people who since early times have been called bishops, priests and deacons" (cf. Kloppenburg, p. 272). The Council will later say that presbyteral powers come to the one ordained from Christ, not from the bishop.

14. Kloppenburg, *op. cit.*, p. 274. The decree seems to give a two-fold basis for the ministry of presbyters: ordination (from God), and the mission they receive (from the bishops). This follows LG, which attributed the three functions of pastoral care, word, and sacrament to ordination, and their exercise to a mission received from the bishop.

15. PO, 5/1. See Kloppenburg, *op. cit.*, p. 275.

16. *Ibid.*

17. *Ibid.*, p. 276.

18. *Ibid.*, pp. 276-277.

19. PO, 7/1.

20. PO, 7/3.

21. Kloppenburg, *op. cit.*, p. 281. The official exposition says, "...the two ways in which presbyteral priesthood has been explained here at the Council are readily harmonized. For a genuine apostolate and an authentic adoration of the Father are closely connected, indeed are inseparable from each other, so that the two aspects must be found in every priest's life."

22. PO, 4/3, 6/4.

23. PO, 6/1.

24. PO, 4/1. This entire section deals with the presbyter's primary duty of proclaiming God's Word.

25. UR, 3. Cf. Kloppenburg, *op. cit.*, p. 281.

26. PO, 2/5.

27. PO, 2/6. From the beginning the council was careful to show that the Eucharist was the source and apex of the whole work of preaching the gospel (5/4).

28. PO, 6/6-7.

29. PO, 2/7.

30. We might note that Trent itself need not be interpreted so narrowly. It considers the forgiveness of sins as a power that comes with priesthood, but relegates its conferral to another day. There is no doubt, however, that Vatican II intended to broaden the perspective of Trent, and to open new vistas for us.

31. Henri Denis, "La théologie du presbyterat de Trente à Vatican II," in *Les prêtres, Formation, ministère et vie*, Unam Sanctam, 68 (Paris: Editions du Cerf, 1968), pp. 193-232. This article analyzes the differences between Trent and Vatican II under five headings. I have slightly modified Denis's schema.

32. Kloppenburg, *op. cit.*, p. 290.

33. PO, 2/4 mentions this character only in passing, when it states that the sacerdotal office of priests is brought about by the anointing of the Holy Spirit though which priests are marked with a special character. See the treatment we give this issue in chapter nine.

34. John Zizioulas, "Ordination—A Sacrament?: An Orthodox Reply," *The Plurality of Ministries*, eds. Hans Küng and Walter Kasper (New York: Herder & Herder, 1972), p. 34. Zizioulas summarizes here material which appears in more expanded form in his book *Being as Communion* (New York: St. Vladimir's Seminary Press, 1985). He and Nicholas Afanasieff are good examples of recent Eastern theologians of the church.

35. *Ibid.*, p. 34.

36. *Ibid.*, p. 34.

37. *Ibid.*, p. 35.

38. This has led to the "private mass" mentality, and the whole issue of clericalism and authority within the church. Conversely, the opposite extreme would make the baptized the source of all ministry within the church, some sort of generic principle of order. The sacraments of initiation already define one's "order" in the community.

39. Zizioulas, *op. cit.*, p. 36.

40. *Ibid.*, pp. 37-38.

41. Augustine, *Sermons*, 340. We might note that any other view of ministry takes the ordained person out of the community. Even in sacramental matters, he is forbidden to absolve the sins of an accomplice. And when a priest confesses, he is like any member of the church in need of mediation. The different functions of priests and laity only exist within the common condition of Christian life.

42. LG, 20/3; 9/1.

43. PO, 2.

44. PO, 4/1.

45. UR, 3/2.

46. PO, 5/2.

47. LG, 37/1.

48. PO, 6/8.

49. PO, 5/3.

50. PO, 6/2.

51. AA, 5/1.

52. Para. 34.

53. PO, 2/4.

54. LG, 10/1, 2.

Chapter 11   Unresolved Problems in Ministry

1. Note that this eschatological witness is especially the role that celibacy has played in the monastic and the newer religious orders. Insisting on it for all diocesan priests as well is a continuing example of the monasticization of the church.

2. LG, 42/5.

3. LG, 11/4-6; 34/2; 35/4.

4. There is a whole volume of *Concilium* devoted to this issue, entitled *The Right of a Community to a Priest*, eds. E. Schillebeeckx and J.B. Metz (New York: Crossroad, 1980). This entire volume is worth reading on this question.

5. See the National Federation of Priests Councils report, "Priestless Parishes: Priests' Perspectives," *Origins*, 21, 3 (May 30, 1991), 1, 43-52. Though dated, see Jan Kerkof's statistical study, "Priests and Parishes," in *The Right of a Community to a Priest*, pp. 3-11.

6. LG, 37/1.

7. This was a thread that ran through the entire meeting. This author was there as secretary.

8. The women's question is sometimes blamed on the feminist movement in the United States. The fact is that it addresses the concerns of intelligent and dedicated women all over the world. See "The Ministry of Women," in William Ra-

demacher's book, *Lay Ministry: A Theological, Spiritual, and Pastoral Handbook,* (New York: Crossroad, 1991), pp. 145-168.

9. Elisabeth Schüssler Fiorenza, in "Breaking the Silence—Becoming Visible," *Concilium* (December 1985) *Women in the Life of the Church,* goes on to say, "We have come to understand that the 'woman question' facing the church is not just a question of ordination but that it requires an intellectual paradigm shift from an androcentric world view and theology to a feminist conceptualization of this world, human life, and Christian religion" (p. 9).

10. Fiorenza, *Concilium,* 171 (1984), p. 32.

11. It seems that the letter itself is not disputed, only its interpretation. See Chapter 4 for further details.

12. "What was not assumed was not redeemed," was the standard argument of Augustine and the Fathers.

13. Sara Butler, "Second Thoughts on the Ordination of Women," *Worship,* 63, 2 (March 1989), 157-165. Butler makes the important point here that many who disagree with the CDF reasoning do not always appreciate what they are trying to refute. Thus the argument goes on without either side ever really joining issue or understanding each other.

The Butler article spawned an interesting series in *Worship.* The first was by Bishop Kenneth Untener, "Ordination of Women: Can the Horizons Widen?" 65 (January 1991), 50-59. This was answered by Charles Meyer and Sara Butler, "Responses to Bishop Kenneth Untener" (May 1991), 256-268, as well as by John Sheets, "The Ordination of Women" (September 1991), 451-461. Finally there is an excellent historical and theological article by Herve-Marie Legrand, "Traditio Perpetuo Servata? The Non-Ordination of Women: Tradition or Simply a Historical Fact?" (November 1991), 482-508.

14. This spousal imagery is not one we attend to much today, but it is extremely powerful as it speaks of completely mutual self-donation. It reminds us strikingly of the humility of Christ, whose love makes us his equals. What really remains to be done is to look into the tradition and see whether the image of Christ as bridegroom and church as bride is prominent enough in the tradition to make it bear the weight given it by the Declaration. It fits, however, within the larger symbol system.

15. This is not irrelevant in the question of women's ordination. That Jesus' sex should be accorded more weight than his height or eye color makes sense because it can't be dismissed as "accidental" to his humanity. We cannot divorce the person of Christ from his humanity without touching the doctrine of the incarnation. Even in his risen state, Jesus remains man because this is integral, not accidental, to his humanity.

16. The *Concilium* volume entitled *The Plurality of Ministries,* eds. Hans Küng and Walter Kasper, has a section entitled "How Can We Arrive at a Theological and Practical Recognition of Ministries?" This is answered by people from the major churches and summarized succinctly by Kasper.

17. The pertinent numbers would be 35-40, 51-55.

18. LG, 8/2-3, 15/1-2.

19. These have been noted in chapter 4.

20. UR, 22/3.

21. For American priests, Robert Schwartz has written a comprehensive compendium, entitled *Servant Leaders of the People of God: An Ecclesial Spirituality*

(Mahwah, N.J.: Paulist Press, 1990). It is the first attempt at a comprehensive spirituality of priesthood in the modern age.

22. Leonard Doohan,*The Lay-Centered Church: Theology and Spirituality* (Minneapolis: Winston, 1984), pp. 105-111. Doohan's efforts to develop an ecclesial spirituality are excellent, and the material on the four trends outlined here are indebted to his analysis.

23. GS, 40/5.

24. GS, 41/4.

Chapter 12 Toward an Evangelical Ministry

1. Raymond Brown, "Rethinking the Priesthood Biblically for All," *The Critical Meaning of the Bible* (Mahwah, N.J.: Paulist Press, 1981), pp. 96-106. The authority question is on p. 98. As with most of Brown's work, this is an excellent article, well worth reading.

2. *Ibid.*, p. 105.

3. See Yves Congar, "My Pathfindings in the Theology of Laity and Ministries," *Jurist*, 32, 2 (Spring 1972), 181-182.

4. *Ibid.*, 178-179.

5. Any Christo-monistic approach tends to result in this. If the priest is related to Christ more directly than to the community, the resultant priestly powers soon become personal privileges, as the theology of the Middle Ages shows.

6. Yves Congar, *Called to Life* (New York: Crossroad, 1987), pp. 68-74. This entire section is well worth reading, and can help correct our skewed perspective.

7. In several locations, the council used the expression *"veri sacerdotes Novi Testamenti."* This is a discreet way of playing down the long-standing custom of associating ordained priesthood with the Old Testament priesthood of Melchisedek or Aaron. The New Testament "sacrifice" is prophetic because the sacrifice we offer is a spiritual (sacramental) one. This is why the council presented the priest as having the Word as his first concern, after the manner of the apostles and in cooperation with the bishops (PO, 4/1-6). See Congar, *Called to Life*, pp. 107-108.

Chapter 13 Reintegrating the Laity

1. LG, 9/5.

2. LG, 10/2.

3. LG, 12/3.

4. *De civitate Dei*, X, 6 [PL 41, 283].

5. Cyprian, 66, 8.

6. *City of God*, 20, 10.

7. *Sermo post Maurinos*, 16, 2.

8. LG, 34-36. Each of the three facets of Christ's priesthood is developed in relation to the laity in these numbers.

9. Denzinger, #956-968.

10. German *Kirchenlexicon*, in its 1852 edition.

308   MINISTRY IN THE CHURCH

11. *Kirchliches Handlexikon* of 1884, after Vatican I.

12. Hans Küng, "The Priesthood of the Faithful, "The Church (London: Burns & Oates, 1968), pp. 183-201. The idea for five areas, as well as many of the suggestions for their possible implementation come from Küng.

13. LG, 12/3. See the very interesting article by James Provost, "Lay Preaching and Canon Law in a Time of Transition," *Preaching and the Non-Ordained* (Collegeville, Minn.: Liturgical Press, 1983), p. 151. The entire article runs from pp. 134-158.

14. AA, 3/1.

15. Homilies on Joshua, 9:9.

16. Canon 766. When the laity are allowed to preach, however, the general stipulation is that it not be done after the gospel, but at some other time—either before the mass or after communion. It is Provost's opinion that the reversal of the 1917 Code means that when the laity preach now, they do so in the name of the church. Cf. p. 151.

17. The Celtic monks used to confess to each other. And it is interesting to note that even Thomas Aquinas held that if there were no priests, one should confess to lay people.

18. SC, 14/1.

19. LG, 10/2; 1967 Synod, 4.

20. LG, 34/1.

Abbott (translation), 294, 302, 303
Abelard, P., 145
Acts of Peter, 69
Administrators, compared with other Pauline ministers, 25
bishops as, 63, 110, 113, 121
Adversus Haereses, 69
Albert, 136, 138, 146, 147, 303
Alexandria, Clement of 55, 60, 115
Amalarius of Metz, 119
Ambrose, 84, 98, 99
Ambrosiaster, 88
Ancyra (Council), 85
Anicetus, 65
Anointing, 60, 77, 166, 225-6, 304
Anselm, 135
Antioch, 21, 23, 33, 47, 85, 87
Ignatius of, 54, 57, 70, 78
Apostle, 17, 18-9, 20. 22, 25, 28-9, 32-4, 38-42, 46-8, 50, 54-60, 63-4, 69, 75-8, 86-8, 97, 111, 137, 182, 227, 258-9, 276, 278, 307
Apostolate, 214
Apostolic Constitutions, 297
Apostolic succession, 38, 48, 56, 64-5 76, 78, 86, 124, 182, 234, 243, 258-60, 273
Apostolic Tradition, 41, 54, 58, 68, 70, 74, 101
Aquinas, 129, 136, 138, 139, 141, 142, 145, 147, 162, 183, 308
Arles, 83, 85, 87
Asceticism, 95, 97, 186, 265
Athanasius, 113
Audet, 96, 104, 297
Augustine, 54, 66-7, 85-6, 92-3, 99, 101, 104, 106-7, 115, 123, 131, 142, 236, 283-4, 296, 305

Authority,
and collegiality, 173, 196, 297
and discipleship, 12, 13, 48, 206, 209
and jurisdiction, 2, 112, 143, 145-6
as presiding, 47, 276
as service, 40, 44, 229, 277
of church, 13, 27, 29, 35, 88, 95-6, 111, 126, 150, 161, 163-4, 177-8, 180, 182, 297, 304, 306
of hierarchy, 56, 60, 85, 91, 111, 113, 130, 150, 152, 195, 206, 208
of ordination, 2, 44, 60, 73, 80, 91, 122, 152, 159, 166
of pope, 114, 127, 129, 184
of Scripture, 33, 88, 163, 171
of teaching, 35, 182, 208, 231
ultimate source of, 2, 12, 13, 44, 80, 168, 173, 218, 228, 233-4, 270-1

Baptism, 10, 53, 105, 159, 161-2, 188-90, 235, 241, 249, 299
and common priesthood, 155-6, 162, 171, 205, 280, 288, 300
and equality, 7, 43, 162, 205, 280, 281
and mission, 9, 12, 188, 209, 212, 214, 251-2, 278, 282, 288, 290-1
and rebaptism, 92-93
foundation of church life, 249, 263, 272, 288, 291, 300
ministers of, 46, 60, 64, 74, 89-90
Basil, 54, 106, 115
Baum, G., 4, 294
Baumgartel, F., 295
Bede, 135
Bellarmine, R., 181, 182-3, 198
BEM, 254